Global Semiotics

ADVANCES IN SEMIOTICS

Thomas A. Sebeok, General Editor

GLOBAL SEMIOTICS

Thomas A. Sebeok

Indiana University Press

Bloomington and Indianapolis

This book is a publication of

Indiana University Press
601 North Morton Street
Bloomington, IN 47404-3797 USA

http://iupress.indiana.edu

Telephone orders   800-842-6796
Fax orders   812-855-7931
Orders by e-mail   iuporder@indiana.edu

The paper used in this publication meets the minimum requirements of American National Standard for Information Sciences—Permanence of Paper for Printed Library Materials, ANSI Z39.48-1984.

Manufactured in the United States of America

Library of Congress Cataloging-in-Publication Data

Sebeok, Thomas Albert, date
Global semiotics / Thomas A. Sebeok.
p.   cm. — (Advances in semiotics)
Includes bibliographical references and index.
ISBN 0-253-33957-X (cl. : alk. paper)
1. Semiotics.   I. Title.   II. Series.

P99 .S323 2001
401'.41—dc21
00-143857

1 2 3 4 5   06 05 04 03 02 01

Contents

Acknowledgments

NATURALLY, THIS WORK owes its existence in part to my genetic constitution, for 50 percent of which I am indebted to my father, Dr. Dezső Sebeők. Born in Budapest in 1891, he died in Washington in 1952. A jurist and practicing lawyer, he had always hoped that I would follow in his footsteps; I take this opportunity to apologize to his spirit for having taken another path. Among his numerous publications, he wrote over fifty allegorical articles between 1919 and 1927, bearing the overall title "For my son Thomas." From these I know that, despite some perfunctory grumbling, he would in the end have supported my choice of a calling. Our ideals were always as one.

"Culturally," this work owes as much to the social environment in which my genes find their phenotypic expression: the serenity of my working atmosphere was created and continues to be nurtured by my life's partner, Dr. Jean Umiker-Sebeok. Jean brings order into my chaotic existence—and that includes the collection of essays that make up this book.

It is a crude mistake to oppose nature and culture, organism to environment. "Culture," so-called, is implanted in nature; the environment, or Umwelt, is a model generated by the organism. Semiosis links them. We use the term *semiosis* to refer to the ceaseless ebb and flow of messages, which are formal, insubstantial concepts, strings of abstract signs. Messages are copied, handed down, from one generation to the next. Hence I think it befitting that this book be also dedicated to our two daughters, Jessica and Erica. The medium I have in common with them is not only our family habitat but, as well, the pivotally transformative, if admittedly changeful, milieu of the College of the University of Chicago. As Robert Maynard Hutchins said: "It's not a very good university—it's only the best there is."

Introduction

A MERE THREE MONTHS before my eightieth birthday, and just about twenty-five years after the appearance of the first edition of my *Contributions to the Doctrine of Signs* (1976), I am racing to complete this introduction to what will perhaps be my last book of a sequence of a dozen or so others in this genre devoted to, broadly speaking, themes in general and applied semiotics. Between 1976 and today, most of these fundamental domains have radically metamorphosed along several dimensions. *Global Semiotics* tries to reflect upon some of the more important reconfigurements.

In *The Sign & Its Masters* (1979b), I introduced my readers to a few of the departed doyens of semiotics, especially ones who most fired my imagination; in *Semiotics in the United States* (1991e), I presented many more—but that was not my point. What I tried to make clear was the fact, not then self-evident, that each and every man, woman, and child superintends over a partially shared pool of signs in which that same monadic being is immersed and must navigate for survival throughout its singular life. I was groping to reformulate for myself an observation by Niels Bohr, responding to a comment that "reality" is more fundamental than the language that it undergirds. Bohr famously countered: "We are suspended in language in such a way that we cannot say what is up and what is down" (French and Kennedy eds. 1985, 302). Evidently, I did not yet grasp in 1979 the full implications of either Jakob von Uexküll's Umwelt-research—that is, his semiotic program of research in subjective universes—or the Moscow-Tartu School's early concept of "modeling systems." I now discuss, in amplified fashion, both of these critical notions in several interrelated parts of this volume (especially in chapters 1–6). In addition, I explore them still further (with my co-authors) in two other recent books: *The Forms of Meaning: Modeling Systems Theory and Semiotic Analysis* (2000, with Marcel Danesi); and *The Semiotic Self* (forthcoming, with Augusto Ponzio and Susan Petrilli; see also chapters 10 and 11 below). For those who prefer to quaff their Semiotics Lite, there are now also my *Signs* (1994a) and two new collections of my essays: *Essays in Semiotics: Culture Signs* (2000a) and *Essays in Semiotics: Life Signs* (2000b).

While, as I continue to insist, all human beings—indeed, all living entities on our planet (see chapter 5)—modulate their environment by means of signs, only a handful grow up to be professional semioticians (and a good thing too). Classic figures in the long and ubiquitous history of this domain were otherwise occupied: for instance, Hippocrates, Galen (chapter 4), and their countless medico votaries subsisted by interpreting (in their parlance, "diagnosing") symptoms and syndromes, which are special kinds of indexical signs akin to the detectival clues sought, observed, and interpreted by the likes of Sherlock Holmes (he called this procedure "the science of deduction")—as the historian Carlo Ginzburg demonstrated in the sparkling chapter he contributed to Eco's and my collection, *The Sign of Three* (1983). The paths leading to academic semiotics are highly diverse, yet finally convergent: many, such as Locke (himself a medical man), Vico (chapter 12), Peirce (while claiming his roots in chemistry), Husserl, Cassirer (chapter 12), Morris, Susanne Langer (chapter 13), Eco, and Deely, arrived via philosophy. Indeed, John Deely recently wrote a substantial tome, *Four Ages of Understanding: The First Postmodern Survey of Philosophy from Ancient Times to the Turn of the 21st Century* (2000), to show how this came about again and again. Others, such as Saussure, Buyssens, Hjelmslev, Jakobson, Prieto, Greimas, Metz, Mounin, Rauch (chapter 13), and I, came to semiotics more or less straight out of technical linguistics. Maritain was a Dominican theologian. Lotman and Voigt detoured via cultural studies (cf. chapters 14 and 15). Marvin Carlson entered from theater studies; Solomon Marcus from mathematics; Eero Tarasti from musicology; Floyd Merrell from chemistry; Milton Singer and Michael Silverstein from anthropology; and so forth.

Although I had my earliest brush with semiotic studies as far back as the mid-1930s, while I was an undergraduate at Magdalene College in Cambridge—where I. A. Richards was then Pepys Librarian and where, wide-eyed, I thumbed through his and C. K. Ogden's *The Meaning of Meaning* (1938), as well as, with bewilderment, tried to make sense of the English translation of Jakob von Uexküll's *Theoretical Biology* (1926, as set forth in chapter 3)—I by no means envisioned semiotics as an immediate career choice. In fact, at the University of Chicago, I later enjoyed the robust discipline of biology, especially genetics, although I kept up a dalliance of sorts with semiotics under the benevolent tutelage of Charles Morris. However, my formal training as a linguist began there, chiefly under the intensive guidance of Leonard Bloomfield, then continued, after I moved to Princeton in 1941 to pursue my graduate education, with increasing fervency under Roman Jakobson (then still working in New York). Both Bloomfield and Jakobson urged me to specialize, inter alia, in Finno-Ugric studies (chapters 16 and 17), a language family to which I eventually devoted not only my dissertation but also several decades of my early teaching and administrative activities at Indiana University.

The meandering road from these relatively straightforward beginnings into the tulgey woods of semiotics was long, labyrinthine, and full of surprises, as well as punctuated by not a few exciting encounters along the way. In the pilot scheme for this very book, I had in fact earmarked for inclusion an additional section, titled "Summing Up." I attempted to sketch out the tale of how it befell that I came to sell my soul—not, Esau-like, for a mess of potage (Genesis 25.29–34) but, rather, for a pot of message. After all, as Jakobson taught us, the core subject matter of semiotics "is the communication of any messages whatever" (1974, 32)! Yet, as this chapter of my book became too hefty, unwieldy even, I decided at the last minute to save it for the eventual diversion of those few readers who might deem such autobiographical tidbits (now incorporated into a separate publication) moderately illuminating.

In the belief that autobiographical episodes tend to enliven narratives by providing a social context, I offer one provocative instance of the chance encounters that impacted on this book. This exemplar bears on the final three sentences of "Nonverbal Communication" (chapter 8), with the intention of expatiating on how one professionally engaged but naive young academic, me, engrossed in a relatively autonomous compartment of knowledge—namely linguistics, or *communication by verbal means*—came, by a sudden insight, to hugely enlarge my field of vision to encompass the shambolic realms of *communication by nonverbal means.* As is quite obvious in retrospect, this pair makes up in the aggregate a tidy portion—though by no means the entirety—of semiotics. In the event, the other shoe dropped in the ensuing fashion.

In the 1940s, while I was a graduate student at Princeton, I also held an evening job, a part-time lectureship at the École Libre des Hautes Études in exile, then quartered at the New School for Social Research. Our faculty—far outnumbering Jakobson and me—consisted of a group of illustrious French refugee scholars, presided over at the time by Jacques Maritain and including my much-admired friend Claude Lévi-Strauss. We would get together after our evening lectures in various combinations to mix informally, often over a meal. In the early fall of 1944, Lévi-Strauss introduced me to an elderly but spry gentleman from Paris, sporting a goatee, whom I had not met before but immediately recognized by name: Jacques Hadamard. I knew him to be a very famous mathematician, a member of the Collège de France. Over dinner, on learning that I lived in Princeton, he told me two salient things: that the Princeton University Press was about to publish a course of lectures he had delivered the year before at the École; and that he was a friend of Einstein's. Indeed, his wonderful work appeared next year under the title *An Essay on the Psychology of Invention in the Mathematical Field* (1945).

The sixth section of his book is especially noteworthy for students of semiotics: it bears the title "Discovery as Synthesis: The Help of Signs." Here Hadamard avowed that he himself did not feel that he understood any mathematical argument "as long as I do not succeed in grasping it in one *global* idea . . . and, unhappily . . . this often requires a more or less painful exertion of thought" (1945, 65–66; emphasis supplied). This portentous sentence is followed by an extended subsection called "Words and Wordless Thought," wherein, among numerous other subtle and fascinating observations, Hadamard claimed:

"As to words, they remain absolutely absent from my mind until I come to the moment of communicating the results in written or oral form, or (very exceptionally) for relay-results" (ibid., 82). He had sent around a questionnaire to elicit the working habits of other mathematicians, and concluded: "The mental pictures of mathematicians whose answers I have received are most frequently visual, but they may also be of another kind—for instance, kinetic. There can also be auditive ones . . . " (ibid., 85).

Hadamard also cited Lévi-Strauss and Jakobson. The former reported that, when thinking about difficult questions in his ethnographic studies, he "sees, as I do, unprecise and schematic pictures, which, moreover, have the remarkable character of being three-dimensional" (ibid., 90). At the risk of being supererogatory, I feel that I should quote the protracted response of Jakobson that, besides being quintessentially semiotic in its taxonomic applications, has hitherto escaped notice. Jakobson told Hadamard in the mid-1940s:

> Signs are a necessary support of thought. For socialized thought (stage of communication) and for the thought which is being socialized (stage of formulation), the most usual system of signs is language properly called; but internal thought, especially when creative, willingly uses other systems of signs which are more flexible, less standardized than language and leave more liberty, more dynamism to creative thought . . . Amongst all these signs or symbols, one must distinguish between conventional signs, borrowed from social convention and, on the other hand, personal signs which, in their turn, can be subdivided into constant signs, belonging to general habits, to the individual pattern of the person considered and into episodical signs, which are established ad hoc and only participate in a single creative act. (in Hadamard 1945, 96–97)

All these penetrating utterances and more were of course unavailable to me while Hadamard and I were chatting, although he did give me a rundown of their tenor. But his account turned downright exhilarating when Hadamard began to speak of Einstein's creativity. That was the first time I heard of "A Testimonial from Professor Einstein," to wit, the letter that was ultimately published in full as appendix II to Hadamard's book (to which I further allude in chapter 8 below). Einstein, referring repeatedly to visual and motor elements in his letter, put it in a nutshell: "In a stage when words intervene at all, they are, in my case, purely auditive, but they interfere only in a secondary stage" (in Hadamard 1945, 143). Nowadays, post–Yuri Lotman, we would term Einstein's secondary stage a "tertiary modeling system" (further discussed in Sebeok and Danesi 2000, 120–157, 187–188).

Now I must note that, at that phase of my academic development—on the eve, as it were, of the conferment of my doctorate—I was by no means virginal as to the manifest processes of human nonverbal behavior; to the contrary, I was probably more attuned to them than most students of linguistics of my generation. This was so because, by another coincidence, I happened to have been a class- and officemate in Chicago's Department of Anthropology of Ray L. Birdwhistell, who later became fashionable as the promoter of *kinesics*. He had minted this term, by analogy with *linguistics,* for the study of body motion from the point of view of how this may function as a communicative code. Month after month, Birdwhistell had obsessively harangued me with his dubious "theory." Despite my early and continuing reservations, I organized twenty years later a conference at Indiana University, held in May 1962 under that rubric combined with *paralinguistics*—another outworn catchword of that era. Some sixty scholars, starring Margaret Mead, attended the meeting, "a discussion designed to focus primarily on paralinguistics and kinesics"; its proceedings appeared in 1964 as *Approaches to Semiotics* (see Sebeok et al. eds. 1972, 6), a cover noun she introduced in her concluding address to the conference (ibid., 279).

It is critical for the readers of this book to grasp the distinction between, on the one hand, the depth of the observations, and their implications, enunciated by Einstein and promulgated (among others) by Hadamard, and, on the other, the shallow scope of kinesics as conceived and advocated by Birdwhistell, shadowed by not a few of his epigones. Although kinesics as a method and as a technical term is effectively moribund, programs investigating human gestures by other means are not only in full bloom but have recently been reinvigorated by an acknowledgment of their roots, for example the classic treatise of Andrea de Jorio (1832) and Darwin's magisterial *Expression of the Emotions in Man and Animals* (1872) (elegant critical editions of both are now available by, respectively, Adam Kendon in 2000 and Paul Ekman in 1998). Furthermore, workshops devoted to scientific studies of human gestures abound. To mention only some: David McNeill's pre-eminent group in Chicago; the so-called GeVoix (a French acronym for "Gesture and Voice") inquirers led by the resourceful Aix-en-Provence team of Isabella Guaïtella and Serge Santi; Cornelia Müller and her colleagues in Berlin; and Geoffrey Beattie's prolific University of Manchester crew. A new journal, devoted to gesture studies, is about to be inaugurated.

But gesture studies constitute only a minuscule fraction of the seemingly unbounded, certainly uncharted purlieus of "nonverbal communication." The sole defining feature of this immense territory thus far is unsatisfyingly passive—it simply reiterates "semiosis-other-than-verbal." Nobody has yet been able to devise a consolidated positive term for the remaining immense, messy hotchpotch of semiosic phenomena. We know little else than that these implicate all manner of our biosphere's indwellers, which ceaselessly barter messages through all available modalities, and that they also comprise all the interlaced communication networks inside and between our cells, the macromolecular engines that are the very *fons et origo* of semiosis. As Loewenstein remarks in his engrossing book: "Communication channels, in one form or other, are behind all organizations in the universe" (1999, 178).

What I found so captivating about Einstein's intuitive account was its immediate derivation from Euclidean spatial models rather than from a line of mediated reasoning with mathematical symbols. Put schematically, the conceit that stunned me was this: the most comprehensive model of the universe—the reinterpretation of gravity in terms of the curvature of space and time caused by matter—could in some sense have originated in Einstein's muscle tissue before being filtered through the bacterial colony lodged in his skull. I espied this as a research problem of the sort that Max Wertheimer wrestled with but did not even come close to solving in his *Productive Thinking* (1945). For surely this riddle is on quite another, much more profound level than the most ingenious experiential inquiries can reveal in most studies of nonverbal communication, because it goes to the very heart of interpretant generation. Interpretants emerge from the murky opacity of neuron populations—the impermeability of the deepest biosemiotic matrix, where, arguably, "meanings" are constructed—before rushing on, as in a dynamical system, like car pile-ups in fog, with each new ghostly representamen smashing into the rear of the one ahead. Shakespeare put it best: "My brain I'll prove the female to my soul, / My soul the father: and these two beget / A generation of still-breeding thoughts; / And these same thoughts people this little world . . . " (*Richard II*, act 5, scene 5). Rarely, if circumstances are favorable, a collision can result in radically new configurations, which may or may not become semiotic models of a glottal kind.

That the normal adult members of our own species are uniquely capable of communicating by *two* disparate orders of semiosic agencies—roughly, nonverbal and verbal—is indubitable. Not even the most jejune advocates of the myth of animal language would maintain, one hopes, that animals are capable of constructing syntactically coherent narratives, whereas we can routinely seesaw such verbal strings to alternate with manual and facial gestures—postural adjustments, say, overlapping, supplementing, or contravening one the other in sundry composites. Superpositions and sequences of configurations like these can be imagined and analyzed as if they were extensions of language games in the manner of Wittgenstein.

Some games of this sort can be designated "intersemiotic transmutations," applicable to certain vernacular literary collections, such as jokes. As a matter of fact, Ted Cohen, who is a professor of philosophy at the University of Chicago, opens his diverting new book, *Jokes* (1999), with a quotation from Wittgenstein's *Philosophical Investigations* (1953). He classifies jokes into several more or less formulaic kinds, but does not cover gesture jokes, which I exemplify in chapter 9 below. In Cohen's scheme, these would appear to be a subset of the sort he calls the kind of "joke that is a very short story" (Cohen 1999, 1). One reason for their neglect has got to be the technical inconvenience of copying them down.

A gesture joke consists of two segments, with possibly some overlay, oscillating between two semiotic repertories. Segment one, which is always verbal, generally begins as either a very short story or as a question: "An American tourist in Paris goes for a walk . . . " or "Why do Italians have short necks?" Segment two, which is always optic, contains the resolution called as a rule "the punch line"; it must, to achieve its intended comic effect, be gestured. Paraphrasing, which is one mode of intralingual rewording, would tend to annihilate or at least radically diminish the joke, as in this debased example:

> "How do you call an elevator in North Korea?"
> "Like this" [pointing one's index finger to press an imaginary elevator button].

Segment two can be visually represented on the page in one of several ways. Géza Balázs, in his article on gesture jokes in Hungary, relies entirely on plates; as he remarks, "I tried to experiment with the impossible by showing some photographs next to certain jokes" (2000, 207). Single plates, however, preclude the depiction of motion, which is why I chose to turn to a cartoonist, Luciano Ponzio, to help me out.

How prevalent are gesture jokes in Western cultures? A quick search turned up, apart from Balázs' piece and my own, none that did not feature the Pope in a never-ending comedic argument with a rabbi. I am thinking of circulating an ethnic questionnaire after this book appears. (Gesture jokes, by the way, are only remotely related to so-called body humor, about which see Nilsen 2000.)

The word "global" used in my title may seem to many like a cliché—see now also Décsy (1999)—a banal adjective currently polluting, for example, economic and political discourse. The English word was used at least as far back as the seventeenth century, but I became acutely aware of it not, as one would suppose, through Marshall McLuhan's renowned village image (1962, 43), but, close to my home in Indiana, the opprobrious off-shoot of Franklin Delano Roosevelt's Hoosier antagonist Wendell Willkie. The tag he used in his best selling book, *One World* (1942)—soon to be echoed by Clare Booth Luce in her first speech before the House of Representatives—was "globaloney."

Although this term, along with its melancholy variant "globa*lonely*," and, of course, the root-word *global* itself, has become today's threadbare platitude, I judged it a befittingly precise attributive accessory to the substantive *semiotics*. I began drafting "Global Semiotics" (chapter 1) in response to a 1989 invitation from Irmengard Rauch to serve as the honorary president of the Berkeley Congress of the International Association for Semiotic Studies (1990–94), at which it was my closing address. Despite the overburdening of "global," I stand by this expression for an assortment of reasons that, I think, sustain recapitulation.

Since the 1980s, my wife and I have put forward several sweeping metaphors —among them "sphere" and "web"—in an attempt to capture what we felt was the all-inclusiveness of semiotics as a *domain* and the catholicity of the empowering network of its supporting *field*. (This pair of terms, in the technical sense used here, come from Mihaly Csikszentmihalyi's acclaimed book, *Creativity* [1996; see further applications in chapters 3 and 15 below].) In 1986, Jean and I co-edited a hefty tome, *The Semiotic Sphere,* which consisted of twenty-seven chapters fashioned to sum up the state of the art from Australia to Venezuela. More ambitiously, in 1987, we launched a series of annual volumes with the overall title *The Semiotic Web,* which ran through 1994, when we gave up in sheer exhaustion (see further chapter 14, below).

"Global" carries a distinctive bundle of unequivocal connotations for me. My principal thematic concerns are:

Geopolitical

In the most mundane sense, "global" refers to the accelerating spread of semiotics over an impressive number of terrestrial tracts. In 1986, we reported on its state in some twenty-seven geopolitical areas. By 1977, I was able to explicitly identify no less than forty-five documented provinces. By 2000, the figure exceeds fifty, including the Basque zone of northern Spain, Baltic nations such as Lithuania, several Islamic countries, and some in sub-Saharan Africa (e.g., Burkina Faso).

Temporal

Chronological considerations are of capital importance as well, but are underrepresented in this volume, for the most part because I am not a qualified historiographer. My essay on Galen (chapter 4) is the principal exception here, although doubtless insufficiently erudite. I attempted it anyhow, as best I could, because of my attraction to iatric symptomatics to begin with and because Galen, next to Hippocrates, was such a towering figure in the annals of our Western medical as well as semiotic progression. As in several of my previous writings, especially my book on *Semiotics in the United States* (1991e), I am not embarrassed to liberally reminisce about colleagues I have happened upon in the course of my life's vocation, and this predilection is again evident throughout these pages. Witness the passages concerning Ernst Cassirer and Suzanne Langer (chapters 12 and 13), Ethel Albert and Margaret Mead (chapter 13), and Yuri Lotman (chapters 14 and 15), to name only a few among those who have passed away.

Academic Traditions

Designer labels, like *L'école de Paris,* pretentiously self-denominated by Jean-Claude Coquet in 1982 but now to most practical purposes defunct, or the Tartu School (alias the Moscow-Tartu School, dispersed in a post-Soviet diaspora but now struggling to be reborn in Estonia) were once commonly invoked landmarks. They strove to ape such formerly fashionable and prestigious Mecca-like archetypal linguists' clusters as the Prague Circle (roughly the *locus classicus* of early structuralism), the Copenhagen Circle (a.k.a. glossematics), or perhaps the logical positivists' Vienna Circle. The Lithuanian lexicologist A. J. Greimas, considered the *spiritus rector* of the Paris School, even castigated a non-existent "Bloomington School of Semiotics" that nobody at Indiana University was aware of.

Then, in a chapter titled "Ecumenicalism in Semiotics," in *A Perfusion of Signs,* I contingently introduced a contrast "between two seemingly antithetical tendencies" in semiotics: a major tradition and a minor tradition (1977a, 182) (ever mindful that so-called twentieth-century traditions are often invented). This distinction has unfortunately been perpetuated either in an ingenuously personified manner as "the Peirce tradition versus the Saussure tradition," or, even more arrantly, in terminologically erroneous forms, as *sem(e)iotic* versus *sémiologie.* Jumbles of inaccuracy lurk in such simplifications. To take the latter first: it is a myth, brought about by the late Max Fisch (after 1978; see Fisch 1986, 322), that Peirce never availed himself of the word *semiotics:* in fact, it is known that Peirce approved of, and contributed to, this very lexical entry for the *Century Dictionary* (1891, 19:5486). As for *sémiologie* —likewise known to Peirce—Saussure used this term only in a handwritten note in 1894, although he was reported to have uttered it once in 1901 to his future father-in-law.

As for the far more convoluted issue of the two "traditions," I pointed out already in 1977 that the differentiation I drew between the two semiotic practices—namely, language-free (or loosely Peircean) versus language-sensitive (or Saussurean)—had "lost its force" (1977a, 182), and explained why. ("Minor tradition" was not meant to be pejorative, but rather to ratify that the verbal paradigm is abjectly based on the *pars pro toto* fallacy.) My intent, as suggested by the title of my essay, was to offer a program for the amalgamation of the main trends: "Semiosis must be recognized as a pervasive fact of nature as well as of culture" (ibid., 183). In addition, I advocated a judicious infusion into the brew of ingredients from all other currents that had something constructive to offer. I think the example I evoked of this possibility I called the Dominican sub-tradition, that is, deriving retroactively from Aristotle, then, via Aquinas, Poinsot, and Maritain, to engaged contemporaries like Herculano de Carvalho,

Beuchot, Deely, and others. However, the Lilliputian quarrel between the Big-Endians and the Little-Endians came to a happy resolution when this doctrine was promulgated: "That all true believers shall break their eggs at the convenient end." Similarly, prospects for a viable comprehensive synthesis of the doctrine of signs, a new paradigm if you will, loom on the horizon in 2001 under the banner of *biosemiotics* (a.k.a. the Jakob von Uexküll "tradition," discussed in chapter 10 of my *Sign & Its Masters* [1979b], and at length further in this introduction and in chapters 1, 3, and 5).

Gender

In the beginning, there was Victoria Welby, who died eight years before I was born, and, quite a bit later, there came Susanne Langer, who died a mere sixteen years ago. In chapter 13, which was written to honor Irmengard Rauch, my Barese colleague, Susan Petrilli, and I speculate why women achieved their professional identity in semiotic teaching and researches—initially perhaps in the anglophone world, but now, as well, in plentiful other venues in Europe and South America—so late in recorded history. Was this due to the intricate interplay of their personal and professional lives in the changed societal circumstances eventuating from World War II, or to some as yet unrecognized factors affecting their, in truth, quite diverse career development? We do not know. Solomon Marcus, a Romanian scholar of note, has argued that there is no significant disparity between the struggles of women in other professions and those in semiotics, yet such difficult questions have to be urgently addressed. Our chapter should be regarded merely as exploratory; it needs to be followed up by a life-course approach by way of focused interviews of the sort pioneered by Csikszentmihalyi in his book on creativity (1996).

Tools

The multiplication of weighty, or even lesser, reference works in any domain is, I think, one symptom of its salubrious condition. For semiotics, this is an unforeseen, unprecedented, powerfully impressive development. There are at least five new encyclopedias or handbooks currently on the market or in the making, plus several journals to boot. Publishers, at least in Canada, the United Kingdom, Germany, and the United States, have evidently decided that semiotics is a sufficiently marketable growth-industry at this time, worth competing for. Let me provide further specifics. The largest undertaking of its kind is the sweeping English and German *Semiotics: A Handbook on the Sign-Theoretic Foundations of Nature and Culture,* co-edited by Roland Posner, Klaus Robering and me, in three volumes totaling approximately thirty-five hundred pages; Volume 1 appeared in 1997, Volume 2 in 1998, and Volume 3 is due to appear in 2002. Concurrently, the totally revised and greatly expanded second German edition of Winfried Nöth's solo *Handbuch der Semiotik* was published in nearly seven hundred pages, and will soon appear in English. Three large-scale encyclopedias of semiotics have in the meanwhile come out almost simultaneously: the first edited by Paul Bouissac (Oxford University Press, 1998), the second by Marcel Danesi (University of Toronto Press, 2000), and the third by Paul Cobley (Routledge, 2001). In the aggregate, the creative energy and both intellectual and financial investments in these separate, and, in many ways, truly worldwide publishing accomplishments are breathtaking—the more so as these quite conventionally formatted print projects were, all five, produced in an era of briskly ameliorating electronic tools. In the afterword to a recent compilation of essays on *The Future of the Book*, one of my most eminent comrades-in-arms in semiotics, Umberto Eco, proclaimed: "I am pretty sure that new technologies will render obsolete many kinds of books, like encyclopedias and manuals" (Nunberg 1996, 299). But evidently not yet; or at least not yet in semiotics!

Conceptual Revolution

To assert that the emergence of biosemiotics entails a "paradigm shift" in the millennial history of semiotics demands fleshing out of a number of labyrinthine entwined issues which I home in on in chapter 3 and adjacent parts of this book. Its advent, under the more restricted German label of *Umweltlehre*, that is, the study of modeling, was far from an epiphany; quite the contrary, it took well nigh a century to season. The word *paradigm*, meaning a pattern or an exemplar, has been a part of English usage since at least the sixteenth century, and soon gathered specialized connotations in linguistics, particularly the structural variety, with reference to substitution classes. Within modern linguistics, a single master, Noam Chomsky, is widely thought to have initiated a revolutionary change of "paradigm" in 1957.

The situation in semiotics is far more complicated. Thomas Kuhn, in his seminal (and to this day darkly controversial) *The Structure of Scientific Revolutions,* used the word *paradigm* in dozens of different ways, but some passages of his could clearly bear on the unraveling of biosemiotics. For instance, he held: "Both normal science and revolutions are . . . community-based activities. To discover and analyze them, one must first unravel the changing community structure of the sciences over time. A paradigm governs . . . not a subject matter but rather a group of practitioners. Any such study of paradigm-directed or of paradigm-shattering research must begin by locating the responsible group or groups" (1962, 179–180). The tangled saga of biosemiotics, as I recount its lineaments especially in chapter 3 of this book, (and as was foreshadowed in Anderson et al. 1984, to which I contributed observations anticipating some arguments bearing on issues raised here), seems to me broadly as well as in many of its particulars to fit Kuhn's portrayal of what he sometimes, if arguably, called a revolution in a "common disciplinary matrix." I find this especially so in the light of what Hadamard, Wertheimer, Csikszentmihalyi, Howard Gardner, and so many other observers of the measures of creativity have taught us. The cutting dissonances between domain and field ring especially true throughout the historiography of semiotics. While it would surely be redundant to retell the story of biosemiotics' prime practitioners, the pioneer Jakob von Uexküll, Heini Hediger, Giorgio Prodi, Thure von Uexküll, and now many others, there might be some profit for me to sketch out in this introduction the highlights of the journey I myself traversed from semiotics to biosemiotics to global semiotics. Much of this has never been recorded.

My role has largely been catalytic and facilitative. It came about more or less adventitiously, starting with an offhand encounter with Ralph Tyler in 1959 at a cocktail party at Stanford, where I was attending a meeting of the Social Science Research Council's Committee on Linguistics and Psychology, of which I had been a founding member in 1952. Tyler and I had known each other while I was a graduate student at the University of Chicago. He was the founding director of the Center for Advanced Study in the Behavioral Sciences (1954–67), and over a casual drink, Tyler abruptly asked me which year I would like to spend at the Center. I had never presumed to apply for a fellowship there, but much later I learned that three very senior anthropologists—Kluckhohn, Kroeber, and Redfield—had nominated me without my knowledge. I asked Tyler what I would have to do at the Center, of which I at that time knew next to nothing. Typically, he responded, "What would you like to do?" Then, I don't know why, I said, "I would like to catch up with developments in biology since my undergraduate years at Chicago." "Fine," he answered. We settled on 1960–61.

On my arrival in Palo Alto, I began to voraciously pore over the biological literature of the 1950s, but soon realized that I had set myself an unreasonably broad goal. Accordingly, I decided to restrict my readings to a review of works on the biology of behavior, or ethology, especially to locate everything there was to be found on how animals communicate. Why? Because I had formed what seemed then a reasonable study hypothesis ripe for refutation: could the communicative behavior of animals shed any light on the communicative behavior of ourselves? Eventually, the answer turned out to be positive, although trivial. If, however, the question was refocused as, can animal communication systems shed any light on language (or its ancillaries, notably speech), the answer was uncompromisingly negative. This last, stark statement appears straightforward enough, although it in fact fuelled a never-ending controversy, while it also became the kernel of a sprawling research program that has taken up decades of my scholarly life (see, inter alia, Sebeok and Umiker-Sebeok eds.

1980; Sebeok and Rosenthal eds. 1981). I culled the tangible fruits of my time at the Center, assembling papers written while there or just afterwards, including a programmatic article on "Animal Communication" for *Science* (1965) and in *Perspectives in Zoosemiotics* (1972), adding more to these about twenty years afterwards in *Essays in Zoosemiotics* (1990a). As well, two major reference books appeared as *Animal Communication: Techniques of Study and Results of Research* (1968), and, nearly double in scope, *How Animals Communicate* (1977).

By the early 1970s, it was clear to me that restricting semiotic inquiry to our species was absurd and that its field of reference had to be extended to comprehend the entire animal kingdom in its maximum diversity. I designated this expanded field *zoosemiotics*. I could envisage the outlines of a fact-finding program, but what zoosemiotics sorely lacked, I thought, was a sound theoretical basis. This uninformed belief, as I soon discovered, or, in fact, rediscovered by the end of that decade, was totally mistaken. The theory was there, in theoretical biology, and it was called Umwelt-research. In chapter 3, I trace, step by step, its trajectory, from its genesis in the first decade of the past century to its present efflorescence.

I do not propose to recapitulate this yarn here, but only to stalk the bearing of Umwelt-research on repeated brachiations within general and applied semiotics as such. At this juncture, then, there were two main branches widely recognized:

a. "Normal" semiotics, or, as this essentially glottocentric enterprise came to be redesignated in some circles for a couple of decades, *anthroposemiotics;* and

b. The vast augmentation thereof, *zoosemiotics,* that was meant to enfold within its purview *Homo sapiens,* that is, man as a biological entity rather than as a cultural entity.

But now there came several dramatic proposals from diverse unexpected, as well as more or less independent, sources. Beginning in 1981, Martin Krampen followed up on the abduction that plants too undergo semiosis, and thus another subdiscipline, *phytosemiotics,* came into being. In 1991, I postulated semiosis in the fungi, and thereby added *mycosemiotics* to the taxonomy. The recognition of far-reaching semiosis in the kingdom Prokaryotae, comprising all bacteria (*microsemiotics),* was triggered by a 1983 book by Sorin Sonea and the late Maurice Panisset, and is being nourished by the inspired writings of Lynn Margulis, recently by her beguiling *Symbiotic Planet* (1998). The most penetrating insight in this vein, with immeasurable implications, is that the body itself is an almost indivisible net of innumerable semioses. A conceptual framework for identifying the pertinent integration levels was presented in a 1993 monograph by the physician son of Jakob von Uexküll, Thure, with two of his medical associates. This domain is now termed *endosemiotics.* (In passing, let me note here that a very significant arena of endosemiotics is entailed in the ultimately immunological issue of "self" and "nonself." Some aspects of this are discussed in chapters 10 and 11, and are further dealt with in my forthcoming bilingual book, *The Semiotic Self* [with Augusto Ponzio and Susan Petrilli].) These newly identified and labeled topics, among others, together now constitute the overall domain of *biosemiotics*. This covers, in my view, the preponderance of the semiosic processes in the terrestrial biosphere, or the *semiosphere,* a concept further discussed in chapter 14 of this book in the context of a critical analysis of this suggestive notion by the great Russian semiotics scholar, Yuri Lotman (cf. also chapter 15).

In sum, *global semiotics* can be seen as composed of two partially overlapping estates: "normal" semiotics, as defined above, the subject matter of which is, intrinsically, Minds, Models, and Mediation; and biosemiotics, all this and much, much more, as presented throughout this book. Needless to point out, practitioners of the discipline may be qualified to work in one aspect or the other, or, as a rule, in one or more fractions of the supervening category. Scarce is the polymath of the magisterial stature of, say, Charles Peirce, capable of reaching athwart more than a couple of divisions, especially across the humanities and the sciences, which are perhaps uniquely bridged by semiotics (as argued in chapter 5).

I conclude this book with three short chapters (15–17) that may appear out of tune with the rest. As was noticed in a staff tribute commemorating the death of Indiana University's visionary chancellor Herman B Wells (Gardiner 2000, 4), it was he who recruited me in 1943 and gave me the support I needed "to lay the foundations for what is today's Hungarian Studies Program" at Indiana University, or more broadly, our ongoing Finno-Ugric (or Uralic) program, which also includes such other languages as Finnish, Mari (or Cheremis), and Estonian. Before 1978, I had written books on Hungarian linguistics and Finnish linguistics, and had a hand in ten books on Mari linguistics and culture. In addition, between 1960 and 1969, I produced one hundred volumes in the Indiana University Uralic and Altaic series. For some twenty years, projects in these areas constituted if not my bread at least my butter. (Last May's "celebrations" of my eightieth birthday in Finland were designated by my hosts as an homage to me "from Fennougrian Studies to Biosemiotics" [Tarasti et al., 2000, 2].) Linguistics having of course been, in Saussure's memorable phrase, *le patron générale* at a critical stage of "normal" semiotics (or semiology)—that is, its underlying model—I thought it not inappropriate to advert to my engagements with three of the major speech communities west of Russia: my native Hungary, Finland (which I have visited annually for the last fifteen years), and Estonia, which really opened up for me only lately. (In the late 1940s, I conducted intensive fieldwork in a Lapp community in the Finnish Arctic but have never written about this exposure.) These experiences are not a negligible part, although but a precursor, of my maturation to semiotics proper.

I have been privileged to be a witness to, and often a part of, the paradigmatic metamorphosis that took place in the twentieth century in semiotics that I tried to ratify and portray in this book. I believe that this "revolution" is now irreversible. At this point, my record might well terminate in the manner of Krapp's last tape (Beckett 1995, 63): "Here I end this reel. Box—[*Pause.*]—three, spool—[*Pause.*]—five. [*Pause.*] Perhaps my best years are gone. When there was a chance of happiness. But I wouldn't want them back. Not with the fire in me now. No, I wouldn't want them back."

Global Semiotics

I

Global Semiotics

My defense at any Last Judgement would be "I was trying to connect up and
use all the fragments I was born with."

—E. M. Forster to Forrest Reid (1915)

Part I

WHEN THE PLAYER who enacted Prospero in 1611 (or thereabouts) famously
recited the expression "the great globe itself" in *The Tempest* (act 4, scene 1),
his audience was aware that the subject of Shakespeare's phrase was at least
doubly denotative: planetary in its habitual, most sweeping sense, but insularly
provincial in the context of that London production, pointing to the famous
polygonal edifice on the south bank of the Thames that Shakespeare called the
"Wooden O," wherein that actual performance was taking place: the Globe.
Earlier, Hamlet had used the expression "this distracted globe" in still another indexical sense, pointing to his own skull, the seat believed to house his
memory (act 1, scene 5).

The denominative adjective *global* is even more abundantly polysemous.
Some of its further connotations which I intend to evoke are "all-encompass-
ing," "comprehensive," "international," "limitless," "pandemic," "unbounded,"
"universal," and maybe "cosmic."[1]

I have always maintained that—at least within the frame of academic
semiotics—it is wise to act locally, in specific terms, but to think in a grand,
holistic manner. (I like sometimes to invoke Wallace Stevens' mysterious line
from "Anecdote of the Jar": "It took dominion everywhere.") And by "global
semiotics" I mean first of all a network—or, to recycle an image I first used in
1975 and since then in the title of seven *Yearbooks of Semiotics*—a web. In the
last analysis, a semiotic web—what Thomas Carlyle, in his magniloquent if

Revised and expanded for publication, this chapter originated as a plenary lecture delivered
on June 18, 1994, in my capacity as honorary president of the Fifth Congress of the
International Association for Semiotic Studies, convened at the University of California–
Berkeley. It was first published in 1997, in *Semiotics Around the World: Synthesis in Diversity.
Proceedings of the Fifth Congress of the International Association for Semiotic Studies—Berke-
ley 1994*, ed. I. Rauch and G. F. Carr, 105–130 (Berlin: Mouton de Gruyter).

mystical rhetoric, might have called organic filaments—amounts to an intricate piece of political negotiation occupying a sort of utopian space, in which personality, historical context, and academic stratagem all play determining roles. It may be appropriate to remind ourselves, as presumptive adherents of the International Association for Semiotic Studies, that the motto for a salubrious federated semiotics community is, or should be, *E pluribus unum*.

To anticipate near the outset my theme's mainspring, I can do no better than to share with you a pair of telling quotations from the semiotically most sensitive and profoundly discerning novel I have read in the last few years. The author is Richard Powers.

First, Powers writes: " . . . the world [is] awash in messages, every living thing [is] a unique signal" (1991, 86). In other words, the world is perfectly semiotic—or, in the more familiar parlance of the *rex et sacerdos* and tutelary spirit of twentieth-century semiotic hagiography, Charles Peirce, the universe is "perfused with signs" (Peirce 1935–66, cited hereafter as *CP*, 5.448n; cf. Merrell 1991). And Powers' next locution is refreshingly tantamount to an exact and true reversal of Peirce's man-sign analogy[2]: "For every symbol is a living thing, in a very strict sense that is no mere figure of speech" (*CP* 2.222 [1903]; cf. Singer 1984 and Colapietro 1989).

Second, Powers writes: "Evolution becomes . . . an intricate switchboard, paths for passing signals back and forth: generation to generation, species to species, environment to creature, and back again. Life [viewed as an] exchange of mail" (1991, 251). It was Jakobson who I think first defined semiotics "as an inquiry into the communication of all kinds of messages," which are in turn composed of signs (1971, 698). But it is preferable to round out this no doubt excessively communication-centered definition to reflect the indissoluble linkage of dissemination with signification. I accordingly proposed to amplify it: "The subject matter of semiotics . . . is the exchange of any messages whatsoever and of the systems of signs which underlie them . . . " (Sebeok 1974a, 212).

But biologists know full well, as for instance the admirable geneticist Cairns-Smith insisted in his scientific detective story (splendidly recounted with a happy recourse to the abductive methodology of Sherlock Holmes), that it is precisely semiosis that provides the breath of animate existence, insomuch as it is precisely messages that are much our most important inheritance; messages coded in DNA render "the only connection between life now and life a million or a billion years ago. Only these messages survive over the long term, because only these messages can persist through the making of copies of copies of copies . . . " (1985, 12, 28; cf. chapter 2 below), spawning an indefinite, if not infinite, temporal progression of interpretants. As for the protein, wherever it goes, it "conveys the meaning of its gene, whether to other proteins, to DNA or even to other cells, and it speaks in a language to which genes, cells, tissue and organs all respond" (Pollack 1994). Peirce, ahead of his time, was right again: "So it is only out of symbols that a new symbol can grow. *Omne symbolum de symbolo*. A symbol, once in being, spreads among the peoples. In use and in experience, its meaning grows" (*CP* 2.302).

As for our novelist's fascinating simile for how the brain's courier service is powered—the "exchange of mail" he picturesquely adverts to, that is, the flow of chemical signs controlling the pattern that has become the crux of modern developmental biology (née embryology)—this too is in perfect conformity with a new scientific discovery by two pharmacologists, Peter Illes and Wolfgang Nörenberg of the University of Freiburg, of a momentous biochemical substance. Adenosine triphosphate (ATP) had hitherto been regarded purely as an energy source, but is now recognized to be a universally applicable fuel found in the body's cells, officiating to transmit messages from one neuron to another. ATP possesses all the characteristics of a real neurotransmitter (see further endnote 13, below).

Although I propose to return to the implications of these and corresponding research results in Part V below, I want to call to mind here at the inception a clearly articulated cornerstone view of Charles Morris. Morris wrote in the first few pages of his favorite book, *Signs, Language and Behavior,* that he believed "that basic progress in this complex field [viz., semiotic] rests finally upon the development of a genuine science of signs, and that this development can be most profitably carried on by a biological orientation . . . " (1946, 4–5). I fully share this presumption and faith with my first major teacher in semiotics, who would be more pleased than astounded at the prodigious stride the life science has enjoyed overall since he wrote that sentence nearly half a century ago, and, more to the point here, the explicit blending of many branches of biology—from genetics and developmental biology to studies in animal behavior—with the sign science. This convergence is easily conceived when one realizes that the same molecules, as enzymes and other key proteins, including the genes that designate those proteins, serve as signs in every living thing from bacteria to humans, and will probably do so beyond humanity.

Too, independently of Morris, Roman Jakobson, my second *maître à penser* semiotically, came after 1967 to increasingly appreciate the robust biological *mise en scène* of the doctrine of signs; he entitled, and explored to the degree afforded at that time, this much more capacious range, "ways and forms of communication used by manifold living things" (1971, 673).

Before I proceed with my would-be irenicon, intimating secure consensus, I had better take note of two general-purpose antonyms of *global*: *local* and, worse, *parochial*. The latter was the opprobrious attribute Jakobson brandished against unnamed—but of course not unrecognized—fissiparous malefactors he called, in the concluding paragraph of his *Dialogues* with Pomorska, "sectarians." Here, in part, is how he phrased it: "As for the question of which genres of signs enter into the frame of semiotics, there can be only one answer: if semiotics is the science of signs . . . then it does not exclude any sign. . . . [O]ne should reject all the unsuitable efforts of sectarians who seek to narrow this vast and varied work by introducing into it a parochial spirit" (1983, 157–158).

Furthermore, I suppose the unavoidably ubiquitous oxymoron combining the two notions into a single powerful conceit, namely McLuhan's phrase "global village" (1962, 43), is worth recalling. Pejorative appellations I conjecture my title will already have viscerally triggered are "imperialistic," "totalitarian," and "megalomaniac."[3] Perhaps some of you may want to keep these in mind as well.

Part II

To begin with, let me consider "global semiotics" in what is perhaps its most basic, pedestrian implication: the more or less systematic planetary proliferation of the doctrine of signs during the past quarter of a century and its crystallization into what looks like nothing so much as a lively guild of transnational scholarship. When the International Association for Semiotic Studies (IASS) was founded in Paris on January 21, 1969, not even the most sanguine among us foresaw the pandemic build-up of semiotic studies we are witnessing today. Now—five IASS Congresses later—there exist multifarious organizations dedicated to the regional advancement of such studies, say, in California, or in the southeastern expanse of the United States, or in Toronto, or over the five Nordic lands of Europe (Rauch and Carr eds. 1997) and in the Balkans, as well as in many separate nations. Too, semiotics these days is diffused and advanced in a concentrated and intensive manner, in a yearly cadence, in at least four extraordinary transnational forums: in Imatra (Finland), in Monterrey (Mexico), in Urbino (Italy), and at the University of San Marino.

Humble, numbing even, chronicles of this sort are impressive if only for their sheer mass and surprising diversity. I list here mainly items which were compiled or edited by myself plus, selectively, a few others explicitly documented in sources known to me first-hand. I have read published reports from or of at least the following countries, standing or lately become defunct (but do not doubt that there are sundry inadvertent omissions):

Argentina (Magariños de Morentin 1987; Rauch and Carr eds. 1997)
Australia (Freadman and Morris 1986; Threadgold 1988; Rauch and Carr eds. 1997)
Austria (Lange-Seidl 1986; Bernard 1987)
Belgium (Martin 1986; Swiggers 1986, Helbo 1979a, 1987)
Brazil (Rector and Neiva 1979; Rector 1986; Braga 1990)
Bulgaria (Bernard 1989)

Canada (Brodeur and Pavel 1979; Bouissac 1986, 1987, 1988; Rauch and Carr eds. 1997)

Chile (Gallardo and Sánchez 1986)

China (Li 1988; Rauch and Carr eds. 1997)

Colombia (Silva 1990)

Czech Republic (Rauch and Carr eds. 1997)

Czechoslovakia (the former) (Osolsobé 1979)

Denmark (Johansen 1979, 1986)

Finland (Tarasti 1986; Rauch and Carr eds. 1997)

France (Coquet and Arrivé 1979; Hénault 1986; Réthoré 1989; Rauch and Carr eds. 1997)

Germany (Bange 1979; Lange-Seidl 1986; Rauch and Carr eds. 1997)

Great Britain (Norris 1986)

Greece (Boklund-Lagopoulou and Lagopoulos 1986; Rauch and Carr eds. 1997)

Hungary (Voigt 1986; Rauch and Carr eds. 1997)

Iceland (Sigurjónsson 1989)

India (Srivastava and Kapoor 1988)

Israel (Tamir-Ghez 1978)

Italy (Ponzio 1976; Bettetini and Casetti 1986; Segre 1979; Petrilli 1993)

Japan (Toyama 1986)

Malaysia (Rauch and Carr eds. 1997)

Mexico (Jiménez-Ottalengo 1986; Garza Cuarón 1988)

Netherlands (Swiggers 1986; Hoek 1992; Rauch and Carr eds. 1997)

Nigeria (Sekoni 1989)

Norway (Storelv 1986; Gorlée 1987)

Peru (Ballón 1986, 1990)

Poland (Pelc 1974; Mazur 1979; Buczynska-Garewicz 1987; Rauch and Carr eds. 1997)

Portugal (Seabra 1986)

Romania (Marcus 1979; Golopentia-Eretescu 1986; Net 1990; Rauch and Carr eds. 1997)

Slovakia (Rauch and Carr eds. 1997)

South Africa (Rauch and Carr eds. 1997)

Spain (Yllera 1979; González 1986; Carrascal and Romera 1987; Rauch and Carr eds. 1997)

Sweden (Ljung 1986; Sonesson 1992)

Switzerland (Grize 1979; "Semiotics" 1986; Pellegrino 1992; Rauch and Carr eds. 1997)

Turkey (Vardar 1979)

United States (Steiner 1978, 1979; Kevelson 1986; Sebeok 1990b, 1991e; Rauch and Carr eds. 1997)

Uruguay (Block de Behar 1987)
USSR (the former) (Lhoest 1979; Rudy 1986)
Venezuela (Carrión-Wam 1986; McCormick 1986)
Vietnam (Trinh 1989)
Yugoslavia (the former) (Skiljan and Velcic 1992)

In the aggregate, surveys like these do represent global semiotics in some tenable geopolitical sense: the underlying principles and the same elements are, after all, held in common. A few are rich in detail and convey a sense of leadership. Other subjects emerge only as blurry caricatures or talking heads in semiotic echo chambers. It would certainly be too simple to assume that the state-of-the-art accounts cited are strictly convertible. While each reporter does tell the story under the same banner, it by no means follows that "semiotics" bears ranges of reference equivalent in Iceland, say, to those in Italy, or in Finland to those in Turkey. Furthermore, the roll call is thought-provoking as well as challenging to action for its slivered perspectives or downright lacunae, for instance as regards such continents as Africa or isolates as New Zealand. Too, despite one's awareness that semiotics currently prospers in the three Baltic countries—in Latvia and Lithuania as well as of course in Estonia—comprehensive reckonings have been hard to come by since their independence. The absence of predominantly Muslim countries is likewise conspicuous, maybe in part for the same reason, although, as Waardenburg implies, there is much more to it than that. For Islam, the primary Koran and the secondary Sunna, or tradition, are "rich both in signs that hint at realities beyond the immediately given and in symbols that associate on a level of feeling and emotion the experience of different kinds of data and represent cores of patterns of meaning" (Waardenburg 1994, 392). Indeed, the Koran has been characterized as "a semiotician's paradise par excellence" (Netton 1989, 321).

In spite of such blanks, the very vastness of this inventory—after all, at issue here are semiotic activities in some forty to fifty nations—provokes a wider, more nuanced reflection, especially when contrasted with such fatiguing twentieth-century experiments in obfuscation and chaos, pomposity or trivial pursuits, as existentialism, structuralism (at least in some of its sea changes), deconstructionism, grammatology (Derrida 1968, not Gelb 1952), Marxism (notably in French literary and university milieus), Freudianism (Crews 1993, 1994), Lacanism, *soi-disant* cultural studies, and the like: buried one by one or, unless I am much mistaken, drooping toward extinction. To be sure, as long ago as the Milano Congress of June 1974, "semiotics" itself, in one version or another, has been declared moribund or dead by persons seemingly unable to distinguish ephemeral Parisian fads from enduring pre-Socratic practices (Kirk et al. 1983).[4]

These compressed ruminations leave two important uncertainties which must be addressed (although not today, not in this context): what were and

remain the sociohistorical impediments to the conventional academic institu-
tionalization of semiotic studies? And is the scantiness thereof a bad thing or,
as I happen to think in spite of certain anxieties this rouses, a good thing?

Part III

At our second Congress, in July of 1979, Eco discussed "the theoretical and
methodological possibility of a unified historical approach to . . . Semiotic
Thought," envisaging diverse approaches to its consummation, the most ambitious of which was "the publication of a complete history of semiotics" (1983,
74). At the same congress, Voigt extended Eco's ideal theses by several further
sound proposals of his own, arguing for a "*long-distance* understanding of
ideas, methods and tradition of semiotics around the world" (1983, 405). And
at the same venue, I likewise pleaded for "a comprehensive history of the vast
semiotic adventure . . . to be recorded in its full panoply" (1983, 354).

Yet even today—fifteen years and three Congresses afterwards—the historiography of semiotics has progressed, if at all, at a disappointing snail's pace.
The major pertinent semiotics reference works (e.g., Rey 1973, 1976; Nöth
2000, 11–76; Sebeok 1994a; Posner et al. eds. 1997, 1998 and 2001) are of limited scholarly utility in this regard. With a smattering of piecemeal exceptions
—such as the dozen or so items enumerated in my *Semiotics in the United States*
(1991e, 87–88), or now Manetti's fine book (1993) dealing with semiotic issues
from the times of Mesopotamian divinatory techniques to the transitory figure of Augustine (d. 430)—embarrassingly little has transpired on this verge
of our either solitary or else collective business. It is as if we had paused, pet-
rified in a time warp, in the first decade of this century, when Peirce characterized himself as "a pioneer, or rather a backwoodsman," who found "the field
too vast, the labor too great, for a first-comer," and who was, "accordingly,
obliged to confine [himself] to the most important questions" (*CP* 5.488).

Our generation plucked from the past and raised aloft only what we
needed, but these apprehensions, these sporadic resuscitations of a few over-
looked giants—whom I once dubbed "neglected figures in the history of semiotic inquiry" (Sebeok 1979b, 187)—temporally inundated, as they were, by
a sea of relatively unremarkable extras, tended to reveal as much or more about
those who engineered revisionist assessments of posthumous reputations than
about those being assessed. Witness, for example, the De Lacys on Philodemus;
Maritain, Herculano de Carvalho, and Deely on Poinsot; Danesi on Vico; Kele-
men on Kant; Ponzio on Peter of Spain and on Bakhtin; Krampen on Piaget;
Rossi-Landi, Mounin, Posner and many others on Morris; Berthoff on Sapir;
or Sebeok on Jakob von Uexküll and on Hediger. These are just a few among
the great or near-great "Euro-American dead white males" who, like Glen-
dower's spirits, have been complacently summoned out of the "vasty deep"

(probably *mea culpa*) for their annual quickening since the October 1983 Snow-bird meeting of the Semiotic Society of America (Evans and Deely eds. 1987, 109–200, et seq.). (Sadly, the only two "dead white females" who have thus been exalted are the English Victoria Lady Welby, by Schmitz, Petrilli, and a handful of others, and, less successfully I fear, our fellow countrywoman Susanne K. Langer, by myself.)

In short, a thorough reconciliation athwart disparate trends in the history of semiotic thought is nowhere near consummation: antique and medieval with modern and postmodern, occidental with oriental, mythic with scientific, laic with theological, iatric with philosophical, glottoperipheric with glottocentric, nonverbal with verbal, endosemiotic with exosemiotic, outward-looking and life-giving with self-enclosed and culture-bound, theoretical with empirical, bi-nary (à la Jakobson) with triadic (à la Peirce) (cf. Andrews 1990), and so on and so forth.

Part IV

Whether semiotics is a science (Saussure 1901 [see Sebeok 1974a, 219 n. 21]; Morris 1946, 253; Jakobson and Pomorska 1983, 157), a theory (Saussure 1981 [see Godel 1957, 275]; Morris 1938 [e.g., title]; Eco 1976 [e.g., title]), a doctrine (Locke [1690] 1975; Berkeley 1732; Peirce c. 1897; Sebeok 1974a, 215; Deely 1982, 127–130), or something else entirely, seems nowadays of even less consequence than heretofore.[5] The further question of whether semiotics is "a discipline or an interdisciplinary method" was luminously discussed by Eco sixteen years ago; he concluded "that semiotics, more than a science, is an interdiscipli-nary approach" (1978, 83). Today's general opinion is often—indeed, often defensively—expressed by clichés like "interdisciplinary," "multidisciplinary," or "transdisciplinary"—ugly artifacts of modern academic cant.

Peirce put the matter at once more personally and more elegantly, as well as more generally and concretely, when he wrote on December 23, 1908, as he was approaching his seventieth year, a long, oft-cited letter to Lady Welby, telling her in part: " . . . it has never been in my power to study anything,—mathematics, ethics, metaphysics, gravitation, thermodynamics, optics, chem-istry, comparative anatomy, astronomy, psychology, phonetics, economic, the history of science, whist, men and women, wine, metrology, except as a study of semeiotic" (Hardwick ed. 1977, 85–86). Elsewhere, in the far less known preface—as gripping as it is tantalizing—to his chimerical "Essays on meaning: By a half-century's student of the same," he wrote: " . . . Signs in general [are] a class which includes pictures, symptoms, words, sentences, books, libraries, signals, orders of command, microscopes, legislative representatives, musical concertos, [and] performances of these, in short, whatever is adapted to making mental impressions virtually emanating from something external to itself" (MS 634, 16–17 [September, 1909]).[6]

Note that Peirce, who was also a playwright, producer, and director (particularly knowledgeable about Shakespeare), as well as "a practiced actor, belonging for many years to amateur performing groups" (Brent 1993, 187, 16), while casually alluding above to music, for the most part skirted the "humanities" and chose to underplay the singular arts—excepting perhaps the semiotic aspects of architectural drawings—even the eminently syncretic theatrical art. For him, the universe was itself a comprehensive global sign, "a vast representamen, a great symbol . . . an argument." Precisely as an argument, the universe was, "necessarily a great work of art, a great poem . . . a symphony . . . a painting" (*CP* 5.119; cf. Merrell 1991, 181).

An explicit and increasingly elaborate study of the particular arts as sign phenomena began only in the second decade of this century, separately in eastern and western Europe, initially spurred, on one side, by the Russian formalists, their scintillating descendants in the Tartu-Moscow School of Semiotics, and the Czech esthetician Jan Mukařovsky, and, on the other, by such "semiotic" philosophers as the German neo-Kantian Ernst Cassirer and his unconstrained American supporter Susanne Langer, and later E. H. Gombrich and Nelson Goodman, to say nothing of a vast number of litterateurs and their critics. In due course these parties were firmly yoked together in sophisticated fashion above all by Roman Jakobson and René Wellek.

But both "folk" artists and professionals in many, perhaps all, communities anticipated them in disposition and execution. I confine myself here to only three exemplary artists: an anonymous Central American "folk" sculptor, a great modern French colorist, and perhaps the most prodigious twentieth-century painter of them all.

As regards the magnificent Mexican statue known as the Great Coatlicue, Octavio Paz recently observed that "What we call a 'work of art' . . . is perhaps no more than a configuration of signs. Each onlooker combines these signs in a different way and each combination expresses a different meaning. The plurality of meanings, however, is resolved into just one *sense*, which is always the same: a meaning that is inseparable from sensory experience . . . " Then he added that a Mayan god covered with "attributes and signs is not a sculpture to be read like a text but rather a sculptured text" (1990, 18, 20).

In Matisse's paintings, also, "signs are not merely signifiers of things; they are also visual embodiments of feelings and concepts that cannot ordinarily be seen with one's eyes . . . Matisse's signs—his own word for his condensed images—are not simply a form of pictorial writing but rather an integral element in the way he transforms lived experience" (Flam 1992, 32).

And this is what Picasso said to Françoise Gilot about a painting: "It isn't an aesthetic operation. It's a form of magic designed as a mediator between this strange, hostile world and us, a way of seizing power by giving form to our terrors as well as our desires. . . . If I telegraph one of my canvases to New York, any house-painter should be able to do it properly. A painting is a sign— just like the sign that indicates a one-way street" (Gilot and Lake 1964, 221).

Inasmuch as semiotic studies steep, illuminate, and confederate everything Locke called "human understanding," it will no longer do to itemize—as Eco once did under the rubric of "political boundaries" (1976, 9–14) and as I was later obliged to do for the United States (Sebeok 1990b), albeit for sound peda-gogical reasons—even a small fraction of its infinite variety. For if, as Peirce held, "the entire universe" is not merely "perfused with signs" but "composed exclusively of signs," it follows that semiotics is *per definitionem* relevant to, and serviceable as an analytical tool for, every actual and conceivable province of knowledge. Naturally, to cite an old German saying, *Der Teufel steckt im Detail!* But for now suffice it to point out that, although the twin endeavors of arts and letters, conjoined in the former Soviet Union, along with other traditional academic pursuits, under a porous umbrella of language-dependent "secondary modeling systems"—actually constituting "tertiary modeling systems," as I ar-gued in Sebeok 1988c—have enjoyed so much semiotic scrutiny, or, in current jargon, have been privileged, they actually form but a microscopic ripple on the measureless oceans of the living. The capacious mind of Roland Barthes was exceptional in its ability to assess the artistic and literary countenance of semi-otics when contemplated side by side with, for instance, the continuous trans-mission belt of medical semiotics (Barthes 1972; see also Th. von Uexküll 1982b, 1986).

Part V

I postulate that two cardinal and reciprocal axioms of semiotics—subject, as always, to falsification—are:

  (1a) The criterial mark of all life is semiosis; and
  (1b) Semiosis presupposes life.[7]

Accordingly, the bailiwick of biology may be viewed as equivalent to "natu-ral semiotics" (Prodi 1988d, 149–170), "nature semiotics," (Kergosien 1985, also in Sebeok and Umiker-Sebeok eds. 1992, 145–170), "semiotics of nature" (Hoffmeyer and Emmeche 1991), or, in a different terminology, biosemiotics (Sebeok and Umiker-Sebeok eds. 1992; Sharov 1992; 345–373; Hoffmeyer 1993b; Kull 1993; Th. von Uexküll 1997; see also Eco [as Alano delle Isole] 1980a, 31–32). Further semiosic unfoldings—such as the genesis of ordered oppositions like self/other, inside/outside, and so forth (Sebeok 1991e, 103)—derive from, or are corollaries of, the above pair of universal laws. These regulations operate exclusively throughout the terrestrial biosphere.

By *biosphere*, we understand that parcel of the planet Earth which comprises life-signs, namely: the lithosphere, or its solid surface; the hydrosphere, or the oceans about eleven kilometers downward; and the atmosphere, the mixture of gases that surrounds our planet about eight kilometers upward.[8] This biosphere is where we live and what we are, but although it is the only domicile we possess thus far, we are not its sole inhabitants, nor do we constitute anything approaching a plurality in occupancy—let alone tenure.

Note that *biosphere*, i.e., Vladimir Vernadsky's 1926 Russian coinage, *biosfera*—by which he meant all of the biota and also the condition for the continuation of life—is far from identical with the late Yuri Lotman's 1984 analogous composite, *semiosphere*. The glottocentric connotations of Lotman's term as a "complex semiotic mechanism which is in constant motion" (1990, 203), and the kind of space encompassing all that cultures do or presumably could do are, to the contrary, much more constricted in scope than Vernadsky's usage or the modern employments of biosphere. In further defining it, while summoning Kant, "as the semiotic space necessary for the existence and functioning of languages," then adding that "the semiosphere has a prior existence and is in constant interaction with languages . . . ," Lotman perplexingly asserts that "[o]utside the semiosphere there can be neither communication, nor language" (ibid., 123–124). Here I must regretfully part company with the seminal Russian master because, by that assertion, he wholly exorcises, puts beyond the pale, not only the prodigious no-man's-land populated by the multifarious speechless creatures but even man himself in his own unalienable animal constitution. In other words, Lotman fails to credit that anthroposemiosis is fastened in zoosemiosis, that human semiosis is played out predominantly in the prelinguistic, extra-verbal mode, or, to repeat, that what in the Soviet Union was called a "primary modeling system" turns out in truth to be a secondary superstructure (cf. Sebeok 1988c).

As a matter of curricular and pedagogical convenience, the earth is often bisected, as it were, into hemispheres.

First: the one which evolved earlier, commencing in the Hadean eon (4,500–3,900 million years ago), is inert and unmarked. As every high school chemistry student knows, its syntax, which obtains throughout the entire cosmos, is displayed in Mendeleev's law of 1869, the periodic table arranged in order of increasing proton number to exhibit the similarities of elements with related electronic configurations (cf. the remarks of Peirce in *CP* 1.289 and 5.469 on "external structure"). This realm is also protosemiotic or, in the words of the late Giorgio Prodi, the "threshold for 'sign,' situated at the very beginning of the biological domain, characterizing its origin and its basic

structure." Proto-semiotics is, moreover, "the basic feature of the whole biological organization (protein synthesis, metabolism, hormone activity, transmission of nervous impulses, and so on)" (in Sercarz et al. eds. 1988, 55; see also
Prodi 1988b and 1988c).

Second: the later one, which issued from the former in the Archean eon
(3,900–2,500 million years ago), is animate and therefore marked (in Jakobson's
sense). Here evidently are the rudiments of the sign-driven realm of biosemiosis.[9]

The earliest, smallest known biospheric module with semiosic potential, the
"semiotic atom," is a single bacterial cell. *Ex hypothesi,* and no doubt debatably,
the largest, most complex living entity may be what the ancient Greeks honored
in their myths as Gaia (Myrdene Anderson in Sebeok and Umiker-Sebeok eds.
1992, 1–13; Ponzio 1993, 379–380). Both units at the polar ends of this *scala
naturae* "display general properties of autopoietic entities" (Sebeok 1991e, 85;
Margulis in Barlow 1992, 237), but it is now the bacteria that merit, in my
opinion, special consideration on the part of all who would work at semiotics
professionally. Any general semiotic theory failing to take into account the fascinating, multiform empirical data of bacterial semiosis is as flawed as would
be one which ignored the complexities of the verbal code and its social manifestations. The bacteria would appear, at first blush, the creatures most alien to
humankind. Yet we dwell in a sea of bacteria. They lodge upon and within us.
In a way that is quite literally mind-boggling, we are composed of bacteria: the
central nervous system is itself a colony of interactive bacteria.

Little wonder then that bacteria are viewed as "the global organism" par
excellence (Sonea 1988). Their semiosis has been most insightfully described by
the eminent microbiologist and immunologist of the Université de Montréal,
Sorin Sonea (1988, 1990, and 1992). The following is a decidedly abridged and
simplified account of his works, interpreted from the standpoint of a semiotician. Sonea's portrayal illuminatingly focuses on bacterial behavior in groups,
"the social dimension of their existence, so to speak—[as] the key to understanding them." This perspective is a crucial one, since, "together, they constitute the communications network of a single superorganism whose continually
shifting components are dispersed across the surface of the planet" (1988, 40).
This amazingly sophisticated grid is in effect the primordial planetary information superhighway: "each bacterium, itself a broadcast station for hereditary
information, is part of a much larger network—a network that," according to
Professor Sonea, "resembles human intelligence . . . , a vast computerized communications network—a superorganism whose myriad parts shift and share . . .
information to accommodate any and all circumstances" (ibid., 45). In short,
bacteria—having "traded" their singular identity to share in a kind of immortality, while individuals of our kind play out our lives between the antipodes
of sex and death—are not at all discrete organisms. In due course, "the super-

organism created environmental conditions (an atmosphere and an array of terrestrial and aquatic nutrients) that favored an entirely different form of life: the eukaryotes" (ibid.).[10] The prokaryotes then took advantage of these new-fangled organisms, "using them as habitats and vehicles for further dispersal," and later as symbionts, acting in concert as a single organism (ibid.).

But the configuration into a single global prokaryotic community is only one of their several modes of semiosic commerce. Another is the ubiquitous formation of localized teams. Such teams adopt multicellular strategies for survival, that is, form an ensemble which acts ad hoc as a single organism for a limited time in order to accomplish particular evolutionary ends. The constitution of such teams, characterized by intense cooperation, eventually had far-reaching evolutionary consequences: via a series of local "symbioses"—or, the word I prefer, *semioses*—the nucleated cells (eukaryotes, composing the bodies of plants, animals, and fungi) emerged over millennia from bacterial ancestors (for details, see Margulis 1993). Plainly put, the membrane-bounded sphere universal in eukaryotes contains remnants of interacting bacteria and, in their turn, the eukaryotes exchange messages with both prokaryotes and other eukaryotes.

Thure von Uexküll and his co-authors adapted the term *endosemiosis* (from Sebeok 1974a, 213) to refer to all processes of sign transmission inside all eukaryotic organisms, and went on to identify any body as a hierarchically structured "web of semioses" (1993, 5, 9). They thoroughly examined these within the immensely productive overall theoretical framework of Jakob von Uexküll's *Umweltlehre,* that is, the study of modeling, his now widely accepted theory of signs (e.g., 1982, 1992; cf. Sebeok 1979b, 187–207), through four ascending levels of endosemiotic integration. Although they do not sift the two levels of integration sketched above, they do allude to and label them: accordingly, we may call the first level of sign processes occurring inside individual cells *microsemiosis,* and the second-level information networks *cytosemiosis* (Th. von Uexküll et al. 1993, 8). The third coding step concerns the combination of cells into organs by a network of nerve cells—a "transport system for high-speed long-distance communication in the body"—which is subtly intertwined by dendrites of nerve cells with a considerably slower transport system for sign vehicles, the bloodstream (ibid., 28). I have previously discussed several endosemiotic systems, such as the genetic code, the immune code, the metabolic code, and the neural code (Sebeok 1991e, Part III, and chapter 2 below), but Thure von Uexküll et al. show in their important study how the neural and immunological counterworlds are tethered by sign processes to form a conjoined unitary inner world, which corresponds to a fourth endosemiotic integration level that is then transmuted into an "experienced reality" (1993, 45).

Eukaryotic cytosemiotics is subsumed under endosemiotics, which is of course entirely subsumed under pure nature-coded semiotics, viz., biosemiotics. However, the scope of the latter might well be extended considerably beyond it, to abut on, though not circumscribe, nature-coded semiotics with culture-coded semiotics superimposed, viz., anthroposemiotics. It would be redundant as well as tedious to recapitulate here, despite their developments with the addition of numerous recent references, my discussion (Sebeok 1991e, Part III) of the basic lineaments of phytosemiotics, zoosemiotics, mycosemiotics, and even cybersemiotics (as to the latter, see Margulis and Sagan 1986; Sebeok 1991f, 97–99).[11] It may, however, be useful to bring to mind some general properties of zoosemiotics which place it in a special category by contrast with the others.

As Martin Krampen has emphasized in his "Phytosemiotics revisited" (in Sebeok and Umiker-Sebeok eds. 1992, 213–219), Jakob von Uexküll's Umwelt theory has pointed to important semiosic commonalities between humans (and other animals) and plants, on the ground that where there is a feature to be found in the botanical world there is bound to be a complementary counterfeature in the zoosemiotic world (or, more generally, elsewhere in the biosemiotic world), and vice versa.[12] One reason for this relation becomes clear from a study by Roth and LeRoith (1987), which also provides clarification for various further biological puzzles. For example, why are there two basic systems of cellular communication in the higher vertebrates—the nervous system and the endocrine system—working separately (although they are linked)? Nerves do sign to other nerves (or to muscles or glands), but, contrary to previous opinion, "they typically do not do so by strictly electrical means . . . but with the help of chemicals called neurotransmitters."[13]

Roth and LeRoith formulate a "unifying theory of intercellular communication" to account for the many coincidences involving plant messenger molecules and human (or vertebrate) cells, and to suggest explanations of such perplexing questions as why pigs can detect buried truffles, or why some chemicals in spinach are almost indistinguishable from human insulin and are also found in some bacteria and protozoans. What they propose is a simple generic semiotic system of which both the nervous subsystem and the endocrine subsystem are specialized evolutionary adaptations; their theory incidentally explains scores of coincidences surrounding cellular semiosis in plants and animals. Semiotically speaking, Krampen concludes, "human sign production is deeply rooted in its symbiosis with plants—the meaning of human (and animal) life is thus being indexically contingent on plant life" (Sebeok and Umiker-Sebeok eds. 1992, 217).

Zoosemiotics is a particularly rich branch of biosemiotics because animals are in some sense semiosic mediators between creation and decay. On a macroscopic scale, they can be viewed as transforming agents fixed midway between the "composer" plants, organisms that set interpretants in motion, and the "decomposer" fungi, which break them down (Sebeok 1988a, 65). In their role as go-betweens, animals process signs through media embracing the entire sensory spectrum, each according to, but only commensurate with, its specific array of sense organs.[14]

Although the inanimate environment as such seems not to assume any semiosic function (but see below), it may act as a quasi message-source when assigned such function by the destination. Thure von Uexküll calls such events "semioses of information" in his "Varieties of Semiosis" (in Sebeok and Umiker-Sebeok eds. 1992, 460; and Th. von Uexküll 1997). He distinguishes these from "semioses of symptomatization" (the same as George Herbert Mead's "unintelligent gesture"), where a living source emits by its behavior or posture signs—called "symptoms" in English, but more accurately "subjektive Zeichen" in German—not directed toward any destination and not claiming any response. He also singles out yet a third category, "semioses of communication" (equivalent to Mead's "intelligent gesture"; cf. Sebeok 1991f, 142), where the source and destination both share the same code.

Biosemiotics, or some of its ingredients, may be called into question from either of the two axiomatic perspectives. As to (1a), *The criterial mark of all life is semiosis*, Eco, in his trail-blazing analysis from a sign-theoretical point of view of the totality of cultural manifestations, relegated zoosemiotics to "the lower limit of semiotics," while conceding that "through the study of animal communication we can achieve a definition of what the biological components of human communication are" (1976, 9). Again, a dozen years later, in a paper on "Semiotics and Immunology," he stood hesitant before "the dramatic problem of the boundaries between Spirit and Matter, Culture and Nature" (in Sercarz et al. eds. 1988, 15). To me, however, the imperium of Nature, or *Weltbuch*, over Culture, or *Bücherwelt*, has always been unmistakable. Only a patent theoretical basis was transcended to resolve what Blumenberg (1981, 17) has called an "alte Feindschaft" between these two semiotic systems, the latter obviously immersed in the former. This is why my "rediscovery" of the *Umweltlehre* came as such a personal revelation.

Semiosis is the processual engine which propels organisms to capture "external reality" and thereby come to terms with the cosmos in the shape of species-specific internal modeling systems. This index-anchored model of the Umwelt operates as a circuit to suit the appropriate evolutionary purposes of each species and every individual (Sebeok 1991f, 142–143). Whenever the model ceases to be compatible with or appropriate to *die Natur*, when disequilibria turn up for example, the organism's environment, somewhat unstable at all times, oscillates radically enough so that the correspondence no longer fits between it and the organism's internal model (Innenwelt)—coded in part in the genome, in part individually learned. Then the organism and perhaps the species, or even the now wobbly, soon turbulent, ecosystem which they inhabit, exits the way of the dinosaurs. Extinction becomes inevitable.[15]

It is arrogant, absurd, and quite inconsistent with the well-researched tenets of the *Umweltlehre* to insist that modeling mechanisms evolved only once, namely, in our sapient species or even solely in the genus *Homo*. Nonetheless, humankind's peculiar secondary modeling device, the one we call language, which is based on inborn neuronal circuitry underlying universal syntactic structures, does seem to have evolved only once. As far as today's evidence indicates—and, *nota bene,* for valid theoretical reasons—nothing remotely resembling language, in the technical sense, exists among other semiotic systems in the alloprimates, let alone the rest of the animal world (Sebeok and Umiker-Sebeok in Sebeok and Umiker-Sebeok eds. 1980, 1–59, 407–427; Chomsky in Sebeok and Umiker-Sebeok eds. 1980, 429–440; Jackendoff 1994, 137, 140; Pinker 1994, ch. 11).[16] This, however, is not to say that more or less congruous syntactic operations do not appear elsewhere in nature, because they demonstrably do, for example, in the generative grammar of the vertebrate immune system (Jerne 1985; cf. Sebeok 1991e, 29–30, 108–109).

As to axiom (1b), the question arises whether semiosis does in fact presuppose life. If the universe is perfused with signs, is there a cosmic "semiophysics," concerned with a broader quest for significant forms, a general theory of intelligibility transcending life (Thom 1990, after Jean Petitot)? According to John Archibald Wheeler, "meaning is the child of physics" (1984, 123). In a figure of a meaning-circuit as a model of existence, this eminent physicist pictures a loop from Physics to Meaning. The former "gives light and sound and pressure—tools to query and communicate." Physics also yields chemistry and biology, and, through them, observer-participators. The loop is tied into closure at one end by fields (spacetime) and particles. At the other end, it is moored by stick-figures of human beings labeled "Communicators," who, "by the way of the devices they employ, the questions they ask, and the registrations they communicate, put into action quantum-mechanical probability amplitudes and thus develop all they know or ever can know about the world" (Wheeler 1988, 5). The universe viewed as an autopoietic "self-excited circuit" is necessarily dependent on life, "mind," and observership. To paraphrase Wheeler, life is as essential to the genesis of semiosis as the universe is to the creation of the observer.

In sum, to come back to Shakespeare once more, this time to a line spoken by Othello to Desdemona: "Tis true; ther's magic in the web of it" (act 3, scene 4).

2

The Evolution of Semiosis

What Is Semiosis?

IN PEIRCE'S USAGE, semiosis, or "action of a sign," is an irreducibly triadic process, comprising a relation between (1) a sign, (2) its object, and (3) its actual or potential interpretant (*CP* 5.473). Peirce particularly focuses upon the way that the interpretant is produced, and thus what is involved in understanding, or teleonomic (i.e., goal-directed) interpretation of a sign. Similarly, Morris defined semiosis as "a sign-process, that is, a process in which something is a sign to some organism" (1946, 253). These definitions imply, effectively and ineluctably, that at least one link in the loop must be a living entity (although, as we shall see, this may be only a portion of an organism, or an artifactual extension fabricated by a hominid). It follows, then, that there could not have been semiosis prior to the evolution of life. For this reason, one must, for example, assume that the report in the King James version of the Bible (Genesis 1.3), quoting God as having said "Let there be light," must be a misrepresentation; what God probably said was "Let there be photons," because the sensation of perception of electromagnetic radiation in the form of optical signals (Hailman 1977, 56–58), i.e., luminance, requires a living interpreter, and the animation of matter did not come to pass much earlier than about 3,900 million years ago.

The Cosmos before Semiosis

The regnant paradigm of modern cosmology is the Big Bang theory of the origin and evolution of the universe (e.g., Silk 1980; Barrow and Silk 1983). The genesis of the cosmos, in a singularity (i.e., a point at which something peculiar happens to a physical process represented by an equation when one or more variables have certain values), is thought to have occurred about fifteen billion years ago. Prior to Planck time 1^0-43, we know nothing. What ensued afterwards is a bit clearer: from the time that the universe was three minutes

This article originally appeared in 1997, in *Semiotics: A Handbook on the Sign-Theoretic Foundations of Nature and Culture*, eds. R. Posner, K. Robering, and T. A. Sebeok, 436–446 (Berlin: Walter de Gruyter).

old until about a million years after its apparent beginning, it was dominated by the influence of photons (heat and light). The elementary particles multiplied, matter became ordered, and the universe organized itself into ever more complex systems. The quasisemiotic phenomena of nonbiological atomic interactions and, later, those of inorganic molecules were consigned by the late oncologist Prodi (1977) to "proto-semiotics," but this must surely be read as a metaphorical expression. Prodi's term is to be distinguished from the notion of "primitive communication," which refers to the transfer of information-carrying endoparticles, as occurs in neuron assemblies, where it is managed in modern cells by protein particles (see, e.g., Fox 1988, 91). The age of the earth is about 4.5 billion years, while the solar system is deemed to be a little older (4.6 billion).

It becomes useful to briefly allude, at this point, to the conjoined ideas of information and entropy, which is a measure of disorder (Brooks and Wiley 1986; Wicken 1987, 17–28; Wright 1988, 87–91). These are mutually implicative technical terms which arguably belong on the margins of semiotics. Cosmic expansion is accompanied by a departure from a state of maximum entropy, and information (as a measure of the nonuniform, orderly properties of physical systems) evolved out of that initial state of utter chaos. Shannon (1948) viewed "information" as a measure of the number of alternative messages, and the biophysicist Gatlin (1972) later applied Shannon's elegant, highly abstract and therefore powerful theorems to a theory of living organisms. She showed that, since information in the living system is transmitted from DNA to protein along a channel of biochemical processes in the cell, it can be subjected to Shannon's equations. On the other hand, Yates and Kugler (1984), eschewing terms like "information" and "communication," because in them lies embedded the elusive property of "intentionality," recently proposed a quite different and very promising scenario for the transition from a physical (kinetic) system to a semiosic (kinematic) system, that is, one incorporating significance.

"Meaning," which is indeed a pivotal term in semiotics, played a crucial part in Niels Bohr's model of a participatory universe, and significance has moved to center stage in the work of such contemporary theoretical physicists as Wheeler (e.g., 1984, 1986). Wheeler's subtle "meaning model" of nature posits a circuit whereby particles owe their definition and existence to fields, fields owe theirs to phases, phases to distinguishability and complementarity, "and these features of nature [go] back for their origin to the demand for meaning . . . " Hence his dictum: "The past is theory." In this model, meaning before the advent of life must, of course, be founded on construction: "Only by [life's] agency is it even possible to construct the universe of existence or what we call reality" (1986, vii). In sum, in Wheeler's grand conception, physics is the offspring of semiosis, "even as meaning is the child of physics" (1984, 123).

The Origin of Life and the Origin of Semiosis on Earth

The question of whether there is life/semiosis elsewhere in our galaxy, let alone in deep space, is wide open; since there is not a single example, one can but hold exobiology and extraterrestrial semiotics to be twin sciences that so far remain without a subject matter. On the other hand, research into the origin and evolution of our terrestrial biosphere has made encouraging progress, although, of course, untold unresolved problems require multidisciplinary analysis in the future (Schopf ed. 1983). The earliest traces of life to be found date from the so-called Archean eon, from 3,900 million to 2,500 million years ago. The story of the quest for the origins of life is detailed in Margulis and Sagan, who then deftly spell out the molecular biological revolution in a chapter tellingly titled "The Language of Nature" (1997a, 59–67). Cairns-Smith has recently shown, especially in his chapter titled "Messages, Messages," that semiosis is at the heart of life, since messages provide "the only connection between life now and life a million or a billion years ago . . . " (1985, 28). Messages are obviously much the most important inheritance, since only they can persist over the vast reaches of time. All living systems are composed of carbon, nitrogen, and hydrogen compounds in water; they are bounded by lipid membrane; and they are autopoietic systems, i.e., they self-maintain their organization and function by a ceaseless exchange of matter, energy, and messages, or, as Maturana put it, "through their interactions recursively generate the network of productions that produced them, and . . . realize this network as a unity by constituting and specifying its boundaries in the space in which they exist . . . " (1980, 53).

The phrase "the language of life" was the title of a book by Nobel laureate George Beadle and Muriel Beadle (1966; the same tag was also used by Berlinski 1986). Much fruitless debate ensued in the following years about whether the genetic code is (like) a language or not. Thus Jakobson asserted that the Beadles' title was "not a mere figurative expression," and then went on to stress the close similarities in the structure of these "two informational systems," i.e., the genetic and the linguistic (1970, 437, 438). By contrast, Lees for example argued that, although there is a very abstract and deep connection between the two, the similarities usually noted are superficial; "I advocate that linguistic competence be viewed analogously to the genetic code as a mechanism invented by minds to serve as a scratch pad . . . " (Lees 1980, 226). There were also somewhat parallel discussions of this issue among some molecular biologists of that time. The question of an analogy between the two codes, the endosemiosic (molecular) and the anthroposemiosic (including a verbal component) seems, however, secondary. What matters is that both are productive semiosic systems.

This is made possible by the principle of double articulation, referred to by the Schoolmen, in linguistic contexts, as *articulatio prima et secunda*. In language, this concept refers (roughly) to the dichotomy between merely distinctive, or phonemic, units, and significative, or grammatical, units (such as morphemes or words). Duality can of course be expressed in radically different substances: for example, polymeric molecules (the four nucleotides, which can generate the proteins which manufacture everything else alive) are distinctive and sound waves are significative. (Double articulation, however, by no means presupposes animation of matter; on the contrary, its fundamental realization is embodied in Mendeleev's periodic table of elements with related electronic configurations.)

The substantive *endosemiotics* was coined in Sebeok 1976 (3; see also Sebeok 1991a, ch. 1, part iii). As a consequence of Jakob von Uexküll's consistent and elaborate doctrine of signs, nothing exists for any organism outside its bubble-like private Umwelt (environment) into which, although impalpably to any outside observer, it remains, as it were, inextricably sealed (see Jerison 1986, 143–144; Sebeok 1989d, ch. 10). The behavior of an organism—behavior being definable as the commerce by means of signs among different Umwelts—has as its basic function the production of nonverbal signs for communication, and first of all for communication of that organism with itself. It follows that the secondary universal sign-relation in the ontogeny of an organism is realized as an opposition between the self (ego) and the other (alter) (cf. Sebeok 1989d). This elementary binary split subsequently brings about the second semiosic dimension, that of inside versus outside. It is this secondary opposition that enables an organism to "behave," i.e., to enter into relations to link up with other living systems in its surrounding ecosystem.

Thure von Uexküll wrote: "The overwhelming majority of objective evidence of a disease belongs to those types of processes taking place within the body, which, in turn, are subdivided into subsystems (organ systems, organs, tissue, cells, cellular organelles). . . . The participants in the exchange of signs that takes place on the biological level are thus given," and this fact is described by the adjective "endosemiotic" (1986, 204). He continues:

> The sign processes use chemical, thermal, mechanical and electrical processes as sign carriers. They make up an incredible number. If one reflects upon the fact that the human body consists of 25 trillion cells which is more than 2,000 times the number of people living on earth, and that these cells have direct or indirect contact with each other through sign processes, one gets an impression of the amount. Only a fraction are known to us. Yet this fraction alone is hardly comprehensible. . . . The messages that are transmitted include information about the meaning of processes in one system of the body (cells,

tissues, organs, or organ systems) for other systems as well as for the integrative regulation systems (especially the brain) and the control systems (such as the immune system). (ibid.)

Semiosis being at the pivot of the immune system, terms like *semioimmunology* and *immunosemiotics* are finding increasing application. Considering that the human immune system consists of about 10^{12} cells, dissipated over the entire body, the problem immediately arises how these cells form an orderly, finely regulated functional network operating via signs consisting of chemical substances. Moreover, the immune system (units of which, the lymphocytes, seem to be excluded from the brain, although they circulate among most other cells of the body) and the nervous system are known to mutually influence one another by means of signs. Niels Jerne, in his 1984 Nobel address, not only proposed a far-reaching model of the vertebrate immune system as exhibiting the properties of any semiosic system, but described it as one that functions as an "open-ended" generative grammar: "The immense repertoire of the immune system . . . becomes a vocabulary comprised not of words but of sentences that is capable of responding to any sentence expressed by the multitude of antigens which the immune system may encounter" (1985, 1058). The context for this approach was provided by Jerne's idiotype network theory twenty years ago, suggested by a remarkable feature of the immune system: namely, that its receptors and specific secreted products, or antibodies, not only recognize the exosemiotic world of antigenic determinants (epitopes), but also recognize antigenic determinants on the immune receptors themselves (the endosemiotic idiotopes). Jerne's theory postulated that within the reflective symmetry of idiotopes, and so forth, formed within the organism's immune system would be found representations, or indexical icons, of most of the epitopes of the external universe. Internal imaging, a fascinating type of biochemical mimicry performed by the immune system, is now of paramount interest to semiotics.

Internal imaging was coined by Gordon M. Tomkins (1975) in the course of his discussion of biological symbolism and the origin of intracellular communication. Tomkins distinguished between simple and complex modes of regulation, both present in modern organisms. By the former, he meant a direct chemical relationship between regulatory molecules and their effects (equivalent to Peirce's secondness). Complex regulation, on the other hand, involves metabolic symbols and their domains (or Peirce's thirdness). By a symbol, Tomkins meant a specific intracellular effector molecule, cyclic AMP, which accumulates when a cell is exposed to a particular environment (or context). This symbol stands for a shortage of carbon; and the live organism, "upon processing the symbol, behaves so as to reconcile its well-being with that environmental condition (by heading elsewhere)" (Wright 1988, 104). The term is appropriate because "Metabolic symbols need bear no structural relationship to the molecules which promote their accumulation . . . "; and, since a particular environmental condition is correlated with a corresponding intracellular symbol, "the relationship between the extra- and intracellular events may be considered as a 'metabolic code' in which a specific symbol represents a unique state of the environment" (Tomkins 1975, 761). Tomkins also points out that in most multicellular organisms (i.e., the eukaryotes), only certain cells are stimulated directly by the environment; but, in higher organisms, these in turn secrete specific effector molecules (the hormones), which signal other cells, presumably sequestered from the *milieu extérieur*, to respond metabolically, via a high number of intermediate steps, to the initial sign. "Specifically, the metabolic state of the sensor cell, represented by the levels of its intracellular symbol, is 'encoded' by the synthesis and secretion of corresponding levels of hormones. When the hormones reach responder cells, the metabolic message is 'decoded' into corresponding primary intracellular symbols" (ibid., 762). It should finally be emphasized that, in many organisms, the endocrine and the nervous systems are intimately connected; thus hormone release is often a function of neural stimulation (e.g., Jankovic et al. eds. 1987, passim).

As Prosser rightly observes, "Communication is what neurobiology is about. The modes of communication include membrane conductances, patterns of neuronal spikes and graded potentials, electric coupling between cells, electrical and chemical transmission at synapses, secretion, and modification of neural function" (1985, 118). Moreover, over the past three decades, neurobiology has moved increasingly into the orbit of semiotics, in the guise of a distinct discipline named *neurocommunications*, regarded by its practitioners, who draw on many basic sciences, as a metascience (see Whitfield 1984, 4). In brief, this new field is apt to represent the (human) mind (the "software" level) and its underlying mechanism, the brain (the "hardware" level of the biological organ which allows cognition), as a pair of semiosic engines, or computational devices for processing verbal and nonverbal signs. However, there remains sharp disagreement about the representation of language and nonverbal systems, ranging from Chomsky's theory that we are born with genetically determined "mental organs," requiring the rules being in some sense innate for generalization to be possible from impoverished samples (a view which received considerable support from the work of David Hubel and Torsten Wiesel, who discovered just such innate connections in the visual system, as well as from the distinguished researches of Colwyn Trevarthen on the prenatal growth of brain parts), to Gerald Edelman and his colleagues' researches on cell adhesion molecules (CAMs). This view accepts that the general patterns of neural connections are shaped by gene action, but suggests that the exact connections of individual cells are not genetically determined.

At any rate, the critical questions—how rules are programmed genetically and how they are carried out by the intricate circuitry of the brain (let alone represented in the mind)—remain unanswered at this time. Cook uses the phrase "brain code" to describe the set of fundamental rules concerning how signs are stored and transmitted from site to site within the brain, to distinguish this from "neuron code," which is reserved for the mechanisms by which large groups of neurons transmit "images, thoughts and feelings which we suspect are the fundamental units of our psychological lives" (1986, xiii, 2–4). Although the decipherment of the brain code remains the ultimate goal of most research in the neurosciences and psychology, in practice this often proceeds by clarification of aspects of the neural code.

Semiosis in the Superkingdoms

According to one standard scheme for the broad classification of organisms, five superkingdoms are now distinguished: protists (including microbes composed of nucleated cells), bacteria, plants, animals, and fungi (after R. H. Whittaker, discussed in Sebeok 1988a; cf. Margulis and Schwartz 1988). In each group, distinct but intertwined modes of semiosis have evolved, some of which are better understood than others. Brief indications of general principles are given below, but no detailed discussion is possible in this chapter.

Microcosmos is the title of a superb book (Margulis and Sagan 1997a) portraying four billion years of microbial evolution, which, of course, is still in progress, both around, within, and, indeed, as us. Human bodies, for instance, are composed of one hundred quadrillion (100,000,000,000,000,000) bacterial cells, and our endosemiosic systems, including the nervous system, are all derived from intercommunicating aggregations of bacteria. The microcosmos began to evolve out of the debris of supernova explosions 4 billion years ago (in the Hadean eon), spread to land 1.3 billion years ago (in the Protozoic eon) as composite organisms, and these microcosmic collectives evolved into our plant and animal ancestors a mere 0.8 billion years ago (in the Proterozoic eon). According to the modern view of semiosis in the microcosmos, or bacterial semiosis, all bacteria on Earth constitute the communications network of a single superorganism whose continually shifting components are dispersed across the surface of the planet. Sonea and Panisset (1983, 85) liken the bacterial world to a global computerized communications network in extent, possessing an enormous database—more than the brain of any mammal—which functions in a manner reminiscent of human intelligence. Bacterial social life takes three forms: localized teams, the global ensemble itself, and as a body interacting with eukaryotes (Sonea 1988, 42–43). Each of these types of associations is characterized by its appropriate form of semiosis, a rapid and continuous shuffling which seems unrestricted by physical, chemical, or geographic boundaries of energy, matter, and signs.

The key to semiosis in the microcosmos is symbiosis. This is a quintessentially semiotic concept (Füller 1958; Margulis 1981; Margulis and Sagan 1997a, especially chs. 8 and 9)—as are such subsumed concepts as parasitism, mutualism, commensalism, and the like. Symbiosis refers to the living together of individuals of two or more species for most of the life cycles of each, and this cohabitation is clearly "often [in fact, invariably] facilitated by simple [?] forms of COMMUNICATION between the participants" (McFarland 1982, 540). Symbiotic alliances, in due course, became permanent, converting organisms (viz., prokaryotes, which share a kind of immortality, but at the expense of lacking individuality) into new, lasting collectives (viz., eukaryotes, which, on the contrary, pursue individuality but at the expense of an existence between the two poles of sex and death) that are more than simply the sum of their symbiotic parts. In brief, all visible organisms evolved through symbiotic unions between different microbes, which subsequently co-evolved as wholly integrated communities, enduring sharing of cells and bodies; such mergers of diverse organisms can be regarded as thoroughly interwoven living "corporations," harmoniously coordinated by means of nonverbal (and, in the case of hominids, also verbal) signs (Margulis and Sagan 1997a, 127). Margulis and Sagan believe that "the concepts and signals of thought are based on chemical and physical abilities already latent in bacteria," and are moved to ask, "Could the true language of the nervous system . . . be spirochetal remnants, a combination of autocatalyzing RNA and tubulin proteins symbiotically integrated in the network of hormones, neurohormones, cells, and their wastes we call the human body? Is individual thought itself superorganismic, a collective phenomenon?" (ibid., 150–151). Although their hypothesis is not proven, it is most congenial to modern semiotic thinking, as is their additional extrapolation, that perhaps "groups of humans, sedentary and packed together in communities, cities, and webs of electromagnetic communication, are already beginning to form a network as far beyond thought as thought is from the concerted swimming of spirochetes" (ibid., 153). It is fascinating that as semiotically informed a student of the "information society" as Beniger suggests the same kind of "integrative machinery we might build from the spare parts amassed by our various disciplines" (1986, 105; semiotics and semiosis are discussed on pp. 89–90), and traces the beginnings of what he calls "the control revolution" to DNA as a three-dimensional control model (ibid., 112–118).

The three categories of multicellular organisms, distinguished by taxonomers according to the nutritional patterns of each class, that is, three different ways in which information (negentropy) is maintained by extracting order out of the environment, are complementary. Plants are the producers, and derive their food from inorganic sources by means of photosynthesis; animals, or ingesters, are the transformers, deriving their food, preformed organic compounds, from other organisms; fungi are the decomposers, and break their food down externally and then absorb the resulting small molecules from solution. On this macroscopic scale, we have two polar opposite life forms: the composer plants, or the organisms that build up, and the decomposer fungi, or the organisms that break down. Animals, which became supreme experts at semiosis in interactions among their many cells, among one another, and with members of other life forms, can be seen as intermediate transforming agents midway between the other two. In passing, the remarkable parallelism between this systematists' P-A-F model and the classic semioticians' O-S-I model should be noted (but cannot be explored here).

Phytosemiotics

The principles of the vegetative world were most thoroughly discussed, under this designation, by Krampen (1981; cf. Th. von Uexküll 1986, 211–212). He argues that these are different from those of the animal world "in that the absence of effectors and receptors does not allow for the constitution of [Jakob von Uexküll's] functional cycle, of object signs and sign objects, or of an *Umwelt*," but that the vegetative world "is nevertheless structured according to a base semiotics which cuts across all living beings, plants, animals, and humans alike" (Krampen 1981, 203). Although plants are able to distinguish "self" from "nonself," they are otherwise brainless solipsistic systems. However, plants "don't really need brains," for, as Margulis and Sagan picturesquely point out, "they borrow ours. They have a strategic intelligence that resides more in the chemistry of photosynthesis and the ploys of the genes than in the tactics of the cerebral cortex; we behave for them" (1997a, 174–175). Plant semiosis, as a matter of fact, incorporates the ancient microcosmos, a circumstance that accounts in part for botanical success. A "unifying theory of intercellular communication" has recently been developed, which aims to explain at a single stroke the many coincidences involving plant molecules and animal (including human) cells, by showing that both the endocrine system and the nervous system descended from a common, more generalized evolutionary ancestor (Roth and LeRoith 1987). This theory provides the explanation, as well, for scores of coincidences in cellular communication in plants and in animals, for instance, the efficacy of various medicinal herbs and modern plant-derived drugs, the presence of an insulin-like substance in spinach, or the production by truffles of molecules identical to a steroid in boars, while sows detect and seek out even deeply buried truffles. Plants have significant interactions with fungi as well as animals (Krampen also described some conspicuous examples of the latter).

There is, however, a great deal of curious folklore about plant communication, the scientific basis of which remains to be investigated (see, for example, Montalverne 1984).

Mycosemiotics

The general features of fungi are presented by Burnett (1968). Mycologists agree that all fungi are heterotrophic organisms, the vast majority of which are constructed of more or less microscopic, cylindrical filaments (hyphae), with well-designed cell walls; but they disagree as to their taxonomic limits. Semiosis in fungi is not yet well understood, but their interactions with other organisms are basically known (ibid., ch. 12): these can occur without actual contact, by secretion or leakage, and by other means as well. Fungi communicate with green plants (especially their roots), with algae, in particularly dense engagements (which have produced up to about 20,000 species of lichens), with warm-blooded animals (to which they are pathogenic), and with insects; "the essential steps in the establishment of any interaction appear to be governed by contact reactions and/or nutritional relationships", and competition among fungi is fierce (ibid., 359). One of the most fascinating forms of semiosis was found in an excitingly relevant model species called *Dictyosielium discoidium* (which many, although not all, taxonomers class with the fungi). This was described in a classic paper by Bonner (1963), concisely pictured by Lewis Thomas:

> Slime-mold cells [join up to form an organism] in each life cycle. At first they are single amebocytes swimming around, eating bacteria, aloof from each other, untouching, voting straight Republican. Then, a bell sounds, and acrasin is released by special cells toward which the others converge in stellate ranks, touch, fuse together, and construct the slug, solid as a trout. A splendid stalk is raised, with a fruiting body on top, and out of this comes the next generation of amebocytes, ready to swim across the same moist ground, solitary and ambitious. (Quoted here from Sebeok 1979b, 23, where see also Fig. 1–11)

The sign carrier is cAMP (the ubiquitous molecule adenosine monophosphate), identical with the one Tomkins (1975) described in his article on the metabolic code, which has assumed the twin functions of (physiological) epinephrine action and (semiotic) mediation of the intracellular actions of almost all those hormones that interreact with the cell membrane or, in the case in point, signify starvation. The aggregation of the slime molds in single-cell form is coordinated by a sign system involving the cAMP receptor, the structure and activity of which is now clear (Klein et al. 1988). Significant homologies link cAMP to sensory processes in higher organisms. The latest findings support the possibility that this relatively simple eukaryotic chemotactic semiosic system and various vertebrate sign systems evolved from a common ancestor. For fuller details of this remarkable story of cell-cell semiosis by cAMP, the earliest symbolic vehicle uncovered thus far, and the implications thereof for eukaryotic chemotaxis in general, see Devreotes 1982 (and in layman's terms, Wright 1988, 196). The same molecule is at work as a so-called "second messenger" secreted by human liver cells as soon as epinephrine molecules ("first messengers") bind to them. Second messengers of this sort, which are common in humans, mean different things in different contexts, but their *Grundbedeutung* ("basic meaning," in Jakobson's sense) is always "emergency."

Zoosemiotics

The term *zoosemiotics* dates from 1963, and is discussed, in some detail, in Sebeok 1972. Observe that it denotes semiosis in animals inclusive of the nonverbal semiosic component in man, in contrast to the anthroposemiosic component, which necessarily and additionally implicates language; for convenience, however, only the languageless creatures will be considered in this section. The literature on this subject—virtually nonexistent before the early 1960s—has since grown hugely: my 1968 survey (Sebeok ed. 1968) ran to almost seven hundred pages; my 1977 survey (Sebeok ed. 1977) ran to more than eleven hundred; and it would now require a multivolume encyclopedia to encompass the accumulated scholarship. At the same time, no one has quite succeeded in producing a biologically informed as well as semiotically interesting synthesis of the essential principles, taking fully into account what we know of intraspecific, let alone interspecific, aspects of how animals communicate. Some useful recent texts on intraspecific communication are Smith 1977, Lewis and Gower 1980, and Bright 1984; varieties of interspecific semiosis, with special emphasis on mutual interactions between man and animals, were more lately discussed in Sebeok 1988a, where further references will be found; see also the special issue of *Zeitschrift für Semiotik* (15 [1/2], 1993) on communication between man and animals. One overblown topic that received exaggerated media attention in the 1960s and 1970s, but which has proved a false trail and has since become essentially moribund, was the search for verbal semiosis in four species of great apes, and perhaps in certain pelagic mammals as well. For critical reviews of the mythology of language-endowed animals, see Sebeok and Umiker-Sebeok eds. 1980, Umiker-Sebeok and Sebeok 1981, Sebeok 1986c, and Bouissac 1993.

Recent instructive researches in animal communication tend to view groupings—in particular, in such social animals as some insects, dolphins, wolves, lions, and of course primates—in a holistic way, as global semiosic systems. For example, honeybee colonies are now perceived as possessing "collective intelligence," but one that arises from fundamentally decentralized sign processing (cf. Seeley and Levien 1987). Complementing the traditional description of the operation of a honeybee colony as one wherein each bee processes information in serial fashion (say, evaluating flower patches one at a time), the colony as a whole is seen as working in parallel (with many patches being rated at once). The analogy is to the massively parallel computers many artificial intelligence researchers are now using, on the assumption (which is in good conformity with neuro-physiological facts) that the human brain is a fundamentally social structure, its semiosic capacity arising from the interaction of many relatively simple sign processors.

Hominid Forms

Cartmill, Pilbeam, and Isaac (1986) wrote a convenient, concise survey of developments in paleoanthropology during the last hundred years. Hominid forms, which evolved out of the australopithecines, are commonly recognized in terms of three principal anatomical features: gradually increasing brain size; the modification of the limb and pelvic bones in adaptation to fully upright walking (bipedal locomotion); and a reduction in sexual dimorphism (i.e., the difference in body size between males and females). As well as from fossils, important arguments derive from the archeological record. Forms which have thus far been identified include *Homo habilis* ("handy man," 2.4 million to 2.0 million years ago), first described in 1964, which is now generally recognized as a transitional form ancestral to all later *Homo*. *Homo habilis* is the first hominid with a distinctly enlarged brain (600–800 cm^3). It appears virtually certain that *habilis* had language, although not speech (this corresponds, if roughly, to the distinction between *Kognition* and *Sprache* [language] drawn in Müller's 1987 book). Language at its inception was not used for exterior communication, but only as an interior modeling device—a modeling device or system being a tool wherewith an organism analyzes its surroundings. Members of early hominid species communicated amongst each other by nonverbal means, in the manner of all other primates (for details, see Sebeok 1986b, 1988c). *Homo erectus* ("upright man," over 1.5 million years ago) had a brain volume of 800–1,200 cm^3, and a far more elaborate tool kit, including fire; there is no doubt that it had language (yet not speech).

Hominids from the upper Middle Pleistocene, starting about 300,000 years ago, with brain volumes of about 1,200–1,400 cm^3, were our own immediate archaic *sapiens* ("wise man") ancestors, with even more elaborate tools (e.g., hafting), ritual burials, and central-place foraging. Evidence for rule-governed behaviors indicates that they not only had language, but manifested this in the form of speech as well. Archaic *sapiens* divided into at least two subspecies, only one of which, modern *sapiens sapiens*, (i.e., ourselves) flourishes today, with an average brain capacity of 1,500 cm^3; *Homo sapiens sapiens*, it is thought, replaced *Homo sapiens neanderthalensis* in Europe 35,000 years ago. Thus verbal semiosis, or language as a modeling system, having emerged on the scene perhaps 2.5 or

3 million years ago, now survives solely in *Homo sapiens sapiens* (a species that appeared only some 100,000 to 40,000 years ago), and seems to have always been an exclusive property of the genus *Homo* (Sebeok 1986b; Sebeok ed. 1994). Jerison's remark, and attendant discussion, of a "uniquely human experience" (meaning species-typical) which arose "from our use of a cognitive system as a communication system" is right on the mark (1986, 155).

The exaptation of language into speech and, later still, into other linear manifestations, such as script—all topics that belong to anthroposemiotics—will not be discussed here, except to call attention to an important observation by Gould and Vrba that applies *a fortiori* to the relationship of language as a biological adaptation (its historical genesis) to its current added utility as a communicative tool: "Most of what the [human] brain now does to enhance our survival lies in the domain of exaptation" (1982, 13). As to why this process of exaptation took several million years to accomplish, the answer seems to be that the adjustment of a species-specific mechanism for encoding language into speech, i.e., producing signs vocally, with a matching mechanism for decoding it, i.e., receiving and interpreting a stream of incoming verbal/vocal signs (sentences), must have taken that long to fine tune, a process which is far from complete (since humans have great difficulties in understanding each other's spoken messages). Hence Geschwind's remark "that the forerunners of language were functions whose social advantages [i.e., communicative function] were secondary but conferred an advantage for survival [the modeling function]," appears well taken (1980, 313).

Biocommunication and the Gaia Hypothesis

The comprehensive German term *Biokommunikation* was employed by Tembrock (1971) to cover the flow of semiosis in the world of the living. While the domain of semiosis is essentially the same, it can also encompass, in any communicative loop, a human artifact, such as a computer, a robot, or automata generally. Moreover, the bold futuristic vision of Margulis and Sagan, according to which it is inevitable that human life and nonliving manufactured parts will commingle in new "life-forms" within the next few decades, with molecules that, instead of turning into cell material "would turn [energy] into information," by a novel progression they refer to as *cybersymbiosis*, likewise opens doors for an extension of evolutionary semiosis beyond biosemiosis (1986, 44).

The term *Gaia hypothesis* refers to a unified planetary world-view proposed by James Lovelock (1979). According to this controversial hypothesis, the atmosphere, the hydrosphere, and the lithosphere mutually interact with the biosphere of the Earth, each being a compound component of a global unitary autopoiesis, i.e., a homeostatic self-regulating system. In this view, all living entities, from their smallest limits to their largest extent, including some ten million existing species, form parts of a single symbiotic ecological body dubbed *Gaia*. Greenstein (1988) is concerned with the more general proposition of the existence of a symbiosis between the universe on the one hand and life on the other. Should a view, along these lines, of a modulated biosphere prevail, it would in effect mean that all message generators/sources and destinations/ interpreters could be regarded as participants in one gigantic semiosic web; and, if so, this would at the very least affect the style of future semiotic discourse.

3

Biosemiotics

Its Roots, Proliferation, and Prospects

Cognition is simply a development of the selective attitude of an organism
toward its environment and the readjustment that follows upon such a selection.
This selection we ordinarily call "discrimination," the pointing-out of things
and the analysis in this pointing. This is a process of labeling the elements so
that you can refer to each under its proper tag, whether that tag is a pointing of
the finger, a vocal gesture, or a written word.

—George H. Mead (1936, 350)

THROUGHOUT WESTERN intellectual history, most semiotic theories and their applications have focused on messages—whether verbal or otherwise—in circulation among human beings, generally within their cultural setting. This kind of semiotic inquiry, characterizable as anthropocentric or, even more circumscribed, as logocentric, has been the rule since ancient times.

A partial if conspicuous, yet until recently by and large undeclared, exception to this tradition has been iatric semiotics, concerned with the arts of healing (symptomatology, diagnostics, prognostics, and the like), practiced and written about by physicians such as Hippocrates of Cos (460–377 B.C.)—called by many the father of medicine but by some also "der Vater und Meister aller Semiotik" (Kleinpaul 1972, 103; on medical theory and sign theory in pre-Alexandrian times, see Langholf 1990, 57–68, 82–93, 150–164)—or the great Neoplatonist Galen of Pergamon (A.D. 129–c.200) (chapter 4 below). As Baer observed of the Greeks: "Signs [*semeia*] are here construed as bodily clues that allow inferences based on observation" (1988, 47).

Iatric semiotics persevered with numberless modern successors of these

This chapter also appears in *Semiotica* 134 (2001), dedicated to the memory and legacy of Jakob von Uexküll (1864–1944). Kalevi Kull, director of the center established in von Uexküll's name at the University of Tartu in 1993, was guest editor of this special quadruple issue of the journal. Sequential talks based on various sections of this chapter were presented in 1999 at the Technical University of Dresden, the University of Copenhagen, the University of Tartu, and during sessions of the International Semiotics Institute (Imatra, Finland).

venerable figures, to name only a few, through Thomas Sydenham (often called the "English Hippocrates") in the seventeenth century; F. G. Crookshank, also of London, emphatic about "the necessity to Medicine of a Theory of Signs" (1938, 354); Harley C. Shands, a distinguished New York cardiologist turned bountiful semiotician; F. Eugene Yates, a Los Angeles specialist in medical engineering who contends that science in general "has been permeated with semiotic issues all along" (1985, 359); and a host of other contemporaries.

But no pillar of the medical establishment would more crisply and trenchantly discern and signal a crucial paradigm shift in, or a consistently comprehensive semiotic overview of, the intellectual landscape than Thure von Uexküll (hereafter in this chapter: Thure). To be sure, his familial as well as medical credentials are unique. So it is apposite and was perhaps foreordained that he would explicitly pinpoint optics as the underlying exemplar for medicine, especially in its aspect as a natural science concerned with "illness as a disturbance of a complicated physio-biochemical machine" (1982b, 206; 1991).

A few years later, he spelled this out further: "The overwhelming majority of objective evidence of a disease belongs to those types of processes taking place within the body, which, in turn, are divided into subsystems (organ systems, organs, tissue, cells, cellular organelles)" (1986, 204). Just as, on the macroscopic level between the organism and its Umwelt, "evolution depends on setting up new systems of communication" (Jacob 1974, 308), so also within the organism. The components listed are among the major participators in the interchange of signs that ceaselessly ebbs and flows on the interior plane; accordingly, the living things are aptly regarded as a web of semioses. In 1976, I tagged such schemes "cybernetic systems within the body" and then termed their operations "endosemiosic" (1985a, 3).

By 1993, the conceptual framework for internal somatic sign transactions was comprehensively expanded by Thure and two of his medical associates. Since, as these authors point out, all sign processes within "are indirectly linked to phenomena in the organism's environment . . . these endosemiotic signs which belong to an 'inner world' have to be translated into the codes of other . . . sign systems" (Th. von Uexküll et al. 1993, 5–7). Such other codes belong to those exosemiosic transactions which were described by means of what Jakob von Uexküll [hereafter in this chapter: Jakob] named a functional cycle (cf., e.g., 1973, 151–156; see also Th. von Uexküll 1987, 166–169).

"Medicine," as Thure highlighted, was ever "a semiotic discipline" (1992, 455). And, as the historian Carlo Ginzburg pointed out, this "model of medical semiotics or symptomatology" and "the 'semiotic' approach, a paradigm or model based on the interpretation of clues, had become increasingly influential [in the nineteenth century] in the field of human sciences." But in fact its "roots . . . were far more ancient" (1983, 87–91). They can be traced to Mesopotamian forms of knowledge and beyond. The medical crafts should thus be seen as the ultimate cradle of—and a lengthy if tacit prologue as well as a vivid backdrop to—not merely endosemiotics but its comprehensively encompassing domain, which has become increasingly known in the last quarter of our century as biosemiotics. This embraces, according to one recent exposition, "all processes that take place in animate nature at whatever level, from the single cell to the ecosystem," as "concerned with the sign aspects of the processes of life itself, not with the sign character of the theoretical structure of life sciences" (Hoffmeyer 1998, 82). In a different but equally valid formulation, "the socio-semiological limits of intentional communication . . . are largely overcome [by means of biosemiotics] as we are introduced to the global logic of the great ecosystem named Gaia where conceptual boundaries finally open up to the encounter between semiosis and life" (Petrilli 1999, 316). Furthermore, as Thure affirms, biosemiotics remains "of central interest for the biosciences and medicine" (1992, 456; for his most extended recounting to date, cf. 1997; for an early map of this then still ill-defined territory, see Sebeok and Umiker-Sebeok eds. 1992). In short, the province of biosemiotics coincides in its entirety with that of the biosphere, which, in this context, is tantamount to the "semiosphere" (but in a sense far vaster than in Lotman's usage).[1]

Terminological issues abound, but this is hardly the place to rehearse the attendant philological niceties beyond acknowledging that the label of this emerging domain of knowledge seems to have been claimed independently at least twice in the United States and once in the former Soviet Union over the past few decades. What remains important is to corroborate that the *domain* of biosemiotics and the *field* of biosemiotics[2] surfaced a long time *avant la lettre;* and that, furthermore, its ripeness did not result from a simple linear progression but surged by fits and starts as a convoluted affair, winding its long but episodic way through at least three successive twentieth-century iterations: I register these with the names of Jakob von Uexküll (1864–1944), Heini Hediger (1908–92), and Giorgio Prodi (1928–87). In the telling, I must make it clear that I intend to proceed not as a professional historian but rather as an implicated deponent, a predisposed witness variously involved in the unfolding chronicle. The following account will therefore have an autobiographical tinge, but I have never before set the better part of it forth in print.

Jakob spent his student days (1884–88) at the University of Dorpat, in Estonia. But all pilgrims' paths eventually lead to Germany—according to the canonical version of his triumphant trajectory—where he became a citizen in 1918, joining (when already in his sixtieth year) the University of Hamburg in 1924. He founded and led the Institute for Umwelt Research there from 1925 to 1940. Although he had produced the first edition of *Theoretische Biologie* in 1920, he prepared a thoroughly revised second edition in Hamburg that

appeared eight years later, to be posthumously reprinted in 1973. The only English translation, published in 1926, was thus calamitously based on the first
edition. This circumstance, aggravated by the poor quality of this rendering,
alas retarded the appreciation (especially, deplorably enough, in the anglophone world) of his Umwelt-science—and, correspondingly, the flowering of
biosemiotics—by about half a century. Thomson, in his review of the English
version, chose, ambivalently, to "congratulate Dr. D. L. Mackinnon on her remarkably successful translation of what we know to have been very difficult
German. No one but an organically philosophical biologist could have achieved
such a conspicuous success. Now the book can ever be easy-reading, in the most
lucid translation." Yet, on the other hand, he grouses that "an unnecessary
difficulty seems to be raised by the use of difficult terms, which perplex the
reader gratuitously" (1927, 419, 415).

I myself first read the book in English in 1936, finding it bafflingly murky;
but then I read the second German edition in 1976, and found that, if not
pellucid, nonetheless electrifying (Sebeok 1998a, 32–34). Some time later still,
this experience led me to instigate and arrange for the publication of two of
Jakob's shorter monographs in English (1982 and 1992).[3]

In the mid-1970s, I resolved to investigate Jakob's writings for my own
edification, and to look at what others had written about them.[4] These exploratory readings resulted in a paper titled "Neglected Figures in the History of
Semiotic Inquiry: Jakob von Uexküll," which I first presented in an abridged
version in August 1977 at the Third Wiener Symposium über Semiotik (Borbé
ed. 1978); the final, much longer version appeared in *The Sign & Its Masters*
(Sebeok 1989e). This chapter, my personal appreciation of Jakob and his principal works, was widely noticed, despite the fact that it was in the main re-
searched and, foremost, composed to educate myself. So one needs to ask: just
what did this piece accomplish for my readership? The answer is: it redefined
and relocated a nonpareil pioneer investigator of a *domain* (*Umweltlehre*, that
is, the study of modeling) and sanctioned his having done so in a *field* (biosemiotics) appropriate to and by that time at last receptive of his creative
achievement.[5]

Thure was among my audience in Vienna. He reacted to my paper about
his father with no cavils, indeed, with enthusiasm. We had an extended talk
over an ensuing dinner, in consequence of which, a few months afterwards, he
came to call on me at my Bloomington home for a further lengthy evening's
discussion. These two talks gave early impetus to, and decisively shaped, the
subsequent unfolding of biosemiotics. Among other things, it was during these
initial dinner meetings that the two of us hammered out concrete publication
plans in English of several works by both Jakob and Thure himself. Most of
these eventually appeared in *Semiotica,* in other series under the auspices of

Walter or Mouton de Gruyter, or were issued by other houses in Germany and the United States.

There were some other far-reaching consequences that flowed from our talks, two among them being especially worth some comments here. First, the idea of launching a series of annual international conferences devoted to biosemiotics was broached and soon realized by Thure. Repeated about five or six times in the late 1980s and early 1990s, these were held on the premises of the Glotterbad Clinic for Rehabilitative Medicine in Glottertal, Baden-Württemberg, Germany, under his leadership, with the signal cooperation of Jörg M. Herrmann, M.D., the clinic's director. Thure, in his introduction to a session on "models and methods in biosemiotics," succinctly stated the aims: "to support the experiment of bringing together Humanities, represented by semioticians; Natural Sciences, represented by experts in molecular biology; and Medicine, a science with an uncertain position between both of them, represented by internists, psychiatrists, and clinical psychologists." He depicted the topic of the conference as "the proposition of an order in nature which has nothing to do with causality, but which canalizes causal processes between living systems and their environment as well as in and between these systems. We maintain," he concluded, "that this order is a semiotic one or at least can be described in semiotic terms" (1990, 1).[6]

Secondly, Thure made arrangements for me to spend a week or so visiting him in Freiburg (in part intended to coincide with Rowohlt's publication of my German paperback, *Theorie und Geschichte der Semiotik*, where I characterized Jakob as "einer der grössten Kryptosemiotiker seiner Zeit" [1979c, 10]). Our Freiburg discussions about multifarious biosemiotic topics were carried out, with rare intensity, from morning late into every night, and were happily augmented by the continuous participation of Giorgio Prodi, director of the Institute for Cancer Research of the University of Bologna. Prodi, an astounding polymath (Eco 1988) who had become my friend several years earlier, encountered Thure for the first time on that occasion; the two of them met only twice more, first in Palermo in the summer of 1984, then in Lucca in the early fall of 1986 (Sercarz et al. eds. 1988). Prodi sparked the third biosemiotic iteration, to which I shall return below after sketching the second.

One of the sundry riddles that mar the gradual coming into view of modern biosemiotics—the second iteration, if you will—is the neglect of Heini Hediger, whose lifelong attempt to understand animals surely marked a milestone in the elucidation of this domain, providing it with a particularly beneficial empirical footing. This seeming indifference—or is it blindness?—to his capital achievements is the more puzzling in the light of Hediger's manifest admiration for Jakob, whose *Umweltlehre* clearly had a decisive influence on his own highly original analyses of the psychology and biology of animal flight response (or negative territoriality). For instance, touching on his 1932 dissertation and work resulting therefrom, he wrote:

> This work was surprisingly successful; it was especially well received by J. von Uexküll at the Institute for Environmental Studies in Hamburg, where I met both him and his successor, F. Brock. For my part, I was extremely impressed by von Uexküll's Umwelt-Lehre. . . . Consequently, I dedicated another paper following that on my flight work, a study of tameness, to von Uexküll . . . these two subjects formed the basis for my later investigation concerning the relationship between animals and man, especially in the zoo. In addition, they led to the founding of zoo biology . . . " (1985, 149)

Hediger's seminal discoveries of the concepts of individual and social space in application to animals of many kinds were later applied to humans and further fruitfully elaborated under such labels as "proxemics" in anthropology (Hall 1968).

Some years afterwards, I myself discussed nine specific circumstances (among no doubt several others) in which man may have "semiotic encounters" with animals (Sebeok 1988a, 68–71). These juxtapositions include taming and training in several interdependent variations (*apprentissage, dressage,* domestication, and the like). My understanding of such procedures was immensely enriched by Hediger's wealth of experience in shaping behavior, especially in zoos and circuses. Hediger totally accepted the principles of zoosemiotics— which of course constitutes a substantial segment of biosemiotics—"[the two of us] have been working together for some time" (Hediger 1985, 151; see further his 1980 book, with numerous examples and references under this heading).[7] As he noted, we "often met in Zürich or Amsterdam," and in 1980 he was my guest in New York City. In all these venues, we frequented zoos and watched the training and performances of animals in circuses, some large enterprises (like Barnum and Bailey) and others small (such as the Swiss Circus Knie). His powers of observation and their subtlety far exceeded mine, so he taught me many things about applied biosemiotics which I could never have learned on my own (see, e.g., his stunning 1974 article, with striking illustrations, on reciprocal semiosis between man and wild animals, viz., panthers, elephants, etc., in the circus). Hediger's appreciation of the quintessentially biosemiotic constitution of the Clever Hans phenomenon was also uncommonly insightful (Sebeok and Rosenthal eds. 1981, 1–17). He foretold "that eventually an explanation for the extremely complex and, so far, under-researched problem of the relationships between man and animals will be obtained by means of signal study or semiotics, specifically zoo-semiotics" (1985, 177). Overall, his legacy is a many-sided, profuse research program for biosemiotics that can easily extend for several generations ahead (his 1980 book is a veritable treasure-house for a research agenda).

Hediger was a visionary innovator who reached from the inside outwards. He felt entirely comfortable within Jakob's Umwelt paradigm, but implicitly with (zoo) semiotics too, which he came increasingly and quite explicitly to embrace and profitably apply in his later years. Giorgio Prodi, to the contrary, was a maverick: a prolific physician and experimental oncologist by profession, a novelist by avocation, but also an intermittent if resolute contributor to biosemiotics. However radically idiosyncratic, Prodi's recreation of a domain for biosemiotics was with little hesitation matched up with an existing field, or academic niche, a luxury not enjoyed by Jakob, and by Hediger only indirectly, and only in his late sixties.[8] His first major book on the subject—which claimed to deal with "la preistoria nelle sue pesanti conseguenze sulla storia e sulla teoria della semiosi" (1977, 5)—was promptly accepted for publication by Umberto Eco; he was asked to deliver a paper on the topic at the Third International Congress of the International Association for Semiotic Studies in 1984 (1988a) and invited to prepare a long English version of the former to appear in *Semiotica* (1988b). He was also chosen to be a key participant in the 1986 workshop on immunosemiotics, organized by Sercarz and others, where he spoke on "Signs and Codes in Immunology".[9] Here he took a decided position against "semiotics as a pure human domain," in contrast to his own perspective of "a general semiotic domain," and introduced the notion of a "protosign," which belongs to "proto-semiotics . . . the basic feature of the whole biological organization"—protein synthesis, metabolism, hormone activity, transmission of nervous impulses, and so on (1988c, 63, 55).

More extensively, he labeled the overall domain *natural semiotics* (1988d, 149–170), which seems to be roughly equivalent to mathematician Kergosien's "nature semiotics" (1992, 145), as well as to the phrase "semiotics of nature," occasionally used by Hoffmeyer and Emmeche (1991, 117–118) (although they currently seem to favor *biosemiotics*). In my judgment, these quasi-synonymous terms are poor substitutes for *biosemiotics*. There are several reasons for this, some narrow, others broader. The narrow reason is that the word *nature* is used with quite different technical connotations by Jakob, as explicated in Thure's glossary: "Systematically ordered and complete structure of all UMWELTS whose meaning is sought in overlapping composition" (1987, 236). Yet, at other times, Jakob equated *nature* with "true reality": "Da die Tätigkeit unseres Gemüts das einzige uns unmittelbar bekannte Stück Natur ist, sind seine Gesetze die enizigen, die mit Recht den Namen Naturgesetze führen dürfen" (J. von Uexküll 1973, 40).

The over-arching context for biosemiotics is our biosphere, in the sense of the organic whole of living matter; and Earth is the only geosphere which contains living matter. Because there can be no semiosis without interpretability—surely life's cardinal propensity—semiosis presupposes the axiomatic identity of the semiosphere with the biosphere. As Short persuasively argued, "there is no basis for the assertion that semiosis occurs outside of living things" (1998, 49), except, one may add, man's inert extensions, such as automata, computers, or robots. Local nature (Gaia), however, additionally comprehends the inorganic matrix for the place wherein organisms dwell—the enveloping gaseous mass, waters, and rocks—while cosmic nature further includes the totality of extraterrestrial objects (chapter 14 below).

Another eccentricity of Prodi's is his avoidance of reference to the works of others. For example, in his English article, although dealing with intrinsically biosemiotic issues, viz., "natural semiology" (1988b, 206), he cites only Frege and the 1923 edition of Ogden and Richards. While this composition style perhaps adumbrates Prodi's striking originality, it fails to align him with any predecessors or successors in semiotics, so his untutored readers may flounder for lack of familiar signposts. But having said this, during the week we spent together in our open-ended 1979 "intensive seminar" in Thure's company on the practical and conceivable ins and outs of biosemiotics, the three of us got along extremely well; as I commented afterwards, "this uniquely stimulating experience enabled me to enhance my writing and teachings . . . in biosemiotics in its various topical subdivisions" (chapter 15 below, p. 170).

In 1988, some months after Prodi's untimely death at the age of 59, I received an invitation from the officers of a medical association in his country to attend a sizable memorial gathering at an isolated resort in southern Italy, where I was to delineate Prodi's contributions to biosemiotics. As it turned out, my fellow participants were all physicians or biologists. His colleagues seemed genuinely respectful of, indeed, fascinated by, the semiotic side of Prodi's scholarly endeavors, yet none publicly declared a commitment to his line of research.

Such appear to me to have been the three principal biosemiotic iterations of our century. But these evidently do not exhaust the prehistory of this domain. Other creative figures could be named (although, arguably, in a minor key): for one, Kenneth Craik (1914–45), the reclusive don of St. John's College, Cambridge, who independently invented "another kind of *Umwelt* theory" (Craik 1943; see Sebeok 1991e, 104); and for another (if perhaps tangentially) René Thom (b. 1923), the mathematician whose catastrophe-theoretical excursions into areas of biological morphogenesis were powerfully impacted by Jakob's theorems of the dynamic of life (Thom 1975).

Biosemiotics tends sometimes to be promoted, though I think mistakenly, to contrast with cultural semiotics. "Culture" is not much more than that realm of nature where the logosphere—Bakhtin's dialogic universe—impinges in infant lives and then comes to predominate in normal adult lives. Yet in fact even mainstream semioticians range over a wide spectrum of attitudes toward biology. Ernst Cassirer's writings are, for instance, not just saturated by biological intimations—Jakob's impress is palpable throughout (e.g., 1944, 23–26; cf. J. von Uexküll 1992, 311, ns. 2 and 3). For A. J. Greimas, zoosemiotics looms somewhere in a hazy if rosy future: "it is destined to become a genuine semiotic realm, both autonomous and promising," he declared (Greimas and Courtès 1982, 376). Umberto Eco, who once banished zoosemiotics to "il limite inferiore della semiotica" (1975, 21), now concedes that "in the depth of biological processes lie the elementary mechanisms from which semiosis springs" (in Sercarz et al. eds. 1988, 15). Louis Hjelmslev remains silent on the matter. And so on . . .

In an attempt to ascertain dispositions in some depth rather than by a mere impressionistic sampling, I was able to persuade an array of colleagues to scrutinize the oeuvre of five pre-eminent semioticians of yore—Charles Peirce, Victoria Welby, Charles Morris, Roman Jakobson, and Yuri Lotman—"for harbingers of biosemiotic discernments, judgments, prognostications, or at the very least congeniality" (from my foreword to Hoffmeyer and Emmeche eds. 1999). Readers interested in pursuing the fascinating results of these searches are referred to Part I of *Biosemiotica* (Hoffmeyer and Emmeche eds. 1999).[10]

In some crudely simple quantitative terms, biosemiotics can certainly be said to have proliferated over the past decade: for example, as compared to the volume *Biosemiotics* edited by Sebeok and Umiker-Sebeok (1992), which ran to less than 500 pages, the Hoffmeyer-Emmeche volume *Biosemiotica* (eds. 1999), ran to 660 pages; but that was, as well, shortly preceded by another over 250-page double issue of *Semiotica* devoted to a closely kindred topic, *Semiotics in the Biosphere* (Vol. 120 [1998]) and followed by a separate volume, to appear in 2001, dedicated to the memory, appreciation, and influence of the domain's chief architect, Jakob. Single-author book-length publications in biosemiotics, like Merrell's (1996) or Hoffmeyer's (1993a), are multiplying, as are collections such as the one by Van de Vijver et al. (1998), with yet others in sight. Significantly, new reference books are now routinely graced by separate entries on biosemiotics, as in Walter de Gruyter's *Handbook of Semiotics* (Posner et al. 1997, 1:436–591), the Oxford University Press's *Encyclopedia* (Hoffmeyer 1998), *Routledge Critical Dictionary of Semiotics and Linguistics* (Cobley ed. 2001), and the expanded second edition of Winfried Nöth's *Handbook of Semiotics* (2000). Too, I have already listed (in endnote 6) scores of recent conventions on biosemiotics, of diverse sizes and varying composition, assembled at venues over four continents.

It is on the other hand also true that biosemiotics—like general semiotics itself—has not typically become a conventional university-based discipline, nor, in my view, should it have.[11] This is not the place to argue again for my preference, but it is clear that such formal units of knowledge production are by no means the only possible, let alone the most desirable, type of reputational system of work organization and control. Semiotics and, *a fortiori*, biosemiotics are, or should be, fields committed to producing novelty and innovations, not much else. Whitley rightly emphasized that there exists an "'essential tension' between novelty and tradition, or co-operation and competition" (1984, 13), a notable feature of certain kinds of modern scientific works, surely inclusive of biosemiotics. He observed that a "broader and more general social unit of knowledge production and co-ordination is the intellectual field." Such fields, conceived as "relatively well-bounded and distinct social organizations which control and direct the conduct of research on particular topics in different ways," possess identities that are by no means always identical with employment or education unit boundaries. They "vary in the degree of cohesion and autonomy from other [academic] structures, but constitute the major social entities which co-ordinate and orient research across a wide variety of situations. . . . They reconstruct knowledge around distinct 'subjects' and their organization and change are crucial aspects of intellectual work and knowledge production in the modern, differentiated sciences" (ibid., 7). By "science," Whitley has of course in mind all forms of modern scholarship, not just the natural sciences; and each intellectual field, or craftwork, he stresses, "has a distinctive language for describing cognitive objects and communicating task outcomes which reduces lay participation in the assessment of contributions and enables results from different production sites to be compared and co-ordinated" (ibid., 34). In a useful tabular form, he differentiates between scientific fields, in which biosemiotics obviously belongs under his type (e), along with bio-medical science, artificial intelligence, engineering, or pre-Darwinian nineteenth-century ornithology (ibid., 158, table 5.2).

Note that each of our three biosemiotics trailblazers was an intrinsically unconventional academic. Jakob, in support of his consecutive faculty engagements in Germany, was, in addition to his affiliation with the Zoological Center in Naples, particularly active in his own Institute for Umwelt Research at the University of Hamburg. Hediger was, to be sure, a professor of psychology at the University of Zürich, but his concentrated intellectual efforts radiated out of a succession of zoological gardens, first at Dählhölzli (Bern), then Basel, finally, effective 1954, his beloved Zürich Zoo. Prodi, who held the chair in experimental oncology at the University of Bologna's School of Medicine, worked out of his own Instituto di Cancerologia. The functions of these distinctions, which may seem to academic outsiders mere subtle refinements, or frosting atop of a cake, are perfectly understood by professors like me, for I too was the chairman of a research center at my institution for thirty-seven years. This is also why the University of Tartu's Jakob von Uexküll Center—a modernized reincarnation (under Kalevi Kull's direction) of the Hamburg prototype—is fraught with such promise of new research departures, supplementing the university's time-honored departmental structures necessarily dedicated to upholding traditional paths of teaching and learning propagation.

An interesting condition specified for the establishment of scientific fields as distinct systems of work organization is that "each field has to control a separate communication system," that is, a benchmark set of shared vocabulary items of its own that differentiates this field from all others as a sort of monopolistic exclusion device (Whitley 1984, 29, 31–32). This is why Jakob's seemingly arcane terminology, often remarked on by biologist commentators and other readers, is so advantageous, even when—or especially because—it provokes an often-felt need to have recourse to an accompanying formal glossary (e.g., in 1982, 83–87). This was pointed out by Thure himself when he insisted that the differences in Jakob's "terminology are not to be regarded simply as a source of difficulty; they may also prove helpful where the various semiotic theories diverge." Here he surely refers to the unavoidable disparities between his father's idiom, Peirce's, and Saussure's (1987, 148; see also Krampen 1997, 512).[12]

Although Jakob's research interests in principle encompassed the comportment of *all* organisms, in fact he spun his theory of models and of the attendant functional cycle almost entirely out of his observations of "the worlds of animals and men," particularly marine animals (jellyfish, sea urchins, octopuses, trout) and insects (annelids, ticks, dragonflies). He is therefore justly counted among the founders of ethology (Bleibtreu 1968, 13), for this "certainly owes more to his teaching than to any other school of behaviour study" (Lorenz 1971, 277); many of the phenomena and operational concepts that "gave focus to classical ethology were first described, or at least anticipated" by him (Dyer and Brockman 1996, 529). His framework was also commonly used by early investigators of synchronic animal communication processes, as well as for the testing of the hypothesis of "ritualization"—or what I have elsewhere called "the semiosis of *gene-dependency*"—an intriguing special case of diachronic sign science (Sebeok 1989e, 29–30, fig. 2–1). Inasmuch as any animal's communication system must be a natural extension of its sensorium, which invokes an understanding of its Umwelt, it is easy to appreciate how indispensable Jakob's insights were to the origins and development of zoosemiotics (Sebeok 1972, 61). Doubtless, the most cited example of the zoosemiotic aspects of Jakob's explorations is his fabled scrutiny of *Ixodes rhitinus,* the cattle tick (with whose story Bleibtreu opens his 1968 book), reinterpreted in a Dresden lecture by Udo Figge as recently as February 1999 in strictly semiotic terms.

Hediger had a sweeping yet intimate knowledge of the behavior of an exceptionally wide range of animals—especially terrestrial vertebrates—based on extensive field work as well as acute observations both in and far beyond the zoo. At the very outset of his remarkable book he specifies: "Insbesondere werden wir uns mit der Zoosemiotik zu befassen haben, also mit den Signalen, die zwischen Tieren und besonders zwischen Tier und Mensch in beiden Richtungen wirksam sind, gewissermassen hin und her schwingen." Later he adds: "Der Zoosemiotik bleibt noch ein weites Feld zu bearbeiten" (1980, 10, 144), but already Hediger himself had impressively contributed to this field. Following in Jakob's footsteps, he consistently applied both biological and semiotic criteria to the study of animal communication. Jakob did so implicitly, Hediger eventually in quite categorical terms.

Peter Cariani, among others, has suggested that "biosemiotics has evolved from the study of animal communication to more general considerations of biological codes" (in Van de Vijver et al. eds. 1998, 360). This, however, simplifies, even skews, the far more labyrinthine sequence of events culminating in biosemiotics to which zoosemiotics is but one contributing factor (Sebeok 1998a, 10). This notwithstanding, zoosemiotics is doubtless "a particularly rich branch of biosemiotics because animals are in some sense semiosic mediators between creation and decay. On a macroscopic scale, they can be viewed as transforming agents fixed midway between the 'composer' plants, organisms that set interpretants in motion, and 'decomposer' fungi, which break them down," viz., between phytosemiosic and mycosemiosic operations (chapter 1, p. 14). Too, in their role as go-betweens, animals process signs through media embracing the entire sensory spectrum, each—in conformity with Jakob's teachings—according to, but only commensurate with, its specific array of sense organs (Sebeok 1997b, 116).

Others chose to pursue different pathways to enhance the biosemiotic superstructure, an enticing case in point deriving from some casual remarks of Jakob's to the effect that plants lack a function cycle. Krampen has shown the predominance of indexicality in plant semioses, that plants nonetheless do have feedback cycles connecting sensors and regulators, and how "meaning factors" function in the vegetal (versus animal) realm—or, in a nutshell, how phytosemiosis differs from zoosemiosis (1981, 1997).

Not surprisingly, the guiding preoccupation of medical practitioners from Hippocrates to our day, notably including both Thure and Prodi, has focused on endosemiosis or "protosemiosis" from the cell up to the highest integration level, the sphere where the non-conscious inner world may in humans and certain other animals become transmutable, by means of sign connections via neurotransmitters, neurohormones, and other neurobiological processes still far from understood, into consciously experienced reality.[13]

Researches at the ephemerally woven frontiers of biosemiotics—the highest and the lowest planetary limits of which are evolutionarily circumscribed by two suggestive metaphors (both, as it happens, of Canadian vintage)—are of quotidian concern. The upper periphery, a virtual community, was dubbed a *global village* by Toronto's Marshall McLuhan (1962, 31). This electronically mediated global forum, located nowhere on the superhighway called the Internet, is a very real, if volatile, network of networks. It is populated by biomimetic creatures with unconventional communication schemes and emotive manifestations actualized by media embodiments, such as animation, robot languages and robot speech, and text. Regular and occasional users are subject to the vagaries of cybersemiotics (cf. endnote 7).

The scalar opposite metaphor was coined by Montreal's Sorin Sonea: the *global organism*. Nor did the similitude with the Internet escape him: "Like an electronic communications network the bacterial world possesses an enormous data base, in this case in the form of bacterial genes. . . . This biological communications network, which possesses more basic information than the brain of any mammal, functions in a manner that sometimes resembles human intelligence" (Sonea and Panisset 1983, 85). Furthermore, the ensemble of bacteria resemble "a vast computerized communications network—a superorganism whose myriad parts shift and share genetic information to accommodate any and all circumstances" (Sonea 1988, 45). The smallest known autopoietic entity is a single self-maintaining bacterial cell, the "biosemiotic atom."

The analogy is powerful, yet not absolute. While being wired is optional— we nonusers think we have rational grounds for our skepticism—the global prokaryotic community inescapably perfuses the earth. In a way that is literally mind-boggling, all of us eukaryotes are fashioned of bacteria; we are both their habitats and vehicles for further dispersal. In particular, our central nervous system may be characterized as a colony of interactive bacteria. For this reason alone, any biosemiotic theory failing to take into account the multiform data of bacterial semiosis is as flawed as would be one that ignored the complexities of the verbal code in its social ramifications (cf. chapter 1 above).

4

Galen in Medical Semiotics

ULLMANN (1951, 161) distinguished among four juxtaposed branches of word-study: "(1) the science of names (lexicology if synchronistic, etymology if diachronistic); (2) the science of meanings (semantics); (3) the science of designations (onomasiology); (4) the science of concepts *(Begriffslehre)*." Although the distinction between designation and meaning, particularly as displayed in the works of German and Swiss semanticists (of the sometimes loosely, as well as erroneously, called Trier-Weisgerber School) is far from consistently drawn or pellucid, I take it that this alterity depends on whether one's starting point is the *name,* the *lexeme,* or, more generally, the *sign;* or whether it is the *concept* or, more generally yet, the *object,* i.e., the constellation of properties and relations the sign stands for. If the former, the analysis should yield a semiotic network responsive to the question: what does a given sign signify in contrast and opposition to any other sign within the same system of signs? If the latter, the analysis should reveal the sign by which a given entity is designated within a certain semiotic system. According to Ullmann, the second inquiry "is the cornerstone of Weisgerber's structure" (1951, 161), but I believe that the two

This article has had a convoluted publishing history. In 1982, I wrote a paper titled "Symptom" for delivery at a symposium on New Directions in Linguistics and Semiotics, convened at Rice University at the initiative of Professor Sydney Lamb. That paper was published, in much expanded form, in a book bearing the same symposium title, edited by James E. Copeland, pp. 211–230 (Houston: Rice University Studies, 1984). A somewhat revised version appeared thereafter in my own book *I Think I Am a Verb: More Contributions to the Doctrine of Signs,* 45–58 (New York: Plenum Press, 1986).

On October 19, 1992, at the Fourth Congress of the Hellenic Semiotic Society at the University of Thessaloniki, Greece, by invitation of the co-organizers, I presented a substantially reworked but still necessarily abridged variant, under the new title "Medical Semiotics: The Legacy of Galen." That version appeared among the proceedings of the congress, in *Anthropos o Semainon,* vol. 1, *Logos Kai Ideologie,* eds. A. Lagopoulos and K. Lagopoulou (Thessaloniki: Pagatigitis, 1996).

In November 1992, while I was both a visiting professor of semiotics at the University of Toronto and a senior fellow in residence at Massey College, I wrote a further elaborated version, incorporating added materials, particularly on Galen. It is this final version that appears here.

I want to thank Professors Alexandros Lagopoulos and Karin Lagopoulou for their generous hospitality in Athens, Iracleo, and especially in and around Thessaloniki.

questions are indissolubly complementary. In any case, the whole enterprise critically hinges upon how the investigator parses the sign/object *(aliquid/ aliquo)* relation, and what the conjunctive *stands for,* in the judgment of the investigator, entails.

The probe becomes at once more intricate, but also more intriguing, when the lexical field *(Bedeutungsfeld? Sinnfeld? Wortfeld?)* being explored happens to be reflexive, that is, self-searching. Such is the case of *symptom* (Sebeok 1986a, 45–58), an ancient technical term in both semiotics and medicine. Thus its examination may begin in the inner realm of the lexicon, if viewed as a name, or in the outer realm of clinical experience, if viewed as sense.

One may properly inquire: what does the lexeme *symptom* mean in language L_1? What does the same lexeme designate, or reveal as a diagnostic intimation, with respect to, say, an actual quality of "diseasehood" (Fabrega 1974, 123) that F. G. Crookshank (in Ogden and Richards 1938, 343) foresightedly portrayed as "a mysterious *substantia* that has 'biological properties' and 'produces' symptoms"? In the end, the results of such dichotomous inquiries amalgamate in a common dialectical synthesis. For the purposes of this exposition, L_1 is American English. However, the semantic field of "medical discourse," which is typically nested within wider sets of concentric frames (Labov and Fanshel 1977, 36f.), is here assumed to be, *mutatis mutandis,* very similar to that in every other speech community committed to the paradigm of medical theory and practice "in the context of the great tradition" (Miller 1978, 184) of thinking marked by a continuity that links modern clinicians with the idea of *isonomia* launched by the brilliant Alcmaeon of Croton during the first half of the fifth century. This heritage was further consolidated by Hippocrates—arguably considered, at one and the same time, the "father of medicine" (Heidel 1941, xiii), and "der Vater und Meister aller Semiotik" (Kleinpaul 1972, 103)—and Plato, Aristotle, and the Alexandrian physicians of the fourth century B.C. (Manetti 1987, 57–134). Equally perceptive studies of *symptom* have, in fact, cropped up in the semiotic literature (e.g., Baer 1982, 1986, 1988) and in the medical literature (e.g., Prodi 1981), undertaken by savants who know their way around both fields (see also Staiano 1979, 1982). One should, however, continue to be mindful of the admonition of Mounin (1981) against a mechanical application of semiotic (especially linguistic) concepts to medicine (especially psychiatry).

Symptom always appears in conjunction with *sign,* but the precise nature of the vinculum is far from obvious (as in MacBryde and Backlow eds. 1970 or Chamberlain and Ogilvie eds. 1974). The basic semiosic facts were perspicuously depicted by Ogden and Richards:

If we stand in the neighbourhood of a crossroad and observe a pedestrian confronted by a notice *To Grandchester* displayed on a post, we commonly distinguish three important factors in the situation. There is, we are sure, (1) a Sign which (2) refers to a Place and (3) is being interpreted by a person. All situations in which Signs are considered are similar to this. A doctor noting that his patient has a temperature and so forth is said to diagnose his disease as influenza. If we talk like this we do not make it clear that signs are here also involved. Even when we speak of symptoms we often do not think of these as closely related to other groups of signs. But if we say that the doctor interprets the temperature, etc. as a Sign of influenza, we are at any rate on the way to an inquiry as to whether there is anything in common between the manner in which the pedestrian treated the object at the crossroad and that in which the doctor treated his thermometer and the flushed countenance. (1938, 21)

The relation of sign to symptom involves either coordination or subordination. If the distinction is between coordinates, what matters less than their inherent meaning is the mere fact of the binary opposition between the paired coordinate categories. This was nicely brought to the fore in a report of an investigation of the symptom "fatigue" by two physicians, Shands and Finesinger: "The close study of . . . patients made it imperative to differentiate carefully between 'fatigue,' a feeling, and 'impairment,' an observable decrement in performance following protracted effort. The distinction comes to be that between a *symptom* and a *sign*. The symptom is felt, the sign observed by some other person. These two terms cover the broad field of semiotics; they are often confused, and the terms interchanged [at least in Li] without warning" (Shands 1970, 52). This passage underscores the importance of separating the "private world" of introspection, reported by the verbal description or nonverbal exhibition of the symptoms on the part of the patient, from the public world of signs, reported by the description of status or behavior observed on the part of the physician. As I have written earlier: "It is a peculiarity of symptoms that their denotata are generally different from the addresser, i.e., the patient ('subjective symptoms,' confusingly called by many medical practitioners 'signs') and the addressee, i.e., the examining physician ('objective symptoms,' or simply 'symptoms')" (1976, 181). Note that only a single observer—to wit, oneself—can relate symptomatic phenomena or events, whereas an indefinite number of observers—including oneself—can observe signs. Accordingly, within this framework the fact of privacy looms as a criterial distinctive feature that demarcates any symptom from any sign (Sebeok 1991e, 36–48). Symptoms could thus be read as recondite communiqués about an individual's inner world, an interpretation that sometimes acquires the status of an elaborate occult metaphor. For instance, the eating disorder anorexia nervosa would appear to be reasonably decipherable as "I am starving (emotionally) to death." Its symptoms are sometimes believed to result from disturbed family relationships and interpersonal difficulties (Liebman, Minuchin, and Baker 1974a, 1974b). One palpable sign of this ailment is, of course, weight phobia, measurable as a decrease in the patient's mass.

The crucial distinction between fatigue and impairment is "similar to that between *anxiety* as a felt symptom and behavioral disintegration often exhibited in states of panic. The latter is a sign, not a symptom" (Shands 1970, 52). The dissemblance exemplified here is obviously related to Thure von Uexküll's notion, maintained both in the life and the sign science, of "inside" and "outside" (1982b, 209). I take the pivotal implication of this to be as follows: "Something observed (= outside) stands for something that is (hypothetically) noticed by the observed subjects (= inside). Or something within the observing system stands for something within the observed system" (ibid.). For any communication, this complementary relationship is obligatory, because the organism and its Umwelt together constitute a single system. The shift from physiological process to semiosis is a consequence of the fact that the observer assumes a hypothetical stance within the observed system *(Bedeutungserteilung / Bedeutungsverwertung)*.

For *symptom* (in L1), there exists an array of both stricter and looser synonyms. Among the former, which appear to be more or less commonly employed, Elstein et al. solely and extensively use *cue*. Although they do so without a definition, their import is made quite clear from passages such as "cues were interpreted by physicians as tending to confirm or disconfirm a hypothesis, or as noncontributory" (1978, 279). Fabrega, on the other hand, seems to prefer *indicator,* but he uses this commutably for either *symptom* or *sign;* and when he remarks that "all indicators may be needed in order to make judgments about disease" (1974, 126), he surely refers to both categories together. The word *clue,* on the other hand, is a looser synonym for *symptom:* generally speaking, where *symptom* is used in medical discourse, *clue* is found in the detective sphere (Sebeok 1981c; Eco and Sebeok eds. 1983).

In the minimalist coupling, *sign* and *symptom* are equipollent; both are unmarked vis-à-vis one another (Waugh 1982). Sometimes, however, *symptom* encompasses both "the objective sign and the subjective sign" (cf. Staiano 1982, 332). In another tradition, *symptom* is a mere phenomenon "qui précisément n'a encore rien de sémiologique, de sémantique," or is considered falling, for instance, in the terminology of glossematics, in the area of content articulation, *la substance du signifiant,* an operationally designated figura that is elevated to full semiotic status only through the organizing consciousness of the physician, achieved through the mediation of language (Barthes 1972, 38f.). However, still other radically different arrangements occur in the literature. In Bühler's organon model (see Sebeok 1981a), *symptom* constitutes but one of three "variable moments" capable of rising "in three different ways to the rank of a sign": *signal, symbol,* and *symptom.* Bühler specifies further that the semantic relation of the latter functions "by reason of its dependence on the sender, whose interiority it expresses" (1965, 28). He clearly subordinates this trio of words under one and the same "Oberbegriff 'Zeichen'" then goes on to ask: "Ist es zwäkmässig, die Symbole, Symptome, Signale zusammenzufassen in einem genus-proximum 'Zeichen'?" It should also be noted that Bühler's first mention of *symptom* is immediately followed by a parenthetic set of presumed synonyms: "Anzeichen, Indicium." (Note that the German verb *anzeigen* bears an ominous secondary judicial connotation, "to denounce somebody"—see Sebeok 1981a, 228f.)

Thus, in acknowledging the importance of the notion of privacy as an essential unmarked feature of *symptom*, Bühler also recognizes that, while it is coordinate with two other terms, it is also subordinate to the (unmarked) generic notion of *sign*, namely, that kind of sign that Peirce earlier, but unbeknownst to Bühler, defined with much more exactitude as an *index* (Sebeok 1991d, 128–143).

Despite his extensive knowledge of medicine (Sebeok 1981c, 37), Peirce did not often discuss *symptom* (nor anywhere, in any fecund way, *syndrome, diagnosis, prognosis,* or the like). For him, a *symptom,* to begin with, was one kind of sign. In a very interesting passage, from the dictionary lemma "Represent," he expands: "to stand for, that is, to be in such a relation to another that for certain purposes it is treated by some mind as if it were that other. Thus, a spokesman, deputy, attorney, agent, vicar, diagram, symptom, counter, description, concept, premise, testimony, all represent something else, in their several ways, to minds who consider them in that way" (*CP* 2.273).

For Peirce, however, a symptom was never a distinct species of sign, but a mere subspecies—or secondness of genuine degree (in contrast to a demonstrative pronoun, exemplifying secondness of a degenerative nature)—of one of his three canonical categories, namely the index. But what kind of sign is this? Peirce gives an example that I would have preferred to label a *clue:* "Such, for instance, is a piece of mould with a bullet-hole in it as sign of a shot; for without the shot there would not have been a hole; but there is a hole there, whether anybody has the sense to attribute it to a shot or not" (*CP* 2.304). The essential point here is that the indexical character of the sign would not be voided if there were no explicit interpretant, but only if its object were removed. An index is that kind of a sign that becomes such by virtue of being really (i.e., factually) connected with its object. "Such is a symptom of disease" (*CP* 8.119). All "symptoms of disease," furthermore, "have no utterer," as is also the case with "signs of the weather" (*CP* 8.185). We have an index, Peirce prescribed in 1885, when there is "a direct dual relation of the sign to its object independent of the mind using the sign. . . . Of this nature are all natural signs and physical symptoms" (*CP* 3.361).

A further detail worth pointing out is that Peirce calls the "occurrence of a symptom of a disease . . . a legisign, a general type of a definite character," but "the occurrence in a particular case is a sinsign" (*CP* 8.335), that is to say, a *token*. A somewhat cryptic remark reinforces this: "To a sign which gives reason to think that something is true, I prefer to give the name of a *symbol*; although the words *token* and *symptom* likewise recommend themselves" (MS 787, 1896). Staiano is undoubtedly correct in remarking that "the appearance of a symptom in an individual is thus an indexical sinsign, while the symptom interpreted apart from its manifestation becomes an indexical legisign" (1982, 331).

Symptoms, in Peirce's usage, are thus unwitting indexes, interpretable by their receivers without the actuality of any intentional sender. Jakobson likewise includes symptoms within the scope of semiotics, but cautions that "we must consistently take into account the decisive difference between communication which implies a real or alleged addresser and information whose source cannot be viewed an addresser by the interpreter of the indications obtained" (1971, 703). This remark glosses over the fact that symptoms are promptings of the body crying out for an explanation—for the construction, by the self, of a coherent and intelligible pattern (which of course may or may not be accurate; cf. Polunin 1977, 91).

Pain is one such symptom that embodies a message compelling the central nervous system to influence both covert and overt behavior to seek out signs of pain, throughout phylogeny, ontogeny *hic et ubique*. Miller befittingly expands:

> From the instant when someone first recognizes his symptoms to the moment when he eventually complains about them, there is always an interval, longer or shorter as the case may be, when he argues with himself about whether it is worth making a complaint known to an expert. . . . At one time or another we have all been irked by aches and pains. We have probably noticed alterations in weight, complexion and bodily function, changes in power, capability and will, unaccountable shifts of mood. But on the whole we treat these like changes in the weather . . . (1978, 45–49)

Peirce once particularized the footprint that Robinson Crusoe found in the sand to be an index "that some creature was on his island" (*CP* 4.351), and indeed an index always performs as a sign with a vector toward the past, or, as Thom put it, "par reversion de la causalité génératrice" (1980, 194), which is the inverse of physical causality. Augustine's class of *signa naturali*, defined—in contrast to *signa data*—by the relation of dependence between sign and the things signified (*De Doctrina Christiana* 2.1.2), beside its orthodox sense (such as a rash as a symptom of measles), is also illustrated by footprints left by an animal passed out of sight. It may thus be regarded as encompassing a portent, or in the most general usage, evidence (for instance, as a southwesterly wind may both signify and bring rain, i.e., give rise to its significatum). Thus symptoms, in many respects, function like tracks—footprints, toothmarks, food pellets, droppings and urine, paths and runs, snapped twigs, lairs, the remains of meals, etc.—throughout the animal world (Sebeok 1976, 133) and in hunting populations, where humans "learnt to sniff, to observe, to give meaning and context to the slightest trace" (Ginzburg 1983). Both tracks and symptoms operate like metonyms. This trope is also involved in *pars pro toto*, as extensively analyzed by Bilz, who spelled out its relevance: "Auch eine Reihe körperlicher Krankheitszeichen sog., funktioneller oder organ-neurotischer Symptome, haben wir unter den Generalnenner der Szene gebracht, einer verschütteten Ganzheit. . . . Hier ist es . . . eine Teil*funktion* der Exekutive . . . wobei wir abermals auf den Begriff der Parsprototo stiessen" (1940, 287).

It is, of course, Hippocrates who remains the emblematic ancestral figure of semiotics—that is to say, semiology, in the narrow, particularly Romance, sense of symptomatology—although he "took the notion of clue from the physicians who came before him" (Eco 1980b, 277). Baer alludes to a "romantic symptomatology," which he postulates may have been "the original one," carrying the field back "to an era of mythical consciousness" (1982, 18). Alcmaeon remarked, in one of the scanty fragments of his book: "As to things invisible and things mortal, the gods have certainties; but, so far as men may infer . . . ," or, in an alternative translation, "men must proceed by clues" (Eco 1980b, 281), namely, provisionally conjecture. And what is to be the basis of such circumstantial inference? Clearly, the concept that has always been central is *symptom* (*semeion;* Ginzburg 1983).

While Alcmaeon is commonly regarded as the founder of empirical psychology, it was Hippocrates, a clinical teacher par excellence (Temkin 1973), who broke with archaic medical practice, where the physician was typically preoccupied with the nature of the disease, its causes, and manifestations, and refocused directly upon the sick person and his/her complaints—in brief, upon the *symptoms* of disease: "Nicht so sehr die Krankheit als das Kranke Individuum" (Neuburger 1906, 196).

For Hippocrates and his followers symptoms were simply "significant phenomena" (cf. Heidel 1941, 62). Their consideration of symptoms as natural signs—those having the power to signify the same things in all times and places—was of the most comprehensive sort. An early discussion of this type is found in Hippocrates' *Prognostic*:

> One must clearly realize about sure signs, and about symptoms generally [peri ton tekmèrion kai ton allon semeion], that in every year and in every land bad signs indicate something bad, and good signs something favourable, since the symptoms [*sèmeia*] described . . . prove to have the same significance in Libya, in Delos, and in Scythia. So one must clearly realize that in the same districts it is not strange that one should be right in the vast majority of instances, if

one learns them well and knows how to estimate and appreciate them properly. (25)

I have previously recalled an enduring example of his method, the detailed description of the famous *facies hippocratica* (Sebeok 1979b, 6f.); another example may here be cited from *Epidemics* I:

> The following were the circumstances attending the diseases, from which I formed my judgments, learning from the common nature of all and the particular nature of the individual, from the disease, the patient, the regimen prescribed and the prescriber—for these make a diagnosis more favorable or less; from the constitution, both as a whole and with respect to the parts, of the weather and of each region; from the customs, mode of life, practices and age of each patient; from talk, manner, silence, thoughts, sleep or absence of sleep, the nature and time of dreams, pluckings, scratchings, tears; from the exacerbations, stools, urine, sputa, vomit, the antecedents of consequents of each member in the succession of diseases, and the absessions to a fatal issue or a crisis, sweat, rigor, chill, cough, sneezes, hiccoughs, breathing, belchings, flatulence, silent or noisy, hemorrhages, and hemorrhoids. From these things we must consider what their consequents also will be. (Heidel 1941, 129)

In *The Science of Medicine,* Hippocrates also stated: "What escapes our vision we must grasp by mental sight, and the physician, being unable to see the nature of the disease nor to be told of it, must have recourse to reasoning from the symptoms with which he is presented." The means by which a diagnosis may be reached

> consist of observations on the quality of the voice, whether it be clear or hoarse, on respiratory rate, whether it be quickened or slowed, and on the constitution of the various fluids which flow from the orifices of the body, taking into account their smell and colour, as well as their thinness or viscosity. By weighing up the significance of these various signs it is possible to deduce of what disease they are the result, what has happened in the past and to prognosticate the future course of the malady. (Chadwick and Mann 1950, 87–89)

However, it was Galen, whose one and only idol was Hippocrates, and whose medicine remained (on the whole) Hippocratic, who attempted to provide prognostics, wherever feasible, with a scientific underpinning, i.e., to base his forecasts on actual observations. This he was able to do because he practiced dissection and experiment: whereas Hippocrates studied disease as a naturalist, Galen "dared to modify nature as a scientist" (Majno 1975, 396; cf. Neuburger 1906, 385). "Empirical method was first formulated in ancient medicine" as systematic and detailed expression in the Hippocratic corpus (De Lacy and De Lacy eds. 1941, 121), and became a part of the theory of signs of the Epicureans and Sceptics, in opposition to the Stoic rationalistic position. Philodemus' fragmentary treatise (circa 40 B.C.) is by far the most complete discussion of a thoroughgoing methodological work uncovered (in the Herculaneum library) and extensively elucidated to date. Galen, despite all of his Platonic training, was later "forced by his profession to be more empirical" (Phillips 1973, 174), even though this open-minded investigator, who continued to speak with the voice and authority of a man of science, did gradually turn into something of a dogmatic mystic (Sarton 1954, 59). He can therefore be regarded as a subtle founder of clinical semiotics. As such, his work therefore constituted something of a watershed, since "die galenische Semiotik verwertet die meisten Beobachtungs-und Untersuchungsmethoden die das Altertum ausgebildet hat" (Neuburger 1906, 385).

Although Galen can, very likely, be reckoned the first "scientific" semiotician, philosophy and medicine are, as well, consistently conjoined in his writings. Barnes (1991, 50) recently reminded us that, according to Galen, "The best doctors . . . are also philosophers," and that he even wrote a pamphlet to show how a competent physician "possesses all the parts of philosophy—logic, natural science, ethics," to which one may dare add: semiotics, or logic in its most technical Peircean sense (on Galen's logic, see Barnes 1991, 54–56 et passim). Galen counted himself among "those who teach the greatest and finest human achievements—the theorems which philosophy and medicine impart." No wonder that the emperor Marcus Aurelius, as Galen himself informed us, referred to him as "the first among physicians, unique among philosophers" (quoted ibid.). He was indeed the first to explicitly articulate, as far as we know, the kind of medical semiotics put in practice by his most eminent predecessors—in fact, he deemed this to have been a platitude in the Hippocratic tradition—and, once reaffirmed, emulated by a veritable legion of professional successors in and beyond his craft.

Particularly intriguing is Galen's usage of the term *endeixis* (roughly "indication") in medicine and logic, as most recently and very revealingly (if not exhaustively) reviewed by Kudlien (1991; see Durling 1991 for added commentary on its prehistory and medieval Latin renderings). This important term, so cherished by Peirce, is very seldom found in the Hippocratic corpus and then never in a technical sense nor in the sense, or rather the broad spectrum of senses, employed by Galen. Kudlien rightly emphasizes that doctors then, as now, do not deem *indication* to be a "a mere 'sign,'" but rather, as he puts it, an action: that is, a sign which points (usually) to the *treatment* of certain symptoms, or the syndrome, of the disease being diagnosed (1991, 103f.). According to him, the evidence confirms that "it was Galen, above all, who used the word in the modern sense," along with such derivatives as *endeiktikos, endeiknynai, synendeiknysthai, antendeiknysthai,* and the like (ibid., 104). In brief, for Galen, *endeiktikon* is by no means the same as *semeion* or *symptomata.* His own usage was quite different from those of the adherents of the Empiricist or again the Methodist schools of physicians (he counted himself a member of the so-called Dogmatist school of medicine). "When seeking for the true 'endeixis', the Dogmatist would not observe all possible signs/symptoms as such (as the Empiricist does), but select only those that are 'indicative of the cause (sc. of the disease) . . . '" (ibid., 106). In brief, in Galen's writings, true *endeixis* is always something "logical." As he clearly remarked: "One must also use the logical [viz., semiotic] method to recognize what all the diseases are, with regard to species and kinds, and how, for every disease, one must take an 'endeixis' of the therapeutical measures ('iamata')" (quoted ibid., 107).

Galen's pen was as busy as his scalpel. In the course of his exceptionally bulky writings, he classified semiotics as one of the six principal branches of medicine ("merè iatrikès ta men pròta esti, to te phusiologikon, kai to aitilogikon è pathologikon kai to hugeinon kai to sèmiotikon kai to therapeutikon" [14.689]), an ordering that had a special, indeed, critical importance for its "effect on the later history of medicine" (Phillips 1973, 172). The strength of Galenism, as Temkin also emphasized, "reposed in no small measure in having provided medical categories . . . for relating the individual to health and disease," including "semeiology (the science of signs)" (1973, 179).

Of semiotics, Galen further specified: "Sèmeiòsis de dai eis therapeia men anakaia, all' ouk estin autè hè therapeia. Dia gar tès hulès hè therapeia sunteleitai kai to men hulikon aneu therapeias ouden heteron sumballetai. To de sèmeiòikon kai aneu therapeias anankaion pros to eidenai tina therapeutika kai tina atherapeuta kai periistasthai pros to eidenai tina therapeutika kai tina atherapeuta kai periistasthai auta, hopòs mè epiballomeomenoi adunatois sphallòmetha." (14.689) At the end of this same chapter, Galen divided the field into three enduring parts: in the present, he asserted, its concern was *inspection,* or diagnosis, in the past *cognition,* or *anamnesis* (etiology), and in the future *providence,* or prognosis ("diaireitai de kai to sèmeiòtikon eis tria, eis te epignòsin tòn parelèluthotòn kai eis tèn epikepsin tòn sunendreuontòn kai eis prognòsin ton mellontòn" (14.690). His clinical procedure was depicted by Sarton thus: "When a sick man came to consult him, Galen . . . would first try to elicit his medical history and his manner of living; he would ask questions concerning the incidence of malaria and other common ailments. Then the patient would be invited to tell the story of his new troubles, and the doctor would ask all the questions needed to elucidate them and would make the few examinations which were possible" (1954, 6). Galen regarded "everything unnatural occurring in the body" as a *symptom* (7.50, 135; also 10.71ff.), and an aggregation of symptoms (*athroisma tòn symptomaton*) as a *syndrome.* He was fully aware that symptoms and syndromes directly reflected clinical observation, but the formulation of a diagnosis required causal thinking (cf. Siegel 1973). He was the master of foretelling the course of diseases: Galen "pflegte . . . die

Prognostik in besonderem Masse und nicht den geringsten Teil seines Rufes als Praktiker dankte er richtigen Vorhersagungen" (Neuburger 1906, 383). Although his prognostications rested essentially and loyally upon the *Corpus Hippocratum,* his own anatomical knowledge and exactitude of mind predisposed him to build up his prognoses from a cogent diagnostic foundation.

It would not appear unreasonable to expect a finely attuned reciprocal conformation between internal states and "reality," between an Innenwelt and the surrounding Umwelt, or more narrowly, between symptoms and their interpretations as an outcome over time, in an evolutionary adaptation—*prodotto genetico,* in Prodi's succinct formulation (1981, 973)—that benefits an organism by raising its "fittingness." But such does not reflect the state of the art of diagnosis. The probabilistic character of symptoms has long been realized by, among others, the Port-Royal logicians (Sebeok 1976, 125); the often vague, uncertain disposition of symptoms was clearly affirmed by Thomas Sydenham, the seventeenth-century physician often called the "English Hippocrates" (Colby and McGuire 1981, 21). This much admired doctor, held in such high regard by his brother in the profession, John Locke, was also known as the "Father of English medicine" (Latham 1848, xi). Sydenham was noted for his scrupulous recognition of the priority of direct observation. He demanded "the sure and distinct perception of peculiar symptoms," shrewdly emphasizing that these symptoms "referred less to the disease than to the doctor." He held that "Nature, in the production of disease, is uniform and consistent; so much so, that for the same disease in different persons, the symptoms are for the most part the same; and the self-same phenomena that you would observe in the sickness of a Socrates you would observe in the sickness of a simpleton" (ibid., 14ff.). This assertion of his was, of course, quite mistaken, although the medical-student jape referred to by Colby and McGuire "that the trouble with psychiatry is that all psychiatric syndromes consist of the same signs and symptoms" (1981, 23), appears to be equally exaggerated. There are, to be sure, certain diagnostic difficulties inherent in the similarities between the symptomatology of functional syndromes and of those of the organic maladies. The marginal, or supplementary, symptoms of the former can, however, be assimilated according to specific criteria, such as are set forth, for instance, by Thure von Uexküll (in Th. von Uexküll et al. eds. 1979).

This set of strictures leads me to a consideration of an aspect of *symptom* that is seldom mentioned in the literature but that I have found both fascinating and, certainly for semiotics, of broad heuristic value. This has to do with anomalies, a problem that was considered in a philosophical context, especially by Peirce. According to Humphries, a naturally anomalous state of affairs is such "with respect to a set of statements which are at present putatively true," or, putting the matter in a more direct way, "any fact or state of affairs which actually requires an explanation can be shown to be in need of explanation on the basis of existing knowledge" (1968, 88, 89). The enigmatic character of semiotic anomalies can be especially well illustrated by clinical examples, where few existing models are capable of accounting for a multitude of facts. Medicine may, in truth, be one of the few disciplines lacking an overarching theory, although local, nonlinear, and hence restricted and over-simple paradigms, such as the "theory of infectious diseases," certainly do exist.

Take as a first approach to the matter of anomalies the spirochete *Treponema pallidum*. This virus, in its tertiary phase, may manifest itself ("cause") aortitis in individual A, paretic neurosyphilis in individual B, and no disease at all in individual C. The last, the patient with *asymptomatic* tertiary syphilis, can be said to have a disease without being ill. Note that a person may not only be diseased without being ill, but, conversely, may be ill without having a specifically identifiable disease. What can we say, in cases such as this, about the implicative nexus conjoining the "proposition," i.e., the virus, with its consequence, whether expressed in some tangible manner or, on the contrary, mysteriously mantled? Are A, B, and C in complementary distribution, and, if so, according to what principle—the constitution of the patient, or some extrinsic factor (geographic, temporal, societal, age- or gender-related, and so forth), or a coalition of these? The influence of context, one suspects, may be paramount. This becomes overriding in the matter of hypertension—not a disease at all, but a sign of cardiovascular disorder (Paine and Sherman 1970, 272)—which is realized in one and only one restricted frame: within that of patient/physician interaction, assuming the aid of certain accessories, such as a sphygmoscope. Semiosis is, as it were, called into existence solely under the circumstances mentioned; otherwise there are no symptoms (asymptomatic, or so-called silent, hypertension lasts, on average, fifteen years), there are no signs, and there is, therefore, no determinate—i.e., diagnosable—object.

Studies have shown that the majority of people who have gallstones—at least fifteen million Americans among them—go through life without palpable problems. These little pebbles of cholesterol that form in the sac that stores digestive juice can clearly be seen on X-rays: the shadows are the "objective signs," but most of them never cause pain, or any other symptom. They remain mute. They are, in other words, diagnosed only in the course of detailed checkups, and thus require no surgical intervention.

Sensory experiences, at times, lead to semiosic paradoxes, such as the following classic contravention. A hole in one of my teeth, which feels mammoth when I poke my tongue into it, is a subjective symptom I may elect to complain about to my dentist. When I inspect it in a dental mirror, I am surprised by how trivially small the aperture—this objective sign—looks. The question is: which interpretation is "true," the one derived via the tactile modality or the one reported by the optical percept? The felt image and the shape I see do not match. The dentist is, of course, unconcerned with the size of the hole, filling the cavity he/she beholds.

It is a common enough experience that the symptom (for reasons ultimately having to do with the chance evolutionary design of the human central nervous system) refers to a different part of the body than where the damage is actually situated. "The pain of coronary heart-disease, for example, is felt across the front of the chest, in the shoulders, arms and often in the neck and jaw. It is not felt where the heart is—slightly over to the left" (Miller 1978, 22). Such a misreport is unbiological, in the sense that a lay reading could be fatal. An even more outlandish symptom is one for which the referent is housed nowhere at all, dramatically illustrated by a phantom limb after amputation. Miller writes: "The phantom limb may seem to move—it may curl its toes, grip things, or feel its phantom nails sticking into its phantom palm. As time goes on, the phantom dwindles, but it does so in peculiar ways. The arm part may go, leaving a maddening piece of hand waggling invisibly from the edge of the real shoulder; the hand may enlarge itself to engulf the rest of the limb" (ibid., 20). What is involved here is an instance of subjective—as against objective—pain, a distinction introduced by Friedrich J. K. Henle, the illustrious nineteenth-century German anatomist and physiologist, and generally perpetuated in classifications of pain ever since (e.g., by Behan 1926).

Subjective pain is described as having "no physical cause for existence," i.e., there is no organic basis for its presence (indeed, with respect to a limb unhinged, not even an organ): it results "of impressions stored up in the memory centers, which are recalled by the proper associations . . . aroused" (Behan 1926, 74f.), which is to say that the pain remains connected with a framework of signification dependent upon retrospective cognizance. Referred pain and projection pain are closely allied; the latter is a term assigned to pain that is felt as being present either in a part that has no sensation (as in locomotor ataxia) or in a part that because of amputation no longer exists.

Certain symptoms—pain, nausea, hunger, thirst, and the like—are private experiences, housed in no identifiable site, but in an isolated annex that humans usually call "the self." Symptoms such as these tend to be signified by paraphonetic means, such as groans or verbal signs, which may or may not be coupled with gestures ranging in intensity from frowns to writhings. An exceedingly knotty problem, which can barely be alluded to here, arises from the several meanings of self and how these relate to the matter of symptomatology. The biological definition hinges on the fact that the immune system does not respond overtly to its own self-antigens; there are specific markers that modulate the system generating antigen-specific and idiotype-specific cell lines—in brief, activate the process of self-tolerance. Beyond the immunological self, there is also a "semiotic self," which I have discussed severally elsewhere (cf. Sebeok 1991f, chs. 3 and 4; chapter 10 below).

Another diacritic category of symptoms deserves at least passing mention. A linguist might be tempted to dub these "minus features," or subtractive symptoms. Here belong all the numerous varieties of *asemasia* (Sebeok 1976,

57; Sebeok 1979b, 58) such as agnosia, agraphia, alexia, amnesia, amusia, aphasia, apraxia, etc., as well as "shortcomings" like blurred vision, loss of hearing, numbness—in short, symptoms that indicate a deficit from some ideal standard of "normality."

In any discussion of symptoms, it should be noted that even a syndrome, or constellation of symptoms—say, of a gastronomical character (anorexia, indigestion, hemorrhoids)—may not add up to any textbook disease labeling or terminology. Ensuing treatment may, accordingly, be denominated "symptomatic," accompanied by the supplementary advice that the patient remain under continuing observation. In some circumstances, "the syndrome might be ascribed to psychologic etiology" (Cheraskin and Ringsdorf 1973, 37). What this appears to mean is that the interpretation of symptoms is often a matter involving, over time, a spectrum of sometimes barely perceptible gradations, entailing a progressively multiplying number of still other symptoms. It is also worth remarking that, temporally, or for predictive purposes, symptoms generally precede signs, which is to say that the orderly unfolding of evidence may be termed *prognostic*.

No one at present knows how afferent neuronal activity acquires meaning, beyond the strong suspicion that what is commonly called the "external world," including the objects and events postulated as being contained in it, is the brain's formal structure (*logos*). For all practical purposes, we are ignorant about how the central nervous system preserves any structure and assigns a meaning to it, how this process relates to perception in general, and how it induces a response. Implicit in this set of queries is a plainly linear model: for example, that fear or joy "causes" increased heart rate. Not only does such a model seem to me far too simplistic, but there is no shred of proof that it exists at all.

The future of symptomatology will clearly rest with program developments using computer techniques derived from studies of artificial intelligence. These are intended to mime and complement, if not to replace, human semiosic processes, such as judgment based on intuition (in one word, abduction). Such automated diagnostic counselors are already operational, for example, the program termed *Caduceus* (McKean 1982). In the simplified example illustrated in figure 1, the program

> examines a patient with fever, blood in the urine, bloody sputum from the lungs, and jaundice. The program adds together numbers that show how much each symptom is related to four possible diagnoses—cirrhosis of the liver, hepatitis, pneumonia, and nephritis—and picks pneumonia as top contender. The runner-up in score is hepatitis. But because hepatitis has one symptom not shared with pneumonia (blood in the urine), *Caduceus* chooses cirrhosis as the first alternative. This process, called partitioning, focuses the computer's attention on groups of related diseases. (ibid., 64)

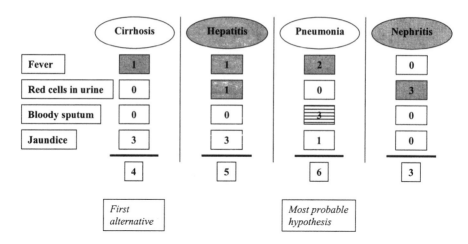

Figure 1. Symptomatology: The program *Caduceus*

The craft of interpreting symptoms has a significance far exceeding the physician's day-to-day management of sickness. As Hippocrates anticipated, its success derives from its psychological power, which critically depends on the practitioner's ability to impress his/her skills on both the patient and their joint environment (the audience gathered in his workshop, which may consist of the patient's family and friends, as well as the physician's colleagues and staff). Dr. Joseph Bell, of the Royal Infirmary of Edinburgh, attained the knack with panache, leaving his imprint not just on clinical practice but, famously, on the detective story, in his pupil Dr. Arthur Conan Doyle's fictional realization Sherlock Holmes (Sebeok 1981c; Ginzburg 1983). According to recent medical thinking, the contemporary preoccupation with diagnosis—that is, the doctor's perceived task, or pivotal drive, to explain the meaning of the patient's condition—rests in the final analysis with the doctor's self-assigned role as an authenticated expositor and explicator of the values of contemporary society. Disease is thus elevated to the status of a moral category, and the sorting of symptoms had therefore best be viewed as a system of semiotic taxonomy—or, in Russian semiotic parlance, a "secondary modeling system."

Lord Horder's dictum that "the most important thing in medicine is diagnosis, the second most important thing is diagnosis and the third most important thing is diagnosis" (Lawrence 1982) must be true, because medical knowledge has risen to the status of a means of social control. Symptomatology has turned out to be that branch of semiotics that teaches us the ways in which doctors function within their cultural milieu.

5

Signs, Bridges, Origins

Bridges

THE LAMENTABLY WOOLLY quality that continues to bedevil semiotic discourse has impelled the spawning of a host of more or less picturesque extended metaphoric models. Some among these, such as the image of a web, have proved sporadically fruitful or at least provocative. *Web* conjures up the organic world of a spider, as well as, in its ineluctable correlations, its inorganic complement, the scaffolding of dry thread that the spider spins. *Web* suggests the reciprocal lives of both invertebrate and vertebrate creatures; it depicts the interplay between hub, spokes, and periphery; it kindles the dialectic of suspense and abatement; and may summon up still further cascades of contrasts or oppositions (Sebeok 1975; Hayles 1984; Seielstad 1989; Sebeok and Umiker-Sebeok eds. 1987–1995; de Duve 1995, 214–221). Thus too, rather usefully, Thure von Uexküll characterized the "body as a web of semioses" (in Th. von Uexküll et al. 1993, 9).[1]

The present conference aims to privilege a different though not unrelated image of a bridge, envisioning, as it were, a *tertium quid,* a sort of linking entity or chainlike substance, even of living bodies: army ants sometimes intertwine and enable, say, silverfish, traversing from "hereabouts" to "yonder," to cross over a chasm.[2] In his eloquent essay about bridges, Rybczynski writes: "Transportation devices, civic symbols, landmarks, and sculptures—bridges are all of these" (1995, 12). But they are also puissant metaphors.

Surely it can be no coincidence that F. Eugene Yates, a distinguished medical engineer, delivered a paper at a symposium sponsored by the Canadian Institute for Advanced Research, held ten years ago this very month at Toronto's University Club (the proceedings of which were published in volume 5 of the

This paper was originally presented to the International Conference on Semiotics as a Bridge between the Humanities and the Sciences, Victoria College, University of Toronto (November 1995) and is to appear in 2000 in the proceedings of that meeting: *Semiotics as a Bridge between the Humanities and the Sciences,* eds. P. Peron, L. G. Sbrocchi, P. Colilli, and M. Danesi, 76–100 (Ottawa: Legas). I acknowledge with appreciation the sensitive and useful comments of Professors Jesper Hoffmeyer, of the University of Copenhagen, and W. C. Watt, of the Department of Cognitive Sciences of the University of California–Irvine, on earlier incarnations of my work in this area.

official publication of the Canadian Semiotic Association). The first four words of Yates's title were "Semiotics as a Bridge" (1985). A bridge is, after all, first and foremost an engineering concept, whether it joins Buda on the Danube's right bank with Pest on its left (helping consolidate the city of my birth) or forms a part of my violin, nose, eyeglasses, dentures, or in the end my coffin.

What Yates attempted to do in his memorable paper—while pointing out that science "has been permeated with semiotic issues all along"—was to "bridge," by means of semiotics, two complementary *Weltanschauungen* of science: the world of dynamics (or physics) and that of information (or biology): "the persistent tension between linguistic and dynamic views of complex systems," he argued, generated an "extraordinary opportunity for semiotics to meld the sciences" (ibid., 359).

Adducing Yates's talk, Rauch and Carr asked why "the metaphor *Bridge* [is] appropriate to semiotic." They went on to answer their own question in part:

> Clearly all the sciences as well as the arts are bridged, whether by single conduit or by network configuration, through the semiotic paradigm.... This is the vital contribution of semiotics, namely, that it entails the inevitable marriage of the arts with the sciences since, as soon as either is touched by man, through his willful choice of a given method, the same human factor influences or interprets the hardest science and the softest art in identical ways." (in Rauch and Carr eds. 1989, v)

This way of thinking presupposes the nowadays common prospect, a truism really, of the humanities, including especially the arts, and of the hard sciences as situated, if edgily, at opposite poles of a disembodied spectrum, with the social and perhaps the so-called behavioral sciences in between. But what appears yet another academic bromide today was not always thus. In the late nineteenth century, for example, a group of "humanists," influenced by new scientific or pseudoscientific trends, claimed that they too should work as "scientifically" as any scientist. The novelist Émile Zola, in a long essay titled "The Experimental Novel"—conceived under powerful allure of the great physiologist Claude Bernard—spelled this thesis out from a writerly angle; in short, Zola pleaded, "we must operate with characters, passions, human and social data as the chemist and physicist work on inert bodies and the physiologist works on living bodies.... We are ... experimental moralists showing by experiment in what fashion a passion behaves in a social milieu" (1880, quoted passim from 1963). Yet who, today, would think of belles-lettres as an experimental science?

And what did John Locke, a close friend of Isaac Newton, think about such matters two hundred years earlier? In the oft-cited chapter 21 of book 4, added as an afterthought to his acclaimed *Essay,* he proposed an epistemological tripartition of the "Sciences," a term by which he meant knowledge, particularly knowledge that is rationally or more fundamentally grounded, as in the title of his book, *Human(e) Understanding* (1975, 720–721).

Locke identified each of the three realms of "Science" which he postulated, also called "the three great Provinces of the intellectual World," stripped to their essentials, by a set of narrower terms: physics, ethics, and semiotics. By physics, or "external" things, he meant that department of knowledge which pertains to the natural sciences, or, roughly speaking, what are now simply called the sciences in the aggregate. By ethics, or ideas (of right and wrong), he meant whatever pertains to the moral sciences, the production of values, or as they are now adverted to more vaguely—but by a floating enumeration rather than by consensual definition—the "humanities."[3] It cannot be stressed enough that the modern word *humanities* derives from the Latin substantive *Humanitas,* meaning "the quality of being human" or "human(e) understanding." Hence this concept subsumed as well the "Sciences" in their absoluteness.[4]

And what of sem(e)iotics, "The Third Branch . . . or *the Doctrine of Signs,*" which, wrote Locke (1975, 720), "is aptly enough termed Logick"? According to Deely's chronicle, what Locke gave us here was "a *distinction which unites:* it distinguishes the different orders only in order to show how they are brought together in the sign" (1982, 64; see also Deely 1994, ch. 5). For, incontrovertibly, Locke claimed that the "business" of semiotics is to "convey" or to "communicate" the mind's knowledge by means of "a Sign or Representation," most conveniently and generally by the use of "articulate Sounds." The true end of speech, Locke emphasized and elaborated in Book III, is that it is "the easiest and shortest way of communicating . . . " (1975, 460). Thus signs are the cognitive instruments whereby "Notions and Knowledge" and "the Thoughts of Men's Minds [are] conveyed from one to another" (ibid., 402–403); or, as Peirce, evidently indebted to Locke (*CP* 2.649), portrayed the identical communicational trope in 1896: "In any case, the deliverer makes signals to the receiver" (*CP* 3.433).

Semiotics—or at least that stock allotment of it which deals with "communication" (Sebeok 1991f, 22–35)—can thus be deemed as spanning or, perhaps more precisely, overarching, Locke's natural sciences and moral sciences. Just as the idea is a sign of—that is, signifies—the thing, so the word, or name, is a sign of—that is, signifies—the idea. In brief, as Charles Morris came to write in 1938: "Semiotic holds a unique place among the sciences. . . . [It] is not merely a science among sciences but an organon or instrument of all the sciences" (1971, 67).

This is not the place to debate whether Vico's "Science of Humanity," however eccentric, is to be understood to constitute a "Zeichen-Wissenschaft" taken as a variant of sematology, as for example Trabant claims in his recent book (1994, 11; cf. Danesi 1993; Sebeok 1995a). Vico was acquainted with most of the philosophical works of Locke but chose not to tag along; in fact, in relevant respects, he was opposed and even tried to undermine them. "New Science," for Vico, was a *pur metafisica* of criticism, a metaphysical history of the human mind. In fact, it was Vico's rigid distinction between the humanities and the natural sciences that Jules Michelet and Benedetto Croce came to exploit and promote as a dam to resist the rising tide of positivist philosophies of knowledge from the early nineteenth century onward.

Which brings me to the gap, or, in C. P. Snow's words, "gulf of mutual incomprehension—sometimes . . . hostility and dislike, but most of all lack of understanding," so memorably highlighted by his expression "the two cultures," and the (tumultuous, on occasion intemperate) debates that ensued (1971). Snow had lamented that "Literary intellectuals at one pole"—for convenience, let me broaden this congregation to humanists in the conventional sense—"at the other scientists, and, as the most representative, the physical scientists" have ceased to communicate (1959, 4). The remedy suggested by Snow entailed a radical reform in educational attitudes without which "the West can't even begin to cope" (ibid., 53), even though he admitted that he didn't know whether the "immense capital outlay, an immense investment in . . . both scientists and linguists" can possibly happen in *laissez faire* economies (ibid., 51–52).[5]

A quick reminder may be salutary here. Unfortunately, although the "two cultures," as ideal assemblages, still by and large "can't talk to each other" (ibid., 17), that is only the lesser part of our—that is, the semiotics community's —predicament. Much more enfeebling is the prevailing estrangement *within* the riven worldwide semiotics commonwealth itself between the many who would style themselves humanists and a scientifically cultivated minority. In a paper, "A Semiotic Perspective on the Sciences: Steps toward a New Paradigm" (Anderson et al. 1984), six of us tried to address this dilemma, but in the short run to little avail. The number of scholars who nimbly scud back and forth between the "two cultures" remains heartbreakingly minuscule. Peirce and Morris were two rare American paragons, exemplars who could do so with the kind of panache mustered by, say, the late Giorgio Prodi (e.g., 1988d), or our colleague Floyd Merrell today (see 1992, 1995, 1996).

The Russian master Yuri M. Lotman has by contrast taken the boldly original step of doing away with the concept of a bridge altogether, replacing it by the semiotically sensitive maneuver of transcoding. A main principle of his research method is the elimination of the opposition between the exact sciences and the humanities by treating the fabrics of these complementary domains as if they were readily transmutable from one semiotic system to another (Lotman 1990, 271).

Semioticians such as these merit our regardful reading and encouragement. For the rest of us, particularly for the sake of our students and successors, I am inclined to support Snow's proposed remedy of learning reform. But let me once again adduce Morris, writing in 1946, antedating Snow by thirteen years: "An education which gave due place to semiotic would destroy at its foundations the cleavage and opposition of science and the humanities" (1971, 246).

Permit me to return for a moment to Snow's concept of the "two cultures," or what Jacob Bronowski later aptly renamed "Two World Systems" (Snow 1971, 53). Because of my predilection for nuanced calibrations and reinforcing scholarly instruction with personal anecdote[6] (where I think it appropriate to mix genres), I would like to report here fleetingly on an extended encounter between Snow and me which took place in California thirty-five years ago, but which I have not owned up to before. That fall, in 1960, Snow was Regents' Professor at Berkeley and I a fellow at the Stanford Center for Advanced Study, where I invited him for drinks and a chat for a Friday afternoon, November 15th. I can date the occasion exactly by his dedication on the title page of his presentation copy of *Two Cultures:* "To Thomas Sebeok with admiration and best wishes for his campaign from C. P. Snow." What campaign was he referring to there?

In the course of our wide-ranging conversation (which I have no room to detail here), I had ventured to advocate that Locke's doctrine of signs might provide the very viaduct Snow had been searching for. This led to a lengthy, attentive discussion about semiotics, which Snow remembered well when we met for some hours for the second and last time the following summer at London's Savile Club. He later came to note that in the United States "the divide is nothing like so unbridgeable" (Snow 1971, 77). By 1971, he thought that though it may be "too early to speak of a third culture already in existence. . . . [t]here are signs that this is happening" (ibid., 58). While, to my knowledge, he never used the word "semiotics" in his own writings, our conversations did resonate in a 1965 novel, *Cork Street, Next to the Hatter's,* the author of which was Pamela Hansford Johnson, Snow's wife (see Sebeok 1972, 180–181).

Elsewhere, I have sifted through the variously coordinated attempts in the United States between the 1930s and 1960s to reconcile the adversarial relationships that Snow tried to palliate. I tried there, illuminating its modern historiography, to accent the role of semiotics as a universal meta-discourse which reverberated like a melody through these heterogeneous endeavors (1977a; 1991e, 70–74). A portion of this colorful, fascinating, but highly involuted story—in which a host of stellar individuals more or less pertinent to the modern unfolding of semiotics on this continent participated, including Roman Jakobson, and Charles Morris with especial vigor[7]—was also competently chronicled, although not entirely captured, in Steve Heims' *The Cybernetics Group* (1991, especially 79, 94). A whiff of semiotics was insinuated even in a 1949 piece by Charles Olson (d. 1970), one of the country's leading poets at the time:

To be in different states without a change
is not a possibility
We can be precise. The factors are
in the animal and/or the machine the factors are
communication and/or control, both involve
the message. And what is the message? The message is
the discrete or continuous sequence of measurable events
distributed in time . . . (fragment after Heims 1991, 271)

Before turning, shortly, to the second section of this paper in order to carry on with a few illustrative applications of the vincular figure of the bridge—which, as a sign itself, exhibits iconic, indexical, and symbolic aspects, depending on contextual conditions—let me say a few words about the notion of *mediation*. In semiotics, the bridge metaphor is one of perhaps half a dozen vivid tropes that can be turned to account as concrete surrogates for the far more abstract *mediation*. However, in semiosis—the sign event itself, in evolution as it were, rather than semiotics, the scholarly study of semiosis—mediation is a sovereignly indispensable core conceptualization, one which has been thoroughly explored in a pair of Richard Parmentier's classic essays (in Mertz and Parmentier eds. 1985, chs. 2 and 15). I wish here merely to underline the distinction between semiotics and semiosis (Sebeok 1991f, 97–99) for two reasons: first, to avoid being misunderstood as to my present topic; and second, to use this opportunity to urge the organizers of this pioneering symposium of the Toronto Semiotics Research Unit that one among those to soon follow be focused on this rich, multi-valued concept of *semiosic mediation*—a no doubt mysterious but rip-roaring journey into the Heart of Thirdness.

Initial Conditions

The life science and the sign science at their conjunction commingle so multiformly, ramify so abundantly, that even sampling such conjunctures in this brief paper risks rendering a disservice to the readership. Biosemiotics, rooted in the West in Hippocratic medical theory and practice, has recently enjoyed a wide-ranging resurgence in Europe, the Americas, and Japan (see, inter alia, Sebeok 1991e, 100–113; chapter 10 below; Eder and Rembold 1992; Kawade 1992; Hoffmeyer 1995a; Th. von Uexküll 1997). Furthermore, even the directly pertinent literature is rapidly proliferating out of control. There no longer seems to be any doubt, as I buoyantly but on the littlest of evidence pronounced in a 1967 seminar held at the Collège de France, that "a full understanding of the dynamics of semiosis . . . may, in the last analysis, turn out to be no less than the definition of life" (Sebeok 1985a, 69). In this judgment, I was of course far anticipated by Jakob von Uexküll, though I was at the time unaware of it. For as his son, Thure, came to write of his father: "Of particular interest to Uexküll was the fact that signs are of prime importance in all aspects of life processes" (1987, 147). For Eder and Rembold, of the Max Planck Institute for Biochemistry, "Biosemiotics represents a new philosophy. Within an overarching framework," they predict, "it will eventually encompass the full range from molecular biology to deterministic chaos" (1992, 66).

This pronouncement has most recently been refined by the Danish molecular biologist Jesper Hoffmeyer when he observed that "[a]dding code-duality to the autopoiesis of living systems immediately makes it clear that life itself is . . . a semiotic phenomenon . . . " (1995b, 18).[8] Too, the theoretical biologist Claus Emmeche, working at the Niels Bohr Institute in Copenhagen, rightly pointed out that it was Peirce himself who inspired the modern view of "sign phenomena as occurring everywhere in nature, including those domains where humans have never set foot. . . . It is a history that dates back to the origin of life," because "living cells, in order to survive as complex systems, had to possess a code or partial description of their own structure, so that they could begin to collect descriptions of survival" (1994b, 126).

If one accepts the intrinsic identity of the life science and the sign science, combining at their root into a "natural semiotics"—as the late Italian oncologist Prodi re-christened biology itself *in toto* (1988c, 55–56; cf. Eder and Rembold 1992, 61–63)—the question still lingers: what is gained thereby? Emmeche addresses this tenable misgiving in a paper which concludes with a sentence highly relevant to the aims of our present assembly:

> It is necessary that the conceptual obstacles to a coherent understanding of life . . . and sign-activity [read: semiosis] can be remedied, and there is indeed some hope that a broader perspective may emerge from the cross-disciplinary gathering around the disciplines of cognitive science, artificial life, biology, semiotics and general epistemology. (1994a, 30)

Hoffmeyer, more generally, speaks of "*The semiotisation of nature*" as an unfolding "important trend" of "semiotic cosmology," and traces some of the far-reaching consequences of the claim that "*the sign rather than the molecule is the basic unit for studying life*" (1995a, 367, 369; author's italics).

In what follows, I choose to concentrate on one set of issues alone, an area of inquiry which is often referred to in traditional biology and other sciences as the problem of "initial conditions" (Barrow 1991, 31–70). It is supposed, or rather hoped, by some scientists that the initial conditions in the world may ultimately be derived from the laws of nature, but the most interesting thing about initial conditions may be that next to nothing is known about them— that they are (by contrast with the physicists' evolution equations) metaphysical mysteries, for the theologians. As the introduction to a popular "series of public lectures by leading authorities" optimistically hedges, "we are far from knowing all about our origins" (Fabian ed. 1988, xiii). Because of their inherent indeterminacy, initial conditions surely belong in Lotfi Asker Zadeh's enter-tainingly fuzzified world of fuzzy sets in fuzzy logic (McNeill and Freiberger 1993). Or, as Barrow says, "the most awkward feature about the influence of initial conditions . . . is the fact that they are the most uncertain aspects of our knowledge"; it may well be, for example, "that we can never know how (or if) the Universe began" (1991, 48).

Another problem with initial conditions is this: pairs of objects in the cos-mos conjectured to have been invested with the same, or nearly so, inceptive endowments turn out on second or third glance to have evolved into dramati-cally different entities. Such are two of the planets in our solar system, Venus and Earth, which are so radically unlike that they even rotate in opposite di-rections.

The classic, and by definition earliest, example comes not from biology but cosmology (Barrow 1991, 44–54), for no one really knows how the uni-verse came into being, although quite a lot is known about the ensuing three minutes (Weinberg 1977). But before the Big Bang, as Einstein's theory in-structs us, there was no "before." Intuitive leaps, such as Peirce's, that the "Universe . . . is necessarily a great work of art, a great poem" (*CP* 5.119), are beautifully evocative, but tell us naught about its provenance. Perhaps the view of the world as a self-synthesizing system of entities, an "idea-account" of the world of intercommunicating existences, "one based on quantum-plus-information theory," offered by the eminent contemporary physicist John Ar-chibald Wheeler—himself influenced by Peirce—provides the most promising clues, although even Wheeler allows that the communicants "thus develop all they know or ever can know about the world" and of its origins (1988, 4–5).

The salient point to register is this: according to Wheeler's intriguing vision of semiophysics—as recaptured for instance by Merrell—"the material world provides the machinery for generating meaning, while meaning contributes the machinery for constructing physics. Existence thus becomes "a closed circle of meaning" (1995, 236 and 1996, *passim;* after Wheeler 1988, 5: fig. 1).[9] In conformity with this perspective of Wheeler, the participatory universe consti-tutes a "self-excited circuit"—or, as I would prefer to express the same idea in terms perhaps better suited to semiotics, the cosmos may be regarded as a *sign-excited loop.*

As one progresses from the age of geochemistry beyond the age of infor-mation—the epochs when Prodi's *protosemiotics*[10] (1988c, 56) held sway—to biotic times, embodied first in prokaryotic then also in eukaryotic cells, in mul-ticellular organisms and then the steps toward humanity and thereafter (as de-picted for example in de Duve's 1995 tour de force account), the "semioticity" of originary events manifests itself ever more conspicuously and persuasively. Professionally, I have occupied myself particularly with those "initial conditions riddles" that pertain to communication and language and speech (see below), but further touch on enigmas or matters of contention ancillary thereto, as the origin of the Hominidae and of certain categories in their semiospheres, notably including their fabrication of tools (Gibson and Ingold 1993) and art (Sebeok 1979a).[11]

Initial conditions, despite, or perhaps because of, their inherent intractability, remain a constant preoccupation among life scientists. A comprehensive recent book (Maynard Smith and Szathmáry 1995), a review article by the same co-authors (Szathmáry and Maynard Smith 1995), and a review article by Maynard Smith (1995) are variously devoted to tracing beginnings viewed as the "major evolutionary transitions." They overlap in good measure with de Duve's concurrent solo chronicle of much the same terrain (1995).

How life emerged is unknown, but that surety does not inhibit unending speculation among biologists (see, e.g., Schopf ed. 1983). As Sonea generalized when asked how life began, "Tout le monde a une explication [mais] tout le monde est d'accord pour dire que la vie ne s'explique pas" (1995, 33). Nobel laureate de Duve's precept, "the universe was . . . pregnant with life" (1995, 9), directly contradicts Nobel laureate Monod's, "the universe was not pregnant with life" (1971, 145). Bada's, and Stanley Miller's, surmise that "life on earth started . . . in a frigid ocean, under hundreds of feet of ice" (Bada 1995, 22) is challenged by other scientists who believe in a contrary dogma: that the first living entities, very likely the progenitors of all microorganisms, were several kinds of extremophile bacteria—especially in the group Archaeobacteria—emanating from submarine hydrothermal springs, alkaline lakes and gas-emitting craters, geysers, and volcanic vents along the mid-ocean ridges. A new candidate for exploration is a hypothesis based on the assumption that life is not rooted in blind chance but in mathematical necessity, deeper than Darwinian natural selection alone—but this too is far from established (Kauffman 1995, 61–66). The currency of borderline phenomena betwixt the abiotic and the biotic ravels this issue further still (Sebeok 1991f, 101). In sum, one can but concur with Davies' dictum: "At the present state of our knowledge, the origin of life remains a deep mystery" (1995, 21)—although, at the same time, very distinguished contributions to the subject do keep appearing (such as Margulis and Sagan 1997a).

The riddle acquires kaleidoscopic reconfiguration when rotated in congruence with semiotic phraseology. We ask how *semiosis* arose—a process I take to have been co-terminous with the emergence of life. Physics has indeed provided communication tools for the living: light, pressure, sound. But it also gave chemistry and biology, "and, through them, observers-participators" (Wheeler 1988, 5) and signifexes/communicators.[12] According to prevailing opinion, this sea change transpired, or became literally viable, approximately 3,800 million years ago.

From its inception, semiosis must have entailed the crystallization of Umwelts, models of purlieus frequented by and appropriate to the survival of each organism and its species (J. von Uexküll 1973). A paramount goal of taxonomy being the pursuit of simplicity amidst a universe of immeasurable complexity (Tort 1983), the earliest constructions (models) of the universe ("reality") must have been binary: a class of things to approach (prey), another class of things to withdraw from (predators), with an immense imperceptible remainder irrelevant either biologically to the organism or socially for the survival of the species (Sebeok 1986a, 13–14). This minimal but sufficient module of distinctive features of +, –, or o, variously multiplied in advanced zoosemiotic systems, like the much misunderstood communication of vervet monkeys (Sebeok 1985b), is a far cry from the exceedingly complex cosmic models Newton or Einstein in due course bestowed upon humanity.

"The common ancestor of all living things most likely was a bacterium, or prokaryote," de Duve informs us (1995, 125). And, thanks mainly to the work of Sorin Sonea of the Université de Montréal, the mind-boggling semiosic comportment of bacteria—about three and a half billion years in depth—is quite well understood. As Sonea recently told the Société de Sémiotique du Québec, "Un système si simple fonctionne à merveille parce qu'il est passé au niveau d'une communication globale, mondiale" (1995, 29; see also Sonea 1988 and 1990, where further references are supplied). Bacteria together "constitute the communications network of a single superorganism whose . . . components are dispersed across the surface of the planet." Yet the semiosic dimension of their existence also comprises associations into countless local teams and interactions with the eukaryotes, using us as habitats and vehicles (Sonea 1988, 40–42). I am unable to recount all the ways and means of prokaryotic social behavior, but I do want my readers to credit that neither comparative nor diachronic semiotics are feasible any longer without a meticulous inventory and full comprehension of the manifold ways of prokaryotic semiosis. Although bacterial communication is radically different from, say, animal communication, we cannot fully grasp semiosis in multicellular organisms (including ourselves)—which, according to recent, very large fossil discoveries in northern China near Jixian, seem to have already evolved on the sea floor at least 1.7 billion years ago—without an appreciation of its ancestral operations, say, 3.8 billion years ago. Our planet was then teeming with huge bacterial colonies of so-called mega-algae, simple single-celled organisms lacking nuclei, but was still bereft of eukaryotes with nuclei, which made *their* appearance only some two billion years later.

Terms such as *symbiosis, endosymbiosis,* and derivatives thereof are commonly used by biologists, especially when discussing the evolution of the eukaryotic cell, to register that mitochondria and chloroplasts are descended from originally free-living prokaryotes (cf. Margulis 1993, ch. 7). So possibly are the microtubular cytoskeletal system (de Duve 1995, 160–168; Maynard Smith and Szathmáry 1995, 125) and even the nucleus (ibid., 136–137), the cardinal feature of eukaryotic cells. Margulis notes "the near ubiquity of the symbiotic state,

the persistence through time of most symbioses, and the profound consequences for the partners," for instance, in that "symbiotic partnerships may
be more fit than individual partners (bionts)" in any environment (1993, 167,
171). When two or more species live together (Margulis and Sagan 1997a, ch.
8), we may be sure that energetic sign transmission (Scannerini 1988), or, as
McFarland intimated (1982, 540), dense communication, solders such alliances.
Therefore, inasmuch as processes of sign transmission outside and inside organisms are at play, it appears not unreasonable to suppose symbiosis to be a
token of semiosis and endosymbiosis to be a token of endosemiosis (Th. von
Uexküll et al. 1993). Nor is this mere word magic: the scrupulous positing of
tokens within the types to which they naturally belong is surely both of heuristic and epistemological import, as applied for example to the quintessentially
transdisciplinary, or rather hybrid, area of psycho-neuro-immunology (Kappauf 1991; Lázár 1991).

We can now state with confidence that, besides bacteria (microsemiosis)
and animals (zoosemiosis), plants exhibit ample (phyto)semiosic functioning.
They therefore communicate as well: "if meaning-based behavior of animals is
classified into matter exchanging behavior, reproductive behavior, information
seeking behavior and defensive behavior, it must be concluded that all four
classes occur likewise in plants . . . " (Krampen 1994a, 727). Notwithstanding
that we lack a present opportunity to consider semiosis ostensively in the remaining two of the five kingdoms of terrestrial life, the Protoctista (semiosic
practices scarcely explored) and the fungi (mycosemiosis; cf. Sebeok 1991e, 112),
we are prepared to formulate the following prime abduction:

THEOREM I: COMMUNICATION

All, and only, living entities incorporate a species-specific model (Umwelt)
of their universe; signify; and communicate by nonverbal (chiefly chemical and/or motor, later also optical and/or acoustic) signs. Many are also
capable of intercommunicating in limited ways with some individuals of
other species.[13]

Lemma IA: Lotman's Schema Modified

Man's nonverbal communicative repertoire, in its totality, corresponds to
the Moscow-Tartu school's "primary modeling system" concept, as now
modified to designate humanity's inborn stock of semiosic devices.[14]

Lemma IB: Popper's Schema Compared

In Popper's schema, man's nonverbal communicative repertoire can be
located at the interface of World 2 and World 3 (Eccles and Popper 1977,
passim; cf. Sebeok 1989e, 203–206).

Bearing the foregoing in mind, let me now turn—I hope with enlightened
but sympathetic agnosticism (a word also used by John Lyons in his circum-

spect discussion of the topic [in Fabian ed. 1988, 141–166])—to one of the busiest areas of research—or abductive inference—namely the zealous revival of an ancient obsession with the "origin of language."[15] As Jakobson said in his 1968 Olivetti lecture in Milano—and not many linguists would disagree with him—"The uniqueness of natural language among all other semiotic systems is manifest in its fundamentals" (1971, 707).

Speculating about the initial conditions of language is admittedly fun, but all deliberations about this matter have led to, *tout court,* dead ends. In the pithy assessment of the English linguist David Crystal, with which I by and large concur, questions like these are "fascinating, and have provoked experiments and discussion whose history dates back 3,000 years. The irony is that the quest is a fruitless one" (1987, 288). A more radical view, which I share, was declared by Marantz (echoing Chomsky): "If language had an origin it might indeed make sense to talk about its creation. . . . But human language cannot be considered to possess an identifiable origin, any more than can the human heart" (1983, 20).

Since, as mentioned, I have argued for my own set of surmises in readily accessible venues, I shall refrain from repeating them to set down instead, in the following three sets of cautionary paragraphs, certain markedly pesky Idols of the Market-place (as Francis Bacon would have called them) which, in my view, have given rise to some of the avoidable clutter which afflicts many—dare I say it—pseudo-scientific proceedings.

1) Resist the temptation to jumble three incommensurate semiosic practices and their corresponding appellations: *communication* (see also Theorem I, above), *language*, and *speech* (Theorems II and III, below). Communication is a universal attribute of the living. Language is a universal attribute of hominids —a "languageless human" verges on an oxymoron. (For speech, see below.) These three phenomena evolved quite separately in phylogenesis and emerged severally in human ontogenesis. The labels are thus by no means interchangeable.

It needs to be emphatically reiterated that language and speech did not co-evolve (cf. Lyons in Fabian ed. 1988, 155–156). On the contrary, speech *presupposes* language, not vice versa. One cannot speak without having a language, but having a language does not enjoin that it be vocally exhibited or indeed externally manifested in any other manner (such as script [Sebeok 1989e, 251–252], sign languages of the deaf [Stokoe 1972], monastic sign languages [Umiker-Sebeok and Sebeok eds. 1987], drum and whistle speech surrogates [Sebeok and Umiker-Sebeok eds. 1976], or the like). Natural languages, Indo-European and others, recognize by encoding on the "folk" level crucial distinctions between terms such as *language/speech: Sprache/Rede, langue/ parole, yazik/rec', kieli/puhe* (Finnish), *nyelv/beszéd* (Hungarian), *hizkuntza/ mintzaldi* (Basque), *dil/geplejish* (Turkmen), *kotoba/hanashi* (Japanese), and so on around the globe.

As a rule, several highly complex sets of successive capacities are tacitly compressed into and entailed by the single word *speech* (or its congeners and derivatives) in common parlance: at the encoding end, the production of sounds, including the airstream process, the phonation process, the articulatory process, and the radiation process; and at the decoding end, the perception of auditory events (hearing) and listening (Handel 1989). Both complementary coding deployments have quite distinct evolutionary histories, with hearing the older propensity by far. In the course of human evolution and history, although the systems for performance and reception of phonemes have coalesced to a degree, they have not to date been perfectly coordinated. One far-reaching reason that a speaker's speech—defined as vocal communication by means of a natural language—is often misheard and misunderstood by a listener is that the integration of these two capacities may still be evolving.

2) Avoid the presumption that just because some transaction is labeled *language* this is equivalent to the technical usage of professional linguists. Expressions such as "language of the bees," even when used by such an authority as Nobel laureate Karl von Frisch, are metaphors. As a rule of thumb, picturesque conjunctions of the word *language* with *ape, dolphin,* the generic *animal* (e.g., Bright 1984), or a category of domestic pets *(cat, dog),* or in phrases like "the language of flowers," are unscientific nonsense, rhetorical tricks designed to mislead by assuming as part of the premise the conclusion that is supposed to be demonstrated *(petitio principii).*

3) Shun pseudo-Darwinian posturings which contend that attempts to inculcate "language" in captive apes (or, more absurdly, in marine mammals; cf. Sebeok 1981c, 170) are motivated, even justified, by the scientifically commendable goal of discovering "The Origin of Language"—the pretentious title, for one, of the chaotically polemic, misinformed no less than irrelevant, penultimate chapter of a book by Savage-Rumbaugh and Lewin (1994, 223–250).[16]

About the status of language in human evolution, let me propose:

THEOREM II: LANGUAGE

All the animals paleontologists classify generically as *Homo,* and only such, embody, in addition to a primary modeling system (Theorem I), a secondary modeling system, equivalent to a natural language. The difference amounts to this: while the Umwelts of other animals model solely a (for each) existent world, man can, by means of the secondary system, also model a potentially limitless variety of possible worlds (containing sentences with alethic, deontic, or epistemic modalities).

Lemma IIA: Twin Modeling Systems

All species in *Homo—habilis, erectus, ergaster, sapiens, neandertalensis,* etc.—possessed this pair of interactive systems, as does the sole extant species, *sapiens sapiens;* but while they were all capable of signifying by *both* nonverbal *and* verbal means (i.e., natural language), solely *Homo sapiens* can, with the eventual development of speech and/or equivalent spatio-temporal realizations, so communicate.

Lemma IIB: Popper's Schema Compared

In Popper's schema, World 3, relating uniquely to man, is the world of language and of its products (cf. Sebeok 1989e, 204). It roughly corresponds to Humboldt's *Sprachwelt,* as well as all I assign to the domain of anthroposemiotics (1974a, 213).

Lemma IIC1: Syntax in Language

The pivotal role of syntax in language has been recognized (if far from fully understood) by linguists from Wilhelm von Humboldt to J. Wackernagel (cf. Sebeok 1966, 2:54) Jespersen (ibid., 168), and Zellig Harris. Humboldt famously pointed out the potential of language "to make infinite use of finite means" (Sebeok 1991e, 29; Pinker 1994, 84), which, after Chomsky, is styled its generative capacity (Mellor 1990, 59). (This needs no elaboration here, but see the next lemma for applications to domains prior to language.)

Lemma IIC2: Syntax in Evolution

Syntax appears to be the hallmark of every "major transition in evolution." The "age of chemistry" was subjected to Dimitri Mendeleev's omnipresent periodic law (1869), the universal syntactic features, or electronic configurations, of which are commonly displayed in the table of elements. In the world of the living, syntax-controlled semiotic systems appear to be, among others such as the verbal code, the following:

- *Genetic Code,* or "language of life" (Beadle and Beadle 1966; Berlinski 1986; Sebeok 1991f, 85–86, 154)
- *Immune Code* (Jerne 1985; Sercarz et al. eds. 1988; Sebeok 1991f, 87, 154–155; Tauber 1994, 169–171; the Hungarian immunologist academician János Gergely recently characterized this as "the most perfect semiotic system in the Universe" [personal remark])
- *Metabolic Code* (Tomkins 1975; Wright 1988, 103–104; Sebeok 1991f, 87–88)
- *Neural Code* (Sebeok 1991f, 88–89): Recent growth of a distinct discipline sometimes named *neurocommunications* has been so dramatic that no account can be furnished in any work short of a handbook. One example is the flurry of discoveries of a range of guidance proteins (semaphorins, netrins), which, in the manner of road signs, usher some ten trillions of neurons on the way to their appropriate destinations in human embryos (Howard 1995, 12, 47). Would not

Crick's "astonishing hypothesis" (1994) of the origin of consciousness also belong under this rubric?

As far as zoosemiotic processes are known to date, no evidence of syntactic structures, let alone of what Chomsky calls a "language organ," has been found, not even in any of the alloprimates; nor has anyone identified any actual "functional intermediates between ape language [*sic*] and human language . . . What was the language organ doing before it acquired its present function?" ask Maynard Smith and Szathmáry, in vain (1995, 47). Accordingly, Jackendoff answers a question of his own—"do apes have a mental grammar that allows them to combine signs in regimented fashion [read: syntax]?"—thus: "The evidence seems to indicate that they don't. . . . In short, Universal Grammar, or even something remotely like it, appears to be exclusively human" (1994, 137–138; cf. Sebeok 1981c, 134–209; Wallman 1992, 139–143).

Theorem III: Speech

Homo sapiens, and only conspecifics, were singularly but not universally able to communicate by language recoded in the acoustic channel by about 160,000 to 180,000 years ago, probably in Africa. But while speech occurs only in modern humans, it doesn't manifest itself in all: not in infants (Trevarthen 1990), mutes, some hearing impaired (Stokoe 1972), some stroke victims, types of aphasics or autistics (on "clinical semiotics," see Sebeok 1977a, 190–192), and some people in their "second childhood"; total speech loss can also be induced by the intake of certain designer drugs which destroy the substantia nigra (also a chronic symptom of classic Parkinson's patients) (Langston 1995).

Erato's Coda

Let me conclude with a characteristically terse but apposite lyric by the incomparable American poet, Emily Dickinson, who, understanding her condition and its boundaries only too well, luminously challenged and miraculously overcame them:

Love is anterior to life,
Posterior to death,
Initial of creation, and
The exponent of breath.

6

What Do We Know about Signifying Behavior in the Domestic Cat (Felis catus)?[1]

I.

To BEGIN WITH, I must register some strictures about what some may deem to be a tautology in the phrasing of my title or, more precisely, an implicit *in adiecto* contradiction which, according to Peirce, "appears as soon as the terms are defined, irrespective of the properties of their objects" (1901, 526). What needs to be made plainer here is the expression "signifying behavior." I am openly appropriating—but not thereby ratifying—the phrasing for my present purposes from this new journal's own gonfalon. The paternity of the phrase remains murky, but I can't avoid taking some responsibility for having perhaps instigated it when titling an early article of my own "Coding in the Evolution of Signaling Behavior," a paper that was originally prepared in 1960 for an international symposium held at Burg Wartenstein, in Austria (Sebeok 1972, 7–33). Yet *signaling* and *signifying* are far from interchangeable terms (for one demarcation, see, e.g., Morris 1971, 366–367).[2]

The issue famously leads back to one of Peirce's far-reaching insights, quoted so often that it has thickened to the status of a maxim, concerning "the fact that the entire universe—not merely the universe of existents, but all that wider universe, embracing the universe of existents as a part, the universe which we are all accustomed to refer to as 'the truth'—that all this universe is perfused with signs, if it is not composed exclusively of signs" (*CP* 5.448n). In the Peircean scheme of things, therefore, and more generally in any semiotic frame of reference, orthodox or not—such as, say, Bakhtin's, who asserts that "everything means, is understood, as a part of the greater whole . . . " (1981, 426)—a living organism survives and steers in its matchless world of significances (its own Umwelt) to which its behavior must accommodate; else it becomes extinct. All behavior must, by definition, be signifying behavior. Put in

This chapter first appeared in 1994, in *Signifying Behaviour* 1, 3–31. An Italian translation was published in 1998 as "Che cosa sappiamo a proposito del comportamento significante nel gatto domestico *(Felis catus)*?" in T. A. Sebeok, *Come comunicano gli animali che non parlano,* ed. S. Petrilli, 75–108 (Bari: Edizioni dal Sud).

Figure 1. Peirce's representation of the semiotic web. Is that a cartoon of a cat in the center of the maze or an impression of his beloved dog, Zola? Or is it perhaps the Minotaur confined to his semiosic Labyrinth? Disregarding the letters "b" and "d," are the letters "c" (top left) and "T"(center left) with the letter "A" (bottom left) intended to spell out *cAT*? Photograph by courtesy of the Harvard University Archives, Joseph Brent, and Indiana University Press. (It may be an intriguing coincidence that Oscar Wilde, Peirce's near-contemporary, in his poem "The Sphinx," which is about a cat, apostrophizes: "Sing to me of the Labyrinth / In which the two-formed bull was stalled, / Sing to me of the night you crawled / Across the temple's granite plinth . . . ")

another way, an animal's ethogram (cf. Part II below) is equivalent to its semiogram.

How, then, could there be configurations of cat behavior which *failed* to signify? Of course, any cat's given behavior segment, a certain feline's particular sign token, may not actually, if ever, be observed, viz., interpreted, by any other animal (the Biblical *vox clamantis in deserto* applies to animals too). But "it would not be a sign unless it were capable of being interpreted, or understood in a certain way. The meaning of a sign is a power to determine observers of the sign to interpret it in a determined fashion" (Hookway 1985, 32–33). Or, in Peirce's own words, "the absolutely incognizable does not exist" (*CP* 5.313).

Now this is tantamount to Peirce's claim that the semiosic relation is irreducibly triadic. To choose an example of the relation

(1)   Y is a sign of Z to X,

any cat's[3] pupil response [Y] (i.e., its marked dilation or marked constriction under normal light) "is telling you that something isn't right [Z]" to any [X], say, to the cognizant Dr. Milani (1987, 90).

The sentence can also be transformed in several other ways, as, for example,

(2)   X interprets Y as a sign of Z,

where "if you [X] see a cat's pupils suddenly expand, without any change in light intensity or proximity of objects [Y], then it is experiencing a strong emotional arousal [Z]" (Morris 1987, 27).

However, the triadic relationship is preserved in one's absence: the cat's eyes will, depending on the situation, change their expression even if you do not perceive or otherwise register the behavioral sequence. In this third kind of transformation, the addresser/interpreter X is merely someone or something hypothetical or potential (Peirce *CP* 1.548). Thus in the following the presence of an "omniscient ethologist observer" is merely implied: " . . . particularly good indicators of an imminent change of mood [are] a sudden narrowing of pupils [Y_1], which announces imminent attack [Z_1], and dilation of pupils [Y_2] which indicates a readiness for escape or defense [Z_2] . . . " (Leyhausen 1973, 300).

Is there a useful working definition of the term *behavior*? To ascertain this, I consulted the pertinent volumes of the *Encyclopedia of Philosophy* (1967), *International Encyclopedia of the Social Sciences* (1968), *Encyclopedia of Psychology* (1984), *Encyclopedic Dictionary of Semiotics* (1994), *Oxford Companion to the Mind* (1987), *International Encyclopedia of Communications* (1989), *A Dictionary of Philosophical Quotations* (1992), *International Encyclopedia of Linguistics* (1992), the *Glossary of Semiotics* (1993), and a number of comparable compendia. These reference books have one negative feature in common: none of them have an entry under the heading "Behavior." Despite its title, neither does *The Ox-*

ford Companion to Animal Behavior (McFarland 1982); and the term remains undefined in the most recent chapter on "Animal Behavior" in the *Annual Review of Psychology* (Timberlake 1993). *Behavior,* it seems, is a prime for many scholars and students, although some reference works do have this entry, as the following examples show.

The brief lemma in the English edition of *Grzimek's Encyclopedia of Ethology* reads:

> The behavior of an animal is defined as the totality of its movements, sound emissions, and body postures; also externally noticeable changes that serve bilateral [*sic*] communication and can therefore release other behavior in the partner (changes in color, secretion of odorous substances, etc.). (Immelman ed. 1977, 687)

In the *Dictionary of Ethology* (1989, 27), the late Immelman (who also wrote the preceding entry), starts off his lemma on "Behavior" by defining it as "What ethologists study in animals," but then goes on to plead that one ethologist's descriptions of an animal's behavior may differ from what another would describe and that these alternative representations may not be reconcilable. He ends the definition with a warning that a description of behavior in terms of motor patterns (say, the pupil response) should not be confused with one in terms of functional categories (say, attack or defense).[4]

In his standard *Dictionary of Philosophy* for students, the English philosopher Lacey sets out the paragraph "Behaviour" by defining it all-embracingly as "What an object, particularly a living creature, does" (1986, 18). He then follows this with a series of cogent, provocative, but in the end as a rule unanswerable interrogatives, or problems and ambiguities as he calls them, which are, effectively, abjurations:

> is intention, or at least controllability, needed? Are heart-beats behaviour? Must behaviour affect the outer world and be publicly observable? Is silent thinking behaviour? Must behaviour described in one way (e.g., waving one's arms) also be behaviour when described in another (accidentally breaking a vase)? Can the utterances of a parrot be called verbal behaviour? Should an uncontrollable reflex action, like a knee-jerk, be called behaviour of the knee but not of the man? (ibid.)

The reason the riddles Lacey poses, and others like them, are insolvable for good is that, as Jakob and Thure von Uexküll have demonstrated, when detecting some other animal's sign-processes we are able to discern solely its message-bearing vehicles with their receptors and some responses of those organisms. To animals, for example to a cat-as-a-sign-receiver, another cat is a black box: a device of which the specified characteristics (its "outside") are knowable but means of operation ("inside") can only be guessed at with less or more confidence.[5] Findings such as this

> stress the fact that observation can show us living systems only "from the outside," that is, as they present themselves "to us." In order to inquire into their "inside," that is, into the sign relationships (with themselves, with their environment and other systems), we must find out how the living system construes its conditions. It should be emphasized here that "outside" and "inside" are semiotic concepts in that they mark a viewpoint outside or inside the system. (Th. von Uexküll et al. 1993)

Conjectures as to why a cat does or fails to respond to this or that sign in such-and-such a manner are merely constructs based on the observers' own repertoire of experiences as sign-receivers, the projections of their own "inner world" upon the cat's "inner world." To put it in a different way, the non-cat outside observer does not know the cat's code; and even another cat shares it only to the limited extent warranted by its own semantic boundaries. Although Fox asserts, as is generally held, that "yes, cats *do* dream" (1974, 111), this is still just a supposition, an attribution, warranted or otherwise, of a mental state of the cat.

Ex hypothesi, I can of course postulate, or intuit, with Fox, that my cats do in fact dream, but, strictly speaking and despite his verbal assurances, I cannot even be absolutely sure—or conceive of an experiment that would conclusively guarantee—that Dr. Fox himself dreams.[6] As Searle has convincingly shown, the attribution of internal, "mental" phenomena to such animals as cats, or indeed to other people, on the basis of their external behavior remains, as it must, nothing more than an inference. Such an inference, according to Searle, is based on the "rough-and-ready principle that we use elsewhere in science and daily life: *same causes—same effects,* and *similar causes—similar effects*" (1992, 75). However, no one knows what engenders dreaming in humans, let alone in cats, whose brains are different from human brains in multiform ways.

What is one to make of all this? It seems to me that, at the very least for us, workers in a zoosemiotic context, there is only one way to get through this thicket, and that is to adhere strictly to Jakob von Uexküll's comprehensive theses about signs. While this is not the forum to review (as I have done elsewhere, e.g., in Sebeok 1979b, 187–207) the overall objectives, scope, or empirical techniques of his Umwelt-research—that is, the biosemiotic exploration of semioses that govern the behavior of living entities from the cellular, or endosemiotic, level on up and outward—it does need to be repeated that his view of ultimate reality is unambiguously compatible with Peirce's. Von Uexküll held that "signs are . . . the only true reality; and the rules and laws under which the signs and sign processes communicate themselves to our mind . . . are the only true laws of nature" (Th. von Uexküll ed. 1992, 281). Living organisms and

Figure 2. From *Love Is a Happy Cat* by Michael W. Fox. Text copyright © 1982 by Michael W. Fox. Illustration copyright © 1982 by Harry Gans. Reprinted by permission of Newmarket Press.

their component parts, including cells, respond, in a cyclical functional process, only to signs, which also have a strictly triadic structure (ibid., 306).

Two of the immediately arresting consequences that arise from Jakob von Uexküll's paradigm of the functional cycle *(Funktionskreis)* are, first, the persuasive elucidation—in conformity with the principles of contemporary no less than classical physics—of the nature of the coupling of an observing entity with the living system observed; "and, second, the mechanisms of mutual influence, or, more precisely, inviolable interdependence, between signs and behavior" (Sebeok 1991e, 102). Nothing at all exists for any organism outside its sequestered, orbiculate Umwelt, its sealed-off, private monadic model of the universe. This model is composed of nothing but signs.[7] "The behavior of every organism—'behavior' being defined as the sign trafficking among different *Umwelten*—has as its basic function the production of nonverbal signs for communication, and first of all for communication of that organism with itself" (ibid., 103).

It appears from this approach that *behavior* is, in semiotic jargon, an indexical sign (Sebeok 1991f, ch. 13) pointing toward its interpretant, viz., another sign, which in its turn is empowered to encode effects of the environment onto its receptors into still further signs, or, in short, to attribute meaning. Writing in his role as a physician, Thure von Uexküll naturally emphasizes what he calls "semioses of symptomatization," equivalent to Charles Darwin's "autonomic effects" (cf. Sebeok 1976, 42, n. 89, 85), as well as George Herbert Mead's category of unintelligent gestures (cf. Sebeok 1991f, 142), by which he betokens indexical signs that are most commonly called *symptoms:* "the emitter is a living being sending signals by its behavior or posture which are not directed toward any receiver and do not await an answer" (Mead in Sebeok 1991e, 67–68; cf. chapter 4). One undeniable (although seldom credited) case in cats of such a symptom, or autonomic effect, or unintelligent gesture, would be their perspiration—yes, cats *do* sweat (Weigel 1975, 281–282).

By contrast, in what von Uexküll calls "semioses of communication"— corresponding roughly to Darwin's "displays" (cf. Sebeok 1989e, 270) as well as Mead's category of intelligent gestures—"the emitter and the receiver share the semiotic task by informing each other about the interpretant (or the code) which gives the emitted signs meaning intended by the emitter. . . . In this case signs attain their 'public character' only through exchange of information between emitter and receiver" (cf. Sebeok 1991f, 142). An example of such display complex in cats is anogenital presentation and tail raising in food solicitation and/or in greeting.

Deportment on this, the third level, is usually labeled a *display* in traditional ethological parlance (where in semiotic terminology *sign* is employed) although sometimes *display* is also applied to demeanor of the second level. Thus Immelman and Beer define *display* as "Behavior having a communication function," but then at once equate this with "expressive behavior, signaling behavior; advertisement behavior" (1989, 75), although, strictly speaking, expressive behavior corresponds to what Darwin called autonomic effects and what Thure von Uexküll calls a symptom. For instance, it is quite clear from Moelk's pioneering study (1944) that when a house-cat vocalizes at times its sound is a display, as when welcoming a familiar person, while at other times it is an autonomic affair, exhibiting, say, a current mood, physical or emotional state—witness that nonpareil observer, Charles Darwin: "Cats use their voices much as a means of expression, and they utter, under various emotions and desires, at least six or seven different sounds" (1872, 128).

Admittedly, the two sorts of semiosis are in practice hard to tell apart since, notwithstanding their involvement in what we tend to read as forms of animal communication, displays are, by and large, genetically determined, species-specific stereotypical motor patterns (McFarland ed. 1981, 133). In any event,

Figure 3. Anogenital presentation and tail raising in a cat soliciting food. Reproduced by permission from Fox (1974, 76: Fig. 19).

"behavior," in this framework, is conspicuously shown to be an emergent phenomenon at a more complex level of system-hierarchy than that of action and counteraction alone (Th. von Uexküll 1992, 460–461). In sum, whenever and however an animal "behaves" it concurrently signifies, and whenever and however an animal signifies it concomitantly "behaves." In Peirce's world, if man is a sign, must not a cat be *a fortiori* a sign too?[8] For consciousness, Peirce observed, "may mean that emotion which accompanies the reflection that we have animal life. This is a consciousness which is dimmed when animal life is at its ebb . . . but which is not dimmed when the spiritual life is at its ebb; which is the more lively the better *animal* a man is, but which is not so, the better *man* he is" (*CP* 5.313; italics are Peirce's).

II.

An ethogram is a behavioral inventory, ideally as complete and accurate a catalogue of all the action patterns that characterize a species as is feasible to register. Immelman and Beer rightly note that the preparation of an ethogram "has to contend with the critical problems of categorizing and labeling behavior patterns, and, if called for, sorting them into principled classes" (in Immelman and Beer eds. 1989, 91). Accordingly, it has become common practice since

Darwin (1872) to distinguish in the compilation of behavioral dossiers (or ethograms) for various creatures a separate heading for communication as a coherent class. Interest in the function of a behavior pattern in the animal's life led naturally to a return to the analysis of animal communication. This renewed regard captured in one and the same grouping both the Darwinian "expression of emotions" and those action patterns whose primary biological function is communication. Studies of animal communication escalated when investigators, such as Julian Huxley, eventually came to supplement the synchronic dimension with a diachronic perspective, or came to focus on the "evolution of displays from nondisplay behavior," the phenomenon he dubbed *ritualization* (Klopfer and Hailman 1967, 35, 38, 74).

Just how complete is, or can be, an ethogram of any species? In contrast with Darwin's informal sketch of the "special expressions" of cats, which took up only about three pages of his paradigmatic book (1872, 126–129) plus three with Thomas Waterman Wood's remarkably vivid drawings[9] (see figures 4–6), a truly comprehensive ethogram of such a familiar household pet would, one would think, have to be voluminous.

Actually, by 1962, a more sweepingly formal review took up thirty-five pages (Rosenblatt and Schneirla), but seven years after that, a follow-up account, "a brief and coherent picture of the behaviour of the cat with an emphasis on neural and hormonal mechanisms" under the same editor (Kling et al. 1969, 482), dropped down to a mere thirty pages. The chapter by Wemmer and Scow on cats in *How Animals Communicate* (Sebeok ed. 1977) was to have dealt with the Felidae in general, but was actually mostly limited to scent marking and contact devices, which together ran to a mere seventeen pages. The English version of Paul Leyhausen's milestone cat ethogram of 1979 occupied 340 pages. Although this was more than twice the size of the original German version (first published in 1956), it dealt amply with wild cats in addition to their domestic kin.

As for the book edited (and written in part) by Turner and Bateson, West described this as "affording a primer on modern ethological methods and outlining an impressive agenda for future research" (1991, 179). Its index refers to issues of "Communication" only once, viz., in lions, and twice to purring in cats, including this somber, veracious, yet in the end quite puzzling comment: "As things stand this most familiar and distinctive feature of the cat remains largely uninvestigated" (1988, 195). And here is all that Darwin had written about it 116 years earlier: "The purr of satisfaction, which is made during both inspiration and expiration, is one of the most curious" (1872, 129). Fox concurred: "No one has been able to give . . . a good explanation of the phenomenon of purring other than to say that a cat does it when it's contented" (1974, 84). But even this is contradicted by the always ingenious, beguiling Desmond Morris in his influential chapter titled "Why Does a Cat Purr?" To Morris, the

Figure 4. "Cat, savage, and prepared to fight. Drawn from life by Mr. Wood." After Darwin (1872, 58: Fig. 9).

Figure 5. "Cat in an affectionate frame of mind. By Mr. Wood." After Darwin (1872, 59: Fig. 10).

Figure 6. "Cat terrified at a dog. From life, by Mr. Wood." After Darwin (1872, 128, Fig. 15).

answer seems obvious enough. A purring cat is a contented cat. This surely must be true. But it is not. Repeated observation has revealed that cats in great pain, injured, in labor, and even dying often purr loud and long. . . . A more precise explanation, which fits all cases, is that purring signals a friendly social mood . . . indicating the *need* for friendship, or as a signal to an owner, saying thank you for friendship given. (1986, 17)

Is purring a so-called contact maintenance sign? And what is one to make of the fact that the ancient Greeks had no word for "purr" (cf. Beadle 1977, 69)?[10]

Compared to what is known of the honeybee, *Apis mellifera,* particularly of its remarkable communicative propensities, our cognizance of corresponding proclivities in *Felis catus* is amazingly scanty, especially considering its longtime intimacy (at least six thousand years) with humans.[11] For a proper perspective, however, it needs to be recollected that semiosis in the honeybee has been far more intensively studied than semiosis in any other animal, with the exception of ourselves. This social insect and its multiform communication systems have thereby achieved for comparative studies of most aspects of their "behavior"—and preeminently their "signifying behavior"—a benchmark observance, so to speak.

III.

Like other mammals, cats, at least during their formative segments (minimally so while weaning), conduct their lives—or, as the saying goes, nine lives (nine, arguably, for the same reason that Peirce showed a predilection for trinities of trinities [see Eco and Sebeok eds. 1983, 1–10 and Morris 1986, 135])—in niches populated by one or several conspecifics, augmented by representatives of a multitude of other species, ranging from the habitual neighborhood microorganismal fauna to animals of various kinds, including, in the domestic scenario, their human companions (Karsh 1983). Their Umwelt teems with—indeed, consists of nothing but—signs, some of which are regulated by species-specific codes, others by interspecific codes. Of the intraspecific code segments, doubtless the most thoroughly explored are, first, the mother-kitten relationship (Beadle 1977, 123–145; Milani 1987, 209–215; Turner and Bateson eds. 1988, 23–39; Haskins 1977, etc.); and second, a characterization of cat society (Fox 1974, 61–66; Beadle 1977, 100–111; Morris 1986, 48–49; Turner and Bateson eds. 1988, part III). Of the interspecific code segments, the hunting practices of the domestic cat and its encounters with such other animals as dogs are of some interest, but, for obvious reasons, most attention has been paid to cats' multiform relationships with humans.

Our propensity for articulated speech conjoined with digitalized hearing,[12] being the most conspicuous species-specific endowment of *Homo sapiens,* predisposes the ingenuous among us to look for semiosis realized through the acoustic modality in other animals (especially avian and mammalian domestic pets), high and low. In an overwhelmingly silent universe, "our planet is only patchily the home of sound"; sound "must be confined to the thin shell of life around the earth's surface, much less than 1 per cent of its radius" (Huxley and Koch 1964, 15).[13] Within this shell (nowadays often called the biosphere) sound is accentuated only in a slim layer hugging the lithosphere, spreading downward a few score fathoms into the upper reaches of the hydrosphere, and extending a few miles upward into the atmosphere. Din may be generated either as an incidental by-product of natural forces at work—whether its origin be inanimate like of a clap of thunder or animate like of the pounding of a herd of antelopes' hooves—or is, to the contrary, "purposeful," that is, functional or biologically useful for the living entity which engenders them. The polar distinction I draw here is between "natural indicative signs" and "conventional signs," which first received considerable attention in classical philosophy and was much later explicated by Hobbes (e.g., 1961, I: 14–15, II: 219) and his Anglo-Scottish successors in the eighteenth century. The salient point to bear in mind here is that both kinds of sounds, regardless of their source and whether wanted (signals) or unwanted (noise), "signify" whenever they impinge on the appropriate auditory circuit of any animal, self or other, thereupon arrogating the office of an interpretant (in Peircean phraseology), or, more accurately, a cataract of such novel signs.

Humans are, moreover, particularly prone to assign the rise of animal sounds to the vocal tract (or to the syrinx, the equivalent voice-organ of songbirds). Not all cat sounds originate in their larynx: for instance, in addition to purring, when appropriate they hiss, they chatter, they sniff (Morris 1986, 62–63, 67–68, 112–113), they "chirrup" (Fox 1974, 159), they spit explosively (Wemmer and Scow 1977, 751), they click ("this clicking noise [is] something of a mystery," [Morris 1987, 24–25]), and produce a variety of noises, which have scarcely been catalogued, with other regions of their body. The male cat in our household conveys his urgency to be let out at dawn by upsetting with much clatter the wastebasket in our bedroom.[14]

Cat vocalizations have been attentively studied, although far from conclusively. Mildred Moelk's admirable article (1944), still unsurpassed, was the culmination of over five years of trial and systematic development, perforce limited by the relatively simple instrumentation available to her in the early 1940s. Today, different investigators cannot seem to agree even on the number of cat calls. Moelk observed sixteen phonetic configurations—organized into three overall groups: murmur patterns, "vowel" patterns, and "strained intensity" sounds—plus three more types in scattered subjects. While Tembrock (1963, 753) claimed that twenty-one groups of sound can be distinguished, Wemmer and Scow (1977, 751) reported, to the contrary, that there are only "six calls that are common to the repertoires of most small cats," which they further subgroup into discrete and graded types (for this opposition, cf. Sebeok 1972). Morris lists "seven of the most important sound messages made by domestic cats" (1987, 25).

To my layman's ears, the matter seems a good deal more perplexing, inasmuch as individual cats appear to differ from one another in their vocal habits at least as much as in many of their other somatic traits; though seldom mentioned, there are probably breed, age (Haskins 1979),[15] and gender differences as well. As Morris so acutely noted, "since the refinement of the different meows as your pet cat grows older is a personal affair between you and your cat, it is not surprising that there is considerable variation from one animal to another" (1987, 21). In other words, while the basic feline sounds are innate, when the cat's Umwelt is pressed in propinquity with the human's novel, variations come to selectively supplement the genetic groundwork.

The frequency, range, volume, and general make-up of the vocalizations of my current pair of cats (of different pedigrees, one male, one female) are so discrepant that they remind this professional linguist of those (nonphonemic, nonconstructive) components of a source's sound wave emissions which Lotz (1950, 714) identified under the rubrics of "characteristics of the . . . organs and the . . . habits," either long-range or short-range, that are constant; plus pragmatic features that are variable, but which, he added, "have never been satisfactorily classified." The latter still require careful analysis, both in cats (Fox 1974, 84) and in humans. But, by and large, nothing much appears to have changed since the time of Topsell, who, at the outset of the seventeenth century, told his readers (seemingly in anticipation of politically correct newfangled usage) about how the cat "whurleth with her voyce, having as many tunes as turnes, for she hath one voice to beg and complain, another to testifie her delight and pleasure, another among her own kind . . . insomuch as some have thought that [cats] have a peculiar intelligible language among themselves" (1607; cf. Beadle 1977, 188).

IV.

Arguably, the most memorable and important pictorial illustrations in generic cat ethograms are the pair devised by Leyhausen (e.g., 1979, 194–195)—drawn from his photographs or films—to drive home the manner in which cats' offensive and defensive behaviors, or "moods," are superimposed. Figure 7 accomplishes this for body posture, figure 8 for facial expression. In both cases, the left to right horizontal, continuous-scale progression is from "neutral" to maximally offensive, while the top to bottom vertical sequel is from "neutral" to maximally defensive. The remaining twelve slots in both diagrams exhibit the corresponding superimpositions in fluctuating degree.

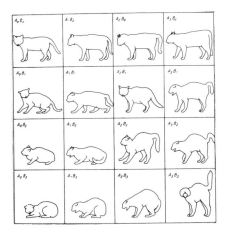

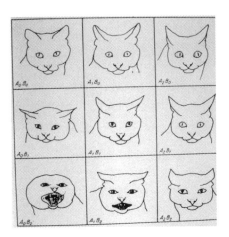

Figure 7. Expression of readiness in body posture for defense or attack in the cat. After Leyhausen (1973, 302).

Figure 8. Facial expressions of offensive and defensive mood in cat facial expression. After Leyhausen (1979, 195).

Mixed motor patterns, displaying two or more conflicting propensities, yield squares such as these, which, in semiotic terms, can be viewed as projections of composite nonverbal sign-assemblies, or supersigns (cf. Martin Krampen, in Sebeok ed. 1994, 2:1025; Eibl-Eibesfeldt 1989, 701). Such supersigns, or sign complexes, are not at all confined to cats, but are configured of visual elementary signs of a sort "found in practically all vertebrates investigated in this connection" (Leyhausen 1973, 301), including humans (Eibl-Eibesfeldt 1989, 467–468, and passim). Salient forms of this graded character (Sapir 1944; Sebeok 1972, 22–27) allow for unique interpretations-as-a-whole produced by the reader,[16] which eventuate from global "rules of grouping" postulating an interaction between tension-enhancing and tension-reducing forces, often called, in the terminology of Gestalt psychology, *Pregnanz*.[17] (Clumsily translated as *pregnance*, this notion shares much indeterminacy with the kindred, predominantly Continental, semiotic/semantic locution *seme*, now rather out of fashion.)[18]

A classic instance of a supersign displayed by a cat is illustrated by the lower right-hand corner square of figures 6 and 7, divertingly deconstructed in the double interpretation—one ostensible, the other esoteric—Morris framed to his own question, "Why does a cat arch its back when it sees a strange dog?" (1986, 59–61). If you sample, as I have done, observers of cat behavior, whether professional or lay (even children), asking them why, under given circumstances, a cat arches its back, there appears to be a wide consensus, as formulated for instance by Morris: "The function of this display is clearly to make the cat look as big as possible, in an attempt to convince the dog [or, for that matter, any hostile creature, including an unfamiliar cat] that it is confronting a daunting opponent" (1986, 59–61). In addition to its savage facial expression, the cat reinforces this canonical "transformation display" by its stance directed broadside at the opponent, its legs elongated and stiffened, typically accompanied by piloerection, inclusive of its tail fur, excepting of course in the genetically deprived tailless Manx breed (if the tail, in cats, is the principal organ of emotional expression, "a Manx cat is the equivalent of a dumb man," according to Huxley [1959, 78]).

Then, however, Morris goes on to speculate as to the supposed origin of the display: "In the case of the cat approached by a dog, there is both intense aggression *and* intense fear. It is this conflicting, double mood that gives rise to the special display. The cat borrows the most conspicuous element of its anger reaction—the stiff legs—and the most conspicuous element of its fear reaction—the arched back—and combines them to produce an 'enlarged cat' display" (1986, 60). In other words, in this context A,

(3) Y_1 ("stiff legs") + Y_2 ("arched back") + Y_n function in concert as
        a supersign of Z ("angry and fearful cat") to X (its opponent)

This functional explanation, even if true, turns out to be incomplete. Thus this same gross bodily display is presented in contexts where there is no need at all to intimidate a putative antagonist. Both my present companion animals, which differ from one another in many of their behavioral repertories, routinely perform their presentation in the shape of an inverted U promptly upon waking up from sleep on my bed, prior to dashing to their food dish. Thus two formally identical (zoo)signifiers—quasi-homonyms, if you will—may be coupled to entirely different context-sensitive (zoo)signifieds. This, in context B,

(4) Y_1 ("stiff legs") + Y_2 ("arched back") function as a supersign
        of Z ("I'm getting up"?) to X (observer)

The ethological implication underlying (3) is that flight, defense, and attack motor tendencies are superimposed in varying degree (Leyhausen 1979, 190–191). This was first proposed by Lorenz:

> The cat threatens dogs . . . by making its well-known "hunch back". Standing on straight, stiff legs and making itself as tall as possible, it ruffles the hair of the back and tail holding the latter slightly to one side in order to make its whole dimensions appear larger to the enemy . . . The cat's ears are laid flat, the corners of its mouth are pulled backwards, and the nose is wrinkled. From its chest a low, strangely metallic growl issues, which culminates in the well-known "spitting", that is, a forced expiration during which the throat is wide open and the incisors exposed. (1954, 177)

The supersign in (4) is a diminished version of the augmented supersign in (3), but this is not mentioned, let alone accounted for, in the literature I have scanned.

Furthermore, the concept of supersign as discussed above fits equally comfortably with Schneirla's theory of biphasic A[pproach]/W[ithdrawal] (1965). The key postulate for this principle of comparative animal psychology is that, by virtue of its A response, an animal orients to and ordinarily *reduces* the distance between itself and a stimulus source, whereas, by virtue of its W response, the animal orients to and ordinarily *increases* the distance between itself and a stimulus source. I have previously argued that Schneirla's A/W theory furnishes a minimal semiotic model that must have been of critical survival value to all species (including primates), because each individual animal imparts its own characteristic set of meanings to those qualities to which it reacts with its specific innate and learned response system (Sebeok 1986a, 13–14; 1991f, 55). Each living entity superimposes a taxonomy upon its universe (the system of signs the von Uexkülls call Umwelt) to filter out otherwise unmanageable environmental noise. Therefore, from its ontogenetic outset, any animal must minimally classify within its inherited cognitive map classes of things to approach (A or +: searching for and identifying prey, for instance), another class of things to withdraw from (W or –: forestalling propinquity with predators, for instance), and an indefinitely vaster category of all remaining objects (o) which appear not to matter either biologically or socially—a brew of plus, minus, and zero signs adequate for survival. Further, Schneirla (1965, 4) speaks of "approach-fixation" and "withdrawal-fixation," by which he appears to refer to neural trace effects which direct and habituate the animal through repetition of reinforcing contiguities by A-processes toward or W-processes away from a given constellation of signs. The cat's hunch back display, as in (4), must then perforce ensue from the synchrony (A/W or +/–) of several of its basic performance patterns. The question that remains to be elucidated is: why is the hunch back displayed as in (5)? What does it mean?

V.

Next, I shall turn to an idiosyncratic question, one to my knowledge totally ignored thus far in studies of cat behavior. Broadly speaking, this pertains to a facet of the pervasive topic of the Clever Hans Phenomenon (i.e., subtly deceptive or inadvertently self-deceptive cueing) that has absorbed me since the great Swiss animal psychologist, Heini Hediger, "first drew me to this inexhaustible magic well," as I have previously often acknowledged (Sebeok 1979b, xiv). My particular aim is to focus here on the language-endowed-animal illusion, which my colleagues and I have sweepingly critiqued, with negative termination, in various earlier publications (e.g., in Sebeok 1979b, 84–106; Sebeok and Umiker-Sebeok eds. 1980, 1–59; Sebeok 1981c, 109–209, 260–265; Sebeok and Rosenthal eds. 1981; Sebeok 1991f, 112–115). By the phrase "language-endowed-animal" I refer to creatures (other than normal hominids) alleged to have been reshaped, or trained, to understand and interpret verbal (not merely vocal) signs and/or to produce them, usually by means of speech. It is important to take note of the fact that all living entities steer in their respective Umwelts by means of species-specific sign action, or semiosis; this is not in question. The issue is rather: can any of them, excepting individuals of the genus *Homo,* be educated to communicate by means of *language* in any of its linear manifestations (speech, graphs, or the like)? Such is the stuff of fairy tales or hoaxes or pernicious self-delusion. There has never existed any corroboration whatsoever for this insinuation that cannot be accounted for otherwise, often in terms of the Clever Hans effect, though on occasion artfully camouflaged. (Saki's Tobermory, a cat who has "this horrible accomplishment," i.e., language, infused in him, is bumped off before he is able to "impart his dangerous gift to other cats" [Munro 1982, 108–115].)

The eponymous Clever Hans of Berlin and of standard psychology textbooks was a stallion, one among a long line of horses that performed both before and after him. Besides countless "talking horses" throughout history, oral and written lore is replete with "learned" pigs and dogs, a wide assortment of birds (like the Prodigious Goose of 1789 in London; Alex, a contemporary African gray parrot; a couple of Chinese chickens; and a salmagundi of woodpeckers, mynah birds, magpies, and crows), a few elephants, a medley of marine mammals (especially dolphins), and, most celebrated of all, a handful of captive great apes: bonobos, chimpanzees, gorillas, and orangutans (about which Wallman's recent independently reached harsh conclusion is the same as ours, to wit, that "none of the ape-language projects succeeded . . . " [1992, 4]).

Note the common presence of domestic animals, especially dogs (for example, in the Ringling Brothers, Barnum and Bailey circuses), in the vast literature on the subject, yet, to the contrary, the all but total absence of domestic cats.[19] This is especially striking since numerous circuses feature so-called big cat acts involving lions, tigers, and other wild specimens of the genus *Panthera,* sometimes in variegated compatible combinations.[20]

The illustrious University of Toronto circus semiotician, Paul Bouissac, confirms that domestic "cats are indeed rarely seen nowadays in circus spectacles," although he adds that "they nevertheless appear in some acts, although as minor, rather passive actors" (personal communication). There does exist a tradition, however slender, of cats trained for the circus, mentioned in the book by Hippisley Coxe, where this scholarly businessman describes his own experiences as an animal trainer—especially of ordinary domestic cats, which, he admits, "are the animals I like most" (1980, 77). His training methods were nothing out of the ordinary: he employed classic conditioning of the Pavlovian kind, slightly adapted to cats.

Bouissac himself has documented one circus act involving a domestic cat (1973, 263). In this article (and in personal communications), from which I recapitulate some of the following, he describes and illustrates a semiotically complex spectacle in which a little cat typically plays a bit part (see figure 9). This number begins with a crocodile perceived by onlookers as making its way across a board in equipoise across the entire ring, attended by a trainer who entices the reptile to do so. Facing the crocodile, there stands a "groom," as he is identified in the spidery French handwriting annotating each of the delicate drawings in the sequence on this page. The sham "crocodile" is then "undressed," revealing a real basset hound underneath (figure 9.1). This hilarious exordium, highlighting the transformation by means of interspecific "cross-dressing" of a ferocious reptile into a harmless pet sets up the more elaborate ensuing seven-episode sequence, likewise involving the application of interspecific transvestitism (ibid., 261).

A lady is next seen outside the cage, carrying a basket of flowers (figure 9.2). The trainer extracts a little cat from the basket, inserts it into a box and closes the lid. He then takes the box inside the cage where a lion seems attached to the bars by a collar (figure 9.3). The groom arranges a table with a plate containing a snack. The humans leave the cage (figure 9.4). The bogus "lion" shakes off his papier-mâché false face and frees himself from his loose collar, revealing a tan-colored Great Dane underneath the disguise. The dog remains in the "head" so long as the trainer is present, but returns later to his initial position. Once divested, he eats the meal on the plate (figure 9.5). The dog opens the box, out of which the cat emerges (figure 9.6), and the dog deposits the cat next to the empty plate. The dog calmly proceeds to replace its own head in the lion's visor (figure 9.7). The trainer returns to the cage and stands stupefied (figure 9.8). The dog, in order to cast blame elsewhere, has "fabricated" evidence by opening the box containing the cat and placing it next to the empty plate. When the man returns to the cage, it indeed looks to him— while the spectators know the cat is blameless—as if the cat has swiped and eaten the food which, the audience assumes, had been served for the man.

Adapting to Greimasian idiom, one might be tempted to say that, in this routine, the (trained) dog/trickster assumes the marked position of an actant, whereas, in an active/passive opposition, the (untrained) cat/innocent occupies the unmarked position of an antactant (Greimas and Courtès 1982, 6).[21]

What I find baffling is that the tame domestic cat, the best-known member of the genus *Felis*—at least as abundantly at hand as its rival companion animal in our affections, the tame domestic dog—so seldom appears in circus acts or, on the rare occasions when it does, as hardly more than a complaisant prop.

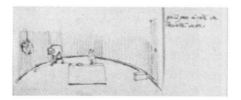
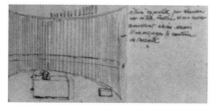
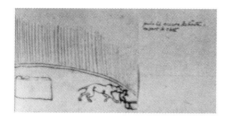

Figure 9. Chas Baron's acts. Fonds Vesque, A.T.P. Iconothèque Atp. classement provisoire V.A. 19. Cl. Atp 73.203.1 & 2. Photo A Guéz. Reproduced by permission from Bouissac 1973, 263.

The facile view is that cats are solitary, "independent" (cf. Fox 1974, 32–34), or headstrong, hence difficult to train. But this is clearly an illogical *post hoc ergo propter hoc* argument. The very fact of their eight thousand years or more of domestication, which presupposes taming, argues otherwise. In truth, an outstanding characteristic of cats is precisely their adaptability (cf. Morris 1987, 136), plasticity even. In a laboratory setting at Pennsylvania State University, for instance, the hierarchical dominance/submission relationships long cemented in a certain group have been shown to be totally reversible by appropriate conditioning.

Figure 10. "Dalila's Wonderful 'Mixed' Group" of lions and leopards. Reproduced, by permission, after Bouissac 1973, 264.

Too, the presumed untrainability of domestic cats stands in manifestly sharp contrast to the taken-for-granted behavioral malleability of the great "roaring" cats in the genus *Panthera,* or packs of them in diverse combinations, including the lion, the tiger, the leopard, and the jaguar (figure 10). Nothing, in principle, would appear to impede construction of an iconic configuration with seven domestic cats of mixed breeds. As a matter of fact, were the same act pictured in figure 10 to be repeated immediately afterwards in miniature, that is, with little cats and a clown (perhaps a midget) standing in for Dalila, the effect could be very amusing indeed. But this was apparently not the case. Yet Hippisley Coxe explicitly states: "There is really no difference in principle between training big cats and little cats" (1980, 128). At times, common dogs, a symbol-laden sacrificial goat (Bouissac 1976, 99–100), or even an adult rhinoceros may be coupled in the ring with, say, a (young female) tiger (Hediger bid me to witness the latter pair being co-trained in Zürich's Circus Knie). Such are among the most common star turns in circuses all over the world. Why then are house-trained cats so seldom found in the lion's den?

One might argue that audiences prefer to shiver to the implied menace of exotic beasts of the jungle—"terrible man-eaters," as they are sometimes proclaimed—and exult at the spectacle of their subjugation by human beings portrayed as valiant. In Bouissac's semiotic analysis (ibid., 97), what we see enacted here is the opposition of two principles: the "identification of the hero" versus the "identification of the hostile force."

A pussy cat, of negligible size and hence hard to see from outside the ring— "[s]mall animals are rarely shown in the circus because the performances lack spectacle" (Hippisley Coxe 1980, 86)—has no such mythological antagonist and can therefore provide no such thrill.[22] But then neither can "man's best friend"—yet clever dog acts do endure. ("The cat will mew and dog will have his day"?) Dogs, certain other mammals (bears, monkeys, apes), and birds are often portrayed as incarnating a different poetic principle: the humanization of animals (Bouissac 1976, 116–118). While cats could also easily embody this latter principle, nowadays they don't; the key, then, can be neither the absence of contained ferocity nor the lack of proportion.

That this benign neglect of cats in exhibitions or performances was by no means always the case is borne out by the illustration in figure 11, where I reproduce (after Sebeok 1991f, 74) an advertisement for just such a gig staged centuries ago at the Bartholomew Fair.[23] Note that the cat identified as the "cleverest" in Signor Capelli's company was professed in this placard (c. 1832) to obey her master's bilingual commands—be they pronounced in French or in Italian—"without any other signal being given than the sound of the voice." This specious disclaimer was intended to forestall possible recriminations of nonverbal cueing. Signor Capelli's other cats "beat a drum, turned a spit, ground knives, struck an anvil and rang bells" (cf. Hippisley Coxe 1980, 79). The backstairs workings of the Clever Hans effect on cats were sensed by so-phisticated English audiences, perhaps especially by those who attended horse acts (typically) at the Bartholomew Fair, at least as far back as the sixteenth century (Sebeok 1991f, 112–115).

One "clever" horse was mentioned by Shakespeare in *Love's Labour's Lost* (act 1, scene 2, line 51). A century after that, on September 1, 1668, Samuel Pepys witnessed, and recounted in his diary, the exhibition of another such "clever" mare. In the late 1920s, Dr. Joseph Banks Rhine was bamboozled by the Won-der Horse of Richmond, Virginia. And Clever Hans lopes on *ad nauseam*—but seldom in the shape of a cat. In short, while cat *apprentissage* is routine, cat *dressage*, although feasible, is very uncommon (cf. Sebeok 1988a, 70–71).

VI.

I purposefully cast the title of my essay as an open-ended question: what do we know about signifying behavior in the domestic cat? The disappointingly pungent answer is: very little. Notwithstanding that the impressive popular and scientific literature—although the ethology is often theory-driven, as in works by Lorenz and Leyhausen—pertaining to cats is vast, these reports tend to be

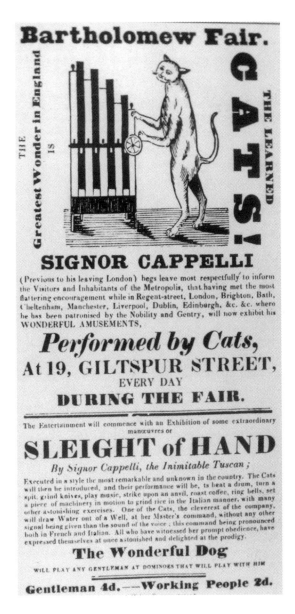

Figure 11. A "learned" (behavior shaped) domestic cat shown performing at the Bartholomew Fair.

replete with redundancies. The alleged empirical "facts" are frequently hedged. Thus the carnal cat in view comes more and more to resemble Lewis Carroll's free-floating Cheshire cat faded to its eyeless phase (cf. Morris 1987, 178–179).

In the special sense that, as I argued in 1979 (1979b, ch. 2, "Semiotics and Ethology"), the biological study of animal behavior is, by definition and historical origin, as well as in contemporary practice, an undeclared branch of semiotics, I provisionally bring to the cat's semiosphere my own host of reticulate interrogative theoretical puzzlements, among them (roughly in the order sifted) these:

- What is the gist of the expression *signifying behavior*?
- Is *behavior* a technical term? In what ways is it an indexical sign?
- What kind of semioses are autonomic effects? And displays?
- What is a *semiogram*? Can a vertebrate's semiogram ever be rounded off?
- What is the biosemiotic import of the opposition "outside" versus "inside"?
- Why are the contributions of Jakob von Uexküll of critical consequence to general semiotics?
- What is the role of sound in the biosphere? And in a cat's Umwelt?
- What is a supersign?
- Is the one-way ethological implication among the three categories of taming/training/domestication analogous to the semiotic categories of firstness/secondness/thirdness? How about Charles Morris's semiotic dimensions of syntactics/semantics/pragmatics (1971, 301–303)?
- What are the differences between *apprentissage* and *dressage* in the domestic cat?
- Why do cats figure so seldom in public spectacles or, more generally, in Clever Hans illusions?
- To what extent can humans communicate with cats and vice versa? (Is there a lesson to be learned from Holst's 1971 tale, "The Language of Cats"?)[24]

7

"Give Me Another Horse"

The form of the horse's hoof is just as much an image of the steppe it treads as the impression it leaves is an image of the hoof.

—K. Lorenz (1973, xi)

THERE HANGS IN London's National Portrait Gallery a 1926 cartoon by Bernard Partridge, depicting Sir Arthur Conan Doyle as "the slave of his creation, Sherlock Holmes" (figure 1). Because "The Adventure of the Lion's Mane" (Doyle 1967, 776–789), first published in the same year, 1926, represents a singularly radical stylistic experiment on the part of its author, then age sixty-seven, this, of all his mysteries, surely became one of the most intriguing in the entire Sherlock Holmes corpus of fifty-six short stories: for Holmes, then living in retirement in his Sussex home, necessarily conducts his investigation there in the absence of Watson. As the great detective notes at the outset of this account, he must therefore serve as his own chronicler. What is lacking here is the venerable cliché of the naive, unreliable narrator, a hoary literary device that Doyle reanimates throughout the rest of his oeuvre with consummate finesse. He uses it, among other goals, to cover up some of the more improbable aspects of his stories.

Apropos of "The Lion's Mane," its creator remarked that, among all his tales, he himself "should put" this very one, about a death-dealing marine coelenterate, "in the front row"—although, he qualified, "that is for the public to judge." "The Lion's Mane," in Doyle's own self-assessment, was admittedly "hampered by being told by Holmes himself, a method which . . . certainly cramps the narrative. On the other hand," he deemed "the actual plot . . . among the very best of the whole series" (1967, 789).

This text alone, then, sets limits to the generalization that all the Sherlock Holmes stories are variants of "one story" (cf. Zholkovsky 1984, 76). Viktor

This is the English version, with English references, of an article with appropriate Japanese references written for a Japanese book dedicated to Umberto Eco, titled in English *Ayukawa and the Thirteen Mysteries of 1900*, published by Tokyo Shogen sha (Tokyo, 1990). The article also appeared in *The American Journal of Semiotics* 8(4), 4–52, published in 1991. The title is taken from Shakespeare's *Richard III*, act 5, scene 3, line 578.

Figure 1

Shklovsky (1925) so claimed, in the sense in which, for example, all Russian fairy tales were said to be uniform in their structure (Propp 1928), or, for another, a myth can be defined "as consisting of all its versions" (Lévi-Strauss 1958, 92). While the plot of "The Lion's Mane" is indeed as ingenious as it is entertaining, this story's thematic development (cf. O'Toole 1975, 148) continues to disconcert in that it largely fails to conform to its readers' presuppositions and expectations. What is the essence of the missing ingredient that troubles the readership of this far-from-favorite tale?

Absent here is Doyle's otherwise inviolate structural principle of *nesting*, omnipresent throughout his other short stories, and accentuated even in such novellas as "The Hound of the Baskervilles." By *nesting* I refer to the organization whereby an ever-variable inner story stands apart from the invariant basic story in which the former lies embedded. "The basic story is what we call that part of the story where Holmes and Watson," the stable pair of foreground characters, are in action or at least present. The inner story is the client's narrative, i.e., the gradually unfolded train of events which has brought him (or, as in "The Speckled Band," her, one may add) "to turn to Holmes for help" (Scheglov and Zholkovsky 1975, 56).

The basic story frames the inner story. Within this elegant but standard touchstone chassis, Doyle was able to put forward and encompass, by way of a "description of the repertoire of images, objects, characters, properties, setting, etc." (ibid., 59), a great many atmospheric and other effects realized in the ensuing linear action, constituting his variegated detectival plots as such. Many of these semiosic devices are listed by Scheglov and Zholkovsky (ibid., 60–65), notably including Holmes's celebrated histrionic demonstrations of abduction from apparently trifling clues (Sebeok and Umiker-Sebeok 1981; Eco and Sebeok eds. 1983)—in short, the method that Holmes himself dubbed "The Science of Deduction" (e.g., Doyle 1967, 152–164). What characterizes all mystery stories, a genre to which detective stories belong *a fortiori* (although the reverse is by no means the case), is that the action progresses with an investigation from indexical signs (Sebeok 1991c) by means of abduction to an analysis and solution of the problem in question.

A particularly pertinent instance of this (in "A Study in Scarlet") is Holmes's observation of two ruts in the dry ground from which he proposes a startling abduction, eventually confirmed ("There is no room for a mistake"), that the murder victim Enoch J. Drebber had arrived at the site of the investigation "in a four-wheeled cab, which was drawn by a horse with three old shoes and one new one on his off foreleg." Afterwards, Holmes explains to the incredulous Watson: "There were the marks of the horse's hoofs . . . the outline of one of which was far more clearly cut than that of the other three, showing that that was a new shoe" (Doyle 1967, 172–173).

In his novel *Il nome della rosa* (1980a), Eco displaces the Baker Street master and his ingenuous friend and aide, Watson, in time and place from Victorian London to an Italian fourteenth-century monastic setting, in the guises of William of Baskerville and Adso. Eco's initial frame opens with what can concisely be designated, after the name of the abbot's favorite horse, as "the Brunellus episode" (1980a, 30–33; English edition 22–25; see also the commentary in Cohen 1988, 66–67 and Daddesio 1990). In this cameo prologue, Eco is able to rapidly but effectively sketch, for his narrator Adso's as well as his readers' benefit, his protagonist's personality and habits of abductive thinking. The cellarer asks William:

> "When did you see [Brunellus]?" . . .
> "We haven't seen him at all, have we, Adso?" William said, turning toward me with an amused look. "But . . . it is obvious you are hunting for Brunellus . . . fifteen hands, the fastest in your stables, with a dark coat, a full tail, small round hoofs, but a very steady gait; small head, sharp ears, big eyes. He went to the right . . . " (Eco 1980a, 31; English edition 23)

It is interesting that Adso's master, William, elucidating his abductions, immediately goes on to instruct his young pupil:

"My good Adso . . . during our whole journey I have been teaching you
to recognize the evidence through which the world speaks to us like a great
book. Alanus de Insulis said that

> *omnis mundi creatura*
> *quasi liber et pictura*
> *nobis est in speculum*

and he was thinking of the endless array of symbols with which God, through
his creatures, speaks to us of eternal life" (Eco 1980a, 31; English edition
23–24)

The pervasive Western metaphor of the Book of Nature (Blumenberg 1986)—
Carlyle (1987, 194f.) referred to it both as "the complete Statute-Book of Nature" and the "Volume of Nature . . . whose Author and Writer is God"—to
which Eco alludes here was in fact deployed in a magazine article, titled "The
Book of Life," written by none other than Sherlock Holmes himself: "From a
drop of water . . . a logician could infer the possibility of an Atlantic or a Ni-
agara without having seen or heard of one or the other. So all life is a great
chain, the nature of which is known whenever we are shown a single link of
it" (Doyle 1967, 159).

William's display of "habits of observation and inference which [Holmes]
had already formed into a system" (ibid., 109) mimics the structure and spirit,
if not the substantive content, of similar passages throughout the Holmes
canon. Thus, for example, at the beginning of "The Red-Headed League":

> Sherlock Holmes' quick eye took in [Watson's pre-] occupation, and he
> shook his head with a smile as he noticed my questioning glances [at Mr.
> Jabez Wilson]. "Beyond the obvious facts that that he has at some time done
> manual labour, that he takes snuff, that he is a Freemason, that he has been
> in China, and that he has done a considerable amount of writing lately, I can
> deduce nothing else." (ibid., 419)

As for the content of the Brunellus episode, Eco found his immediate inspiration for this incident of the abbot's horse in Voltaire's *Zadig* (discussed at
length in Eco and Sebeok eds. 1983, 207–15), where the Master of the King's
Hounds asks Zadig "if he had not seen the king's horse pass by":

> "The horse you are looking for is the best galloper in the stable. . . . It is
> fifteen hands high, and has a very small hoof. Its tail is three and a half feet
> long. The studs on its bit are of twenty-three carat gold, and its shoes of
> eleven scruple silver."
> "Which road did it take? . . . Where is it?"
> "I have not seen the horse," answered Zadig, "and I never heard speak
> of it." (Voltaire 1926, 9)

The retroduction practiced here was unequivocally designated in an 1880 lecture delivered by Thomas Huxley (1881) at the Working Men's College as "Zadig's method." But long before Voltaire, there were Arabic, medieval, and other variants of Zadig's abductive exploits, where the authors' *rei signum* of choice (*Quintiliani Institutio oratoria* 8.6.22) involved one horse or another. Among recent post-Voltaire but pre-Eco illustrations of this equine intertextuality, my last parodic pick fastens upon Dorothy L. Sayers's book, *Have His Carcase* (1932). In chapter 16 of this novel, Harriet Vane hands over to Lord Peter Wimsey a horseshoe she has just found on the beach. He then proceeds to reconstruct yet another horse—*ex alio aliud etiam intelligitur* (ibid.)—in this sparkling cascade of synecdoches:

> He ran his fingers gently round the hoop of metal, clearing the sand away.
>
> "It's a new shoe—and it hasn't been here very long. Perhaps a week, perhaps a little more. Belongs to a nice little cob, about fourteen hands. Pretty little animal, fairly well-bred, rather given to kicking her shoes off, pecks a little with the off-fore."
>
> "Holmes, this is wonderful! How do you do it?"
>
> "Perfectly simple, my dear Watson. The shoe hasn't been worn thin by the 'ammer, 'ammer, 'ammer on the 'ard 'igh road, therefore it's reasonably new. It's a little rusty from lying in the water, but hardly at all rubbed by sand and stones, and not at all corroded, which suggests that it hasn't been here long. The size of the shoe gives the size of the nag, and the shape suggests a nice little round, well-bred hoof. Though newish, the shoe isn't fire-new, and it is worn down a little on the inner front edge, which shows that the wearer was disposed to peck a little; while the way the nails are placed and clinched indicates that the smith wanted to make the shoe extra secure-which is why I said that a lost shoe was a fairly common accident with this particular gee. Still, we needn't blame him or her too much. With all these stones about, a slight trip or knock might easily wrench a shoe away."
>
> "Him or her. Can't you go on and tell the sex and colour while you're about it?"
>
> "I am afraid even I have my limitations, my dear Watson." . . .
>
> "Well, that's quite a pretty piece of deduction. . . . " (Sayers 1932, 209–210)

Animals of the most various ilk—since Poe's errant orangutan (1841) of the Rue Morgue, identified by abduction (then called "ratiocination")—abound in detective fiction, notably Doyle's, as well as in Eco's novel. A privately printed paper by Ewing and Pattrick (1965) attempted to list every speechless creature, of which there are many, actually appearing in the Sherlockian zoo, under headings such as "Stables," "Kennels," "Cattery," "Aviary," "Menagerie," "Reptile House," "Aquarium," "Insect Cases," "Farmyard," and

Figure 2

even heraldic and tavern-inn beasts, as well as a "worm unknown to science" and the unfathomable "giant rat of Sumatra," alongside the Sussex vampire.

"Give me another horse . . . ! Great reason why," cried out Richard III. Horses are especially common in the Holmes saga. They have also been featured in literally scores of modern detective novels, since Doyle's Shoscombe Prince, and notably his chronicle of Silver Blaze, John Straker's race-horse "from the Isonomy stock" (a real horse, by the way), pictured by Sidney Paget in the December 1892 issue of *Strand Magazine* (figure 2). To cite just a few by others, such novels include Creasey's *Death of a Racehorse* (1959), Giles's *Death at the Furlong Post* (1967), Gruber's *The Gift Horse* (1942), Palmer's *The Puzzle of the Red Stallion* (1937) and *The Puzzle of Happy Hooligan* (1941), Philips's *Murder Clear Track Fast* (Pentacost 1961), Platt's *The Princess Stakes Murder* (1973), Van Dine's *The Garden Murder Case* (1935), Wallace's *The Flying Fifty-five* (1922) and *The Green Ribbon* (1930), and, of course, some three dozen racing books, through his current *Longshot* (1990), by Dick Francis.

Indeed, horses—about fifty in all, in rich synonymic assortment—"bay," "cab-horse," "chestnut," "cob," "gray," "mare," "mule," "mustang," "pack-horse," "pony," "trotter"—turn up in so many roles in the Sherlock Holmes cycle that they have engendered quite a respectable secondary literature, including a thirty-one-page illustrated Danish monograph (Lauritzen 1959). They have also inspired all kinds of speculative meditations about Holmes's private life: "that his young days were spent among circles which were interested in the turf" and that, like Watson, Holmes perhaps patronized bookmakers (Bridgeman 1969, 59–60); or at least that the stories provide ample indication of

Holmes's "full knowledge of and interest in the equine branch of the animal kingdom" (Holstein 1970, 112).

Why are horses, which were, during the late Neolithic era, the last among the five most common livestock animals to be domesticated, yet which remain the least affected by human manipulation and artificial selection, featured with such predilection in detectival fiction? "The horse evolved as a fast-moving ungulate capable of migrating over great distances" (Clutton-Brock 1981, 80). The earliest accounts of riding and the management of horses date from the Iron Age; especially noteworthy are the essays on hunting and horsemanship from the fourth century B.C. by Xenophon, an adviser of Philip of Macedon, the father of Alexander the Great, who, together with his war-horse Bucephalus, conquered the world.

In his remarkably rewarding study titled "Clues: Morelli, Freud, and Sherlock Holmes," Carlo Ginzburg (in Eco and Sebeok eds. 1983, 81–118) has shown that the "conjectural or semiotic paradigm"—embracing divination through tracks and eventually the scientific analysis of footprints, gnawings, hairs, scat, and comparable pointers (body parts, separable or not)—is connected with Mesopotamian divination and ancient hunting techniques:

> For thousands of years mankind lived by hunting. In the course of endless pursuits, hunters learned to reconstruct the appearance and movements of an unseen quarry through its tracks—prints in soft ground, snapped twigs, droppings, snagged hairs or feathers, smells, puddles, threads of saliva . . . Successive generations of hunters enriched and passed on this inheritance of knowledge. (Eco and Sebeok eds. 1983, 88)

In the mythic landscape of the Indian world of the American wilderness, the Prairie (Lawrence 1985, 57–77), as depicted by James Fenimore Cooper, the last of the Mohicans, Uncas, and his friend Leatherstocking practiced the art of pathfinding (discussed in Sebeok 1991e) as the real-life Indians used to track in the Old World of their forefathers. And Peirce's most striking instance of an indexical symbol was, as well, of this kind:

> The . . . Perceptible may . . . function doubly as a Sign. That footprint that Robinson Crusoe found in the sand . . . was an Index to him that some creature was on his island, and at the same time as a Symbol, called up the idea of a man. (*CP* 4.531)

Thomas writes: "Tracking is an ancient science. It was probably practiced to a far greater extent by prehistoric man than it is today simply because it was a skill necessary for survival . . . Tracking or learning to read signs is no easy task" (1985, 129, 131). The distinguished field-naturalist Niko Tinbergen, ever mindful of the powerful Book of Nature metaphor, called tracking "countryside detection," based on "a vast map of such records, printed overnight . . .

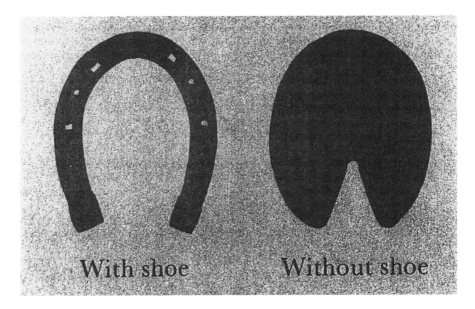

With shoe   Without shoe

Figure 3

tracks and traces of immense variety, often of wonderful clarity . . . written in footprint code." (Ennion and Tinbergen 1967, I). The track of a horse—an animal with non-cloven hoofs—is easily recognizable, whether shod or not, as pictured in Bang and Dahlstrom's abundantly illustrated, useful guide: when shod, "one sees only the impression of the shoe and identification is easy" (1972, 64, 74). Without shoes, a horse leaves large, almost circular tracks, each more or less deeply indented at the back; but the size varies considerably, depending on the race, which takes an expert to tag.

The survival of all species, and of each individual member of every species, depends on the correct decipherment of indexical signs ceaselessly barraging their Umwelts. Trackers of horses or of other animals, augurs and diviners, detectives, art historians, physicians and psychoanalysts, and modern scientists are, each in their own way, avid readers and interpreters of metonyms in the Book of Nature—just as the rest of us experience signs throughout our daily lives, only in a perhaps less concentrated, less specialized way. As the Italian physicist Giorgio Carreri wrote,

> Our senses pick up . . . events that cannot be arranged within . . . a simple measurable framework, thanks merely to the yardstick and the clock. For these events, the signs are the most appropriate expressions, and so the correlation among these signs can be perceived as a sense of immeasurable order, for example, in the unity of a work of art. (1984, 156)

8

Nonverbal Communication

ALL KNOWN LIVING organisms communicate exclusively by nonverbal means, with the sole exception of some members of the species *Homo sapiens,* who are capable of communicating, simultaneously or in turn, by both nonverbal and verbal means. The expression "by verbal means" is equivalent to such expressions as "by means of speech," "by means of script," or "by means of a sign language" (e.g., for use in a deaf group), that denote manifestations of any prerequisite natural language with which human beings are singularly endowed. However, not all humans are literate or can even speak: infants normally do develop a capacity for speaking, but only gradually; some adults never acquire speech; and others lose speech as a result of some trauma (e.g., a stroke) or in consequence of aging. Such conditions notwithstanding, humans lacking a capacity to verbalize—speak, write, or sign—can, as a rule, continue to communicate nonverbally.

A terminological note might be in order at the outset. The word *language* is sometimes used inappropriately in common parlance to designate a certain nonverbal communicative device. Such usage may be confusing in this context where *language* should be used only in a technical sense, in application to humans. Metaphorical uses such as "body language," "the language of flowers," the language of bees," "ape language," or the like, are to be avoided.

Nonverbal communication takes place *within* an organism or *between* two or more organisms. Within an organism, participators in communicative acts may involve—as message sources or destinations or both—on rising integration levels, cellular organelles, cells, tissue, organs, and organ systems. In addition, basic processes in the whole biological organization, conducted nonverbally in the *milieu intérieur,* include protein synthesis, metabolism, hormone activity, transmission of nervous impulses, and so forth. Communication on this level is usually studied (among other sciences) by subdomains of bio-

---

This article has not previously appeared in print. It is modified after an encyclopedia entry commissioned for *The Routledge Companion to Semiotics and Linguistics,* edited by Paul Cobley (London: Routledge, 2001). Similar materials were covered in my inaugural talk for the annual Thomas A. Sebeok Lecture Series in Semiotics, presented at the University of Toronto, Victoria College, on November 22, 1999.

semiotics labeled *protosemiotics, microsemiotics, cytosemiotics,* or, comprehensively, *endosemiotics.*

Internal communication takes place by means of chemical, thermal, mechanical, and electrical sign operations, or *semiosis,* consisting of unimaginably busy trafficking. Take as an example a single human body, which consists of some twenty-five trillion cells, or about two thousand times the number of living earthlings, and consider further that these cells have direct or indirect connections with one another through messages delivered by signs in diverse modalities. The sheer density of such transactions is staggering. Only a minuscule fraction is known to us, let alone understood. Interior messages include information about the significance of one somatic scheme for all of the others, for each overall control grid (such as the immune system), and for the entire integrative regulatory circuitry, especially the brain.

The earliest forms of interorganismic communication in our biosphere are found in prokaryotes—that is, mostly one-celled creatures lacking a nucleus. These are commonly called bacteria. In the last two decades, bacterial associations have come to be viewed as being of three sorts: localized teams; a single global superorganism; and interactions with eukaryotes (which are familiar life forms composed of cells having a membrane-bounded nucleus, notably animals and plants, but also several others). Localized teams of great complexity exist everywhere on earth; there are intestinal bacteria, dental plaque bacteria, bacterial mats, and others. There is of course a very large bacterial population both in soils and in the sludge at the bottom of bodies of waters. Such teams busily draw upon information fitting particular sets of circumstances, especially as regards the exchange of genetic information. Sorin Sonea has noted that, in this way, a local bacterial team can adopt sophisticated communicative survival strategies, that is, it can function for a certain period of time as a single multicellular organism.

Importantly, all bacteria, worldwide, have the potential to act in concert, that is, in the manner of a boundless planetary aggregation, as a sort of vast biological communications network—an Internet, if you like. This ensemble has been characterized as a superorganism, possessing more basic information than the brain of any mammal, and whose myriad parts are capable of shifting and sharing information to accommodate to any and all circumstances.

This bacterial superorganism created the environmental conditions conducive to the evolution of an entirely different life form: the eukaryotes. Bacteria exploited the eukaryotes as habitats as well as used them for vehicles to advance their own further dispersal. Indeed, eukaryotes evolved in consequence of a succession of intimate intracellular associations among prokaryotes. Biologists call such associations symbioses, but as these crucially entail diverse nonverbal communicative processes, they might more generally be characterized as forms of biological *semioses*. Biosemioses between bacterial entities started more than a thousand million years ago and are thus at the root of all communication.

Both in form and in the variety of their communicative transactions, animals are the most diverse of living creatures. Estimates of the number of animal species range from about three million up to more than thirty million. Since the behavior of each species—most of which are in any case scarcely fathomed—differs from every other, it will be evident that only a few general observations about these transactions can be made here.

Animals communicate through different channels or combinations of media. Any form of energy propagation can, in fact, be exploited for purposes of message transmission. The convoluted ramifications of these channels can only be hinted at here, but take acoustic events as one set of illustrations. Since sound emission and sound reception are so ubiquitous in human communication, it may come as something of a surprise how rare sound is in the wider scheme of biological existence. In fact, the great majority of animals are both deaf and dumb. True hearing and functional sound-production are prevalent—although by no means universal—only among the two most advanced phyla: the invertebrate Arthropods and the vertebrate Chordates (to which we belong). Insects, among the former, far outnumber the rest of the animal kingdom. Sound is most widespread in the Orthoptera, including grasshoppers and especially katydids, mantises, and cockroaches, and in the cicadas of the order of Homoptera. Possessing the most complex sound-producing mechanisms of any Arthropod, cicadas also have well-developed hearing organs on the forepart of their abdomen. The Coleoptera, or beetles, also contain quite a number of noisy forms. By contrast, sound-use is rather rare among the Arachnids, which include ticks, mites, scorpions, and spiders.

As we move on to the vertebrates, it becomes useful to distinguish not only nonverbal from verbal but also nonvocal from vocal communication, and to introduce yet further discriminations with the advent of tools. The vocal mechanism that works by means of a current of air passing over the cords, setting them into vibration, seems to be confined to ourselves and, with distinctions, to our nearest relatives, the other mammals, birds (endowed with a syrinx), reptiles, and amphibians; although some fish do use wind instruments as well, they do so without the reed constituted by our vocal cords. So far as we know, no true vocal performances are found outside the land vertebrates or their marine descendants (such as whales).

The functional advantages or disadvantages of the different channels of communication have never been fully analyzed, but certain statements can be made about acoustic communication in these respects which, other things being equal, apply to animals including man. A clear disadvantage, in contrast for instance to molecular traces such as pheromones, or chemical messengers, which tend to persist over time, is the short-lived character of sound. To counteract this transience, humans eventually had recourse to writing and, more recently, introduced all sorts of sound recording devices. This apparent defect may be outweighed by several advantages sound has over other media. For one thing, sound is independent of light and therefore can be used day or night. For another, it fills the entire space around the source. Accordingly, it does not require a straight line of connection with the destination. Too, it involves a minuscule expenditure of energy. In most animals, solely the body produces sound— ordinarily, no tool is requisite. In the case of humans, it can also be modulated to vary from intimate whisper to long-distance shouting.

In summarizing what is known of the acoustic behavior of vertebrates, we can only scratch the surface here. Among fish, as in the insects, sound production seems to occur but sporadically. Almost all are in the Teleosts, and their methods are, Huxley tells us, of three distinct kinds: by stridulation of one hard part against another (grinding their teeth, for instance); by expulsion of gas (a sort of breathing sound); or by vibrating their gas bladder (Huxley and Koch 1964). Some fish hiss like a cat, some growl, some grunt like a pig, others croak, snore, or croon, some bellow, purr, buzz, or whistle, and one even vibrates like a drum. And of course fish can hear (although their auditory powers vary considerably).

Most amphibians cannot hear and seldom produce any sound other than a weak squeak, but frogs and toads are quite noisy in highly diverse ways. Reptiles can in general hear better, yet few produce sounds (though crocodiles roar and grunt).

Birds signify by sounds, given and received, but, more comprehensively, by *displays*—stereotyped motor patterns involved in communication—which also include visual movements and posturing. Birds produce a huge variety of vocalizations, ranging from short, monosyllabic calls to long, complicated sequences, their songs. Some birds can more or less faithfully reproduce, that is to say "parrot," noises of their environment, imitating those of other species, notably even speech-sounds. The communication systems of birds, which have been well studied for many centuries, are so heterogeneous that they cannot be dealt with adequately here. The same must be said of their multifarious, often dazzling, visible displays, including their sometimes spectacular plumage, (e.g., peacocks or birds of paradise) and their constructs (e.g., bower-birds).

Mammals have elaborate auditory organs and rely on the sense of hearing more than do members of any other group, but they also, like many birds, communicate by non-vocal methods as well, if sporadically. A familiar example of this is the drumming behavior in the gorilla, produced by clenched fists beating on the chest. In echolocation, the emitter and receiver of a train of sounds is the same individual; this is found in bats as well as marine mammals, such as certain species of whales and dolphins. (The capability of blind people to navigate by echolocation has not been proved.) Some vertebrates, such as rats, mice, gerbils, and hamsters, communicate in a range inaudible to normal human hearing, by ultrasonic calls. (Analogously, the most effective color for the social bees seems to be ultraviolet, a spectrum beyond unaided human vision.)

All carnivores (cats, dogs, hyenas, etc.) as well as all primates, including man's closest relatives, the apes, more or less vigorously vocalize. But the characteristic performances of these creatures are both so rich and so varied—ranging from the relatively silent orangutans to the remarkably diverse "singing" gibbons—that describing them would demand a book-length treatment. Instead of attempting a sketch here, it is worth emphasizing that apes do *not* communicate verbally in the wild and that, furthermore, even the most strenuous undertakings to inculcate any manifestation of any natural language in captive apes—contrary to insistent claims made in the media—have uniformly failed.

Attempts to teach language-like skills to apes or to any other animals (such as captive marine mammals or pet birds) have been extensively criticized on the grounds that the Clever Hans effect, or fallacy, might have been at work. Since this phenomenon has profound implications for (among other possible dyads) man-animal communications of all sorts, some account seems in order here. In brief, a stallion named Hans, in Berlin in the first decade of the twentieth century, was reputed to be able to do arithmetic and perform comparably impressive verbal feats, responding to spoken or written questions by tapping out the correct answers with his hoof. Ingenious tests eventually proved that the horse was in fact reacting to nonverbal cues unwittingly given by the questioner. Ever since that demonstration of how unintended cueing can affect an experiment on animal behavior, alert and responsible scientists have tried to exclude the sometimes highly subtle perseverance of the effect.

It later turned out that there are two variants of the Clever Hans fallacy: those based on self-deception, indulged in by Hans' owner/trainer and other interrogators; and those performances—with "wonder horses," "talking dogs," or "learned" pigs or geese—based on deliberate trickery, performed by stage magicians and common con "artists" (over many centuries). Deceptive nonverbal signaling pervades the world of animals and men. In animals, basic shapes of unwitting deception are known as *mimicry*. This is usually taken to include the emulation of dangerous models by innocuous mimics in terms of visible or auditory signals, or distasteful scents, in order to fool predators. In humans, deceptive communication in daily life has been studied by psychologists, and on the stage by professional magicians. Various body parts may be mendaciously involved, singly or in combination: gaze, pupil dilation, tears, winks, facial expression, smile or frown, gesture, posture, voice, etc.

Humans communicate via many channels, only one of which is the acoustic. Acoustic communication among us may be *both* verbal *and* vocal, such as of course very commonly when we speak. But so-called alternative sign languages developed by emitters/receivers to be employed on special occasions or during times when speech is not permitted or is rendered difficult by special circumstances are, though generally verbal, not vocal. In this category are included North and South American Indian sign languages, Australian Aboriginal sign languages, monastic communication systems actualized under a religious ban of silence, and certain occupational or performance sign languages as in pantomime theater or some varieties of ballet. Unvoiced signing may also be freely chosen in preference to speech when secrecy is wanted, for instance, when a baseball catcher prefers to keep the batter ignorant of the next type of pitch to be made, or when a criminal attempts to keep certain messages from witnesses. More complex sign languages used for secrecy are employed by religious cults or secret societies where ritual codes are meant to manipulate problematic social relationships between "insiders" and "outsiders."

Acoustic communication in humans may, moreover, be somatic or artifactual, produced with tools. For example, contrast humming or so-called "whistle talk," produced by the body alone, with "drum signaling," which requires some sort of percussion instrument (or at least a tree-trunk). Acoustic somatic communication might be vocal, like a fearsome shriek, or nonvocal, like snapping one's fingers to summon a waiter. Sometimes nonverbal acoustic messages—with or without speech—are conveyed at a remove, from behind masks, through inanimate figures, such as puppets or marionettes, or through other performing objects. Furthermore, in humans, acoustic communication in all known communities has been artfully elaborated into a large variety of musical realizations. These might be accompanied by a verbal text (as in a song), crooned without lyrics, produced by all sorts of musical instruments, or embedded in an enormously complex, multi-dimensional work of art, like an opera. Thus while the overture to Mozart's *Don Giovanni* is a pure sonata-allegro, the enchanting duet between the Don and Zerlina, "Là ci darem la mano" (act I, scene 7), immediately following a *secco* (i.e., purely verbal) recitative, gives way to a melody solo, then voices intertwining, and climaxes in a physical gesture (a touch) and dancelike (i.e., 6/8 meter) skipping off-stage arm in arm ("Andiam, andiam mio bene . . . "). Opera being the supremely syncretic art form, Mozart's musical code, with Lorenzo da Ponte's libretto, is in this scene supported by a host of additional nonverbal artistic codes, such as mime, scenery, setting, costuming, and lighting, among others (elsewhere in the same opera these include dancing, the culinary art, and even statuary).

Perhaps somewhat less complicated but comparably fused artistic structures include sound films. These usually partake of at least four codes: one visual and three auditory, including speech, music, and sound effects. Circus acrobatic performances, which are realized through at least five codes—the performer's dynamic behavior, his social behavior, his costume and other accessories, the verbal accompaniment, and the musical accompaniment—furnish still another example of blended artistic achievement. The dazzling complexity of the messages generated by theatre events (Hamlet's " . . . suit the action to the word, the word to the action" providing but a modest start) can only be hinted at here.

Another interesting sort of nonverbal communication takes place during conducting, which can be defined as eliciting a maximum of acoustical results from an orchestra with the most appropriate minimum choreographic gestures. In a public setting, the conductor connects not just with the members of the orchestra but also with the audience attending the concert. The gestures shaped by his entire upper body—including hands, arms, shoulders, head, and eyes— are decoded by the onlookers through the visual channel, and transformed by the players into sound, which is then fed back to the audience. (Operatic conductors often mouth the lyrics.) And, as the eminent pianist Charles Rosen recently wrote, "For all of us, music is bodily gesture as well as sound, and its primitive connection with dance is never entirely distilled away" (1999).

A consideration of mainly acoustic events thus far should by no means be taken for neglect of other channels in which nonverbal messages can be encoded, among them chemical, optical, tactile, electric, thermal, and others. The chemical channel antedates all the others in evolution and is omnipresent in all organisms. Bacterial communication is exclusively chemical. Plants interact with other plants via the chemical channel, and with animals (especially insects, but humans as well), in addition to the usual contact channels, by optical means. While the intricacies of plant communication (technically known as *phytosemiosis*) cannot be further explored here, mention should at least be made of two related fields of human communication: the pleasant minor semiotic artifice of floral arrangements and the vast domain of gardens as major nonverbal semiosic constructs. Formal gardens, landscape gardens, vegetable gardens, water gardens, coral gardens, and Zen gardens are all remarkable nonverbal contrivances, which are variously cultivated from Malinowski's Trobriands to traditional *kare sansui* (dry gardens) of Japan, to Islamic lands, China, Europe, and so forth.

Smell (olfaction, odor, scent, aroma) is used for purposes of communication crucially by, say, sharks and hedgehogs, such social insects as bees, termites, and ants, and such social mammals as wolves and lions. It is less important to birds and primates, which rely largely on sight. In modern societies, smell has been roundly commercialized in the olfactory management of food and toiletry commodities, concerned with repulsive body odor and tobacco products. Perfumes are often associated with love and sexual potency.

The body by itself can be a prime tool for communication, verbal as well as nonverbal. Thus, in animals, it is well-known that dogs and cats display their bodies in acts of submission and intimidation, as famously pictured in Charles Darwin's *The Expression of the Emotions* (1872; the cat illustrations are reproduced in chapter 6 of this volume). There are many striking illustrations in Desmond Morris' *Manwatching: Field Guide to Human Behaviour* (1977) and in the photos assembled by Weldon Kees of how the human frame is brought into habitual play (Ruesch and Kees 1956). Professional wrestling is popular entertainment masquerading as a sport, featuring two or more writhing bodies, groaning and grunting, pretending in a quasi-morality play to pit good against evil; the players obviously interact with one another, but, more subtly, communicate with a live audience. Performances like this differ from legitimate bouts like boxing and collegiate wrestling, or sports like tennis, soccer, or cricket, in that the outcome of the contest is hardly in suspense.

Dance is one sophisticated art form that can express human thought and feeling through the instrumentality of the body in many genres and in many cultures. One of these is Western ballet, which intermingles sequences of hand and limb gestural exchanges and flowing body movements with a host of other nonverbal protocols that echo one another, like music, costumes, lighting, masks, scenery, props, etc. Dance and music usually accompany pantomime or dumb shows. Silent clowns or mimes supplement their body movements by suitable make-up and costuming.

Facial expressions, like pouting, the curled lip, a raised eyebrow, crying, and flaring nostrils, constitute a powerful, universal communication system, solo or in concert. Eye work, including gaze and mutual gaze, can be particularly important to understanding a range of quotidian vertebrate as well as human social behavior. Although the pupil response has been observed since antiquity, in the last couple of decades it has matured into a broad area of research called *pupillometry*. Among circus animal trainers it has long been an unarticulated rule to carefully watch the pupil movements of their charges, for instance tigers, to ascertain their mood alteration. Bears are reported to be "unpredictable" and hence dangerous precisely because they lack the pupil display, as well as owing to their inelastic muzzle which cannot "telegraph" an imminent attack. In interpersonal human relationships, a dilation of the pupil acts in effect as an unwitting message transmitted to the other person (or an object) of an intense, often sexually toned, interest.

Many voluminous dictionaries, glossaries, manuals, and sourcebooks exist to explicate and illustrate the design and meaning of brands, emblems, insignia, signals, symbols, and other signs (in the literal, tangible sense), including speech-fixing signs such as script and punctuation, numerical signs, phonetic symbols, signatures, trademarks, logos, watermarks, heraldic devices, astrological signs, signs of alchemy, cabalistic and magical signs, talismans, technical and scientific signs (as in chemistry), pictograms, and other such images, many of them used extensively in advertising. Regulatory signs ("No smoking"), direction signs deployed at airports ("Passport Control," "Men," "Women") or in hospitals ("Pediatrics"), and road signs ("No passing") are commonly supplemented by icons under the pressure of the need for communication across language barriers, certain physical impairments, or comparable handicaps.

The labyrinthine ramifications of optical communication in the world of animals and for humanity are boundless and need to be dealt with separately. Such sciences as astronomy and the visual arts since prehistoric times naturally and mainly unfold in the optical channel. Alterations of the human body and its physical appearance, whether non-permanent (e.g., body painting, make-up, or hair styling) or quasi-permanent metamorphoses by dint of procedures such as body sculpture (e.g., the past Chinese "lotus foot" or Western "tight-lacing" customs; infibulation, cicatrization, or tattooing; and, more generally, plastic surgery), all convey messages by nonverbal means. The art of mummy painting in Roman Egypt was intended to furnish surrogates for the head by which to facilitate silent communication of a deceased individual during his or her passage to the afterlife.

An intriguing variety of nonverbal human communicative-behavior-at-a-remove features a bizarre form of barter known since Herodotus, modern instances of which are still reported, labeled by ethnographers *silent trade*. None of the common direct channels are usually involved, only the abstract idea of exchange. What happens is something like this: one party to a commercial transaction leaves goods at a prearranged place, then withdraws to a hidden vantage point to watch supposedly unobserved. The other party then appears and inspects the commodity. If satisfied by the find, it leaves a comparable amount of some other articles of trade.

The study of spatial and temporal bodily arrangements (sometimes called *proxemics*) in personal rapport, the proper dimensions of a cage in the zoo or of a prison cell, the layout of offices, classrooms, hospital wards, exhibitions in museums and galleries, and a myriad other architectural designs—involve the axiology of volume and duration. A map is a graphic representation of a milieu, containing both pictorial (iconic) and non-pictorial (symbolic) elements, that can encompass a few simple configurations or highly complex blueprints, diagrams, and mathematical equations. All maps are also indexical. They range from the local, such as the well-known multicolored representation of the London underground, to the intergalactic metal plaque on the Pioneer 10 spacecraft speeding its way out of our solar system. All organisms communicate by use of models (Umwelts, or self-worlds, each according to its species-specific sense organs), from the simplest representations of maneuvers of approach and withdrawal to the most sophisticated cosmic theories of Newton and Einstein. It would be well to recall that Einstein originally constructed his model of the universe out of nonverbal signs, "of visual and some of muscular type." As he wrote to a colleague in 1945: "The words or the language, as they are written or spoken, do not seem to play any role in my mechanism of thought. The psychical entities which seem to serve as elements in thought are certain signs and more or less clear images which can be 'voluntarily' reproduced and combined." Later, "only in a secondary stage," after long and hard labor to transmute his nonverbal construct into "conventional words and other signs," was he able to communicate it to others (see Hadamard 1945, appendix II).

Suggested Readings

Because all living things communicate nonverbally, the literature on the subject as a whole is astronomical. Therefore, the following references are arbitrarily restricted to just one English entry for the main topics discussed in this article. Topics are listed in alphabetical order.

Aboriginal sign languages: Umiker-Sebeok and Sebeok eds. 1978

Acoustics: Busnel ed. 1963

Acrobats: Bouissac 1985

Advertising: Nadin and Zakia 1994

Animal communication: Sebeok ed. 1977

Animal sounds: Huxley and Koch 1964

Animals and humans: Sebeok 1990a

Apes: Sebeok and Umiker-Sebeok eds. 1980

Bacteria: Sonea and Panisset 1983

Bird display: Armstrong 1965

Bird song: Catchpole and Slater 1995

Clever Hans: Sebeok and Rosenthal eds. 1981

Clothes: Lurie 1981

Communication (general): Sebeok 1991b

Conducting: Schuller 1997

Dance: Hanna 1979

Deception: Schiffman 1997

Echolocation: Busnel and Fish 1980

Emotions: Darwin 1998

Endosemiotics: Th. von Uexküll et al. 1993

Faces: Landau 1989

Film: Metz 1974

Gardens: Ross 1998

Gaze: Argyle and Cook 1976

Gestures: Morris et al. 1979

Hands: McNeill 1992

Infants: Trevarthen 1990

Light: Petrilli and Ponzio eds. 2000

Lying: Ekman 1985

Manwatching: Morris 1977

Maps: Turnbull 1989

Modeling: Anderson and Merrell eds. 1991

Monks: Umiker-Sebeok and Sebeok eds. 1987

Music: Wright 1996

Objects: Krampen 1995

Performing objects: Proschan ed. 1983

Piano: Rosen 1999

Pictorial communication: Sonesson 1989

Plants: Krampen 1994a

Proxemics: Hall 1968

Pupils: Janisse 1977

Road signs: Krampen 1983

Semiochemistry: Albone 1984

Sign languages (deaf): Stokoe 1972

Signs and symbols: Frutiger 1989

Smell: Classen et al. 1994

Social organs: Guthrie 1976

Space: Sommer 1969

Speech surrogates: Sebeok and Umiker-Sebeok eds. 1976

Tattooing: Sanders 1989

Theatre: Carlson 1990

Visual communication: Ruesch and Kees 1956

9

Intersemiotic Transmutations
A Genre of Hybrid Jokes

DRAWINGS BY LUCIANO PONZIO

THE LABEL *TRANSMUTATION,* as used here, refers to intersemiotic translation, defined as "an interpretation of verbal signs by means of signs of nonverbal sign systems" (Jakobson 1971, 261). Jokes, as a rule, are considered "one form of narration" (Miller 1995, 66), hence a type of verbal art, even though (in their telling to hearing and sighted people when in the presence of a light source) they are normally accompanied by various gestural elements as accessories, including coupled manual and facial expressions, postures, and the like, which tend to complement in unison, indeed often to reinforce, the facetiousness conveyed by the primary verbal thematic strand. Notwithstanding that all jokes are thus intrinsically pansemiotic configurations, the verbal twist is typically primary. The joke can be fecundly, if perhaps less amply, told in the dark, but not, on the contrary, conveyed solely by means of the nonverbal adjuncts, which, for instance in an Italian consummation, play "an essentially adverbial function with respect to the meaning manifested by the mimicked expression" (Ricci Bitti 1992, 195).

There exists, however, another category of jokes, of which this article relates five examples. Jokes belonging to this subgenre are narrated like any other, but only up to a point: the climax—or, in instances such as "The Dead Cat" (joke 4 below) several punch lines building up from one climax to another—can be delivered only by means of simple gestures, as in jokes 1 and 2 below, or an aggregate of gestures, e.g., joke 3. Their humor cannot be satisfyingly imparted in the dark or over the phone, nor easily disclosed in written form (including e-mail). Such hybrid jokes, if delivered face-to-face, must be accompanied by appropriate gesticulation; or, if communicated in script, must be illustrated by

This article was originally published in Italian as "Trasmutazioni intersemiotiche: Un genere di barzellette ibride" in *La traduzione,* ed. S. Petrilli, 153–166 (Bari: Meltemi Editore, 1999). It was in part inspired by a set of photographs in which Jean Umiker-Sebeok, Erica L. Sebeok, and I modeled the gestures.

pictorial displays of various sorts, sometimes representing motion, as in "Jesus Christ on the Cross" (joke 3). The funniness of the verbal portion of a hybrid joke falls off rapidly in proportion to the quantity of visual elaboration its inscribed unfolding demands; this will be evident to would-be readers of jokes 3 and 4.

The interlaced semiotic transmutations of jokes belonging to this genre depend for their graspable performance on the principle of successivity (or indexicality) superimposed over that of simultaneity (or iconicity). They are therefore semiotically more complex formations than the run-of-the-mill, orthodox witticisms that brighten our daily lives.

1. The Danish Photographer[1]

Ost, the Danish word for "cheese," is pronounced "oost," with a distinct moue on the vowel. The joke goes as follows:

A young Dane wants to make a career as a professional portrait photographer, but the pictures he takes are inept (figure 1.1). He is advised to study the art of portrait photography with a celebrated master in New York City (figure 1.2). He crosses the Atlantic to apprentice with this master (figure 1.3), who teaches him a simple rule: instruct models to say "CHEESE" before he snaps the picture (figure 1.4). The Dane returns to Copenhagen (figure 1.5). He tells his models: "Say OST" (figure 1.6). [Here the joke teller exaggerates the decidedly unsmiling pout of "oost." Figures 1.7 and 1.8 picture what the joke's audience imagines will happen as a result.]

2. Les Baguettes[2]

An American tourist in Paris goes for a walk, and, wanting to return to his hotel, loses his way. He accosts a Frenchman who is carrying a baguette under each arm and asks him where he can find the Hotel d'Iéna (figure 2.1). The Frenchman asks the tourist to hold his two baguettes (figure 2.2). To the consternation of the American, the Frenchman goes [here the joke teller shrugs his shoulders in a typically French manner, spreading his arms outwards from his sides, conveying that he hasn't any idea. (figure 2.3)].

3. Jesus Christ on the Cross

Jesus Christ is condemned to death by Pontius Pilate. Pilate says to him: "Look, I am a merciful man. Die you must, but I will give you a chance to choose the manner of your execution. Your two options are: (a) we can bury you in the sand up to your armpits, then smear honey on your head and arms, letting insects sting you to death; or (b) we can nail you to a cross" (figure 3.1). As is

Figure 1.1

Figure 1.2

Figure 1.3

Figure 1.4

Figure 1.5

Figure 1.6

Figure 1.7

Figure 1.8

Figure 2.1

Figure 2.2

Figure 2.3

Figure 3.1

Figure 3.2

Figure 3.3

Figure 4.1

Figure 4.2

Figure 4.3

Figure 4.4

Figure 4.5

Figure 4.6

Figure 5.1

Figure 5.2

well known, Christ chose the second option, which is why all Catholics remember Christ by making the sign of the cross (figure 3.2) rather than by [here the joke teller waves her arms wildly about her head, as if fending off biting insects (figure 3.3)].

4. The Dead Cat

A man is driving his car too fast and inadvertently runs over a cat (figure 4.1). He stops to search for and apologize to the cat's owner. He stops at the house of an old lady (figure 4.2), thinking she must have been the owner. He says to her: "Madam, I am very sorry indeed but I think I killed your cat." The lady asks, "Well, what did the cat look like?" (figure 4.3). [Here the joke teller simulates a dead cat (figure 4.4).] The old lady then says: "No, no, young man! I meant: what did the cat look like *before* you ran over him?" (figure 4.5). [Again the joke teller says nothing but mimics the astonished expression of a cat that's about to be hit by a car (figure 4.6).]

5. Short Necks[3]

An American asks an Italian: "Why do Italians have short necks?" (figure 5.1). [The joke teller does not say anything, but simply makes the Italian gesture for "I don't know," which raises his shoulders and makes his neck seem to disappear (figure 5.2).]

10

"Tell Me, Where Is Fancy Bred?"
The Biosemiotic Self

IN *The Merchant of Venice,* Bassanio amplifies his query to the caskets, "Tell me, where is fancy bred," with two further sets of rhetorical questions: "Or in the heart, or in the head? How begot, how nourished?" He demands: "Reply, reply," but then settles these issues for himself: "It is engender'd in the eyes, / With gazing fed; and fancy dies / In the cradle where it lies: / Let us all ring fancy's knell; / I'll begin it,—Ding, dong, bell. / Ding, dong, bell" (act 3, scene 2, lines 63ff.). In early English usage, the word *fancy,* or *fantasy,* was roughly synonymous with "imagination"; yet, by the end of the sixteenth century, certainly in this passionate context, it plainly also meant "love." Love is evoked neither in emotion or in the intellect but springs from a moment of visual apprehension: in Bassanio's view, the eye, transcending all other modes of human perception, such as sound or smell, serves as the supreme organ of erotic inclination.

This belief is not necessarily shared by everyone, not even by other Shakespeare characters, such as Helena, who claims, to the contrary, that "Love looks not with the eyes, but with the mind" (*A Midsummer Night's Dream,* act 1, scene 1, line 144). Diane Ackerman, in her delightful if eccentric recent book about the senses, makes no mention of love in her chapter on vision. Whimsically perhaps, she associates love with the sensation of taste, particularly of chocolate (following some inconclusive work by the psychopharmacologist Liebowitz [1984] and others): "A sly beau once arrived at my apartment with three Droste chocolate apples, and every wedge I ate over the next two weeks, melting lusciously in my mouth, filled me with amorous thoughts of him" (1991, 154).

Shifting sharply to a commonplace sphere of observation from the cascade

This article was written in honor of the late Milton Singer. It originally appeared in 1992, in *Biosemiotics: The Semiotic Web 1991,* eds. T. A. Sebeok and J. Umiker-Sebeok, 333–343 (Berlin: Mouton de Gruyter). In 2001, Italian translations of this and four other articles of mine on the semiotic self (including the following chapter) will be published in T. A. Sebeok, S. Petrilli, and A. Ponzio, *La semiotica dell'io* (Rome: Meltemi), to be followed by an English translation of that book.

of lofty questions Bassanio toyed with, note that police officers in American cities, and perhaps elsewhere, when they arrest someone and invite him for a ride "downtown" in the back seat of a police car, firmly press a palm on the handcuffed suspect's head when ushering him into a back seat. This practice is so familiar that actors impersonating cops and robbers in a movie or a television show use this very gesture, often, I hear, not knowing or fully understanding why. Police officers explain their action as routine preventive procedure to make sure that the suspect doesn't contuse his or her head on the car frame while in custody and thereby later claim physical abuse.

To me, however, this behavior suggests an interesting and empirically quite accessible research problem: are human beings—or, for that matter, vertebrates in general (Hediger 1980, 44f.)—consistently aware of our body size, viz., our changing height? Given that we grow in stature at a relatively leisurely pace from childhood to adulthood, then tend to diminish somewhat as we become yet older, how are these changes registered in consciousness and implemented so as to, for instance, know when to duck entering a car? (For that matter, how do drivers internalize their fairly accurate knowledge of the perimeter of their vehicles so as to avoid scraping surrounding objects?)

More generally still, how are self-images established, maintained, and transmuted into performances? Sensory experiences may at times pose semiosic ambiguities, as in the following seemingly paltry example. I have a hole in one of my teeth, which feels mammoth when I poke my tongue into it. When my dentist lets me inspect it in a mirror, I am surprised how trivially small the aperture—the objective sign—looks. The question is: which interpretation is "true"—the one derived via the tactile modality or the one reported by the optical percept? (cf. chapter 4, p. 55).

The felt image and the lesser configuration I see reflected in the dental mirror—or, rephrased in semio-medical usage, the private symptom *(subjektives Zeichen)* and the public sign *(objektives Zeichen)*—do not quite tally in this case. These convey distinct intimations—messages with implications that are at odds. Such a mismatch, confusing if perhaps negligible here, can also on occasion, as in the myriad interpretations of severe and always terrifying chest pains, have grave or even fatal consequences for the patient.

A pain in the chest, as a diagnostic entity, is a signifier with multifarious and often hard-to-sort-out signifieds. Sharp chest pains, accompanied by profuse sweating, dizziness, shortness of breath or smothering sensations, accelerated heart rate, and a sense of impending doom, form a coherent set of indexical signs (Sebeok 1991f, ch. 13), dubbed, at least since Galen, a *syndrome*; together, they frequently denote a true cardiac emergency. In 1722, William Heberden coined the phrase *angina pectoris* to describe recurrent chest pains (usually due to a disease of the coronary arteries, caused by excessive deposits of low-density lipoproteins or vessel spasm). The Atlanta cardiologist-essayist

John Stone, in his illuminating survey of the various presagings of chest pains, quotes from this English physician's classic account: "They who are afflicted with [*angina pectoris*] are seized while they are walking . . . with a painful and most disagreeable sensation in the breast, which seems as if it would extinguish life, if it were to increase or continue; but the moment they stand still, all this uneasiness vanishes" (1989, 53). Much later, the novelist Nabokov described it thus: "A certain unpleasant and frightening cardiac sensation . . . not pain or palpitation, but rather an awful feeling of sinking and melting into one's physical surroundings" (1957, ch. 5: 5).

In fact, as Stone points out, severe chest pains may signify a whole range of other maladies, such as "pleurisy" or inflammation of the pericardium, but also precordial stabs and other conditions that may be caused by physical activity (including plain coughing), a pinched nerve, or muscle cramp, and may be harmless. However, an entirely different medical condition, a supposed psychiatric disorder officially recognized only in 1980 and known in laymen's idiom as a panic attack, closely mimics the symptoms of a heart attack, although not such objective signs as may show up, for instance, in a treadmill stress test, angiography, or thallium scan.

A seriously complicating risk factor for cardiac predicaments is the widespread inability to perceive, or at least to accurately construe, the body's own internal signs, such as heart rhythm disturbances, and of course the total incapacity to be aware of the level of one's asymptomatic blood pressure. The pain of coronary heart disease may be felt across the front of the chest, in the arms, or in the neck and jaw, instead of where the heart is situated, to the left. In such dangerously deceptive "displaced signs," as I once called them, the signifier does not accurately, or at all, "point to" the requisite signified (to be sure, for reasons that are respectably rooted in evolution; cf. Miller 1978, 22f.). Indeed, according to the investigations of Rainer Schandry (1990) of the University of Munich, only 10 percent of people have a "precise heart perception"; many innocuous cardiac reactions, unrecognized, can lead to disabling fears.

In trying, since 1977, to come to terms with many more or less anomalous semiosic phenomena, only a sampling of which I can recount and illustrate here, I began to explore the notion of the semiotic self. Cited instances have to do with the somatic localization of passions like love or feelings like anxiety; the incorporation (as it were) of such faculties as one's own body-size; and the association of other private experiences, such as light-headedness, pains, twinges, nausea, hunger and thirst, "funny feelings," or what Hungarians call, in a well-nigh untranslatable idiom, *közérzet* (a generalized but amorphous state of good or ill health), with their respective outward manifestations or referents. The effects of wrongly parsed sign processes or their impairment, including long-persisting images of amputated extremities, constitute another profoundly enigmatic class of events, as in the eerie case of the one-armed Paul

Wittgenstein's—Ludwig's brother—amputated but lingering phantom right limb with its reportedly still virtuoso fingering technique for some new composition (Otten 1992, 45).

My initial concern was with what has been called signal anxiety, which, at least since Freud, has been deemed a classic human semiosic predicament. It has been correlated, as the recent sensitive studies of Verres in the context of cancer have stressed especially, with certain disturbances in accurate message transmission from patient to physician (see also the pertinent remarks of Th. von Uexküll in Verres 1986, vii–x):

> Viele Menschen haben durchaus den starken Wunsch, offen über ihre Angst zu kommunizieren. Sie trauen diesen offenen Austausch aber ihrem sprachlichen Kommunikationsvermögen nicht zu und sind dabei auf Hilfe angewiesen. (Verres 1990, 2)

> (Many people have a compelling desire to communicate openly about their anxiety. However, they do not entrust such open exchange to their verbal communicative competence and are therefore in need of help.)

These difficulties of communication arise in part, I believe, from the fact that bodily sensations and the like, most saliently those connected with illness, are not amenable to verbal expression because they lack external referents; insistent intrusions though they may be into the routines of one's day or night, they can at best be denominated, for they resist unfolding into narratives, which are, by definition, always verbal.

For a life scientist, however, the self is delimitable in the first instance in terms of a nonverbal network of interpretation, labeled by the late Giorgio Prodi (in Sercarz et al. eds. 1988, 53) the body's *immunocompetence,* an overall processing function of a large (although, in principle, enumerable), highly specific but adaptable array of molecular defining entities, the autoantigens, that is, antigens or nonself substances that are a natural part of the host of an eukaryotic immune system. (Note that protists lack an immune system, but have other effective means of safeguarding their own cells from autodigestion.)

In short, self-recognition is an intrinsic property of the immune system. This system compels a continuous discrimination of immune cell from foreign protein, self from nonself, except when pathology supersedes normal physiology, as for example in an allergy, which the Medawars characterized as "a miscarriage of the immunologic process in which something that begins as a protective device has deleterious consequences that range in severity from itching to sudden death" (1983, 9). In other words, "cells infected by a virus or . . . transformed to a malignant state are recognized as modified self antigens and eradicated" (Battisto et al. eds. 1982, 178), but of course mistakes—which may, alas, prompt serious challenges to the animal's biological integrity—do happen;

for example, it is credible that an error in how antigens are prepared for presentation to the immune system may contribute to the development of a disease (say, type I diabetes, an autoimmune condition).

By "mistakes," I mean to focus here on semiosic miscarriages, for instance, a genetic defect that incapacitates normal cells from passing routine inhibitory messages (neurotransmitters or changes in cell membrane potential) to adjacent cells through the tiny ion tunnels (or protein channels) that connect them, thereby causing uncontrolled growth leading to a cancerous tumor. Ion channels are a property inhering in all cells; they perform special tasks and are, among other operations, directly involved in both the elementary and manifold advanced functions of life.

The immune system is criterial for the definition of our biological self. As such, it is an *endosemiosic* organ (Jerne 1985; Sebeok 1985a, 3), along with such kindred, intertwined structures (each discussed in these terms in Sebeok 1991e, 108f.) as the genetic code, the metabolic code, the neural code, and even the verbal code, at least when the latter is deemed, as it was by Chomsky, a "mental organ" (1980, 241). "The term 'endosemiosis'," Thure von Uexküll writes, "refers to processes of sign transmission inside the organism," which are all, it should be emphasized, "indirectly linked to phenomena in the organism's environment" (Th. von Uexküll et al. 1993, 5).

Where, then, is the "semiotic self" located? Clearly, in the organism's *milieu extérieur,* on the level of an idiosyncratic phenomenal world, tantamount to Jakob von Uexküll's Umwelt (1973, 334–340)—a technical appellation I prefer to render as the "model" of a species-specific segment of individual reality (Sebeok 1991f, ch. 5)—made up of *exosemiosic* processes of sign transmission. Miller, in a nice figure of speech, tells us that sensations happen "in an isolated annexe called the self, and if that annexe is missing . . . the sensations float around in a sort of elsewhere" (1978, 20). This semiotic self, which of course enfolds and thus "contains" in its *milieu intérieur* some body's immunocompetence, occupies, as it were, a sphere of space/time bounding the organism's integument, although the programs for the fabrication of subjective constructs of this sort are surely stored within the subjacent realms of its endosemiosic organs (semiotic aspects of pertinent boundary conditions were recently discussed in Hoffmeyer 1992). This semiotic self, furthermore, is composed of a repertoire of signs of a necessarily sequestered character; as Jakob von Uexküll—claiming that even a single cell has its *Ich-Ton* ("ego-quality")—remarked, "bleibt unser Ich notwendig subjektiv" (our ego remains necessarily subjective) (1973, 68).

Peirce, in his canonical amplification of the classic definition of a representamen, wrote that a sign "is something which stands to somebody for something in some respect or capacity" (*CP* 2.228). It is his addition precisely of the tag "to somebody" which illuminates the semiotic self, and which doubtless engendered Peirce's Shakespearean notion of "glassy essence" (Singer 1984), that each living organism is enswathed in a private Umwelt: an impalpable, solid, withal context-sensitive and environmentally supple, carapace, or, as I have previously dubbed it, a Hediger bubble (cf. Sebeok 1989e, 45, 46; 1991f, 40). This invisible, malleable proxemic shell amounts to nothing less than what laymen call "reality," to which all sign users and sign interpreters are knit by a formidable array of indexical representamina (Sebeok 1991f, ch. 13).

By "Hediger bubble," I allude to the subtle amalgam of what this greatest of animal psychologists has variously called, since the early 1940s, "biological distance," "individual distance," or "social distance." These are quintessentially semiotic concepts which lie at the heart of, among other exploits, human training of animals for circus performances. The trainers' work

> consists of a masterly judgment of biological distances and symbols . . . [A] performance is a continuous and very delicate interplay of provocations and reactions of the animal, an elegant weaving together of movement and counter movement . . . The observer can often hardly distinguish between deliberate, carefully calculated movements and involuntary accompanying ones. This is the secret . . . " (Hediger 1968, 130f.)

Nature's indexicals are universally nonverbal, but in our glottocentric genus indexicals may increasingly, if always selectively, be enhanced—in a phylogenetic as well as an ontogenetic sense—by verbal elements, including especially deictics, designators, reagents, metonyms, symptoms, clues, cues, synecdoches, and *pars pro toto* expressions. In *Homo*, nonverbal and verbal indexicals may be either vocal or nonvocal. Nonverbal vocal indexicals such as groans and moans are public signs of latent discomfort, as are nonverbal nonvocal expressions such as frowns or writhings. Signs of both kinds are *promulgations* of, for instance, pain, in contrast to *exposures,* which are usually out of self-control, such as yellow skin exhibited by a jaundiced person.

It is interesting to reflect in passing that the plasticity of the Hediger bubble, the parochial responsiveness of the semiotic self, or its remarkable ability to adjust its performance depending on its semiosic input, is a process wholly governed by appropriate signs emanating from within that same Umwelt.

Accordingly, a body can be pictured, in an arabesque of interlocking convolutions, as "a web of semioses" (Th. von Uexküll et al. 1993, 8). This powerful master metaphor is also widely applicable to all manner of biosemiosic transformations, such as the cybernetic interplay in the first semiosic dimension, which is one of complementarism between ego and alter (Pais 1991, 438–447), and in the second semiosic dimension between inner and outer, which is a relationship of embedding (Sebeok 1989e, 42–45; 1991e, 103), i.e., the immune self comes to be integrated as a constituent part of the surrounding semiotic self.

The barriers which occlude and thereby separate each and every windowless monad from all the rest are such as to prevent any self from fully fathoming any other. Hurdles between egos—unlike those between cells, which are surrounded by semipermeable membranes, allowing the passage of certain chemicals and thereby certain information—are insurmountable. We can, of course, and regularly do, spin fantasies about, or "image," the situation of an "other," or even perhaps empathize with a fellow-human's or some pet's singular individuality, but our respectively impenetrable semiosic orbits are perpetually kept apart by a frigid intergalactic void: the self's perception of any other is composite, partial, and forever incomplete. We can approach the "real" richness of the universe only by entertaining multiply contending, mutually complementary visions. I believe this is the quotidian implication of Niels Bohr's celebrated adage that it is "wrong to think that the task of physics is to find out how nature is. Physics concerns what we can say about nature" (Pais 1991, 427).

The semiotic self, as was already noticed by Thure von Uexküll, is the recondite interpreter of our world in the semiosic chain of transmission, and therefore continually engaged in meta-interpretation, viz., interpreting interpretations. Any self can and must interpret the observed behavior of another organism solely as a response to *its* interpretations of *its* universe, "behavior" meaning the propensity that enables it to link up its Umwelt with those of other living systems within its niche.

An act of interpretation is an act of as*sign*ment, that is, the elevation of an interpreted phenomenon to "signhood"; indeed, this is what the word *encoding* betokens. Interpretation is an autopoietic (i.e., actively self-maintaining) process, and one that operates, moreover, on the product of its own operations (Maturana 1980, 47–52, 253); that is, it is recursive, as both Peirce and the von Uexkülls undeniably understood. The elder von Uexküll was the earliest to actually postulate a biological mechanism for the elucidation of the process (1973, ch. 5 and passim), namely, the well-known "functional cycle" *(Funktionskreis)*, in the course of which a meaning is not merely con*sign*ed *(Bedeutungerteilung)*, but also pragmatically verified *(Bedeutungsverwertung)*.

It is evident, then, that passions, deficits (and kindred minus signs), feelings, and the rest of the experiences alluded to above are not "located" in any one organ of the body, even the brain, but are, in a vague sense, semiosic reverberations of the neural circuits operating throughout the creature's Innenwelt (ibid., 150)[1] in ceaseless feedback interplay with its Umwelt. People (and some other organisms, such as domestic animals) may react positively in equal measure to iatric ministrations, with opiates perhaps (which affect not only the spinal cord and the brain, but also receptors and nerve fibers) and to placebo control (symbolic healing), in which I would include psychological or religious counseling such as culturally variable manifestations of shamanism (Sebeok 1981c, ch. 10). The placebo effect poses further intriguing problems for the entire field of PNI (psycho-neuro-immunological) researches as much as for semiotic theory and applications. PNI is an essentially multidisciplinary endeavor, concerned with the bidirectional bioregulatory and clinical interactions between the central nervous system and the immune system (Kappauf 1991) in sickness and in health, with thought-provoking implications for speculative semiotics, its current paradigms, and its far-flung, traditionally established practices (Sebeok 1981c, ch. 10; 1989e, ch. 5).

II

The Cognitive Self and the Virtual Self

WHEN A MAN, such as me, reaches his seventy-sixth year, he has earned the right to glance at himself or—in the case at hand—his "self." It was a little over twenty years ago, in fact, when I became attentive to, as so many have before me, the notion of identity or, to be more precise, interested in the problem of what I dubbed the "semiotic self" (in Sebeok 1979b; cf. 1989c, 1989d, and chapter 10 above). That the "self" is a sign—or, rather, an amalgamated projection of composite nonverbal sign-assemblies called *supersigns*—is hardly in doubt (cf. chapter 6 above; Krampen 1994b). Of course, in man, verbal signs contribute, though optionally so, as well. By the latter I refer to certain idiosyncratic habits of any speaker, which are constant markers, plus certain variable factors which the linguist and semiotician John Lotz classified together as "pragmatic features" of the sound wave (1954, 378–380). These may include exhibitions of the emotional attitude that the message source maintains while speaking (anger, conviction, irony, or the like). Although such studies, building upon classical rhetorical texts, recommenced in the early 1950s (Moses 1954; see also Stankiewicz 1972), acoustic features of this kind, or kindred ones, have never been satisfactorily explored, let alone systematized. Most recently, and quite aptly, Schiffrin (1966, 167) has shown the role of narrative as a valuable resource for self-portraiture, that is, "the display of self and identity." *Mutatis mutandis*, verbal expressions realized in other media, or channels such as, notably, calligraphy, can be analyzed for "self-revelations" in comparable ways.[1] Even the manner in which a Morse code operator taps out the code as a linear series of dots and dashes betrays his identity to an experienced listener or seasoned "watcher" of a distant instrument that faithfully reproduces the encoded pulses at their genesis.

Peirce's scattered views on the human self, along with George Herbert Mead's and Royce's, were effectively reexamined, following Colapietro's accomplished integrative effort (1989; see also Short's far-reaching 1992 review article), in a recent book by the Berkeley sociologist Wiley (1994, 30–32, 171,

This article is the fourth of my essays on the semiotic self. It was written in honor of the late Roberta Kevelson and was published in 1998, in *New Approaches to Semiotics and the Human Sciences: Essays in Honor of Roberta Kevelson*, eds. W. Pencak and J. R. Lindgren, 307–321 (New York: Peter Lang).

and passim). While I acknowledge the heritage and the scholarly merits of these and other recent works that deal with semiotic antecedents, I do not pursue them here, aside from one fascinating paradox. This aporia (to apply a fashionable term), which was studied separately by Mary Haight (1980) and Karen Hanson (1986, 105), refers to the literally impossible or, at best, oddly incoherent conceit of "self-deception." I believe that questions of the sort both of these authors raise could be further elucidated by semiotics and immunology, especially in the light of such molecular deceptive phenomena as camouflage, mimicry, perverse morphology, and the like. A strategy of defensive evasive structure, a concealment of lethal binding sites, has been hypothesized, among others, for the HIV virus. But I have not tried to provide here even a minimal survey of other considerations of the "self," for plenty of those already exist. I prefer instead to explore some novel aspects of the broader biosemiotic perspectives introduced in my previous papers on this topic, as well as to consider some implications that the pair of complementary titular attributes *cognitive* and *virtual* may pose in this context.

Biosemiotics, firmly rooted in classical and modern medical semiotics, is a contemporary offshoot of general semiotics on the one hand, yet, on the other, it became viable as a new "Paradigm of Biology." Two German scientists—Eder and Rembold of the Max Planck Institute for Biochemistry (Martinsried)— elected, at the Twenty-second International Ethological Conference held in Kyoto, to so style converging developments they perceived in this respect. Energetic inquiries are crowding in from both sides of an often erroneously grasped divide: erroneous because, on deeper analysis, the general sign science turns out to embed the life science to constitute a comprehensive conjoined science—a "natural semiotics," in the words of such sophisticated observers as the late Italian oncologist and prolific writer on semiotic themes, Giorgio Prodi (in Sercarz et al. eds. 1988, 55–56; also Eder and Rembold 1992, 61–63).[2]

From the semiotics verge, I attempted to capture the state of the art in several books and two consecutive conference reports (see Sebeok 1991e, 100–113; chapter 10 above). The far more diversified biomedical side, in its burgeoning incarnations, harks back pre-eminently to the pioneering labors of Jakob von Uexküll in theoretical biology (e.g., 1973), to those of his son, Thure von Uexküll, chiefly in the medical applications of the doctrine of signs (e.g., Th. von Uexküll and Wesiak 1988, 123–150), and to the equally seminal work of Heini Hediger in animal psychology (e.g., 1980).

This century's pertinent proliferating developments can be emblematized, inter alia, by the following series of declarations:

- Peirce's well-known axiom, "that all this universe is perfused with signs, if it is not composed exclusively of signs" (*CP* 5.448 [1905]);
- Mead's view, that "through the medium of communication with a self . . .

the biologic individual becomes essentially interrelated with the self" (1934, 372);

- Thure von Uexküll's remark about his father, Jakob: "Of particular interest to Uexküll was the fact that signs are of prime importance in all aspects of life processes" (1987, 147);
- Jacob's statement, "The genetic system and the immune system . . . function as memories of the past of the species and of the individual respectively" (1982, 54);
- Edelman's observation, "By selfhood I mean not just the individuality that emerges from genetics and immunology, but the personal individuality that emerges from developmental and social interactions" (1992, 167); and
- János Gergely's characterization of the human immune system as "the most perfect semiotic system in the Universe" (personal communication, 1995).

Of the dozen or so branches of biosemiotics, only the last mentioned was called upon in my 1977 paper (1977b). This hybrid has since been dubbed both *semioimmunology* and, better, *immunosemiotics* (Sebeok 1991e, 108). The latter term is associated with Tomio Tada, a renowned immunologist of the Faculty of Medicine at the University of Tokyo. Tada had "framed the definition of this science as the study of the general principles underlying the structure of sign systems perceived by different cells of the immune machinery." Thus, in all mammals, "restrictions in partner cell interactions must exist as part of an intracellular semiotic system" (Sercarz et al. eds. 1988, v, vii; see also P. A. Bretscher, ibid., 293–303). The reason for having invoked immunosemiotics as aforementioned should become evident from the main propositions advanced in 1977, where I argued approximately as follows:

1. There are two ill-defined (see 2.ii below) comprehensions of the animal "self":

    a. *immunologic,* or biochemical, with semiotic overtones; and
    b. *semiotic,* or social, with biological anchoring.

Gloss to (1)

These coupled, complementary perspectives (a-b) appear to be in good conformity with the passage from Edelman quoted above, but only as a first approximation to a very intricate matter. As F. Jacquemart and A. Coutinho, of the Pasteur Institute, pointed out, "The notion of the self is perhaps one of the oldest in human history. This is precisely what makes it difficult to analyse" (in Sercarz et al. eds. 1988, 173).

2. The arena of the immune reaction (Ir) is contained within the skin. The arena in which the semiotic self officiates—and which contains the former—is between an ill-defined region of the body beneath the skin of an organism and the outer perimeter of what I have labeled the "Hediger bubble," discussed,

and provisionally redefined, thus: "a variably shaped impalpable sphere of personal space that admits no trespass by strangers and is defended when penetrated without permission" (Sebeok 1977b, 1063).

Glosses to (2)

i. The late Heini Hediger, successively the director of the Bern, Basel, and Zürich Zoos, was the most remarkable animal psychologist of our times. He wrote an impressive dissertation in 1935 on (among a host of other topics) the specificity of animal flight-reactions, the measurability of flight-distances, and space-time systems in animal social behavior. In the course of a highly productive scientific career, Hediger came to hone and reshape the discipline that he founded and christened zoo-biology ever more in accordance with semiotic principles (1990a, 415–439). He came to write: "I believe that eventually the explanation for the extremely complex and, so far, under-researched problem of the relationship between man and animals will be obtained by means of signal study or semiotics" (1985, 177).

Although adherents of the *Umweltlehre,* that is, the study of modeling, seem unaware of the personal connection between the two men, von Uexküll *père* in fact received the younger scholar in Hamburg in 1934 with utmost cordiality. Many years afterwards, Hediger acknowledged that he was "extremely impressed by von Uexküll's *Umwelt-Lehre*" (ibid., 149). His own extensive researches on animal "biological distance," "individual distance," or minimum remove within which one may approach another, and "social distance," or maximum separation between the members of any animal group—plainly semiotic concepts, all three—were in a fertile sense logical extensions of the *Umweltlehre.*[3]

ii. By "ill-defined," I mean that the immune code, along with the genetic code and the neural code (brain/mind), is only one of three or four powerful intercommunicating mammalian pattern-recognition systems, each with capabilities of learning and memory, housed within our bodies (Sebeok 1991f, 85–86, 88–89). In addition, the bloodstream carries around within the organism, reliably if relatively slowly, valuable packages of information. The properties of these systems are, however, as yet far from our capacity to comprehend or precisely represent. As Edelman has emphasized (1987), the three are architectonically much the same, differing mainly as to the time scales on which they function. "The evolutionary system works on a time scale of hundreds of thousands of years, the immune system in a matter of days, and the brain in milliseconds" (Pagels 1988, 135). Furthermore, of the mammalian body's three information systems—biosemiotic systems par excellence—two evolved from the same bacterial ancestry and all three are governed by a language-like generative syntactic device (Chomsky 1980, 136–139; Jerne 1985; Sebeok 2000d).

I now provisionally suggest combining the meshwork of this triad of selves under a single designation: the supersign *cognitive self*. The much abused adjective *cognitive* is meant here to suggest unlimited semiosis, in Peirce's sense, with respect to a potentially infinite string or cluster of interpretants. Too, metaphorically, I intend *cognitive self* to be roughly equivalent to Jacob's master image for his own fascicle of inner selves, *la statue intérieure* (1987). The expression further implies a competence on the part of the central nervous system, or "brain," to discriminate the organism, or "self" within which it is lodged, from its Umwelt, or, broadly, from "the rest of the world." This discriminative capability evolved from the *primal ontogenetic as well as phylogenetic sign relation,* namely, the opposition between *ego* and *alter* (Sebeok 1991e, 103), realized chemically in the earliest free-living cells.

3. Invasion of (1a) is signified by the immune reaction—recognition followed by a triggered response; of (1b) by anxiety (as used in Sebeok 1989c; see also gloss), with the latter serving as an early warning system for the former.

Gloss to (3)

Anxiety, defined by Freud in explicitly semiotic terms "as a signal indicating the presence of a danger-situation" (Sebeok 1989c, 263), is indeed an indexical sign (Sebeok 1995b).[4] Anxiety is activated when the self is at peril from an event assigned sufficient, marked weight by the endangered organism. The triggering index may take a quasi-biological, nonverbal shape, such as the olfactory trace of a leopard predator for a baboon prey, or be of a semantic character, such as some verbal assault whereby a stranger intrudes upon the territorial preserves of the self (in the sense of Goffman 1971, 28–61).

4. Transmission errors may occur in both processes, with potentially devastating effects on the self. The capacity of a human immunodeficiency virus to impede or destroy the immune self through docking to the self-recognition receptor CD4 may be the most notorious contemporary example among many other autoimmune diseases.

In 1989, several opportunities encouraged me to reconsider and add to what I had written a decade before. My interest now refocused more narrowly: "The body has—or rather consists of—a veritable armamentarium of more or less palpable indexical markers of unique selfhood" (Sebeok 1989d, viii). The ones I came to discuss included phenotypic fingerprints and, on the genotypic plane, DNA "fingerprinting." Species odors and group odors—metonyms for distinctive functions in humans and other animals, and singular personal scents of particular individuals—are in part biological, in part cultural (e.g., diet-derived) tokens of selfhood. Le Guérer reminds us that "Humans produce a characteristic odor in the air around them that reflects [read: indexes] their diet and/or health, their age, their sex, occupation, race . . . the most direct and profound impression we can have of another person is his (or her) smell"

(1992, 23). Napoleon, for one, allegedly became so enamored of eau de cologne (originally a plague prophylactic) that he splashed a vial of it over his head every morning (Classen et al. 1994, 73).

I have also raised the empirically testable question whether speechless creatures are capable of internal self-representation. Is an animal aware of its appendages, its shadow upon the ground, its body-size? Such items can be semiotically charged features in a bundle of deconstructable idiosyncratic features of the self. The same is true of proper names, which, in humans, take a predominantly verbal form but in the rest of the animal kingdom are indexed by a wide variety of nonverbal means (Sebeok 1986a, 82–96).

In a 1992 paper (chapter 10 above), I examined the establishment and maintenance of self-images in terms of symptoms and the coherent sets of indexical signs called, at least since Galen, syndromes. I also raised this question: where, with respect to the body's *milieu extérieur,* is the "semiotic self" located? I also claimed that the semiotic self is engaged in continual scanning, or monitoring, or a process of meta-interpretation of its modeling system: "Any self can and must interpret the observed behavior of another organism solely as a response to its interpretations of its universe, 'behavior' meaning the propensity that enables it to link up its Umwelt with those of other living systems within its niche" (chapter 10, p. 126).

A book edited by Alfred I. Tauber on the *Organism and the Origins of Self,* containing several important articles by various authors on "The Immune / Cognitive Self," appeared too late for me to take into account when the above paper went to press in 1991. This collection has since been superseded by Tauber's own reflective book, *The Immune Self: Theory or Metaphor,* which considers the Sercarz conference report in a brief discussion of how "semiotics . . . might be applicable to immunology with respect to the kind of phenomena both study" (1994, 169). Unfortunately, however, evidently under the impression that Saussure "has had a decisive influence in semiotics" (ibid.), Tauber's analysis is flawed by his blurring of the crucial differentiation between linguistics, a model which pertains only to humans, and semiotics, which bears upon the immune systems of other species as well.

In the meantime, there appeared a rich and stimulating book by Synott—who, alas, seems to be unaware of either the Sercarz or Tauber books—on "the meaning of the body." Synott argues that it and the senses, like the organs and "parts" of the body, are socially constructed, and that the body is also, and primarily, as Sartre (1966) among others had held as well, "the self" (1993, 1 and passim).

Lastly, I want to consider what significations, if any, such expressions as "virtual self" or "virtual subject" may have. In the most straightforward, uncomplicated way, I take the phrase "virtual reality" (VR) to refer to the three-dimensional representation of "*object* worlds."[5] Although René Descartes deemed "object worlds" questionable, he never did doubt his own "subjective" thinking substance, his mind; hence the dictum *Cogito ergo sum* (*Discourse*, 1637, Part 4). VR upgrades, as it were, pseudo-reality (e.g., that achieved by TV, with such now-standard extensions as cable networks, satellite dishes, and videocassette recorders). Similarly, drug-induced states, whether by use of stimulants such as cocaine or depressants such as alcohol, bring mankind a step closer to controlled escape from reality, and hallucinogens, such as mushrooms containing psilocybin, fly-agaric, cannabis, LSD, etc., promote the fabrication of VRs even more (cf. O'Flaherty 1984; Wright 1987).

Gödel's Incompleteness Theorem fuses subject with object. It entangles the observer with the observed (cf. Hofstadter 1979, 699). By doing so, it demonstrates how self-reference can produce either paradox or indecision, or both. The lingering dilemma has always troubled semioticians: this is the distinction, or duality, between the *private character of signs* (notably of symptoms, like the Freudian feeling of anxiety; see above) and the *public character of their signified objects*. It implies limits to which the human self has the plasticity to become "disembodied" (beyond a paranoid-schizoid mode), or externalized, that is, "objectified" in any meaningful way, so as, for instance, to enable one to modify the style, color, material, or sex of her/his own body—morphing by cosmetic surgery, maybe like Michael Jackson, or turning into a "borg," a hybrid entity combining life forms, like the neurons of a leech, coupled by a signaling channel through which information is exchanged with an inorganic element like a silicon chip (cf. Sebeok 1991f, 98–99; and also thoughtfully envisaged in Dery 1996).

The clandestine interpreter of symptoms is, by definition, the semiotic self. This interpreter corresponds to what Jakob von Uexküll identified, on the cellular level, as *Ich-Ton*, usually rendered into English as "ego-quality." He wrote: "The ego-qualities of the cells that are concentrated in our sense-organs . . . are perceived as signs. . . . All these signs consist exclusively of ego-qualities" (1982, 34, 84). Clearly, the notion of *Ich-Ton* corresponds in all particulars to the substantive I now italicize in Peirce's classic definition of a sign: "A sign . . . is something which stands to *somebody* for something in some respect or capacity" (*CP* 2.228). Again, that "somebody" is of course the semiotic self.

One can quite comfortably contemplate an infinite number of object worlds in VR as a limitless number of "possible worlds" (à la Leibniz) that are made feasible by information-driven and rich syntax-endowed combinatorial systems like the genetic code, the immune code, the neural code (Black 1991, 161–162), the verbal code, and comparable natural and cultural devices of copying of information from one site to another. However, the postulation of multiple *subject* worlds would seem to lead back to the blind alley mentioned at the outset—the apparently insoluble paradox inherent in the notion of "self-deception."[6]

12

Some Reflections on Vico in Semiotics

IN PREPARATION FOR this article, dedicated to my friend Sydney Lamb, I re-read some of the principal works of Giambattista Vico which I had had no opportunity to consult closely since my formal and informal studies and con-versations in the early 1940s at the University of Chicago with my teacher, the Italian classicist Giuseppe Borgese. My overall interests have recently refocused on the Continental roots of semiotics in the United States. This contribution reflects this current preoccupation and concern (as do, more extensively, several recent works of mine: Sebeok 1990b; 1991a, 21–93; 1991e).

In making the claim that "Peirce was the heir of the whole philosophical analysis of signs . . . ," we know that Charles Morris (1971, 337) was surely ex-aggerating. Peirce neglected to mine, for one source, the foundational semiotic of the seventeenth century's John Poinsot (Deely 1988). He also seems to have been unaware, among his American predecessors or contemporaries, of the likes of Alexander Bryan Johnson (Fann 1990), Frederick A. Rauch (Sebeok 1991e, 8–11), and Garrick Mallery (Sebeok and Umiker-Sebeok eds. 1978), who, each in his own way, clearly made substantive and noteworthy contributions to semiotics, including the philosophy of language.

Had Peirce read Vico? Fisch tells us that Peirce nowhere mentions Vico (although, in 1905, he did refer once to Robert Flint's 1884 book, *Vico;* see Tagliacozzo and Verene eds. 1976, 430, n. 1). Fisch himself, following hints by Feibleman, attempted "the outline of a tentative approach to a more compre-hensive and more historical comparison which goes back to the origins of prag-matism and therefore compares Vico primarily with Peirce . . . " (1986, 201). John Michael Krois has essayed to confront Vico's and Peirce's *sensus communis.* He also brings Victoria Lady Welby into the picture, claiming that it was a consequence of his correspondence with her that Peirce came to connect his "semeiotic" with Vico's theory of the *sensus communis* (Tagliacozzo ed. 1981, 58–71). Many years earlier, Feibleman had found it "interesting to observe the similarities in the reactions of Vico and Peirce toward the Cartesian innova-tions" (1956, 69f.).

This article was written in honor of Sydney Lamb and was first published in 2000, in *Functional Approaches to Language, Culture and Cognition,* eds. D. G. Lockwood, P. H. Fries and J. E. Copeland, 555–568 (Amsterdam: John Benjamins).

While Vico endeavored to reconcile scholastic philosophy with the new empiricism of the eighteenth century, efforts at refuting Descartes overshadowed such attempts at an accommodation in Peirce's own development. Peirce's insistence that for claims to be true they must have practical consequences is certainly in line with Vico's condensed formula, *verum factum convertuntur,* that the truth is in the deed. Yet, well beyond such amorphous and uncredited resemblances, Peirce obviously, if implicitly, built on the heritage of Giambattista Vico. As Masani justly remarks, the pragmatism, viz., pragmaticism, of Peirce —whom he calls "America's first Leibniz"—was in essence Vico's, in that "the understanding of theory is deepened by its use in concrete construction" (1990, 62). Discussing the achievements of Norbert Wiener—whom Masani calls "America's second Leibniz"—he also points out that the cybernetic attitude of studying the inaccessible internal structure of organisms by observing their responses to different stimuli (the so-called black box approach), namely, their behavior, and by fabricating a model organism exhibiting the same behavior, was also emphasized by Vico, and then "it was reiterated by C. S. Peirce" (ibid., 255). Too, it is provocative that Bertrand Russell likewise perceived Vico—especially with respect to his radical criticism of the rationalist line of thought and in setting up his new principle of epistemology—as having been an inheritor and enhancer of Leibniz's suggestion that only God had perfect science (1959, 206).

Eco (1984, 107f.) reminds us that Vico, in the context of the production and interpretation of metaphors, "seems to put into question the existence . . . of a preestablished process of semiosis" (as, by the way, did Locke in his *Essay*). Blumenberg's rehabilitation of metaphor—especially of the pivotal metaphor of the Book of Nature (1986)—parallels other modern returns to rhetoric. This too received its impetus from Vico:

> der Anfang der Weisheit sei Dichtung gewesen und die Erfinder der Sprache hituen *in poetischen Charakter* gesprochen." (1986, 171, emphasis in source)

> (the beginning of knowledge was supposedly poetry, and the inventors of language presumably spoke *in a poetic character*.)

Blumenberg's further observation, that the central problem posed by Vico— concerning the ability of men to form law-governed communities and to exercise altruism—was, *mutatis mutandis,* solved by Kant, is well taken (ibid., 176). Accordingly, it is hardly surprising that Ernst Cassirer and his neo-Kantian semiotic, or philosophy of the symbol—being itself an enlargement on Kant's necessary doctrine of schemata—is closest to "metaphorology," the label Blumenberg coined to account for the operations of figurative thinking in changing historical conditions (see further Blumenberg's 1974 overall evaluation of Cassirer).

Herzfeld's book, with its epigraphic citations from Vico, pursues, while it perhaps overvalues, the pseudo-philological uses to which Vico put etymology (1987, 22), such as for instance his obeisance to the doctrine of divine nomathesia—that the names for all objects Adam signified mirrored their "essence" or their "nature" (Bedani 1989, 47). The Cartesian expectation that ordinary language shall forge ever-sharper tools for the purposes of scientific discovery, and its concomitant demand for clear and distinct ideas, was not understood by Vico, who "therefore missed the significance of rationalist philosophy for science" (Russell 1959, 209). In any event, however, the Vichian project as such has not had much directly traceable effect on modern semiotic inquiry or methodology. This is so despite the fact that Vico was interested, at the very least programmatically, in the most diverse applications of signs; he states, in his *De constantia jurisprudentis,* that humanity is "the affection of one man helping another. This is done most effectively through speech—by counseling, warning, exhorting, consoling, reproving—and this is the reason . . . that studies of language are called 'humanities' *[studia humanitatis],* the more so since it is through language that humanity is most strongly bound together" (Mooney 1985, v). For the purposes of this essay—more about Cassirer and Langer, less, in truth, about Vico—it is sufficient to understand that the several versions of Vico's "New Science"—"a mixture of various ingredients that are not properly distinguished," as Russell excoriated (1959, 207)—are wide open and therefore subject to any number of interpretations. The opacity of Vico's style, and what Russell also called "the obscurity of his message" (ibid., 206), invite more or less dubious claims of his having been a precursor of the most disparate intellectual movements, including anthropology and social sciences in general; historiography (from Trotsky to Toynbee) and a kind of romantic historicism (rediscovered and reinforced by Jules Michelet and Thomas Carlyle); literary criticism, theory, and practice (Yates and Joyce); and philosophy (Comte and Collingwood) (White 1968, 316). Croce (1913), in particular, projected onto Vico notions which characterized his own rather than his subject's extreme idealistic position, and thus managed to misdirect, to a degree, two generations of his readership.

For Vico, as is well known, art, myth, and poetry were important genres, or means for understanding the spirit of culture. As Bedani put it, "'Poetry' and 'myth' in the *Scienza Nuova* are concepts which describe *necessary* forms of primitive linguistic and mental processes," but these terms are "anthropological/historical rather than 'aesthetic' categories," which is to say, "they describe forms of language and thought characteristic of early historical epochs" (1989, 35). In other words, in Vico's frame of reference, "poetry" was, as a part of the world of nature, a more rudimentary form of language than narrative, particularly scientific, prose or any other language tending toward context-freedom. Poetry was not by any means, for Vico, a "higher" form of aesthetic expression: to the contrary, he compared the mental processes of the early poets with those of feeble-minded idiots and, more particularly, of women (1948, 456f.)!

Comparably, as Dorfles came to testify (1968), Cassirer was later to insist on the precedence of figurative over utilitarian language, and to maintain that such Vichian concepts determine the way we experience the natural world for every manifestation of culture—that, for example, shapes of mythical thought can be unearthed by examining the forms of language. In this way, as in other aspects of his methodological strategy, Vico had inverted traditional conceptions of natural and conventional signification.

It was this diachronic view of signification, according to which poetry was early man's natural form of expression, that Vico regarded as the "master key" to his new science. Iconicity, or what Peirce later elaborated as the category of firstness, is inherent in such passages as this one: "Mutes make themselves understood by gestures or objects that have natural relations with the ideas they wish to signify" (1948, 225).

The consonance of Vico's view in this respect with Francis Bacon's semiotic (cf. Sebeok 1987a, 22f.) is especially conspicuous. Bacon, in his *De dignitate et augmentis scientianum,* remarked that it is evident "that hieroglyphs and gestures carry a certain likeness to the signified object," and further that "Signification of objects, which is either without aid or by means of words, is of two kinds; of which the first relies on congruity or likeness. The other signifies by convention. Hieroglyphs and gestures belong to the first whilst the others are what we call letters or words" (Bacon 1815, 281).

It is not at all surprising nowadays to find Vico's name linked with Cassirer's as his forerunner in this or that respect, although Vico scarcely figures in Schilpp's collection (1949) of some twenty-three descriptive and critical essays (by various hands) about Cassirer's philosophy. In Schilpp's massive tome, Vico was accorded a mere handful of inconsequential entries, once as the founder of the "new philosophy" of language and mythology (ibid., 368). We owe the link to Verene, I think, who first elaborated on the fact that Cassirer looked upon Vico "as the founder of a theory of knowledge based on a philosophy of the humanities and cultural ideals" (Cassirer 1979, 43). Although Cassirer seldom cited Vico directly, he had nonetheless been familiar with his writings since 1922. Verene also made accessible to a wide anglophone readership Cassirer's short but illuminating Yale seminar lecture (c. 1941) on "Descartes, Leibniz, and Vico" (ibid., 95–107). In this presentation, Cassirer interpreted Vico's philosophy of civilization as unified and progressive, and as being at the root of romantic fascination with the myth of origins of culture. All the same, one is compelled to agree with Paci's overall observation that Vico's presence in Cassirer's writings is like that of "a ghost, which acts without revealing its human story or its name" (1969, 457).

As Domenico Vircillo (1970) observed, Cassirer "closed his life" with a lecture on "Structuralism in Modern Linguistics" (Cassirer 1946b), reverting to the theme of—and, as it were, coming full circle from—his classic trilogy of the 1920s on symbolic forms. As I relate more fully in my book on *Semiotics in the United States* (Sebeok 1991e), I was privileged to attend that lecture in the fall of 1944. Since I must surely be one among the vanishing handful of survivors—I am unaware of any others—who spent that evening with Cassirer, I now offer some of my personal impressions of him. These I propose to follow, and thus conclude, with some notes about Suzanne K. Langer.

In 1981, on Friday, April 10, having barely landed in Hamburg where I had flown to take part in the Third German Colloquium of the Deutsche Gesellschaft für Semiotik, I received a phone call from Klaus Oehler, the organizer, my friend and host, asking me to accompany him immediately to a wreath-laying observance beneath a bust erected in memory of Ernst Cassirer. This piece of sculpture stands in the foyer of the University of Hamburg's *Philosophenturm* (the same building where my own office was located during my visiting professorship in 1966) (see figure 1). Cassirer had been professor of philosophy (that is, he had occupied the same chair that Oehler, a foremost German specialist on Peirce, then held) at the University of Hamburg from 1919 until his dismissal and departure for Oxford and eventually Göteborg, in 1933. Those standing around at this ceremony included members of the board of the Deutsche Gesellschaft für Semiotik, plus a scattering of senior American semioticians. I was taken aback when I was unexpectedly called upon to make some commemorative remarks, but then it turned out that, fragile as this link may have been, I was the only one present who had ever come face to face with Cassirer. This affair spurred impromptu recollections much along the lines of the following.

I recounted, off the cuff, that I had attended Cassirer's lecture, in the fall of 1944, on "Structuralism in Modern Linguistics." He delivered this, at Roman Jakobson's invitation, before the Linguistic Circle of New York, at the New School for Social Research, some months before his sudden death on April 13, 1945, near the campus of Columbia University.

Cassirer and Jakobson had chanced to cross from Göteborg to New York on the same freighter, *Remmaren,* May 20–June 4, 1941. What I remember vividly even to this day is that these words, adapted from Genesis 27.22, pressed on my mind throughout Cassirer's lengthy lecture: "The voice is Cassirer's voice, but the hands are the hands of Jakobson." After his lecture, in the course of which Cassirer stressed both the word and concept "semiotics," Jakobson and I dined with him, in the company of a few others. Both the linguist and the philosopher gave an animated account of their daily conversations aboard ship, and I concur that "these talks no doubt influenced Cassirer's interest and work on structuralism . . . " (Krois 1987, 30, 222, n. 86). On the other hand, I

Figure 1. The author at the 1981 dedication of a bust of Cassirer, University of Hamburg

never could find any trace of Cassirer's reciprocal influence on Jakobson's thinking, to which Vico was also totally alien. In this odd couple, Jakobson, then at his cerebral pinnacle, was doubtless the dominant personality, although Cassirer, in his younger days, could be quite self-assured in public.

Not long after Hitler had come to power, Cassirer's senior colleague, Jakob von Uexküll, read a paper tinged with the classic semiotic flavor of his Um-welt-research. He reported, at a Hamburg Congress of Psychology, on a piece of research he had recently concluded on the cognitive maps of dogs. As these are constructed of and demarcated by scent-signs, he asserted that a dog takes everything located within its olfactory field for its property. Cassirer opened the discussion by recalling that Rousseau had said that the first man who erected a fence and declared "This is mine" should have been beaten to death. "After the lecture of Professor von Uexküll we know," he then expanded, "that wouldn't have sufficed. It was the first dog which should have been beaten to death." This bandying about territoriality was attacked in next morning's *Völkische Beobachter* by Herr Göbbels himself, under the punning headline: "Kötereien eines deutschen Professors!" (The phrase can be approximately translated as "mongrelisms of a German professor." The punning reference is between *köter* (cur, mongrel) the base of the first word, and *kot* (dirt, manure, excrement).

Cassirer, whom von Uexküll, a profoundly original idealist yet empirical semiotician, deemed the greatest living German philosopher, one who shaped an entire generation of students in neo-Kantian ways of thinking, left for Vienna at the beginning of May 1933. In his *Essay on Man,* a condensed American reworking of his *Philosophy of Symbolic Forms,* Cassirer's argument is avowedly, although metaphorically, based on von Uexküll's biosemiotic principles (Sebeok and Umiker-Sebeok eds. 1992) extended into the human world: man's acquisition of the "symbolic system," he contended, transforms the whole of our existence; accordingly, Cassirer designated man *animal symbolicum* (1944, 26).

The neo-Kantian von Uexküll's impact on the neo-Kantian Cassirer (ibid., 23f.) cannot be overestimated, even though a careful study of the writings of the senior scholar will, I am convinced, show that Cassirer (and generations of his followers) failed to grasp the fundamental idea of the former's "functional circle" (briefly, a construct made up of signs arrayed in a negative feedback circuit), or his independently innovative fashioning of a new pragmatic, sensory semiotics; (he also, more mysteriously, rechristened Jakob von Uexküll "Johannes"). Readers can verify this adverse judgment for themselves by reading von Uexküll's works (which, by the way, evince no awareness of Vico). While I concur with Verene (1976, 311) that it is mistaken to think of Cassirer's philosophy as merely a form of Kantianism, it is equally erroneous to leave unmentioned, as it has thus far generally remained, the powerful, if to a degree muddled, impact of von Uexküll's thought and personality on the junior (by a decade) Cassirer.[1]

Susanne Langer, like Sydney Lamb (Regan et al. eds. 1992) a follower of Kant and Whitehead, has also long been regarded as the American "philosopher most influenced by Cassirer" (Krois 1987, 12), although his conception of the symbol seems to have eluded her, as did its derivation reaching back to Vico. If Vico was a ghost for Cassirer, he evanesced into a sheer shade of a wraith for Langer. "This symbol concept, as it emerges in use, in the course of work," she wrote (1962, 56), "cannot be defined in terms of denotation, signification, formal assignment, or reference. The proof of the pudding is in the eating, and I submit that Cassirer's pudding is good; but the recipe is not on the box."

Morris also put Langer down, together with Wilbur M. Urban (cf. Schilpp 1949, 403–441), as a "follower" of Cassirer (1946, 189). And she herself has told us as much: "In many years of work on the fundamental problems of art," she wrote, she found Cassirer's philosophy of symbolic forms, however slippery, "indispensable; it served as a key to the most involved questions" (1962, 58). In 1946, she translated Cassirer's little book *Language and Myth,* characterizing it in her preface as imbued "by a final flash of interpretive genius" (1946a, x). And her appraisal of his theory of language and myth (Langer 1949) is both sympathetic and insightful. "Symbols are the indispensable instruments of conception," she reaffirms in connection with Cassirer's "greatest epistemological contribution," which lay in "his approach to the problem of mind through the study of the primitive forms of conception." If she was aware of Vico's seminal role in Cassirer's formulation of this central problem, that is, "the diversity of symbolic forms and their interrelation in the edifice of human culture" (ibid., 386–387), she passes over it in silence.

After World War II, because of the easy accessibility of her attractive paperback, *Philosophy in a New Key* (1948), Langer became something of a campus celebrity, but her work, while never regarded as trivial, seldom seems to have been taken for more than "a point of departure" by such professionals as Morris (1946, 50). Thus Charles S. Stevenson dissected her arguments ascribing "a symbolic function to the arts," viz., music, "that other writers have often denied to them" (in Henle ed. 1958, 202), and judged them implausible. Stevenson tried to show, more generally (as Abraham Kaplan did earlier, in 1943), "that the importance of the theory of signs to all the arts, rather than merely to those commonly classified as representational, is seriously open to question" (ibid., 210). Similar difficulties, he stated, "arise in any theory of signs" (ibid., 219), yet he concentrated his specific criticisms on Langer's views alone. Years later, Morris, while completely ignoring Langer's thesis, found Stevenson's arguments not compelling (1964, 67).

In mid-May 1969, Langer was a featured speaker at a symposium held at the Smithsonian Institution, where I was also a guest. She read a paper titled,

"The Great Shift: Instinct to Intuition," the guiding concept of which turned out to be her assertion that language began "with symbolic utterance" (Eisenberg and Dillon eds. 1971, 325). She held that

> Speech is not derived from animal communication; its communicative and directive functions, though all-important today, are secondary; its primary function is the symbolic expression of intuitive cognition. (ibid., 326; she had made the same point in Langer 1962, ch. 2)

In other words, language evolved, in her view (though the terminology here is mine; cf. Sebeok 1986a, 10–16; 1991f, ch. 5) as a uniquely human modeling system. In spite of its unfortunate delivery—Langer was tiny, dwarfed behind the lectern, and practically inaudible because of the placement of the microphone—I was enthusiastic about her talk (some participating biologists, I gathered, were, by and large, not) and told her so at one of the social functions we attended afterwards.

It is fascinating to note a clue *in nuce* lurking in this very quotation to Langer's equivocal position in American semiotics. Her frame of reference was sharply at variance with views promoted by simplistic physicalist technicians (some of whom are mentioned in Demers 1988, but there are others, especially Lieberman [1988]), who strove to pursue an illusory comparison of language and animal communication systems. On the other hand, it is in line with critical doubts expressed by thinkers as different as Popper (1972, 121), Chomsky (e.g., 1980, 229f.), and many others (e.g., Sebeok 1991f, 81, n. 5). This kinship is not at all surprising, considering Langer's proximal intellectual lineage, including the pervasive (although riven) impact of the neo-Kantians, via Wilhelm von Humboldt and Peirce or, as the case may be, von Uexküll and Cassirer, on the parties involved.

The only comments known to me specific to Langer's "properly" semiotic project, which is said to focus "on the foundations of the theory of signs from within a highly differentiated philosophical matrix," are Innis' (1985, 87–89). But Innis' allusion to Nelson Goodman's ideas of notationability and similarity, to which, he alleges, "Langer's position . . . bears remarkable similarities" (ibid., 89), was stated with quite a different emphasis by Goodman himself: "I am by no means unaware of contributions to symbol theory by such philosophers as Peirce, Cassirer, Morris, and Langer. . . . I reject one after another . . . the views common to much of the literature of aesthetics . . ." (1968, xii). Goodman acknowledged congruencies between his different ways of "worldmaking" and Cassirer's effort to distinguish various "symbolic forms," but added that "Cassirer undertakes the search through a cross-cultural study of the development of myth, religion, language, art, and science. My approach is rather through an analytic study of types and functions of symbols and symbol systems" (ibid., 6).

Clearly, Langer's semiotic work merits detailed reconsideration in the near future, especially in its implications for music and the whole range of the fine arts—the creation of symbols of value, of apparent forms expressive of human feelings—in short, aesthetics, the vast estate where she perhaps unknowingly caught up with Vico (see chapter 13 below; Berthoff 2000).

13

Women in Semiotics

WITH SUSAN PETRILLI

0. Introductory Notes

THIS STUDY IS DEDICATED to Irmengard Rauch—located at the epicenter of our present quincunx of women in semiotics—upon her sixty-fifth birthday. Part 1 was contributed by the junior author: it seemed appropriate to co-opt Petrilli, a leading authority on Victoria Lady Welby—the legendary English foremother and prime mover of "significs" and "sensifics," species of turn-of-the-century (and subsequent) semiotics—to collaborate on this article dealing with an important social issue alluded to by our title. These introductory notes, then parts 2 and 3 concerning four disparately illustrious twentieth-century American trailblazers in our domain—each having pursued a quite distinct career path which, however, converged with his—were sketched by the senior author.

On August 30, 1998, in São Paulo, I was a luncheon guest of Lucia Santaella Braga—herself one of the most astute women internationally active in today's Peirce studies and the academic furtherance of semiotics. When I informally foreshadowed the argument and proposed structure of this (perforce brief) article, Winfried Nöth, the other luncheon guest that day, reminded me, with his customary artful erudition—although perhaps jestingly—of the Oracle of Delphi, to wit, a priestess called the Pythia, the spokeswoman for Apollo Didymeus' messages to his consultants. Was not this oracle-speaker, he asked, this medium (Sebeok 1995c), the first recorded female semiotician in the post-fourth century B.C. Western world (cf. Fontenrose 1988, 55–56)?

Any medium, whether "real" or *fausse,* is of course professionally engaged, *ipso facto,* in semiosis of a very particular sort: the arcane processing of signs. From the gods or the spirit-world at the supposed originary end of a communication chain, signs are delivered ultimately in a natural language, if am-

This article was written in honor of Irmengard Rauch and first appeared in 1999, in *Interdigitations: Essays for Irmengard Rauch,* eds. G. F. Carr, W. Harbert & L. Zhang, 469–478 (New York: Peter Lang).

biguously, to a certain clientele at the receiving end. In principle, the Pythia appears no different in action from, say, the notorious Mina ("Margery") Crandon. She greatly impressed the credulous Sir Arthur Conan Doyle but was ultimately destroyed by Houdini (Brandon 1993, ch. 16), who debunked "trick" mediums—alas, far more often than not, females of the breed.

There is, however, one basic distinction between the prophetess and the likes of Margery, or even, if you like, the triple "weird sisters" who interpreted portents for Macbeth. To apply a dichotomy often ascribed to Peirce, whereas the Pythia clearly functioned as a woman playing a pre-assigned role—thereby being a type or *legisign*—false mediums, including Shakespeare's fictional witches' collective of "imperfect speakers," are each a token woman or *sinsign*.

Speaking of Peirce: according to extant chronicles of his dolefully truncated teaching stint in Baltimore, he seems to have had but one female student, the logician Christine Ladd (Mrs. Fabian Franklin). Over sixty years later, in the mid-1930s and 1940s, when I set out on my graduate studies with Leonard Bloomfield, Manuel Andrade, Charles Morris and others in Chicago, and then Roman Jakobson in New York City, I had no women cohorts (let alone teachers) in any linguistics or semiotics classes I attended. Today, such manifest bias is unlikely: women abound in semiotics seminars, indeed exercise leading positions within most local, national, and global organizations. To parochially mention only the Semiotic Society of America, this has been piloted for the past quarter of a century by at least as many elected women presidents as men, the first being—who else?—Irmengard Rauch herself (1983). (The three SSA presidents elected for 1996, 1997, and 1998 were women.)

A question we intend to raise in this context is this: can we account, at least abductively, for this massive shift in gender ratio, so accelerated after the end of World War II, in the semiotics community? We defer this intriguing inquiry to the end of our study.

1. The First Lady: Victoria Welby (1837–1912)

Lady Welby, who belonged to the highest circles of English nobility, was keenly aware of the exceptional status of her position as an open-minded female intellectual of the Victorian and Edwardian eras. Given that not only was she a woman but a woman without any formal education, she often discussed her status as a scholar with her friends and correspondents, humbly searching for the conditions which made her scholarly work possible. In this perspective, she highlighted the importance to her mind of the extensive travels with her mother that often occurred under dramatic circumstances. These came to a tragic end with her mother's death in the Syrian desert, leaving Victoria alone and unaided until help arrived from Beirut. To Peirce she famously wrote at the end of 1903:

I may perhaps mention that I never had any education whatever in the conventional sense of the term. Instead of that I traveled with my mother over a great part of the world under circumstances of difficulty and even hardship. The present facilities did not then exist! This I think accounts in some degree for my seeing things in a somewhat independent way. But the absence of any systematic mental training must be allowed for of course for any estimate of work done. . . . I only allude to the unusual conditions of my childhood in order partly to account for my way of looking at and putting things: and my very point is that any value in it is impersonal. It suggests an ignored heritage, an unexplored mine. This I have tried to indicate in "What is Meaning." (Hardwick 1977, 13–14)

The studies leading to her first monograph ([1903] 1965), mentioned at the end of this passage, were devoted to problems of expression and communication through signs, as was her second monograph, *Significs and Language* (1911). In spite of her illustrious social background and contacts with many of the most important people of her time, Welby was not at all attracted to the mundane life of the court and, as a married woman, was content to retire to private life in Denton Manor in Grantham (Lincolnshire), where, in addition to carrying out her duties as a wife with prescribed social obligations and mother to three children, she quietly pursued her semiotic studies. From 1863 to her death on the eve of World War I, Welby often acted as a friend, source of inspiration, fellow student, and correspondent of numerous intellectuals from the worlds of science and literature throughout Europe and North America. A feature that characterized her research was that she maintained constant dialogic communion with others, using her letters as one of her principal venues for theorizing. While maintaining her distance from the social matrix to which she belonged, she used her epistolary contacts to cultivate relations with approximately 460 correspondents, a fact that testifies to her determining presence in the cultural ambience of her time. Furthermore, she also gave hospitality to many of her friends and acquaintances, welcoming often more than one person at a time in her home, sometimes over weeks, so that they could meet and continue their discussions through direct confrontation.

However, as her various contemporary biographers took occasion to note after her death, even though there was a widespread general awareness of the importance of Welby's work on the theory of signs, meaning, and interpretation, for which she coined the neologism *significs* (cf. Saussure's similar *signologie;* she also minted *sensifics*), and of the deep-running presence of her views among intellectuals of the time, the importance of her work went, more often than not, at least publicly, unrecognized. On her part, in an attempt to avoid being taken into consideration and flattered simply because of her title, noble lineage, and hospitality, she tended to publish either anonymously, with various combinations of initials, or simply as "Victoria Welby." And, as she continued in the above-quoted letter to Peirce, "the only honour I value is that of being treated by workers as a serious worker" (ibid.).

Welby's vast epistolary network continued to multiply and accelerate rapidly after 1880 both locally and internationally, but most of it remains to be published. For now, her correspondence may be consulted in the archives of Toronto's York University.

A few years before her death, Welby thought to have found an enthusiastic student and promoter of significs in C. K. Ogden, who corresponded with her intensively in 1910 and 1911. As a young university student Ogden chanced to come across Welby's 1903 book and consequently visited her at Harrow, spending several weekends consulting her rich library. Despite such privileges, Ogden was to be counted among those who were to marginalize Welby and their intellectual debts to her. Despite such neglect, Welby succeeded in making her work known to diverse eminent scholars, many of whom appreciated their special focus on the interaction between signs and values, or, more broadly, semiotics and axiology. The favor she gained for significs was such that, in 1911, an entry, "Significs," was at last published in the *Encyclopaedia Britannica*. This editorial event represented for Welby an official recognition for which she had tenaciously striven over some thirty years of arduous research, the publication of numerous articles, a copious correspondence, as well as in her two volumes mentioned.

(For discussions of Welby, significs, and the post-mortem movement these engendered in the Netherlands, see, e.g., Schmitz 1985; Petrilli 1988.)

2. Three North American Pioneers

Susanne K. Langer (1895–1985)

By contrast to Victoria Welby, an adventuresome autodidact who transcended the binding social conventions of her set to gloriously dream up and memorably label a brand of semiotics, Susanne Langer's academic career began at Radcliffe College, where she remained as a tutor in philosophy for fifteen years after earning her Ph.D. She also taught at a score of American universities, settling at Connecticut College for Women in 1954. Highly indebted to her teacher Alfred North Whitehead, but afterwards under the powerful spell of Ernst Cassirer (Sebeok 1995a), she was the author of the best-selling paperback classic *Philosophy in a New Key* (1948) widely read on campuses all over the country, as well as of the monumental but for the most part unread *Mind: An Essay on Human Feeling* (1982), several other books, and an important collection of essays, *Problems of Art* (1957). However, she was generally treated by her colleagues with "condescension," as Berthoff (1999, 112) aptly remarks in the only perspicacious, fair assessment of Langer's oeuvre known to me. "The reasons for the neglect are . . . complex," Berthoff expands in her penetrating essay, to which I would add that feminist theory is not the only loser by this disdainful disregard, even nescience.

It is sad enough that neither Welby nor Langer figure, or are even alluded to, in such desultory discussions about women philosophers as, for instance, *Hypatia's Daughters* (McAlister 1996). But one would think that historiographers of the semiotics can *a fortiori* ill-afford to consign to oblivion our eminent female pioneers in accounts of our domain, which so earnestly strives to be integrated into (at least American) curricula. Berthoff believes that Langer lost her influence

> because her enterprise of developing an aesthetic consonant with Cassirer's philosophy of symbolic forms, a biology of feeling, and a philosophy of mind ran counter to the scientism which in the post-war years was everywhere on the rise—in structural linguistics, in ethology, in both behavioral and cognitive psychology, and in all other disciplines for which "the end of ideology" was a slogan. (1999, 113)

I am able to support this view of Berthoff's by citations of critiques on the part of Charles Morris, Charles S. Stevenson, Wilbur M. Urban, and B. F Skinner, all noted in my previous considerations of Langer's distinctive, cogently argued semiotics (cf. Sebeok 1991e, 42–44, 75; chapter 12 above). Her contemporary assailants (two of these four were professors of mine, both of whom I otherwise recollect with much affection) were myopic: Langer deserves to be reinstated without further delay into the welcoming annals of semiotics, a restoration which, in my view, is even more pressing in the light of her foresighted sensitivity to biological issues and therefore to the soundest of contemporary frames of reference.

Margaret Mead (1901–78)

Why Margaret Mead? A reasonable question, to which there are various answers. This intellectually restless, indeed, omnivorous anthropologist was one of only two women (the other, a psychologist, soon quit) among twenty-one founding members of the Cybernetics Group (1946–53), a high-level, ambitious collaborative venture the pertinence of which to the development of semiotics in the United States in the post–World War II decade or so I have previously attempted to emphatically delineate (Sebeok 1991e, 71ff.). This group's free-wheeling panache suited to perfection what became a hallmark *modus operandi* of Mead's, who carried on whenever she could by way of "a community of seminal 'insiders,' an informal elite talking to one another and significantly shaping and informing the direction of the social sciences in the United States" (Heims 1991, 68). Her biographer, Jane Howard, put it engagingly:

> As methodically as Mead had once surveyed new classrooms and new bunches of playmates, she now assessed the cast of characters in American social science, to figure out who among them would be most worth meeting and how she could best get to know them. . . . Interdisciplinary convocations, from this point on, would be one of the sustaining delights of her life. (1984:165– 166)

Interestingly, it was only in May 1962, starring at yet another transdisciplinary conference of more than sixty participants, that Mead had a spur-of-the-moment sweeping insight: to apply the term *semiotics* "to this whole field . . . which in time [would] include the study of all patterned communication [that is, institutionalization] in all modalities. I am not enough of a specialist in this field to know what word to use," she continued, "but many people here, who have looked as if they were on opposite sides of the fence, have used the word 'semiotics'. It seems to me the one word, in some form or other, that has been used by people who are arguing from quite different positions" (Sebeok et al. eds. 1972). One of her acolytes, Ray L. Birdwhistell, the creator of *kinesics* (see p. xiii), promptly chimed in: "I agree that 'semiotics' is a special word, a dignified word" (ibid., 275–276). Ironically, a principal reason why Birdwhistell's "work in kinesics remained largely programmatic" (Kendon and Sigman 1996, 232) was that he failed to grasp the decisive theoretical implications of Mead's sagacious, if ad hoc, observation for his studies of human bodily movement.

Some of Mead's voluminous writings were characterized by a palpably semiotic awareness and tincture—her war-related explorations of "culture at a distance," for instance. These surely merit future concentrated semiotic scrutiny.

Mead's lifelong interest in the paranormal, her embarrassing occult beliefs (among others, including her conviction that the earth is under observation by extraterrestrials orbiting in flying saucers) (Gardner 1983), and her posthumous exposure as the victim of a prank—with far-reaching consequences for the field of ethnography—by a pair of her Polynesian "informants" (Gardner 1993), are relevant here, if only in the light of her deathbed participation in a bizarre, literally terminal shamanistic routine, with an anonymous female medium, referred to only as "the healer." By pretending to feed her encouraging prognostications from "the beyond" and thereby playing cruelly upon Mead's superstitions, this medium set in train a cascade of interpretants that were bound to finally disappoint. By the testimony of her daughter, "Margaret had gradually lost the ability to balance her insistence that she was not dying against the knowledge that in fact she was, making herself, by self-deception, vulnerable to deception and exploitation" (Bateson 1984, 216).

Only when the sentinels of death were palpably at hand and she at last interpreted their indications truly, did Mead become angry at the medium "who had kept promising healing and found herself suddenly busy with other engagements at the moment of hopelessness" (ibid., 217). This melancholy episode shows that Mead was by no means immune to the universal semiotic purchase of interpersonal expectancy effects; as Rosenthal said: " . . . when deception cues [are] being emitted, women [are] substantially less accurate in their decoding and [are] more likely to interpret these cues as the deceiver wanted them to be interpreted rather than as the deceiver really felt" (1981, 196).

Ethel M. Albert (1918–89)

Four years Mead's junior, Clyde Kluckhohn became, arguably, the second most charismatic leader in anthropology on the American scene next to her. Author of a splendid, now classic, study on *Navaho Witchcraft* (1944), Kluckhohn attained an extremely influential position at Harvard after World War II. His theoretical work with culture patterns and "universal values"—to which he attempted to apply, in the late 1950s, Jakobsonian "binary distinctive features" —was well funded. I got to know him in his administrative capacity as the first director of the Russian Research Center at Harvard, which, among more recondite tasks, sought to conduct research of the "culture at a distance" type, via signs given off by Soviet émigrés.

A few years before his death (in 1960), I happened to be in his impressive Cambridge offices—I remember that he asked me to "confidentially" expatiate on the comparative assets of "Bloomfield the technician" versus "Jakobson the theoretician"—when Ethel Albert, by profession a cultural anthropologist, by avocation a self-taught semiotician, by employment then a research associate on Kluckhohn's staff, happened by. We were introduced, and thereafter kept in touch regularly for about a decade, until a crippling progressive disease forced her into early retirement from normal academic pursuits.

Although Albert's 1968 C. V. identified among her then-current research interests "semiotics: theoretical models and methodology for comprehensive analysis of continuous discourse" (Sebeok 1991e, 96), her publications were not what secured her place in late twentieth-century American semiotics. Her teaching did that (Sebeok 1995d). After Kluckhohn's sudden death, Albert went first to the University of California–Berkeley, but soon joined the department of anthropology at Northwestern University, where she was listed as a professor in that institution's catalog for 1966–67. Indeed, their bulletin featured her as having offered three successive "graduate seminars on semiotics," devoted respectively to discourse analysis, systematic lexicography, and, perhaps surprisingly, "animal communication." Albert's accomplishment was, in effect, to revive semiotics as such in an American university curriculum—or maybe even *any* university curriculum—after Charles Morris' trio of seminars at the University of Chicago offered a quarter of a century before her. Colleagues who have tried to re-introduce semiotics elsewhere before Albert or since will appreciate the magnitude of her achievement, with deep regret at her premature fade-out.

3. American Gothic: Irmengard Rauch (b. 1933)

With Rauch's advent on the semiotic scene, the kaleidoscopic tableau assumed a novel configuration. At the time she commenced her public activities in the semiotic domain—toward the end of the 1970s—Rauch was already an established linguist, specializing chiefly in diachronic Germanic topics, with perhaps five books and a score of articles to her credit. Recall that, by contrast, Langer was a philosopher, while both Mead and Albert were trained as anthropologists.

Rauch's earliest articles on semiotic subjects date from 1978. The first major international conference she organized, attended by about two hundred persons, was tellingly captioned "The Signifying Animal," and convened at the end of June of that same year. Her lead article in the proceedings of that conference, published two years later, was formulated as a challenge, "What Is Signifying?" This essay concluded with seven augural words which aphoristically foreshadowed the *biosemiotics* mandrel that supports and, in the manner of an axle, now drives much of what is best in contemporary sign theory: "To signify . . . is ultimately to be alive" (Rauch and Carr eds. 1980, 8).

Twenty-two further studies of hers, coupling in one synoptic vision semiotics with linguistics, newly gathered in a fecund collection "bottom-up-style" (Rauch 1999)—a phrase I commented on in application to Rauch's work in Sebeok 1999a—further consolidate the two mutually dependent tendencies, both of which she commands separately and also with impressive ease in combination.

The history of women, including women in American scholarship, emerged as a legitimate field of inquiry about a decade and a half after the end of World War II, almost coincidentally with the culmination of Rauch's studies for her doctorate at the University of Michigan between 1958 and 1962. With the arguable exception of the discrimination that, in my judgment, Langer could have propounded on several grounds and in more than one venue but never did, few have to our knowledge claimed that women in the Western tradition of semiotics were ever marginalized or victimized before the war or after. Gender separatism in this domain has never been proclaimed, let alone formally charged (which is by no means to assume that it does not exist).

To obtain hard evidence for his highly enlightening and deservedly influential book on creativity and the psychology of discovery and invention, the University of Chicago's Mihaly Csikszentmihalyi (1996) interviewed ninety-one exceptional individuals, worldwide, in the arts, humanities, sciences, business, education, and government, a dozen of them Nobel laureates, about thirty of them women. The oldest female subject interviewed was born in 1906, the youngest in 1943, but the preponderance were born in the 1920s and five in the 1930s.

"Almost all the women scientists interviewed mentioned that without World War II it would probably have been impossible for them to get graduate training, fellowships, postdoctoral positions, and faculty appointments" (ibid., 186). A critical factor seems to have been the admission, albeit grudging, into higher education of women needed as graduate assistants by the professorate not directly engaged in war-related tasks. Too, most of the married women in this same sample reported "that their husbands had freed them to concentrate on their work [and in addition] often served as mentors to their wives and helped them to get started on their careers" (ibid., 190). Moreover, we are told, most creative women "enjoy their work [and] are in awe of its importance" (ibid., 228).

These and the other distinctive features associated with creativity as adduced and recounted by Csikszentmihalyi identifiably mark Rauch's personality and her protean contributions to the scholarly advancement, teaching, and both local and global organizational aspects of semiotics. Too, her career evidently eased the way for generations of younger women who endeavor to emulate, indeed, perhaps to surpass her remarkable achievements.

14

The Music of the Spheres

THE FOLLOWING BRIEF passage from Vilmos Voigt's obituary of Yuri M. Lotman prompts these needfully compressed bipartite meditations. Voigt wrote that, in the 1980s, "the central 'new' term coined by Lotman was *'semiosphere'*. I am inclined to think," he added, "this was his first personally invented term . . . his brainchild, however, modeled after the term 'noosphere'. (Sebeok noted that Lotman's term stems perhaps from Vladimir Vernadsky's 1926 Russian coinage 'biosphera'—quoted by some Soviet semioticians as an early case for holistic and system theoretical notion)" (1995, 197).

Scenario I: Culture

In an earlier paper (chapter 15 below), I described why, on October 3, 1986, and under what circumstances, Lotman entrusted to me, several years before it was actually available in print for the perusal of Western readers, a typescript copy of his paper "O semiosfere," although this piece bore a nominal publication date of 1984 in Russian. In a confused publishing sequence, two German versions appeared only several years afterwards, in 1989 and 1990 (cited under Lotman 1984); Lotman 1999 (cited under Lotman 1984) constitutes the earliest French version, translated by Anka Ledenko from the canonical Russian version first published in Moscow in 1966, after which Ann Shukman had also prepared her English translation (Lotman 1990).

By way of an inceptive detour, let me now record that, in that very same year, 1986, a co-edited book by ourselves (Sebeok and Umiker-Sebeok), titled *The Semiotic Sphere,* had appeared in New York. Included among the twenty-seven chapters in this volume was a chapter by Vilmos Voigt on semiotics in Hungary, and one by Stephen Rudy on semiotics in the USSR. Our book had of course been in preparation for well over two years prior to the date of its printing, so our choice of a concordant title was clearly unconnected to Lotman's Russian coinage of some time during the same decade. Note that we did not perpetuate our newly minted phrase "semiotic sphere" beyond the title of

This article was written in honor of Vilmos Voigt and originally appeared in 2000, in *Semiotica* 128(3/4), 527–535.

the 1986 book, favoring quite another—*The Semiotic Web*—for the continuation of their series through six more volumes (ending in 1994). But that is another story for another time.

Rudy, in the afterword to his chapter, remarks that "The East-West dialogue has expanded the 'semiotic sphere' considerably" (in Sebeok and Umiker-Sebeok eds. 1986, 582); and Voigt, in his, alludes in a highly interesting way—without, however, any reference to either Lotman's "semiosphere" or to Michael Halliday's "social semiotic"—to the expressions "semiotics of culture" and "social semiotics" as synonyms in (then) current use in Hungary (ibid., 291–292).

It is also worth pausing here to point out that Halliday, who gave currency to the phrase "social semiotic" in his famous book of 1978, commenting on that very expression in an interview published in 1987 (Steele and Threadgold eds. 1987, 616), ascribed it to a prior oral usage by A. J. Greimas in 1969, who in fact employs the French equivalent *socio-sémiotique* repeatedly in a much later book of his (1976, 57). This in itself might be another coincidence, were it not for the fact that Greimas, a few pages earlier (ibid., 47 f.), mentions Lotman as having "vite abandonné" a cultural semiotics which Greimas, all appearances to the contrary, came to embrace.

To refocus on Lotman's concept *semiosphere,* this was finally elaborated and knit into a much wider English frame by his translator, Ann Shukman, in 1990. Lotman himself died, after a lingering illness, three years later. Many pages before part 2 of this book, which is titled "The Semiosphere," Lotman defined this term—chary as he tended to be of precise demarcations—as "that synchronic semiotic space which fills the borders of culture, without which separate semiotic systems cannot function or come into being" (1990, 3).

In fact, the central concept of part 2 is, he explicitly tells us, culture. Then, as if to underline his exclusively anthroposemiotic preoccupation with human society "in constant interaction with the individual intellectual world of human beings," he insistently draws upon the "legacy of Saussure whose works . . . remain in force as the foundation stones of semiotics" (ibid., 5). As Grzybek sums up the extension of Lotman's semiosphere, this "covers the totality of sign users, texts, and codes of a given culture" (1998, 377); yet note that, by implication, the "totality of sign users" slims his glottocentric point of departure to an even narrower segment of the human population. To boot, as Sturrock has pointed out, the culture Lotman has in view is yet more compacted: being predominantly literary, "it might be quite another matter to adjust his informational model to incorporate music, let us say, or sport, or other cultural forms not touched on" (1991, 10). Furthermore, Lotman's acknowledged debt to Mikhail Bakhtin's notion of *logosphere*—that "dialogic sphere where the word exists" (Mandelker 1994, 386)—pervasively informs the glottocentricity of his entire semiospheric enterprise. The unit of semiosis, Lotman claims, "the smallest functioning mechanism, is . . . the whole semiotic space of the culture in question. This is the space we term the *semiosphere*" (1990, 125).

In everyday English parlance—and so, *mutatis mutandis,* in all other European languages—one may speak metaphorically of "a sphere of influence," "the economic sphere," "the social sphere," "the cultural sphere," or the like, in brief, of the province, domain, or range of a thing, quality, activity, or operation. Is Lotman's semiosphere then simply, or at least at first approximation, identical with "the cultural sphere"? From remarks such as the above, it is difficult to escape the conclusion that "the integrated unity of the semiosphere" is in truth tantamount to "the creation of a general and historical semiotics of culture" (ibid., 273). Most of Lotman's readers have understood that, in his usage, semiosphere is indeed basically the same as culture, even if it is a concept of culture wielded by him with a unique sensitivity, technical mastery, and immense erudition from a very special, highly sophisticated semiotic standpoint.[1]

But what exactly is "culture"? Kroeber and Kluckhohn, in their comprehensive critical review of the concept, adduced close to three hundred definitions (1963, 291, n. 4a)—most of which need not detain us here—in application to human societies and history. However, given that the suggestively glamorous term *semiosphere* is undeniably Lotman's, the interesting question in this context becomes: where else in the vast literature on the subject has a juxtaposition of "culture" with, or within, the realm of signs been propounded? The answer unmistakably points to Leslie White's pioneering argument, as he wrote in 1940:

A culture . . . is but a particular kind of form (symbolic) which the biologic, life-perpetuating activities of a particular animal, man, assume. (463)

In 1949, he elaborated:

"culture" is the name of a distinct order, or class, of phenomena, namely, those things and events that are dependent upon the exercise of a mental ability, peculiar to the human species, that we have termed "symbolling." (quoted and discussed in Kroeber and Kluckhohn 1963, 137–139, 186)

The glottocentricity of White's notion of "symbolling" is later emphasized, apparently on his own initiative, in his observation that "articulate speech is the most important and characteristic form of symbolic behavior" (ibid., 193).[2]

Scenario II: Living Matter

In this section, I turn, beginning with the Austrian geologist Eduard Suess's 1875 monograph on the origin of the Alps, to certain philological and related considerations. Almost at his book's end, Suess sections the earth into three concentric *Hüllen* (zones, circles, or, if you like, spheres): "Die erste ist die Atmosphäre, die zweite die Hydrosphäre, die dritte die Lithosphäre" (1875, 158)—that is, the terrestrial gaseous mass, waters, and rocks.[3] On the next page, referring to the "spherical" covering of living matter, Suess casually adds: "es lässt sich auf der Oberfläche des Festen [i.e., the crust] eine selbständige Biosphäre unterscheiden" (ibid., 159).[4]

Since Suess's brief mention, the term *biosphere* has acquired a far expanded set of meanings, thanks in the first place to several remarkable works by the earth scientist V. I. Vernadsky, including especially several editions of his book *The Biosphere* during the 1920s. "The biosphere is the envelope or upper geosphere of . . . the crust. By definition [it] is the only geosphere which contains living matter" (Bailes 1990, 190)—the most powerful of all geological forces, chemically the most active part of the earth's crust, decisively shaping the other three spheres with its activities. Vernadsky deemed the biosphere the zone where "life acts as a geological force," not only "the place where organisms dwell, but also the interactions among those organisms and between them and the environment" (Guerrero and Margulis 1998, 35). He held that organisms must be studied not only alone or in taxonomic groupings but in their overall mass effects. "We can gain insight into the biosphere only by considering the obvious bond that unites it to the entire cosmic mechanism" (Bailes 1990, 190).[5]

There can be no doubt how Lotman came to coin *semiosphere,* for he explicitly tells us: "By analogy with the biosphere (Vernadsky's concept) we could talk of a semiosphere . . . we justify our term by analogy with the biosphere, as Vernadsky defined it, namely the totality and the organic whole of living matter and also the condition for the continuation of life" (1990, 123, 125).[6]

Eduard Le Roy, the French ethicist who succeeded Henri L. Bergson at the Collège de France in 1921, in a lecture delivered there in 1927 coined the quasi-philosophical appellation *noösphere.*[7] This new formation was then appropriated and popularized by the French Jesuit mystic paleontologist Teilhard de Chardin in his 1959 book, *Le Phénomène humain* (180–184). He described it as "really a new layer, the 'thinking layer'" and spelled out, "outside and above the biosphere there is the noösphere" (ibid., 182). Here we have another unequivocal quintessentially anthropocentric concept—a "noöspheric form . . . becoming hominised" (ibid., 225). Teilhard de Chardin is never named, nor is the word *noösphere* to be found, in any of Lotman's writings with which I am familiar. This does not of course exclude Lotman's having read the man himself or, more likely, registered *noösphere* via some citation from Vernadsky, who in the 1920s was acquainted with Le Roy, then said to have been a friend of Teilhard de Chardin's (Vernadsky 1945, 9).

Vernadsky was well known to have long had "a mystical bent . . . which drew him to Eastern religions and philosophy" (Bailes 1990, 122). This perhaps

explains his affinity for Teilhard de Chardin. It may also provide us with a telling clue as to why he recorded (on his Cyrillic typewriter) a three-sentence
message on the eve of his death (January 6, 1945), the last of which read: "We
live in a transition to the noösphere" (Vernadsky 1945, 12). Instead, forty years
or so later, we arrived at the semiosphere.

Semiosphere

"Semiosphere"—which basically invokes the conceit of a semiosis-saturated sec-
tor—can have but one of two applications, one local, the other global.[8] Lotman's uncomfortable paradox is that, while he chose to confine his usage to
much the more attenuated—if more privileged—of these two zones, the wider
resonance of his coinage could, for his scientifically sensitive readers, have been
pandemic in scope.

According to Scenario I, Lotman's "semiosphere" is evidently interchangeable with "culture" in one or more of the three hundred senses of the latter,
presumably closest to precursory semiotic models like Cassirer's, White's, or
even in part Morris', or those by such near-contemporaries as are enumerated
in Foster's article. Even "Cultural Studies," Sturrock notes, "are simply applied
semiotics" (1991, 9). Whether anything of substance has been gained by Lotman's substitution of his glittering, kindling locution for the overburdened
traditional nomenclature, or whether we remain still only in "the sphere of
rhetoric" (Lotman 1990, 46), will in the end depend on the degree of its ac-
ceptance by professional students of *Homo loquens*.

Vernadsky delineated sixteen criteria for the fundamental differences in the
spatio-temporal manifestations of living and inert matter, leading to the "natural laws of the biosphere, the only terrestrial envelope where life can exist,"
emphasizing that, basically, "man cannot be separated from it." Man is indissolubly a part of the totality of "living matter," a part of the biosphere which
stands "revealed as a planetary phenomenon of cosmic character" (1945, 4). All
this we now know, but we know a good deal more, thanks to Vernadsky's almost exact contemporary, Jakob von Uexküll.[9] Von Uexküll's great contribution
derived from his recognition of "the fact that signs are of prime importance
in all aspects of life processes" (Th. von Uexküll 1987, 147), his refusal to separate the human sciences from the natural sciences, and his establishment of an
original, independent, and powerful general semiotics which he designated as
the Umwelt-research (Sebeok 1989e, 187–215). I recently had occasion to comment on the potential relations of Lotman's Umwelt to von Uexküll's Umwelt,
or, to put the matter in another terminology, of semiotic studies to biosemiotic studies (chapter 15 below, parts 2 and 3). The proper range of Lotman's
semiosphere, had he regarded it operationally, according to Scenario II, from
a biological perspective—to wit, not as a dialogic but as a cyclic process—could

have enhanced by synergy von Uexküll's so-called "functional circle," the model for this scheme in which the functions of receiving and transmitting messages are brought together within the subject in a single, truly universal semiosphere (Th. von Uexküll 1987: 168, 172).[10]

The present terminological requirement to subsume a semiotics of culture, or just plain semiotics, under a semiotics of nature, or biosemiotics, might have been obviated decades earlier. As things are going now, the boundaries between the two are already crumbling, giving way to a unified doctrine of signs embedded in a vast, comprehensive life science.

15

The Estonian Connection

Exordium

THE TOPIC FOR this highly personal account was suggested, with Peeter Torop's concurrence and encouragement, by my colleague Kalevi Kull, director of the University of Tartu's Jakob von Uexküll Center. Its purpose is to chronicle my direct involvement with certain segments of scholarship in or derived from Estonia during the past thirty years or so. In what follows, I shall focus mainly on three quite disparate figures: Paul Ariste, né Berg (1905–90), an "Estonian" from Torma, who pursued his calling, after 1940, essentially in the Soviet Union; Yuri Mikhailovich Lotman (1922–93), a "Russian" from Petrograd, who settled in Estonia in the 1950s; and Jakob von Uexküll (1864–1944), a Baltic "Prussian" from Keblas, who emigrated from Estonia to Hamburg in the 1920s.[1]

The order in which I list and deliberate about them herein is obviously not in the order of seniority, that is, according to their respective dates of birth, but is meant to reflect the rough chronology of my own successive associations with their person and/or the realization thereof through family and oeuvre. This idiosyncratic arrangement is to be understood to track, and thus to roughly mirror, Estonian aspects of three consecutive stages in, or engagements with, three diverse but still in retrospect congruent domains of my academic career: (1) Finno-Ugric studies; (2) semiotic studies; and (3) biosemiotic studies.

Finno-Ugric Studies

When I joined the faculty of Indiana University in 1943, I was pigeonholed as a professional linguist in general, and, more narrowly, a specialist in Finno-Ugric studies. In a pair of recently commissioned articles (chapters 16 and 17 below), I recount how, beginning in the mid-1940s, I eventually came to formally, that is, administratively, establish our Program (later Department) of Uralic and Altaic Studies, as well as, on the national level—in close collabora-

This chapter first appeared in 1998, in *Sign Systems Studies* 26, 20–38.

tion with my late friend John Lotz—a set of related activities, comprehending a vast publication program.

There is no need to rehearse these events once more here beyond noting the participation, in various respects and capacities and at various stages, of a number of Estonian scholars (for details, see chapter 16 below), including Paul Ariste, George Kurman, Ilse Lehiste, Felix Oinas, Ants Oras, Valter Tauli, and Alo Raun (whose son, Toivo Raun, now chairs the Department of Central Eurasian Studies, the present avatar of the same department).

Miklós Zsirai, in his ambitious, enduringly monumental book (if now in many ways rather quaint) about "our"—that is, the Hungarians'—kinship and affinities, devoted a fair amount of space to the Estonians (1937, 442–471) and, in a separate section, to comparative linguistics as practiced in contemporary Estonian workshops (570–573). In the concluding sentence of the latter, he rather pompously foretold that, among the activities of the "younger Estonians, much is to be expected from two well-trained ones," naming Paul Ariste and Alo Raun. A decade or so afterwards, this pronouncement, having made a strong impact on me, led to several local consequences—as well as another which eventually came to play a pivotal role in this story. Having been eager to establish a strong Estonian presence at this institution from the outset of Uralic and Altaic Studies, I invited both Alo Raun and Felix Oinas, with at first different titles but eventually with tenure leading to full professorial rank, to join in our efforts as of 1951.

This parochial narrative thread stops right here, because, by the middle of the 1950s, I had already turned to other scholarly activities, among them psycholinguistics, computer research, and the barely nascent area of zoosemiotics. But another narrative trend now kicks in, marking Ariste's entrance into the frame of my activities, leading in due course, as will presently become clear, directly to Tartu.

From 1933 to 1988, Ariste was a professor at the University of Tartu (with which he had been affiliated since his student days in the mid-1920s). His tenure thus overlapped for some four decades with Lotman's, who had received a teaching post in Tartu in the 1950s. (Ariste had spent 1932 in Hamburg, but there is no record of his having crossed paths there with Jakob.) My own contacts with Ariste commenced in 1968, when I published his grammar of Votic as the sixty-eighth volume in the Indiana University Uralic and Altaic series. I had, in fact, edited one hundred volumes in that series between 1960 and 1970, including books by each of the seven Estonian scholars listed in the fourth paragraph of this article. I had also run into Professor—later Akademik— Ariste at various international congresses and other meetings, where we exchanged friendly greetings.

Notwithstanding that we didn't really know one another all that well, I turned to him in the spring of 1970 on the basis of our slender acquaintanceship—yet also in full awareness of the political clout he exercised in academic spheres of and beyond the Estonian Soviet Socialist Republic—to request a considerable favor: that he help persuade the ruling authorities in Estonia to allow me and my wife Jean to visit Yuri Lotman *in situ,* preferably while the Summer School on Secondary Modeling Systems would be in session. It will be remembered that Tartu was a "forbidden" city during Soviet rule, so foreigners, particularly Americans, but even most citizens of the Soviet Union or from other "socialist" countries (Voigt 1995, 201), were ordinarily denied access. It was greatly to Ariste's credit that he graciously, and rapidly, acceded to my plea, and a bit later helped us out in an acutely suspenseful instant of need, as I shall presently recount.

Semiotic Studies

My first, remote contacts with Lotman date from 1966, when he joined the Committee on Publications and Development of the Studies in Semiotics section, for which I had been asked to assume overall editorial responsibility, lodged within the organ of the International Council for Philosophy and Humanistic Studies and of the International Social Science Council, *Social Science Information* (see volume 7[2], 101–169, April 1968). Our appointments ran concurrently through the end of 1968 (7[6], December issue); the section was superseded the very next month by the advent of *Semiotica.*

The International Association for Semiotic Studies was founded in Paris on January 21, 1969. Lotman, *in absentia,* was elected one of its four vice-presidents. I was elected editor-in-chief of the newly created journal, whereupon I promptly moved to carry Lotman over to our new international Editorial Committee (Sebeok 1974a, 230–231). On this he served until his death, that is, through no less than ninety-eight volumes. He himself published six articles in *Semiotica* (one in collaboration with A. M. Piatigorsky, another with B. A. Uspensky).

Voigt noted in his necrology of Lotman that he was "one of [those] scholars who do not maintain regular correspondence" (1995, 201), which was in general true enough. Nevertheless, in the course of our early contacts, coursing to and from our concurrent but divorced worlds—his in the USSR, mine in the United States—we found other means to keep in touch via circumspect postings of the outmoded kind; yet they tended to revolve almost exclusively around innocuous editorial matters of a technical sort. But after August 17, 1970, our mutual, if intermittent, relationship was radically transfigured.

During this same decade, Lotman's reputation steadily accrued. He soon ripened into "one of the first Soviet scholars who became famous abroad" (ibid., 200). This maturation coincided with, was even impelled by, the second phase in the development of Soviet semiotics, which quickened with the shift from

Moscow to Tartu. This phase was observed most authoritatively by Vyacheslav Ivanov in his engrossing autobiographical sketch, which adds, "many of our works which could not be published in Moscow were [hereafter] published by Lotman in Tartu" (1991, 36). In 1964, Lotman launched the yearbook *Trudy po znakovym sistemam* (Sign system studies, reanimated now with the present twenty-sixth issuance). It became known worldwide under the portentous catchword *Sémeiótiké* (cf. Voigt 1995, 192). Accompanying the geographic displacement noted by Ivanov, there came a transfer of focus to "secondary modeling systems . . . characterized by an extremely wide-ranging subject matter and bold theoretical thinking" and a concern with the larger questions of "world-view" or "world-model"; "[b]y the time of the fourth summer school [cf. Revzina 1972] this tendency was given formal expression in the program for the study of semiotics of culture" (Shukman 1994, 560).[2]

Throughout my teaching career, I attempted to persuade my students, my colleagues, and anyone who would listen that it is important for us all to comprehend what the eminent University of Chicago psychologist Csikszentmihalyi has recently delineated under rubrics he identifies—and discusses at great length, with many examples—as *domains* and *fields*. Creativity, in his definition, "results from the interaction of a system composed of three elements: a culture that contains symbolic rules, a person who brings novelty into the symbolic domain, and a field of experts who recognize and validate innovation" (1996, 6).

To simplify considerably, a *domain,* on the one hand, constitutes a set of symbolic rules and procedures, such as semiotics, or, at a finer resolution, semiotics of culture, Paris semiotics, Tartu-Moscow School semiotics, medical semiotics, biosemiotics, or musical semiotics—or what Eco once similarly distinguished as "limiti politici [del] campo semiotico," within "fenomeni 'culturali' complessi" (1975, 21). A *field*, on the other hand, comprises "all the individuals who act as gatekeepers to the domain," who decide "whether a new idea . . . should be included in the domain" (Csikszentmihalyi 1996, 27–28)—such personages as, for instance, editors of major journals or book series, compilers of widely used reference books, officers of international organizations, leaders of important institutional centers or "schools," organizers of colloquia, conferences, congresses, popular lecturers, and the like. From another perspective, a field may be viewed as a contemporary avatar, or modern expression, of what used to take the form of a medieval guild, in short, the entity that controls the workplace in professions such as the various academic disciplines (or law or medicine) (Haskell 1997).

Complementary domains and fields can of course affect each other in a variety of fundamental ways, but my point here is that any pensive and resolute would-be practitioner of a *domain,* viz., semiotics, must make every effort to become thoroughly familiar as well with "the gatekeepers to the domain," such as I have instanced, controlling the *field*. In short, ideas and the personalities who embody and propagate them are, in my view, kept asunder at one's peril. It will be evident to the readers of this article that I aim to address here (subcontinents of) the field of semiotics, not its global domain (see chapter 1 above).

According to my own precepts and standards, therefore, I felt an urge to seek every opportunity and pursue any opening to get to know Professor Lotman in person, and preferably to visit him in his adopted domestic setting, which was then a singular Mecca-like field for us "pilgrims" laboring in the domain of semiotics. My first chance came in 1970, and Academician Ariste turned out to be the provider of, as it were, an unassailable convoy to Tartu. The framing event was a call I had received to address, in Tallinn, an international congress in Finno-Ugric studies.[3] As soon as my invitation arrived from Estonia, I realized that the dates of the Tallinn congress would actually coincide with those of the Fourth Summer School on Secondary Modeling Systems: both were to take place August 17–24, 1970.

Therefore I immediately contacted Lotman, who had indicated that we would be cordially welcome at the summer school, provided we could ourselves secure the necessary papers. I next wrote to Ariste, pleading for his intervention and assistance. He did not respond in writing, but, the day after we had disembarked and checked into our Intourist accommodations in Tallinn, a telegram was delivered to our room, clearing the way for the two of us to spend the following day, the 18th, in Tartu. I alluded to some of the ensuing adventures in a new foreword to Lucid's anthology eleven years ago (Sebeok 1988b), but that appeared before the death of Ariste two years later (Domokos ed. 1990), the liberation of Estonia one year after that (1991), and Lotman's death in October of 1993. Now, five years later, I feel free at last to furnish my recital with some particulars.

On Tuesday morning, barely at dawn, a car driven by a KGB man picked us up in the deserted lobby of our Tallinn hotel. Several hours later, it pulled up in front of the main building of Tartu State University. Jean and I kept conversation to a minimum during the drive. We mostly dozed.[4]

At this point, it is necessary to mention that, during our entire stay in Estonia, and *a fortiori* in Tartu, neither of us took any notes, let alone photographs. My report of this crowded, exciting day may therefore contain some misapprehensions. Take, for example, the composition of the impressive gathering that greeted us on our arrival outside the gate: there were, to my best recollection, over twenty men and women there, only a few of whom I had met before, swarming around us introducing themselves. I transcribed their names from memory several days later on the ship returning us to Finland. Here is what I do remember.

The very first colleague to come forward to greet me was Petr Bogatyrev, who seemed by far the most senior personage present and who was introduced, for the record (I guessed), as being the "president" of the school.[5] Next, Lotman was introduced as the "secretary" of the school, and he in turn presented us to his wife, Zara Minc.[6] I was then informed that D. M. Segal would be my interpreter for the day, and he was thereafter at my side until our departure. To the best of my recollection, the following individuals were also in the group: T. V. Civ'jan, B. F. Egorov, T. J. Elizarenkova, B. M. Gasparov, V. V. Ivanov, M. B. Mejlax, A. M. Piatigorsky, B. Ogibenin, I. I. Revzin, O. G. Revzina, V. N. Toporov, and B. A. Uspensky.[7]

As I have summarized previously, our searching discussions and debates of many semiotic topics were "freewheeling and never less then rousing." They continued through lunch, and, most productively, "through the course of a leisurely, intimate amble outdoors, and finally during a farewell tea" (Sebeok 1988b, vii). Indeed, confidential talks with our hosts took place typically in the course of leisurely strolls in the woods. They constituted the most productive, memorable, and cherished moments of our exhilarating (if exhausting) day.

We returned to Tallinn at dusk to resume my normal responsibilities to the Finno-Ugric Congress, but now faced a new—although, to me, not unprecedented—problem. While in Tartu, a number of colleagues handed me manuscripts to convey to the West. Most of these were intended for publication in *Semiotica;* some were meant for delivery to other editors. Such scholarly papers (the only kind I ever accepted) were entrusted to me to sidestep nightmarish Soviet bureaucratic restrictions. I was aware of the illicit nature of such dodges and the risks if I were caught, but abetted them because of my refusal to condone censorship of intellectual property of any kind. Too, many of the pieces by authors such as the ones I list in endnote 7, which would soon come out in *Semiotica,* would scarcely have appeared in English otherwise and, very likely, would have remained unknown to all but a very limited readership.

However, in this instance, while I had been entrusted with a larger than usual number of works, I had relatively little luggage space. I knew that all incoming and outgoing baggage was subject to search in the customs shed of Tallinn harbor. So I decided to discreetly consult with Ariste: should I gamble on endangering the several authors of these manuscripts, likely being myself apprehended, putting my wife in jeopardy, and, not least, embarrassing the congress organizers? I thought he would advise me not to. On the contrary, he told me not to worry. Indeed, thanks to Ariste's propitious and imaginative succor, these manuscripts got out of the Soviet Union.

What transpired on our departure, as recollected after more than a quarter of a century of tranquility, takes on, in retrospect, the coloring of a farce. At the harbor, we noticed that all passengers ahead of us were ordered to pile their bags on a stand and open them. All were thoroughly searched. On being summoned by a Russian officer to step forward and submit likewise, I braced myself for serious trouble. At the very moment I placed our luggage on the counter, the entrance to the shed burst open and Ariste rushed in with a large bouquet of flowers, handing them to my astonished wife. At the top of his voice, he proclaimed what an honor it was for his country to have had two such distinguished and gracious American visitors in attendance at the congress. While holding up the line behind us, the noisy hurly-burly fomented such befuddlement and delay that the impatient officer hurriedly waved us, with our untouched luggage, through to board the ship. I thanked Ariste warmly, saying goodbye. I never saw him again.

In 1973, responding to initiatives from the Academy of Sciences of the USSR to come for an approximately six-week sojourn in Russia, and conjoined but separate invitations from the Armenian and Georgian Academies for lectures, I was awarded an exchange professorship by the U.S. National Academy of Sciences for studies in Moscow, Leningrad, Erevan, and Tbilisi. My specific requests for additional visits in the Estonian and Mari Republics were rejected without explanation.

Soon after our arrival in Moscow, I made contact with several local members of the Moscow-Tartu School to set up an "unofficial" get-together with those willing to attend. An all-afternoon tea was arranged in Ogibenin's flat. To my surprise and pleasure, Lotman, who came by train from Tartu, was there among half a dozen or more Muscovites, including Ivanov and Uspensky. Topics of mutual interest were discussed—notably having to do with the publication of various books and articles bearing on semiotics.

However, one important, novel topic, not broached with me in Tartu, was insistently raised in Moscow. This had to do with the fact that several of the colleagues I met in Tartu had since left to live in foreign parts or were just now preparing to emigrate. I was quizzed at length about conditions, particularly job opportunities, in several major Western capitals and in the United States. One of those present declared his interest in coming to Indiana University. It later became possible for me to arrange that he come to Bloomington for an interview, and even, on his receiving favorable mention from Roman Jakobson (who was coincidentally also here at the time), to offer him a permanent faculty appointment in semiotic studies. To Jakobson's fury and my own disappointment, this gifted young man declined our offer for the flimsiest of reasons. Reputedly living in Paris, he has since vanished from the academic scene.[8]

My next encounter with Lotman, most intimate, most interesting—but, as it turned out, the last—was an extraterritorial happening for both of us. It happened so.

In 1986, the Norsk Forening for Semiotikk (Norwegian Association for Semiotic Studies) convened in Bergen, upon the initiative of Dinda L. Gorlée and Sven Storelv, a symposium on Semiotics in Theory and Practice. I delivered the keynote speech on the first morning, October 2 (Sebeok 1987b). After some uncertainty about his whereabouts, Lotman landed late in the afternoon, on what was his first journey ever to the West. Not surprisingly, he at first appeared exhausted and nervous, but he performed with his customary brilliance the next day.

He spoke extempore in Russian (ably rendered into English on the spot by Professor Jostein Børtnes)—in electrifying fashion albeit with a touch of whimsy—during the second day, the third of the symposium, to "situate semiotics within the Slavic cultural tradition" (Lotman 1987). The local organizers assigned us parallel roles, but there wasn't any doubt of Lotman's star quality. We both wrote special introductions to precede the communications, published in the third issue of *Livstegn* (1987), Lotman's entitled "Semiotics and Culture in the Second Half of the Twentieth Century."

That evening, Lotman and I had a protracted dinner together at the Hilton, addressing one another mostly in German, with snatches of French, interspersed by his shaky English and my faltering Russian. Yet, as the evening progressed, palliated by some toasts, a mutual rapport and sympathy came to suffuse and envelop us as if we had been the oldest of friends.

In the course of the evening, Lotman handed me a typescript of his now classic, highly sophisticated if rather controversial essay "O semiosfere," which would appear in volume 17 of *Sémeiótiké,* dated 1984. He rightly considered this to be an exceptionally important paper, though it was hardly available to Western readers even two years afterwards. He asked that I arrange to have it promptly translated and printed in *Semiotica,* to which of course I enthusiastically assented. Unfortunately, although in the past he had left the assignment of translators to my judgment, in this instance he expressly stipulated a specific individual. After my return home, I phoned this man (whom I knew and respected for his skills) in New York, and, after some haggling over his fee and the timing, he took the job on—but, in the event, he neither delivered the English version nor, to this day, returned the original typescript. This was, needless to say, mortifying as well as a grievous disappointment to me, scarcely made up for by my modest role four years later in promoting the publication by the Indiana University Press of our colleague Ann Shukman's definitive presentation of Lotman's *Universe of Mind* (1990). Part two of this book, titled "The Semiosphere," conveys his most mature statement of what he apparently intended by this concept, which seems to have recourse to a kind of multi-faceted universal semiotic "culture engine."[9]

Voigt later claimed that *semiosphere* was Lotman's "first personally invented term . . . his brainchild." If so, this may in part account for his fondness for and attachment to it. However, there is no evidence for Voigt's further suggestion (1995, 197) that Lotman's term was "modeled after *noösphere*," a fuzzy contraption by the French Jesuit and metaphysician Pierre Teilhard de Chardin. To the contrary, there is plenty of internal evidence in Lotman's writings for my repeated contention (e.g., Sebeok 1991f, 8, 142; chapter 14 above) that Lotman coined his term by analogy with Vernadsky's 1926 term *biosfera*.

Here it should be noted that Kull wrote an exploratory inquiry—based in part on extant texts, in part on interviews—titled "Towards Biosemiotics with Yuri Lotman," which appeared in a special issue of *Semiotica* devoted to biosemiotics (Hoffmeyer and Emmeche eds. 1999). Two companion articles in the same issue take up comparable concerns of, respectively, C. S. Peirce (by M. L. Santaella Braga) and Charles Morris (by Susan Petrilli).

Lotman, in his introductory speech to *Livstegn*, rightly underlined the contemporary emergence of syncretic tendencies in semiotic investigations. "In the humanities," he said, "different disciplines combine into a single science of man, centered around the semiotic study of culture" (1987, 10). Commute *science* for *the humanities, life* for *man,* and *nature* for *culture*—and this great, charismatic thinker and I might have consummated a transcendental disputation. I had hoped to argue my basic case, and ancillary issues, at our next scheduled encounter, at the Twenty-fifth Symposium of the Tartu-Moscow School of Semiotics, held in Imatra, Finland, July 27–29, 1987 (Sebeok 1988c), but, alas, Lotman could not attend, and I never saw him again.

Biosemiotic Studies

I first came across von Uexküll's name in 1936, when I was still in my teens and he was to live for eight more years. I chanced to catch his name on the verso of the half-title page to Ogden and Richard's *The Meaning of Meaning,* the fourth edition of which I purchased when I was an undergraduate at Magdalen College in Cambridge, where Richards was Pepys Librarian at the time. Ogden was also associated with Magdalen, according to the same page, which also listed him as the "General Editor of the International Library of Psychology, Philosophy and Scientific Method." This consisted at the time already of some eighty-five volumes. Von Uexküll's *Theoretical Biology* was listed as the thirty-fourth book from the top, or fifty-second from the bottom. The title having caught my attention, I obtained a copy from the library and found that it was a 1926 translation of a German book published in 1920, and that it was beyond doubt over my head. Not until some thirty years later did I come to realize that this judgment was premature as well as very wide of the mark. The English translation had in fact been carried out "wretchedly . . . under Ogden's eccentric auspices" (Sebeok 1991e, 104). In the mid-1960s, when at last I read the original German version,[10] I came to believe that Ogden, the very animator of anglophone semiotics in the twentieth century, had either known little or no German or, with all his polymathic gifts, had failed to understand what *Theoretische Biologie* was really about: not biology, not psychology, not physiology, but semiotics. What's more, it unfolded a wholly unprecedented, innovative theory of signs, the scope of which was nothing less than semiosis in life processes in their entirety. It created and established the basis for the comprehensive new domain that we now call *biosemiotics* (for definition, cf. Sebeok 1973, and Th. von Uexküll 1987, 214).

Jakob von Uexküll, who single-handedly brought biosemiotics about— *avant,* so to speak, *la lettre*—received his basic academic training in zoology at the University of Dorpat (now Tartu) (G. von Uexküll 1964, 25–30; see also his portrait facing p. 32 as an Estonian student). It is therefore highly appropriate that a research institution dedicated to this domain named the Jakob von Uexküll Center, has functioned since 1993 under the auspices of the master's *alma mater.*[11]

His had been a signal achievement. As Csikszentmihalyi noted in his book *Creativity,* the term *domain* ordinarily "refers to the act of changing some aspect of a domain . . . But of course there was a time when domains did not exist . . . So, in a sense, the most momentous creative events are those in which entire new symbolic systems are created" (1996, 291). Such a novel system was Umwelt-research, that is, *biosemiotics,* rooted in no antecedent semiotic theory or practice at all; it was, rather, connected to the thought of Plato, Leibniz, (especially) Kant, Goethe, and a handful of biologists, such as Johannes Müller and Karl Ernst von Baer.[12]

Furthermore, as Konrad Lorenz himself has pointed out (1971, 275), "the research programme mapped out [by von Uexküll] is pretty nearly identical with that of ethology." This should surprise no one who remembers that von Uexküll was "one of [Lorenz's] most important teachers" (ibid., 274; cf. G. von Uexküll 1964, 198); nor anyone able to get to the bottom of the congruence between ethology, specifically the study of ritualization, and diachronic semiotics (Sebeok 1989e, 27–34).

On occasion, I have tried to get a fix on whether the practitioners of the Tartu-Moscow School were aware of the writings of Jakob. While I do not think that Lotman and I exchanged views about this particular question, I did pose it to Ivanov on several occasions, once in Berlin and another time over lunch when he visited me in Bloomington. Yet a clear-cut answer continues to elude me. It is a fact, however, that the Russian semiotician Stepanov devoted an entire chapter of his book to "Biosemiotics" (1971, 27–32), a discussion which opens with a survey of some works by von Uexküll (to whom he refers as a "German" biologist). His scrutiny is vitiated by a ritual obeisance to Lenin. This is followed by a misestimation of the psychologist and primatologist Zhinkin, who, in a review of one of my books (Sebeok ed. 1968), made two remarks: he correctly surmised that "one gains the impression that there is no branch on the tree of genetic evolution where living beings fail to engage in communication," but he incorrectly supposed, and his view misled Stepanov, "that the roots of language lie deep in the layers of the evolution of animal life" (Zhinkin 1971, 75).

In brief, it is difficult to accept that, although the notion of "Umwelt" was evidently known in Moscow circles by the 1970s, it still remained hermetic to Lotman. One hopes that further inquiries on the part of Kull and others may resolve this conundrum, with possibly far-reaching bearings on ambitious overarching conceptual twosomes such as *semiosphere / biosphere, semiotics / biosemiotics,* and the like, in their intricate interplay.

However that may be, in August 1977 I attended the Third Wiener Symposium über Semiotik to present a paper titled "Neglected Figures in the History of Semiotic Inquiry: Jakob von Uexküll" (Sebeok 1979b, ch. 10, 187–207, 290–291). Thure was in the audience. Afterwards, we had a long talk, subsequent to which he paid a call on me in Bloomington, and, still later on, made arrangements for me to spend a week or so visiting him in Freiburg, accompanied by my late friend, Giorgio Prodi. Prodi, a distinguished oncologist by profession, a novelist, and a prolific contributor to general bio- and endosemiotics[13]—he favored the comprehensive expression "natural semiotics" (e.g., in Sercarz et al. eds. 1988, 55; cf. Prodi 1988b)—had forged, without explicit reference to any other previous or contemporary thinker, still another variant of this sprouting, or re-emerging domain. Prodi was another remarkably creative individual (Eco 1988). While the three of us were together in Freiburg (with Thure's sister, Dana, visiting him from Finland, "keeping house"), we conducted an intensive week-long, open-ended seminar, so to speak, on the practical and conceivable ins and outs of biosemiotics. Over and above redefining and sharpening my overall perception of this semiotic domain, this uniquely stimulating experience enabled me to enhance my writings and teachings (Sebeok 1995d) in biosemiotics in its various topical subdivisions.

Our intensive triadic "brainstorming" led directly to the series of pivotal seminars held annually in the late 1980s and early 1990s in Glottertal, on the outskirts of Freiburg. These thought-provoking international get-togethers were held at the Glotterbad Clinic for Rehabilitative Medicine, under Thure's overall aegis and the superintendence of a student and associate of his, Jörg M. Herrmann, M.D., its director. They were attended by many German, Swiss, and other physicians, and on occasion by the biologists Jesper Hoffmeyer (of Denmark), and Kull, now two of the leading figures of the biosemiotics movement.

The paper I had presented in Vienna and published two years later as chapter 10 of my book *The Sign & Its Masters* (1979b) was my attempt to come to terms with the historical fact that there were certain men in the history of ideas, and several women, who, unawares, turned out to have been seminal figures in the history of semiotic inquiry. Much later, I dubbed this phenomenon the *Jourdain factor* (Sebeok 1991e, 45), offering a host of examples, but none more amazingly conspicuous than Jakob, now all but universally granted redefinition.

"The Estonian Connection," as I choose to call this article, endeavors to set in motion the seeds of a fascinating dialectic between Jakob von Uexküll, emigrant from Dorpat to the West, renowned as the scientist who had the creative power to imagine and delineate what we now call biosemiotics, and Yuri M. Lotman, emigrant from Russia to Tartu, the celebrated visionary humanist who invented the notion of what we now call the semiosphere. Seemingly polar opposites, they both formulated and brought into being vast subcontinents of global semiotics (chapter 16 below): von Uexküll life itself in its multiform complexity, Lotman the universe of the human mind in its profusion of profound discernment. At bottom, of course, the biosphere and the semiosphere must be the same, for semiosis is the criterial attribute of all life, inclusive of the mind observing the universe, which comprehends life, the biosphere (Vernadsky 1926). The two together are linked in a closed cybernetic loop, or what the physicist Wheeler, remarking that "meaning itself powers creation," has called a self-excited circuit (1988). How the two are to be reconciled in their rich minutiae into a global synthesis is open to debate by their disciples at University of Tartu and elsewhere.

Coda

In sum, there is far more that could be said about the issue of "domain-semiotics" versus "field-semiotics." A field-semiotic standpoint was exemplified in this mapping of some of the multifarious genealogical filiations, in their quite diverse ramifications, of three major scholars whose points of convergence or intersection—actual or symbolic, synchronous or otherwise—chanced to be the University of Tartu.

However, another, on the surface quite different, charting could be projected if these same scholars were to be reconsidered from a domain-semiotic standpoint—for example, the Peircean category of Indexicality (Sebeok 1995b). Were one to attempt an approach like this—more common, perhaps, in traditional academic publications—one would have to zoom in, for instance, on Votic demonstrative pronouns (Ariste 1968); on "how, for example, umbrellas, coaches, dinners, and card-playing occur (and can be understood) in literature" (Lotman, in Voigt 1995, 191); and on such biosemiotically dramatic events as predation (Jakob and Thure von Uexküll, passim; cf. Thom 1983, 267–269).

At the time of writing, I am trying to think through the implications of what I am calling "the genealogical method to semiotic historiography," or what I have elsewhere elaborated under the ensign of "The Semiotic Web." (Two months ago, I presented another fragment of this possible *modus operandi,* dealing with semiotic anthropology.)[14] For the time being, however, I remain content to leave the domain-semiotic facets of this and other possible such exercises for future occasions.

16

My "Short Happy Life" in Finno-Ugric Studies

MY TWENTY YEARS or so in Finno-Ugric (FU) studies, as reflected in my list of publications, began in 1942 and, except for a few oddments, appear to have come to an end in 1962. In later years, I did issue, responding to special requests—seldom for original work but rather for scattered reminiscences about this portion of my early academic life—some pertinent reports. Thus, in a pedagogical vein rather than intending to contribute to scholarship, I wrote in 1969 on "The Study of Finnish in the United States," and in 1992 on "Uralic Studies and English for Hungarians at Indiana University" (chapter 17 below). More generally, in my retirement address to my colleagues at a festive convention on March 22, 1991, informally looking over my half-century academic career, I included a synoptic account of my "Finno-Ugric years" at Indiana University (1992a).

In the fall of 1993, I was a visiting professor at the University of Helsinki, also lecturing at the Universities of Tampere, Turku, and Vaasa, as well as to various Finnish learned societies, including the Suomen Kirjallisuuden Seura. After my talk to this group one afternoon, a lady approached me from the audience introducing herself as having come from Ioshkar-Ola, the capital of the Mari (Cheremis) Republic in Russia, and as being a native speaker of the Cheremis language. Since, from the second half of the 1940s into the early 1960s, I had conducted an intensive study of this language and culture, publishing two additional books on Cheremis subjects as recently as the 1970s (1974b, 1978), she allowed that my name was well known among her people. However, because I had published nothing more about them lately, the conclusion had been reached in Mari-land that I must have died two decades before. Determined to prove the contrary, Dr. Lidia Tojdobekova (whom I have met with several times since) insisted on taping a lengthy "live" interview with me for transmission to and deposit in Ioshkar-Ola's archives.

Any narrative of my activities as an FU practitioner has necessarily two

This article was originally composed as a speech at the invitation of Mihály Szegedy-Maszák and published in 1999, in *Snow, Forest, Silence: The Finnish Tradition of Semiotics,* ed. E. Tarasti, 16–25 (Bloomington: Indiana University Press).

aspects: a private one and a public one. The latter is bound to be the more interesting, but makes little sense without the former to illuminate it. So I will begin with some personal background.

In my beginning years at the University of Chicago, I had every intention of becoming a biologist, viz., a geneticist. Not to belabor my academic trajectory here, the outbreak of World War II in 1939 inexorably impelled me toward linguistics instead. My eminent professor, Leonard Bloomfield, advised me to build upon my native knowledge of Hungarian and to expand upon that base by learning as much as possible about Finnish and the other accessible languages of the family to which both belonged. This was sensible advice, except for what soon loomed as an insuperable quandary: none of the FU languages were taught, programmatically or otherwise, at Chicago or, as far as I could ascertain, anywhere else in the Americas. Not long before Professor Bloomfield left Chicago for Yale, he somehow found the time to read with me and critique a just-published *Outline of Hungarian Grammar,* but it soon became obvious that, were I to expand my glottal horizons in the directions he counseled, I would have to fall back on my own resources and devices. The theoretically obvious option of continuing my studies somewhere in Europe was blocked by the inaccessibility of all regions, even Swedish Lapland, where FU populations were indigenous.

In 1941, I too left Chicago for the east coast to continue my formal studies at Princeton University, supplemented by semi-formal but demanding studies with Roman Jakobson at Columbia University and vicinity. I was also appointed civilian chief of the War Department's Hungarian and Finnish desks at one of its New York City offices, and was, moreover, busily engaged in other kinds of war work. However, before the war ended in 1945, I was able to publish, besides more than a dozen papers on FU topics, two hefty pedagogically oriented books plus a monograph constituting my doctoral dissertation. My first book, which ran to about five hundred printed pages, was titled *Spoken Hungarian* (1945a), and was enhanced by twenty-five twelve-inch vinylite recordings, as well as a separate *Guide's Manual.* My second book, of about the same size, was titled *Spoken Finnish* (1947a); comparable recordings accompanied it. On the bilingual recordings for my Hungarian book, the English voice was that of the American linguist Henry Lee Smith, Jr. (d. 1972), the Hungarian my own; to the contrary, on those to go with my Finnish book, while I spoke the English parts the native voice was that of His Excellency, the Ambassador of Finland to Washington, Mr. Jutila.

In a special study I was invited to prepare at the time for the *Modern Language Journal* (1945b), I described the pedagogical and other uses to which the materials on which these twin manuals were based had been put to train large numbers of armed personnel as well as, after the war, foreign service officers of the U.S. Department of State; the books eventually became available for civilian uses in a somewhat different, commercial version, and both may still be in print.

During my residency in Princeton, I frequently commuted to meet with Jakobson and to attend various lectures and colloquia he offered at several institutions in New York, including a semester he spent leading an advanced evening seminar at Columbia devoted entirely to the typology of case systems. Since case constitutes a pivotal grammatical category in several FU languages, he asked me to prepare detailed accounts of relevant materials for a series of class presentations and discerning discussion. In this way, the idea for a dissertation topic came to me, namely, an inquiry into the shape of the case system in the FU protolanguage as reconstructed by a comparison of the case systems of extant daughter languages.

Jakobson urged me to establish contact with John Lotz, who was at the time (1936–57) director of the Hungarian Institute at the University of Stockholm. I wrote to Lotz immediately and he responded promptly. Massive correspondence and thoroughgoing exchange of ideas between us ensued, in spite of wartime delays and interruptions. "Lotz asked to see my dissertation, then offered to publish a portion of it, edited by himself. I accepted his assistance with gratitude, but asked to see my proofs. These never reached me, however, for, as we learned afterward, the ship bringing them [from Sweden] was torpedoed. The monograph was therefore published in the raw [1946] and I received my authors' copies only some two years after the war" (1989a, 235).

In the spring of 1945, I received a Ph.D. from Princeton University's Department of Oriental Languages and Civilizations, with probably the first dissertation on a FU topic awarded to anyone by any North American institution; and, the following year, I joined the peacetime faculty of Indiana University. I proposed to Herman B Wells, this institution's president, that we build upon the resources that had serendipitously accumulated here during the war years, and he enthusiastically supported all such endeavors (see chapter 17 below), among which I shall concentrate here only on developments that bear directly on FU studies.

By now, it was amply clear to me that no one, anywhere in this country, could receive anything approaching adequate professional training in the full extent and depth of FU studies. I therefore resolved to proceed along two tracks simultaneously, one *personal,* the other *institutional.*

To realize my personal goal, I initiated conversations with the American-Scandinavian Foundation, and presented a coherent plan that would enable me to visit Sweden and Finland for three or four months in 1947 in order to:

1. Spend as much time as was necessary to get a feel for the shape of the field, overall, from John Lotz, who, by dint of his assignment to the University

of Stockholm since 1936, was at its sole neutral epicenter throughout the war years;

2. Get acquainted with as many FU specialists in the Nordic countries, or, as it turned out in practice, mostly in Finland;

3. Conduct a summer's worth of all-out but as yet preliminary fieldwork among one of the FU groups of the region (I chose to settle in a Lapp speech community in Outakoski, on the Finnish shore of the Teno River across from Norway); and

4. Determine, in consultation with Lotz and others, to which of the extant dozen or so FU language-and-culture configurations I could most productively devote my own research energies in the decade or more ahead. For various reasons, I settled on the Cheremis (Mari), pursuing my intensive studies initially with Paavo Siro in Helsinki, thereafter moving on for some months to what turned out to be a remarkable one-on-one learning experience with the controversial but surely greatest living specialist of those times, Odön Beke, in Budapest. (See further below.)

The American-Scandinavian Foundation approved all the facets of my application, enabling me to obtain some of the training post-doctorally that I was unable to get in my graduate years. This, however, was the lesser, personal part of my strategy, which would have been relatively worthless without the institutional part of the scheme.

To prepare the ground locally, I first submitted an internal proposal to President Wells, calling for the creation of a curricular Program in Uralic and Altaic Studies. This entity, which was rapidly approved by the Board of Trustees, grew organically out of my wartime duties and experiences. (The term "Uralic" is a well-established linguistic concept that comprehends all of the Finno-Ugric languages plus several languages spoken in Siberia, together called Samoyedic; on the other hand, "Altaic" is a much looser areal concept. This logical incongruity notwithstanding, these two concepts are sometimes combined mainly for institutional convenience, as they were, by mutual agreement with Lotz, at both Columbia and Indiana Universities.)

Now armed with the authority of the chairmanship of this new academic unit, I turned for assistance to the Rockefeller Foundation. "Fortunately," as I have reported elsewhere (1992a, 7), "I had befriended an exceptionally farsighted officer . . . , Mr. Stevens, who most bountifully financed the launching of a sound academic program in this arcane field, then and again today uniquely featured at Indiana University, with a multi-year donation which enabled me to invite a series of senior visiting professors from Scandinavia and Finland to help give it a durable shape." The first of these visiting scholars, Björn Collinder, was a Swede, and two who succeeded him, Asbjörn Nesheim and Knut

Bergsland (both Lapp specialists) were Norwegians; the rest were prominent Finns: Paavo Ravila, Lauri Posti, Aimo Turunen, Osmo Ikola, and Valentin Kiparsky (a Slavist). Most of them taught in our program for about a year, usually taking a vigorous role in building up basic resources, mainly our library holdings. The Rockefeller Foundation and the university both provided liberal funding for stockpiling books and other research materials, which enabled me to purchase large private libraries and special collections on sale, notably, in Finland. To cite just a single example, rich materials from the heritage of Professor Yrjö Wichmann were transferred here wholesale. There were so many books available at the time that Wichmann's Hungarian widow, Julia, having wearied of preparing catalogues, preferred to sell them to me by weight—so many kilos of printed matter for a price she chose to set.

To veer from the main story line, I should mention here that, in 1960, I inaugurated, and edited for nine years, a unique *Uralic and Altaic Series*. By 1969, when I retired as the editor, one hundred numbered volumes had appeared, with Vol. 67 alone, however, consisting of twenty-one separate tomes. Contributors of Hungarian provenance—living and dead—included, inter alia, Péter Hajdú, Kálmán Keresztes, Béla Kálmán, Károly Rédei, Gyula Décsy, János Gulya, Stephen Erdély, Ioannes Sylvester Pannonius, Vilmos Diószegi, János Eckman, János Zsilka, Edith Vértes, László Szabó, Ferenc Kiefer, Stephen Foltinyi, György Lakó, Lajos Tamás, Erzsébet Beöthy, László Arany, Joannes Sajnovics, Sámuel Gyarmathy, Denis Sinor, Klára Magdics, and Szenciensis Albertus Molnár, besides John Lotz and myself. Among the Finnish contributors were Alexander Castrén, Lauri Hakulinen, Valter Tauli, Meri Lehtinen, Toivo Vuerela, Paavo Ravila, Elli Köngäs, and Jaako Ahokas. And among the Estonian contributors were Ants Oras, Felix Oinas, Alo Raun, Ilse Lehiste, Paul Ariste, and George Kurman. There were also Russian, Ukrainian, Latvian, German, Swedish, French, Turkish, Mongolian, and Chinese authors, to say nothing of the dozen or more native Americans. The series enjoyed an immense domestic and worldwide popularity, with scores of volumes selling out their print runs or achieving multiple editions. A long time afterwards, when I spent some time in Ulan Bator, I found these many volumes in the library of the Mongolian Academy of Sciences; but I was truly astonished, although not displeased, to be widely introduced by my hosts as the editor of the series!

Returning to Paavo Ravila: he was an admirable linguistic technician, a warm human being, and a visionary organizer who returned to Finland to eventually serve as the chancellor of the University of Helsinki. While he was at Indiana University, I proposed to him the establishment of a permanent, rotating Chair for Finnish Studies within the frame of our Uralic and Altaic Program. Indeed, such a chair was created, even financed, on Ravila's initiative, largely by the Finnish government, but these fruitful arrangements were some years afterwards abrogated because of the destructive internal political machinations of a later administration.

The visiting professors—especially the Finns, who generously shared with me facets of their vast collective scholarly expertise as well as their individual friendship—contributed to my education in varying degrees. Via this unconventional route—since (to paraphrase the Russian proverb) the mountain could not come to Mahomet, a throng of Mahomets graciously came to the mountain, such having been the only practical avenue open to me in those times—I gradually secured my footing in the FU field at large. At the same time, however, I was busy forging a particular specialty on and of my own, to wit, the language and culture of a particular FU population situated mainly in the Mari Republic of the Soviet Union, better known to Western scholarship as the Cheremis. In this endeavor—having been coached as to the basics by my Finnish tutor, Siro, and thereafter guided far beyond by my Hungarian mentor Beke (see above)—I henceforth came to increasingly rely on the services of a native speaker, Ivan Jevsky.

Jevsky had fortuitously landed in the United States in February 1952. It soon became possible for me to secure the necessary funding for importing him to and supporting him in Bloomington, and to formally embark upon what became known as the Cheremis project (under circumstances described elsewhere, e.g., in Sebeok and Ingemann 1956, 7). The attendant intensive researches, which concluded in 1963, were funded by a substantial grant from Indiana University, with additional aid, to name only some of the major contributors, from the U.S. Department of State, Department of the Air Force, Office of Education, the Arctic, Desert, Tropic Information Center of the Research Studies Institute, located at Maxwell Air Force Base, the National Science Foundation, the American Philosophical Society, the American Council of Learned Societies, the Social Science Research Council, the John Simon Guggenheim Memorial Foundation, the Wenner-Gren Foundation for Anthropological Research, and the Newberry Library. I enumerate these in some detail to attest that, in the decades whereof I write, many U.S. funding agencies—federal, state, and private—were concerned with the national development of not just FU studies in general but such specialized branches of it as Cheremis studies.

A deserter from the Red Army to a German camp from which he was in due course "liberated" by advancing American forces, a semi-literate barber by trade, Jevsky was the first member of his culture and the first speaker of his language ever to have come to this continent; beside his native Cheremis, Jevsky spoke only some Tatar and a little Russian. Although, by and large, he cooperated with my team of assistants and students cheerfully enough, he complained with some regularity that "work with the head is almost unbearably fatiguing as opposed to work with hand." He seemed relieved to finally be allowed to revert to his tonsorial slog at the conclusion of our dedicated undertaking.

Some half a dozen students participated in the Cheremis project, three of them (one a Finn, Eeva K. Minn) earning their doctorates with dissertations on relevant topics. In 1952, I launched and edited a mini-series, *Studies in Cheremis*, in which eleven volumes, by members of the faculty or advanced graduate students at Indiana University, appeared before the series petered out twenty-six years afterwards (for a list, see Sebeok 1978, 5). I should also mention that, in the course of some half a dozen professional trips to the Soviet Union in the 1950s and 1960s, I managed to purchase hundreds of books published in the Mari Republic, anything from grade school textbooks to technical training manuals to novels and poetry to transcribed folklore texts of various genres, etc. I eventually donated this unique stockpile to the Indiana University libraries, along with my entire FU collection, which included not only hundreds of grammars, dictionaries, and the like, but complete bound runs of practically every journal series, both Hungarian and Finnish, in the field, plus many items from Soviet times and well before.

It would be erroneous to conclude from the foregoing account that FU studies constituted my exclusive academic preoccupation during the twenty years covered here. In addition to a host of articles having to do with the Cheremis and other FU groups and their languages, I wrote, as early as 1951, several papers eventuating from parallel investigations of a language spoken by the Aymará, a large community of Indians in Bolivia. Among the latter, I compiled a sizeable collection of materials for a modern dictionary (1951). And, as far back as the mid-1940s, I had conducted extensive fieldwork, under the auspices of the Cranbrook Academy, among the Winnebago, a Siouan population in the Green Bay area of Wisconsin (see, e.g., 1947b).

By the mid-1950s, I was also, and remained for more than a decade to come, thickly involved in collaborative work, under the auspices of the Social Science Research Council, with several colleagues in psychology and linguistics (Osgood and Sebeok eds. 1954)—but this is not the place to recount these attendant experiences. Furthermore, during the 1950s and 1960s, I became engaged in problems of stylistics, along with Lotz, Jakobson, I. A. Richards, and a host of others, including several prominent psychologists (Sebeok ed. 1960). This aspect of my work is particularly relevant here because it served as one bridge— although I was not explicitly aware of it being so at the time—between my fading efforts in the FU field, on the one hand, and my fumbling entry into the domain of general semiotics, on the other. Let me briefly describe one such Janus-like project, which resulted in a major—although, for FU studies, highly unconventional—book: the *Concordance and Thesaurus of Cheremis Poetic Lan-*

guage, which became the eighth in the *Studies in Cheremis* series (Sebeok and Zeps 1961).

As a part of the overall Cheremis project, I had assembled a rather large corpus of about 1,200 folksong texts, which I began to analyze off and on throughout 1958–59, while I was in residence at the Department of Anthropology of the University of Arizona and a fellow of the John Simon Guggenheim Memorial Foundation. Then, for 1960–61, I was unexpectedly appointed a fellow of the Center for Advanced Study in the Behavioral Sciences, with absolutely no restrictions as to my activities there. In consequence of this total freedom, my year's stay at the Center had a momentous, if unforeseen, effect on the remainder of my scholarly career. While, on the one hand, I saw this as a singular opportunity to strike out in a wholly novel research direction—to examine how animals communicate—I also felt bound to finish up, albeit in an innovative way, the analysis of the corpus of folksong texts I had been working on for the past few years.

As to the latter, I was fortunate to be accompanied to the Center by one of my "postdocs," the late V. J. Zeps, supported by two consecutive grants I obtained for him from the National Science Foundation for "computer research in psycholinguistics." Zeps was a member of my team which had worked with Ivan Jevsky, but his true talents and inspired enthusiasms lay in computational linguistics, at the dawn of the era—almost forty years ago—when such predilections and preoccupations became the rage. Zeps was a quintessential hacker *au pied de la lettre,* who conceived and implemented our programs. Based on an empirical exploration of large quantities of Cheremis verse and other such devices in the light of considerations of problems of poetic language in the widest sense, this investigation was, for its time, a pioneering effort in the automatic compilation of concordances and related scholarly tools with a then-state-of-the-art IBM 650 electronic data processing system, equipped with four magnetic tape units, three index accumulators, and a host of peripheral equipment. While the overall design of and prose passages in the resulting book (finished on New Year's Eve in 1960) were mine, Zeps accomplished most of the computational work, thus becoming its junior author. Perhaps not surprisingly, this particular work of ours was greeted with complete silence by all FU media— who, after all, would have been competent to review it?

Over a decade, I faithfully attended international congresses of FU studies, for instance, in Helsinki (1965), Tallinn (1970), and Budapest (1975); in due course, I was even elected to represent the United States on the worldwide body that was responsible for organizing them. At each of these conventions I gave a paper on some traditional topic, most often on a Cheremis theme. However, at the Budapest congress I decided to tackle a seemingly unfamiliar subject: in my presentation I argued that since human beings communicate amongst each other by both verbal and nonverbal means—indeed, according to some scholars (notably John Lotz), most messages by far are transmitted nonverbally—it would be instructive to scrutinize the nonverbal behavior of each extant FU population and to juxtapose this with their corresponding verbal behavior as well as to compare every system with every other. There was of course nothing radical about this proposal, which had been implemented with rich multiple inflections by ancient orators and actors (Hamlet's "Suit the action to the word, the word to the action") and by countless others: for example, Garrick Mallery assiduously explored "the systematic use of gesture speech" among North American Indian tribes in the 1880s; and David Efron, the Argentinian Ph.D. of Franz Boas, famously carried out in the 1930s an exemplary comparison of facial expressions and body movements among Italian and Jewish immigrants in New York City (cf. Sebeok 1991a, 27–32). Notwithstanding a highly respectable pedigree for probes of this sort, the reception for my Budapest overtures was so uncompromisingly frosty that I knew, for me, a change of venue had become henceforth mandatory.

My paramount preoccupation at the Center for Advanced Study started out with a youthfully naive premise. As I have noted elsewhere, I always considered myself a biologist *manqué*—a student who, frustrated by World War II, had missed his true vocation. So, having been told by Ralph Tyler, the Center's director, to spend my time during my residence doing what I liked, I mistakenly imagined that I could, in a single year, "catch up" with developments in the life sciences over the past twenty years. Soon I was so overburdened that I had to strictly confine my readings to a narrow segment of biology. The wedge of the pie I settled on was ethology, the biological study of behavior, which led me straight to a review of the literature on animal communication.

Readings in this domain led me to formulate the following abduction: the attentive, empirically founded, study of communication systems in the other animals will clarify fundamental questions about the evolution of language in hominids. By way of a series of publications since then (periodically collected, e.g., in 1972; Sebeok and Umiker-Sebeok eds. 1980; Sebeok 1990a), I satisfied myself that this hypothesis has been *falsified*. Nonetheless, this literature, supplemented by my own observations of animals in the wild and in captivity, led me, through multifarious fascinating detours and occasional blind alleys, to develop what I regard as my principal contribution to general semiotics, the field which I (and now many others) call biosemiotics (Sebeok and Umiker-Sebeok eds. 1992). That, however, is a convoluted story that would carry us far beyond—in Ernest Hemingway's evocative 1936 attribution to Francis Macomber—my "short happy life."

17

Uralic Studies and English for Hungarians at Indiana University

A Personal View

SEVERAL PARTICIPANTS IN this assembly have asked me, in casual conversations since last Saturday evening, how it came about that Indiana University, located in a rural area on the southern border of midwestern America and with very few original residents of Hungarian extraction, came to be so closely associated with Hungarian affairs of considerable variety, ranging from education to business, from the arts to the sciences, and from high cultural affairs—our School of Music comes to mind—to puerile political posturing.

While I cannot begin to address this question fully this afternoon, I should like to relate just two episodes of this long and convoluted story, in both of which I was deeply and personally involved: the earlier from the third term of President Franklin Delano Roosevelt, i.e., the early 1940s; the later from the second term of Dwight D. Eisenhower, i.e., the late 1950s. I selected these because of their inherent and general interest. Both have to do with language and linguistics, which is my academic specialty.

Before World War II, Hungarian linguistics in America simply did not exist; and in no institution of post-secondary education was the Hungarian language ever taught. Robert A. Hall, Jr.'s highly original *Outline of Hungarian Grammar* was printed by the Linguistic Society of America at the turn of the decade, and Leslie Tihany's *A Modern Hungarian Grammar* was privately published shortly thereafter. At Leonard Bloomfield's request, I reviewed these, as well as John Lotz's *Das Ungarische Sprachsystem*, in the 1942 issues of *Language*.

With the quickening of the war, the situation of American universities grew increasingly precarious. The departure of male faculty members and students, who had been called up for service in large numbers, left our campuses more and more depopulated and in academic disarray. At the same time, as the global nature of the war became evident, the Washington administration real-

This article was originally composed as a speech at the invitation of Mihály Szegedy-Maszák and published in 1991–92 in *Hungarian Studies* 7(1/2), 149–152.

ized that the country simply lacked the most elementary expertise in pertinent foreign areas and languages of the world.

These two seemingly unrelated problems—how to arrest the degradation of university life and how to meet the pressing demands of our commanders in the field—were brilliantly solved in a single stroke by U.S. Army Chief of Staff George C. Marshall. In 1942, Marshall created an Army Specialized Training Program (ASTP), which, on the one hand, quickly repopulated enterprising university campuses, notably this one, and which, on the other hand, provided intensive training in dozens of languages which had never previously been studied on this continent. In addition, Marshall devised and his staff designed a farsighted infrastructure to fuel this voracious language-learning machine with teaching materials. It so happened that I became deeply enmeshed, with a service ranking but in an essentially civilian capacity, with both enterprises: on the supply side as well as at the consuming end.

In 1941, the War Department established a large office in New York City, at 165 Broadway. I was appointed civilian chief of the Hungarian and Finnish desks. It was my primary task to rapidly produce textbooks suitable for intensive Hungarian and Finnish language instruction for military personnel, in addition to several other types of language aids, including sizeable dictionaries. *Spoken Hungarian,* a book of about five hundred pages, supplemented by four sides of audio materials, appeared in 1945, and the comparable *Spoken Finnish* in 1947.

By the fall of 1943, the ASTP became fully operational at this university. At various periods, the program involved about a dozen different languages, including particularly those of Eastern Europe in the broad sense, comprehending also Russian, Finnish, and Turkish. I was originally hired to be in charge of the Hungarian and Finnish groups; eventually, I was made responsible for the entire operation, overseeing a large faculty of linguists and their corps of native speakers, the instructors for area studies, and of course the thousands of officers and enlisted men who were our students. The Hungarian faculty in Bloomington comprised six civilians, plus Army support personnel.

The language materials these students devoured in up to forty-four contact hours per week over a period of from nine to twelve months were normally the product of the New York staff, rushed to us here in mimeographed form practically daily. I myself commuted between my offices and billet in New York and my Bloomington home. (Parenthetically, one of my more entertaining assignments was to locate and hire reliable native speakers from ever more recondite language communities, at various times involving Azerbaijanis, Cheremis, Uzbeks, and the like, in search of whom I occasionally had to undertake hazardous trips overseas and to several prisoner of war camps.)

The vast Indiana University segment of the national ASTP, including particularly its Hungarian component, was in part based, as we were to learn some years afterwards, on Winston Churchill's strategic intent and hope to launch the invasion of Europe via its southern soft "underbelly." In the event, and to their disappointment, most of the Hungarian alumni were sent to Africa or to Italy to monitor radio broadcasts in Hungarian, to digest and interpret printed materials in that language, or to perform other remote intelligence functions. Some of our students joined the Foreign Service after 1945, many went into business, and a few are still pursuing academic careers.

Even before the war ended in 1945, I proposed to Herman B Wells, our visionary and international-minded president, that we immediately commence building, solidly and with an eye to permanence, upon the resources that had serendipitously accumulated here during those years. He strongly supported all such endeavors, which ultimately flowered into an amazing diversity of research, teaching, and publication schemes, including sizeable Departments of Anthropology, Linguistics, and others, plus a global variety of area-and-language programs. It would take a moderate tome to chronicle all of these, so let me briefly dwell only on the Hungarian programs.

Here, credit must go first of all to the Rockefeller Foundation, which committed large resources toward the creation of what in due course became our Department of Uralic and Altaic Studies. A bit later, an allied programmatic activity developed under the direction of my close friend and partner, John Lotz, at Columbia University. Eventually, especially in the early 1950s, the two of us, as well as a growing number of European émigré scholars, were given invaluable moral assistance by the American Council of Learned Societies, which translated into heavy financial provision on the part of the (then) U.S. Office of Education.

By the mid-1950s, I considered Uralic and Altaic studies adequately launched here at Indiana University, and, my attention having turned to other fields of study, I ceded my duties to my colleagues. The rest, as the saying goes, is history—literally so, in contrast with linguistics.

Eleven years then passed. The revolution had run its bloody course in Hungary just as the Eisenhower-Nixon team was being returned to the White House. In December of 1956, Eisenhower set up a high-level commission, headed by his vice president, to deal with the flood of Hungarian refugees by then pouring into Austria, many hoping to enter the United States.

At the outset of 1957, between the fall and the spring semesters, I was summoned to the office of our president, Dr. Wells, who informed me that, at Eisenhower's direct request, Indiana University was being designated to organize an emergency intensive spoken-language training program for those Hungarian refugees who would shortly be heading either for this country or perhaps for other anglophone countries, such as Australia, Canada, or Great Britain. I was that day being relieved of all my normal administrative and teaching duties for the next eight months and ordered to devote my full time and energies toward this goal. Next day, I left to consult with the Nixon team, already at work in Vienna.

The Hungarian refugees whom I interviewed overseas were, by and large, of college age, but not on the whole very well schooled. Practically none of them, as I recall, spoke any second language, save a little Russian. Considering the group's overall educational profile, I decided, on my return to Bloomington a week later, to set up three personnel modules.

The pivotal module was headed by an extremely able Ph.D. candidate of mine in the Department of Linguistics. Elaine Ristimen's duty was to spend her days compiling an English-language training manual aimed specifically at Hungarian learners. Her partner was Victor Hanzely, a Hungarian graduate student of ours, whose duty it became to translate at night into Hungarian the drafts produced by Elaine during the day. Their joint product was typed and mimeographed the following morning, and copies were dispatched to Washington for distribution to all anglophone training centers, worldwide, who requested them. The manual written by this team eventually well exceeded one thousand pages.

A second team was formed to use the same materials in the English for Hungarian classes here at IU. These classes, never exceeding ten individuals, received forty-four hours of language instruction per week for over seven months.

I also set up a third group, responsible for the day-to-day welfare of our Hungarian students, including their accommodations and feeding and their local social life, and also seeing to our complex liaisons with off-campus training centers using our materials. The short-range goal of this program was to enable those Hungarians who wished to do so—as was generally the case—to enter a college of their choice by the fall of 1957. An added duty of the third module thus became channeling the students' entry into the normal higher educational life of this country.

By next August, this project, having fully met its integrative goal, came to an end. All of the Hungarians who had studied English on this campus, at least, were settled in college communities across the nation. I still keep in touch with some of them.

Notes

1. Global Semiotics

1. In his recent book, a Swiss colleague (Mahmoudian 1993, 91) coined as his preferred synonym for the concept of universality this intriguing choice of words: "semiotic omnipotence."

2. The "man-sign analogy" is not, contrary to what many Peirce scholars suppose, unique to him. Cf., for instance, this pronouncement by Hölderlin: "Ein Zeichen sind wir, deutungslos, Schmerzlos sind wir und haben fast die Sprache in der Fremde verloren" (1959, 204).

3. A calumniatory fabrication which I first heard in the 1940 Presidential campaign leveled at the Indiana politician Wendell L. Willkie—who in 1943 formulated a passionate plea for international cooperation in his book *One World*—was "globaloney."

4. As for Stanley Fish's would-be witticism, "Deconstruction is dead in the same way that Freudianism is dead . . . It is everywhere"—well, especially so under the beds of America's hand-me-down literature departments. I am also reminded of a dinner I attended in Paris, in the mid-sixties, with a cheerful Roman Jakobson and a grumpy Lucien Goldmann, who growled at us: "I hate structuralism!" To which Jakobson shot back: "And I hate all '-isms.'"

5. The intent of this sentence is not to question the utility of taxonomy, viz., identifying where semiotics belongs in the architectonic of knowledge. The relatively humble joys of classification are essential prerequisites to analytical investigation and to the understanding of the internal logic of both the sciences (cf. Peirce's non-exhaustive outline classification in *CP* 1.180–283) and the arts (cf. Sebeok 1981c, 210–259) of sign interpretation, but such preoccupations must not be allowed to hinder the pace of the chase proper.

6. Alas, to our loss, Peirce went on to augment his suggestive and intriguing passage thus: "the definition will be worked out more carefully when the method of doing so shall have been considered" (MS 634, 18–20). Further he added, in presumable clarification, that the definition of Sign

> is a delicate affair; since if one excludes from consideration any class of Signs, one will condemn himself to a maimed understanding of them, while to include too much is necessarily to overlook some essential character of the Sign. . . . [A] few remarks may conveniently be appended here. Every Sign represents or is in some sort a substitute for an Object, always regarded as Real and, for the most part rightly so; every Sign is capable of being interpreted through the mind. Must the Object always be other than the Sign? In some sense this diverseness seems quite essential to the idea of acting as a Sign; an Object that merely presents itself represents nothing. (ibid.)

Note that Peirce did not deny that the universe we experience is made up of Objects, but of course all Objects, when (re)cognized, must be Signs: "Every sign stands for an object independent of itself; but it can only be a sign of that object in so far as that object is itself of the nature of a sign" (*CP* 1.284; cf. Sebeok 1991b, 17–18). Note further that Peirce's "Sign" seems to roughly correspond here, as elsewhere, to what some other scholars call *signans*, and his "Object" to *signatum* (or translations thereof).

7. Inorganic artifacts that imply life—such as automata, robots, computers, or the like—may undergo semiosis as well. Herein lies the deep meaning of the idiom "ghost in the machine." In William Gibson's cyberpunk fiction, "semiotic ghosts" are a series of failed images, like "the personal anti-gravity belt," or "the bubble-base on the moon," or "the atomic-powered razor" (introduced in his 1981 story, "The Gernsback continuum"). By 1986, in Bruce Sterling's *Mirrorshades*, "semiotic ghosts" have become "semiotic phantoms, bits of deep cultural imagery that have split off and taken on a life of their own" (Slusser and Shippey 1992, 211).

8. The first biosphere known to humans is the earth. There is no evidence for the existence of any other; it provisionally follows that semiosic processes are confined solely to our own planet. Here, the domain of the inanimate is routinely subdivided into three "spheres," corresponding to the three states of matter (at low temperatures or energies, or under ordinary terrestrial conditions). Together these constitute the interactive environmental matrix for the biosphere: (1) the solid lithosphere; (2) the liquid hydrosphere; and (3) the gaseous atmosphere (plasma, a fourth state of matter, is found mainly in interstellar space, under laboratory conditions, or in such industrial applications as fluorescent lamps). However, it has recently been reconfirmed (cf. Sebeok 1991b, 111, n. 2) that our planet has a hidden biosphere extending many more kilometers down into the earth than previously thought. This subterranean biomass—existing under conditions of extreme temperature and pressure—may well exceed that on the surface and may indeed have been the birthplace of life. It is not yet known how deep this biomass may lie and how much there is. However, semiosis in the lowest reaches of the biosphere, in hot springs, volcanoes, ocean vents, and oil reservoirs, is sure to be quite different from the processes we are accustomed to on the surface.

9. This distinction is admittedly blurred at the interface (Sebeok 1988b, 64; Margulis in Barlow 1992, 236–238).

10. Prokaryotes (bacteria) are organisms composed of cells with no nucleus. All the other life forms (including plants, animals, fungi, and protoctists) are eukaryotes; their cells have nuclei.

11. Admittedly, the terminological glut is unfortunate but hard to do without.

12. This refers to Jakob von Uexküll's contrapuntal notion, sometimes called "matching" (1982, 65–73). It later became dogma in ethology and beyond. Thure von Uexküll cited several examples in his manuscript, "Models and methods in biosemiotics" (delivered at a conference I attended in Glotterbad on June 8, 1990). One example: "Where there is a mouth, there is also food"; or conversely: "Without a mouth, there can be no food." In an endo-semiotic domain, immunology, the mutual constitution of antigen and antibody is an important case of point/counterpoint (F. Jacquemart and A. Coutinho in Sercarz et al. eds. 1988, 178).

13. Human body cells apparently rely in part on a startlingly simple but versatile chemical, nitric oxide (NO), to act as a powerful sign-vehicle in a "pantheon of messenger molecules," tying neuroscience, physiology, and immunology together in a single semiotic model by implicating it in an array of different activities, "from communication to defense to regulation" (Culotta and Koshland 1992). The so-called hedgehog genes belong to another newly identified class of "semiotic molecules," invigorating sign-vehicles which produce morphogens ("structure makers") of great importance for vertebrate development, enabling the fertilized egg to effloresce into a complete animal.

14. In considering the countless varieties of human semiosis, it is well to be aware of this limit, as was emphasized not long ago by an astute analyst of preliterate or marginally literate jurisprudential expression: such folk "express their legal meanings in myriad permutations of sound, gesture, touch, and savor. . . . Because this practice enables legal meaning

to be distributed among different media instead of being concentrated in a single channel, we must take care to consider the totality of verbal and nonverbal information in any given performative legal transaction" (Hibbitts 1992, 955).

15. In Jakob von Uexküll's schema, Subject and Object are dovetailed into a systematic whole, a relation which he pictured in a diagrammatic "functional cycle" (1982, 32, 84; 1992, 324); after all, Subject and Object alike (as Short 1994, 247 re-emphasized) depend upon their mutual opposition. This "systematic whole" is the proper arena for semiosis, or signs in action, in all animals. Chomsky's notion (1980, 188) of a system of grammatical rules as a kind of interactive "mental organ" has its general analogue in semiotics, where nonverbal and verbal signs or systems of signs operate as quasi-filters linking "the reality outside" to "the mind inside," the two of course functioning as one system bound in solidarity. "Mind" is equivalent to an ensemble of neurons in action (viz., semiosis) which are, in turn and as remarked above, composed of a community of reciprocally busy bacteria. It is not too fanciful, in my judgment, to claim that signs perform, in another body-space, in the manner of an organ like the gill in crustaceans (including the land isopods) or fish. A gill functions as a special mediating surface which is exposed toward an (as a rule) aquatic animal's environment on the "outside," and toward its circulatory system on the "inside." The gill surface, which must be kept wet, allows oxygen dissolved in water to pass from the outside to the inside. Later vertebrates, including ourselves, must likewise transfer oxygen into our circulatory system via wet surfaces—the lungs—but these are "consigned," for safety, deep inside our bodies.

16. The large literature, old and recent, on allegedly language-inculcated apes (cf. Wallman 1992) and other animals is based on either self-deception or outright fraud. The scientific status of the currently popular, cruelly irresponsible efforts at "facilitated communication" with autistics is likewise nil. The latter is a phenomenon akin to the movement of a Ouija board, table tipping, and automatic writing, and the magic trick known as "muscle reading" (e.g., Gardner 1957, 109).

3. Biosemiotics

1. For the contrast between Y. M. Lotman's anthropological usage and V. I. Vernadsky's global usage, see chapter 14 below.

2. For this important distinction—which is particularly pertinent to biosemiotics—between "domain" and "field," see chapter 15 below or Csikszentmihalyi 1996.

3. Ironically, Klopfer and Hailman wrote of Jakob's earliest classic work, *Umwelt und Innenwelt der Tiere* (1909, 2d ed. 1920), that it has "had relatively little effect on animal behavior studies compared with the great originality of its content" (1967, 126). One reason for this seems to have been that it was far ahead of its time; or, in Csikszentmihalyi's parlance, that there was no field competent in the domain to take control over it: "There are several ways that domains and fields can affect each other. Sometimes domains determine to a large extent what the field can or cannot do . . . No matter how much a group of scientists would like their pet theory accepted, it won't be if it runs against the previously accumulated consensus" (1996, 44).

4. That research was in large part conducted at the Netherlands Institute for Advanced Study, where I was a fellow during 1973–74.

5. See again Csikszentmihalyi (1996). Note my continued emphasis on the availability of a responsive field, which was by no means at hand in 1934, when Bühler first recognized the semiotic character of the *Umweltlehre*, "welcher von vornherein in seiner Grundbegriffen 'Merkzeichen' und 'Wirkzeichen' sematologisch orientiert ist" (1965, 27).

6. Those attending the Glottertal conferences included Swiss, Danes (e.g., Hoffmeyer), Estonians (e.g., Kull), and me, besides many Germans. A prominent German semiotician

whom I remember being there on each occasion was Martin Krampen, who substantiated phytosemiotics, i.e., the semiotics of plants, putting this then novel domain on an equal footing with other recognized branches of biosemiotics (1981, 187; see discussion in chapter 2 above). A large wind-up gathering in this series was organized in the 1990s by Hoffmeyer; this took place in Denmark, with an expanded attendance on the part of Scandinavian semioticians as well as natural scientists. More recently, biosemiotics get-togethers (enumerating here only those which I myself was asked to participate in, several repeatedly) were scheduled in Berkeley, Denver, Dresden, Gaithersburg, Imatra, Guadalajara, Las Cruces, São Paulo, Tartu, and Toronto.

7. At the risk of being overcome by terminological surfeit (or vertigo), I can offer the following non-exhaustive rundown—with a basic reference or two—of the currently labeled component branches of biosemiotics that I am aware of: protosemiotics ("the basic feature of the whole biological organization [protein synthesis, metabolism, hormone activity, transmission of nervous impulses, and so on]," cf. Prodi in Sercarz et al. eds. 1988, 55); microsemiotics (in prokaryotes, cf. Sonea 1988, 1990, 1995); cytosemiotics (in cells, renamed microsemiotics by Yates 1997); endosemiotics (in the *milieu intérieur,* cf. Th. von Uexküll et al. 1993); phytosemiotics (plants, cf. Krampen 1981, 1997); zoosemiotics (speechless animals, cf. Sebeok 1972, 1990a); mycosemiosis (fungi, cf. Kraepelin 1997); and cybersemiotics (androids, robotics, cyborgs, sensor and muscle augmentation, prostheses [eye-glasses, hearing aids, dentures, artificial limbs, mirrors, etc., cf. Eco 1986, 220–222], cf. chapter 1 above). Anthroposemiotics (speechifying animals) is usually excluded. Exosemiotics has been used in two different senses: as the opposite of endosemiotics, or in passing reference to the sign behavior of putative extraterrestrial creatures.

8. A reminder: one of the central components of creativity is the field, "which includes all the individuals who act as gatekeepers to the domain. It is their job to decide whether a new idea or product should be included in the domain." Publishers and journal editors figure prominently among the "field of experts" who recognize and validate innovation, as are academic administrators, officers of public and private sources of financial support, or, to put it briefly, persons with control over access to critical resources (cf. Csikszentmihalyi 1996, 28, 6).

9. Tomio Tada's definition of immunosemiotics is: "the study of the general principles underlying the structure of sign systems perceived by different cells of the immune machinery," according to which "restrictions in partner cell interactions must exist as part of an intercellular semiotic system" (in Sercarz et al. eds. 1988, vii).

10. Two among these subjects were my former teachers. To gain a still more rounded historical perspective of this cardinal domain of learning, we hope to arrange for similar probes of writings by other such respected figures, for instance, Susanne Langer.

11. For glimpses of the relation of semiotics and biosemiotics, see Th. von Uexküll 1998, 2189–90.

12. There is no evidence that these three masters of the sign were aware of one another. The meandering, diffuse arguments at June 1999's twin von Uexküll-related meetings (Tartu and Imatra) over matters of basic terminology underline these points. There were sharp debates about the meaning even of such a pivotal term as *Umwelt* and its correct rendering into English, ranging from such approximations as "perceptual universe," "self-world," and "phenomenal world," to such absurdities as "environment" (but see Immelman and Beer eds. 1989, 88) and "niche." Despite the fact that the closest English equivalent is manifestly "model," the only palpable group consensus reached was the unhelpful surrender that the German word should be retained in English. Nevertheless, seemingly recondite concerns about technical vocabulary, leading toward a standardized symbol system, tend to reinforce the unity of a field like biosemiotics.

13. On nitric oxide, that "pantheon of messenger molecules," and so-called "hedgehog genes," cf. chapter 1, n. 13 above.

5. Signs, Bridges, Origins

1. Beside the use of *Web* to designate the user interface known as the *World Wide Web*, there is the metaphor *Internet*, or simply *the Net*, for a system designed originally for data exchange between small local networks. (The Web is sometimes described as the Internet with pictures.) Then there are variations on the metaphor *highway*, as in "data highway," or "infohighway," or "global digital highway," each roughly equivalent to "global information infrastructures," and of course *roads*. Kindred popular motifs include *landscape, maps,* and the like. A separate study on the prevalence of figures of speech and, broadly speaking, their uses in semiotics cries out to be written (cf. Keller 1995).

2. As captured in a dramatic photograph reproduced in Wilson 1971, 62. Although ants do not actually construct "bridges" to cross obstacles, some bacteria do transfer, along an extruded bridge called F pilus, genetic material (plasmids) communicating packages of information emitted by a donor cell to a recipient cell.

3. Eschewing definition in the enabling legislation that created the National Endowment for the Humanities in 1965, the United States Congress stated:

> The term "humanities" includes, but is not limited to, the study and interpretation of the following: language, both modern and classical; linguistics; literature; history; jurisprudence; philosophy; archeology; comparative religion; ethics; the history, criticism, and theory of the arts; those aspects of the social sciences which have humanistic content and employ humanistic methods; and the study and application of the humanities to the human environment with particular attention to reflecting our diverse heritage, traditions, and history and to the relevance of the humanities to the current conditions of national life. (National Foundation on the Arts and Humanities Act of 1965, Sec. 3[a])

Evidently, semiotics was licensed to receive the support that it has enjoyed over the past thirty years by virtue of the clause "but is not limited to." I can claim some credit for having persuaded the first (1966–70) chairman of the Endowment, Barnaby Keeney (a medieval historian, d. 1980), in the course of a petrifying flight the two of us shared in a tiny plane from Washington to Princeton, to look with favor on semiotics (if we survived our mercifully brief journey) and to pass this tradition on to most of his successors.

Sometimes lobbyists for the NEH and others use this puny visual pun-like slogan (which looks more like a misspelling): "'Humanities' means 'Human Ties.'"

See also, defying summation, Peirce's "Outline Classification of the Sciences" (*CP* 1.180–202) and his detailed modifications thereto (*CP* 1.203–283). Interactions between "natural science" and "social science" in general, with some clarification of these expressions, is discussed by I. B. Cohen (1994); see especially his terminological note (189–196).

4. Locke knew perfectly well that the antithesis of *Humanitas* was never *Scientia* but *Divinitas*. Although the antagonistic confrontation of the humanities and the sciences, based on an etymological perversion, can be ascribed to Vico (among others), it became commonplace by the middle of the nineteenth century. "Divinity," loosely speaking, then and thereafter found a home among the humanities.

5. Snow also cautioned in his 1959 Rede Lecture (wrongly, as it turned out) that, "if we don't do it, the Communist countries will in time" (53).

6. "Never underestimate the power of anecdotes; they can be more profound, more creative, than generalizations" (Rosen 1995, 52).

7. Among these were Gregory Bateson, Rudolf Carnap, Yuen Ren Chao, Karl Deutsch, Heinz von Förster, Warren S. McCulloch, Margaret Mead, I. A. Richards, Jurgen Ruesch, Claude E. Shannon, Norbert Wiener, and numerous others.

8. Autopoiesis is defined as "the imperative set of continuing energetic biological processes . . . by which all living beings maintain themselves" (Margulis and Sagan 1986, 283; cf. Margulis 1993, passim, and Maturana and Varela 1992, passim). Briefly put: living systems create themselves. Code duality, as used in various works by Emmeche and Hoffmeyer concerning the construction of body cells and organism, refers to the transmutation of the digital genetic code of DNA into an analogue code.

9. "Semiophysics is concerned in the first place with the seeking out of significant forms; it aims to build up a general theory of intelligibility" (Thom 1990, vii). The term appears to have been coined by Jean Petitot in 1985. Merrell, like myself, was strongly impressed by Wheeler; see especially Merrell 1995, xiv, chs. 9, 10, and 1996, passim; and Sebeok 1991a, 48, 135; 1991b, 21, 84, 143, 153.

10. Prodi applied his neologism *protosemiotics* in a phylogenetic sense. This must of course be distinguished from the study of *protosigns*, as Trevarthen calls the signs of *infant semiotics* in ontogenetic perspective (1990, 716, 689).

11. On March 30, 1995, I conducted a seminar at the Institute for Advanced Study (Collegium Budapest) that dealt largely with such conundrums as the foregoing. I want to thank my colleagues at the Institute, particularly the members of the Theoretical Evolutionary Biology group working with Eörs Szathmáry, and the audience at large, for valuable input during the discussion that followed. Some of this is reflected in my subsequent work, including the second section of this chapter. Brief remarks about tool use and language in *Homo*, a relationship Maynard Smith and Szathmáry (1995, 293) claim was suggested by P. M. Greenfield in 1991, may be appropriate at this point. In fact, I made the same association in a talk I gave in Montreal in December 1964, subsequently published as Sebeok 1967, 363–369 (reprinted in Sebeok 1972, 84–92; see also Bickerton 1990, 138–140). Paleoanthropologists are currently focusing on a set of dates for tool-making 2.6 million years ago; it is not yet clear whether these remarkably early stone tools, from the desiccated fossil fields of Ethiopia, were forged by a variety of *Homo*—presumably *habilis*—or by hominid australopithecine ancestors. The distinction is an important one for students of initial conditions of human (and thus language) origins especially because the period between three and two million years ago is still rather opaque.

12. In this connection, Hoffmeyer (1995b, 372) called my attention to the following passage in a paper by Swenson and Turvey (1991): "the world is in the order production business, including the business of producing living things and their perception and action capacities, because order produces entropy faster than disorder."

A *signifex* is any organism performing semiosis. This useful locution—redundant in the framework that I advocate, because every organism, *ipso facto* and whether *in esse* or *in posse*, does perform semiosis—appears to have been coined by Watt (1993, 428), presumably to steer clear of the equivocality of *signifier*, which more commonly means (as used for instance by Morris) to act as a sign in a process of semiosis or (as in the Saussurean tradition) a sign-emitter, intended to translate the Latin *signans* or French *signifiant*.

13. Jakob von Uexküll's *Umweltlehre*, put forward as a theory and technique for the biological analysis of species-specific modeling of the universe, in fact constitutes this century's most original, coherent, fecund, and far-reaching theory of signs (1973). The semiotic implications, distorted and misconstrued for nearly half a century, were elucidated in modern terms and much extended by his elder son Thure in various publications; see especially 1980; also 1982a, 1987; cf. Sebeok 1989e, 187–207).

The term *communication*, as used here, specifies one of the three forms of semiosis, "the only sign process in which emitter and receiver share the semiotic tasks," namely, by informing one another about the interpretant, or the code, which attaches to the emitted signs the meaning "intended" by the source (Th. von Uexküll 1997; Th. von Uexküll et al. 1993, 48). George Herbert Mead, in the early 1930s, called this same process "intelligent gestures" (Sebeok 1989e, 142). More generally, see Sebeok 1991f, 22–35.

It is worth recalling that many speech communities have no native equivalent to our Latin-derived *communication,* but only borrowings (Basque *komunikazio*) or calques (Hungarian *közlés,* Finnish *tiedonanto*), etc.

Let me record in passing that I concur with Maturana and Varela's conclusion that "The Metaphor of the Tube for Communication . . . is basically false," for the very reasons that they give, and their conclusion that, biologically, communicating "is a very different matter from 'transmitting information'" (1992, 196). However, this fallacy is still widely held, even by biologists as perspicacious as Maynard Smith, as for example in his statement: "A meme is an idea that can lodge in a person's mind, and can be transmitted, in print or by word of mouth, to other minds . . . What is peculiar about humans is that they can hold ideas in their heads, and transmit them to others . . . " (1995, 47).

14. Actually, by the expression "Primary Modeling System" the Soviet scholars meant language. Their proposal was emended by me in a 1987 study titled "In What Sense Is Language a 'Primary Modeling System'?" (Sebeok 1991f, 49–58), where I argued that language is a temporally and hierarchically secondary superstructure over humanity's inborn stock of nonverbal semiosic devices. What the Soviet colleagues called the "Secondary Modeling System" (roughly: culture) thus necessarily becomes a tertiary superstructure over both underlying strata.

15. By "zealous revival," I refer mainly to the foundation a decade or so ago of the Language Origins Society and its many publications, one recent item being Wind et al. (1994). The "ancient obsession" becomes apparent, *inter alia,* from browsing through Gessinger and Rahden's twin tomes (1989), running to 1,263 pages; see also Hewes 1975, with over eleven thousand entries.

The surest, most sophisticated linguist's guide to the subject thus far remains Bickerton's; his account of the "Origins of Representational Systems" (1990, 75–104) is in good conformity with the *Umweltlehre,* although he seems to be unaware either of the work of the von Uexkülls or the sprawling literature engendered by the innovatory thrust of their writings, especially in recent years. Kenneth Craik's influence, however, does make itself strongly felt (cf. 1990, x). Craik was a singular Cambridge don, a crypto-semiotician who independently invented a version of the Umwelt theory in the late 1930s, and who thought that "the organism carries a 'small-scale model' of external reality and of its own possible actions within its head" (see Sebeok 1991e, 104–105).

Biologists Szathmáry and Maynard Smith wrestle with the issue of the emergence of language, though arguing from sources of uneven reliability, for some thirty pages (1995, ch. 17; see also Maynard Smith and Szathmáry 1995), only to head, along with everyone else, towards a black hole; so does de Duve, blithely passing over elementary distinctions between apples, oranges, and bananas when he leaps from "the tantalizing question [of] the origin and evolution of language" to the "ability to speak and, with it, the power to communicate" (1995, 234).

A number of talks by fellows and guest speakers (including, serendipitously, me) were devoted, in full or in part, to this topic during the 1994–95 session of the Institute for Advanced Study (Collegium Budapest); versions of these were published under the editorship of Jürgen Trabant (1996). For some of my own previous narratives, see, e.g., Sebeok 1986a, 10–16; 1991f, 83–96.

16. The senior author is modestly identified on the jacket as "one of the world's leading

ape-language [*sic*] researchers," while her co-author is a journalist. For an informed critical discussion, not mentioned by the foregoing, of "Pursuing the Roots of Language" and related matters, see Wallman 1992, 113–115 and passim. Pinker (identified on *his* book's jacket as "one of the world's leading scientists of language and the mind") thinks that, within the field of psychology, "most of the ambitious claims about chimpanzee language are a thing of the past," but this sanguine sentence was written before the appearance of the book about Kanzi, whose "language [*sic*] abilities, if one is being charitable," Pinker grants, "are above those of his common cousins by a just-noticeable difference, but no more" (1994, 341). Incidentally, the widespread allegation that certain apes have been taught ASL is another fairy tale.

6. What Do We Know about Signifying Behavior in the Domestic Cat *(Felis catus)?*

1. By (as it were) "exercising indexicality" (Sebeok 1991f, ch. 13), a cat, by virtue of being assigned a personal name (Sebeok 1981b), can be dragged, if only to a degree, through the periphery of and into our Umwelt. Once named, we tend to redefine our cat as "tame," in recognition of the fact that its flight reaction from man has been appreciably reduced or perhaps even eliminated—an indispensable precondition for both training and domestication (Sebeok 1988a, 70). Thanks for assorted assistance are due to Paul Bouissac and Martin Gardner.

2. The ethologist Smith, writing in the first volume of *Semiotica*, justly observed that, with respect to the evolution of communication in animals, "All activities are potentially informative" (1969, 358). In his standard book published eight years later, he initially used the wording "communicative behavior" (1977, 563), upgrading, in fact, a kindred expression to the title, *The Behavior of Communicating*. Alas, however, he then (ch. 6) arbitrarily and confusingly divided messages into "Behavioral and Nonbehavioral." The psychologist Paul Ekman repeatedly rejected the expression "nonverbal behavior" as a "terrible term," but adds he knows "no better phrase" for his purposes (e.g., in Sebeok and Rosenthal eds. 1981, 270, n.). The social anthropologist Willis' suggestively multivalent titular word play, *Signifying Animals*, is to a degree disambiguated by his subtitle, *Human Meaning in the Natural World;* see especially his interesting elaboration of J. von Uexküll's *Umweltlehre* in this context (1990, 11–12). The unfortunate tautology "semiotic behavior," some of its extensions, and the like, abound in and mar a recently edited text by Gibson and Ingold (1993, 39, 344, 401–403, 437, 481).

3. Several celebrated exceptions include Rudyard Kipling's "cat that walked by himself" (cf. West 1991, 180); Baum's Glass Cat, that was so transparent "that you could see through it as through a window" (cf. Baum 1981, 41); and Edwin Schrödinger's long suffering 50 percent alive and 50 percent dead quantum physical cat (cf. Gribbin 1984, and now see especially Kanitscheider 1992, 41–51). Notwithstanding the metaphorical status of these cats, each is highly pertinent to our semiotic assessment of reality—but that's another *Just So Story* (some aspects of which Merrell 1991 recently explored).

4. These examples are mine.

5. Marcel Proust wrote: "A real person, however deeply we may sympathize with him, is . . . perceived through our senses; that is, he remains opaque, offers a dead weight that our imagination cannot lift" (cf. Sebeok 1991e, 34). And Aldous Huxley, writing apropos his she-cat who, while her expressive black tail lashes the air in a tragical gesture of despair goes about mewing Debussy's "Je ne suis pas heureuse ici," remarks: " . . . in spite of language, in spite of intelligence and intuition and sympathy, one can never really communicate anything to anybody. The essential substance of every thought and feeling remains incommuni-

cable, locked up in the impenetrable strong-room of the individual soul and body. [Thus his cat's] life is a sentence of perpetual solitary confinement" (1959, 81).

6. Or whether I myself dream. This is the well-known conundrum of the Chinese Taoist Chuang Tzu, of the third century B.C., who wrote, "Once upon a time, I, Chuang Tzu dreamed I was a butterfly flying happily here and there . . . suddenly I woke up and I was indeed Chuang Tzu. Did Chuang Tzu dream he was a butterfly, or did the butterfly dream he was Chuang Tzu?" Perhaps more to the point is that the REM sleep (with presumptive dreaming and theta-rhythm) which is known to occur in all mammals (cats included) is not identical with the REM sleep (with presumptive dreaming but minus the theta-rhythm) which is known to occur in all primates (us included).

7. For this reason alone, the title of Ferruccio Rossi-Landi's posthumous book, *Between Signs and Non-Signs* (1992), contains a solecism.

8. In the Peircean universe, every cat is *eo ipso* a sign, but this becomes most conspicuous in the world of the theater, where, as Veltrusky once put it, all that is on the stage is a sign (1940, 154). See, for example, Harold Pinter's short comedy of menace, *The Collection* (1962), in which an actress is expected to hold a cat through much of the play, or the Roger O. Hirson and Stephen Schwartz musical, *Pippin* (which opened on Broadway in 1972), where a cat has a perilously amusing if minuscule supporting role in act 2. This passive cat, which exhibits no overtly "trained comportment" at all (it is in fact intended in the story to function, of all things, as a surrogate for a dead duck), is of course behaviorally unpredictable, thus functioning in this musical as a pure token representamen; should the cat unexpectedly become active, i.e., "naturally (mis)behave" onstage, its conduct would at worst enhance hilarity. The prevalence of iconic cats on film merits a separate study; one memorable example is the opening sequence of Hitchcock's *To Catch a Thief* (1955), with shots of a cat stalking across rooftops, a metaphor foretokening the narrative's "cat-burglar" theme.

9. Disconcertingly, there are two Mr. Woods involved in Darwin's book. The animal engraver was very likely Thomas Waterman Wood (1823–1903), whose monogram signature consists of an intertwined T, W & W (with the last name sometimes spelled out). The other Mr. Wood, who appears as "Wood, J." in the index, seems (as Darwin refers to his knowledge of anatomy and his patients) to have been a surgeon. He was probably John Wood (1825–91).

10. For one phonetic description of the purr, but no speculation about its putative function, see Moelk 1944, 188–189.

11. There is a substantial if controversial literature on practically every aspect of the history, taming, and domestication of the cat. There is much uncertainty, for instance, about their domestication: some hold that they domesticated themselves, others, Serpell among them, that they were domesticated by design of the Egyptians to exploit their adroitness in hunting. Most recently, see James A. Serpell's brief but well-documented narrative in Turner and Bateson eds. 1988 (151–158).

12. On what little is known about hearing in cats, see, inter alia, Fox 1974, 49–51, Beadle 1977, 49–52, or Milani 1987, 96–102; these contain essentially the same information. The speculations of Morris (1987, 6–13) on, for instance, the reactions of cats to music, are characteristically amusing.

13. Huxley's elegant yet little-known non-technical account of semiosis in the acoustic modality in Animalia—of the uses of animal sounds, the methods and evolution of sound-production, and the sounds of mammals (on cats, see Huxley and Koch 1964, 50–51)—is among both the most comprehensible and the most comprehensive in the vast literature on this subject. For details, see Busnel 1963.

14. Cats endeavor to stalk their prey in silence, of course, but their bird-loving masters "bell the cat" to forestall such a stealthy approach.

15. Haskins' experiments demonstrated "that kittens produce cries with different physi-

cal characteristics depending on their age and the stimulus condition" (1979, 734). He thinks that "kitten cries may contain information that elicits particular types of maternal behaviour," but this needs to be confirmed (see also Haskins 1977).

16. Cf. Riffaterre's comment with respect to his similar but predominantly literary notion of hypersigns: "It is the reader who puts together and builds into a system a number of signs that are discrete . . . and that can be analyzed separately by the semiotician. These signs, however, have common elements thanks to which they lead to an interpretation that could not be arrived at from the same signs if they were kept separate" (1987, 5).

17. Chiefly Max Wertheimer 1922; but see now the critical refinements introduced by catastrophe theorist and semiotician René Thom (1990, 6, and passim).

18. *Seme* has been variously promoted by Continental semioticians such as Eric Buyssens, Luis J. Prieto, Louis Hjelmslev, Algirdas J. Greimas, and discussed, albeit with due caution, by Eco; although Sydney Lamb's American usage is substantially discrepant, this has also not gained any favor. See further Henry G. Schogt's thorough lemma in Sebeok ed. 1994 (2:879–884).

19. Notwithstanding that Krall's book is chiefly about horses, he has quite a lot to say about great apes, dogs, elephants, seals, walruses, as well as miscellaneous birds, but he mentions "'sprechende' Katzen" only in passing, eccentrically yoked to talking oxen and deer (1912, 210).

20. The potentially trainable and docile (but in many ways uncatlike) cheetah, which accompanied man on hunts in antiquity and is sometimes used as a household pet even today, belongs to a third genus, *Acinonyx*, of which it constitutes the sole species, *jubatus*. Although readily amenable to training for sport, cheetahs have not appeared in the circus to my knowledge.

21. Incidentally, in this same encyclopedia, the authors make the preposterous claim that animal "languages," i.e., zoosemiograms, number about six hundred (e.g., Greimas and Courtès 1982, 376). In fact, in the phylum Chordata alone—to which the genus *Felis* belongs—there are at least forty-five thousand known species and hence no fewer corresponding systems of communication.

22. Save in fiction, as for example in Ira Levin's 1991 novel *Sliver* (recently turned into a movie).

23. This was held every summer from about 1123 to 1855, becoming, in the seventeenth century, the entertainment center of London during the three-day session. There were always numerous booths, in some of which animal acts were performed.

24. Martin Gardner (personal communication) tells me that cats, in fact, are very obedient if you give them the right sort of command, such as "Come here or not!"

9. Intersemiotic Transmutations

1. John Lotz, then at the University of Stockholm, told me this joke in July 1947, supposedly to illustrate the difference between the Saussurean "signifier" and "signified."

2. Jessica A. Sebeok, then at Brasenose College, University of Oxford, told and demonstrated this and the two following jokes in November 1998.

3. Professor D. N. Rudall, of the University of Chicago, recounted this joke to me in August 1999.

10. "Tell Me, Where Is Fancy Bred?"

1. *Innenwelt* is a structure composed of cell and organ "subjects" and the texture of signs connecting them. By "subject," the point of reference for meaning *(Bedeutung),* von

Uexküll referred to the core of an *Umwelt,* a model or set of signs interpreted according to a species-specific code.

11. The Cognitive Self and the Virtual Self

1. The foregoing is not to imply the scientific adequacy of graphology, which, "from an objective and dispassionate evaluation," according to Furnham's critical conclusion, "is quite simply invalid" (1988, 69).

2. The phrase "nature semiotics" is used by Kergosien (in Sebeok and Umiker-Sebeok eds. 1992, 145–170) in a similar, but not identical, sense to Prodi's "natural semiotics."

The book edited by Sercarz et al. (1988) contains the contributions from an unprecedented workshop on the semiotics of cellular communication in the immune system. This meeting took place in September 1986, near Lucca, Italy. Professor Sercarz, of UCLA, was kind enough to invite me to be among the semioticians from Italy (Eco, Prodi, Violi) and Germany (Thure von Uexküll) who did participate. I keenly regret my inability to have joined them, owing to a prior commitment to the World Archaeological Congress being held in Southampton that same week (see Ingold ed. 1988, 63–76).

3. The term *Umwelt,* which I prefer to render in English as "model [of 'reality']," corresponds, in the human context, to Shakespeare's celebrated locution, "[man's] glassy essence" (*Measure for Measure,* act 2, scene 2). The tag was garnered and fascinatingly applied to man's nature by Peirce—for instance, in his Lowell Lecture of 1866—and then was featured in the title of Singer's astute book-length meditations on this theme (1984). However, Singer did not make the connection with the concept of a subjective Umwelt, or semiotic "bubble," for he knew of its von Uexküll-Hedigerian bio-psychological roots only from our conversations, viz., by hearsay.

In other directions, Hediger's ideas about various types of "distance" in the world of animals, came, after the mid-1960s, to provide a rationale for a semio-anthropological inquiry known as proxemics, launched by Edward T. Hall (e.g., Watson 1974, 317, 340). They also strongly influenced, although this is seldom properly credited, zoosemiotic investigations everywhere.

4. The indexical character of this sort of relationship is interestingly analyzed by Thom (1983, 267–269), showing that even a false index can have semiotic value for an organism, as in Pavlov's well-known conditioning experiments.

5. Both the "real" and fictive literature of VR and related subjects has become very large and sprawling. For two recent anthologies favoring the "real," see Gray 1995 and Markley 1996. I found the measured contribution of Katherine Hayles, "Boundary Disputes: Homeostasis, Reflexivity, and the Foundations of Cybernetics," on pp. 11–37 in the latter collection, typically useful, although several other pivotal sources should expand her account, some of them adduced in my own survey (1991a, 68ff.) For some technological aspects, see also Schroeder 1996.

6. Rue's definition of self-deception (1994, 88) in his otherwise comprehensive guide to deception in nature and human societies is so abstract and schematic as to be bootless.

12. Some Reflections on Vico in Semiotics

1. For further particulars on Cassirer, who is currently undergoing a kind of mini-revival in the United States as well as in western Europe, see Krois's recent splendid book (1987). As to Cassirer's brand of semiotics, see Verene's authoritative lemma (1994). The secondary sources about Cassirer are staggering in quantity, as the nearly five-hundred-page annotated bibliography by Eggers and Mayer (1988) testifies. An edition of Cassirer's com-

plete works, including his many unpublished remarks on semiotic topics, is in preparation under Krois's direction.

14. The Music of the Spheres

1. This identification notwithstanding, his term is now being bandied about in various venues, evocatively enough but in suspiciously adulterated senses. One recent resourceful commercial illustration of this is the advertisement under the cover title *Semiosfera*—"una nuova collana semiotica di testi semiotici"—for a new series launched in 1998, with seven initial volumes, under the co-editorship of Gian Paolo Caprettini and Guido Ferraro, by the Roman publishing house Meltemi.

2. It is doubtful whether White had read the works of Cassirer, such as his *Essay on Man* (1944), where similar notions on culture-bound symbolism are plentiful. Note in passing that chapter 2 of this work, titled "A Clue to the Nature of Man: The Symbol," is largely devoted to the principles of Jakob von Uexküll, about which Cassirer remarks: "Between the receptor system and the effector system, which are to be found in all animal species, we find in man a third link which we may describe as the *symbolic system*" (ibid., 24). It is this mediating domain which Cassirer, like White a few years before, dubbed "the world of human culture" (ibid., 35), and which Lotman came to rename, much later still, the "semiosphere."

As semioticians we should also take note of the fact that Charles Morris, who knew the works of Cassirer but evidently not those of White, averred just two years later "that culture is largely a sign configuration" (1946, 207).

Forty years or so after these innovative views of White, Cassirer, and Morris, Mary Foster undertook a state-of-the-art survey of "Symbolism: The Foundation of Culture," a formulation which is now widely taken for granted in and on the margins of anthropology, insisting, for example, that "the whole of culture is organized by a single, coherent semiotic principle" (1994, 368). Sadly, neither the ideas of Cassirer nor of the trailblazing American anthropological (viz., semiotic) theorist, let alone of the originator of the "semiosphere," are acknowledged in Foster's piece. Notwithstanding this sort of neglect, White's demarcation of culture is nowadays commonly taken "to be the most important fundamental definition ever offered," for instance in the view of the late Roy Rappaport (1999, 464, n. 5).

3. The word *sphere* derives from the Greek word for ball. Ancient astronomers conceived the visible vault of heaven as the "celestial sphere," consisting of concentric hollow globes, in which the "music of the spheres" was sounded. The various "spheres" recounted in this article—and additional ones that might have been touched upon, such as *barysphere, stratosphere, troposphere, mesosphere,* etc.—had each best be pictured as geometrical entities of quasi-fractional dimensions, orbicular, although far from perfectly round, in shape.

4. According to Vernadsky (1945, 7, 10, n. 1), the concept of *biosphere,* that is, "area of life," was introduced into biology by Lamarck in 1802.

5. The notion of biosphere is also indirectly linked to the "Gaia hypothesis" that Earth, "including both its biotic and abiotic components, functions as a single self-regulating system, in which the growth and activities of living organisms in response to the environment regulate the reactive gas composition, acidity-alkalinity and temperature, bringing about changes that make the Earth continuously habitable" (Margulis and Sagan 1997b, 350; cf. Guerrero and Margulis 1998, 36).

6. Inevitably, Bakhtin too—on "dialogic structure" (1990, 164) or "the folklore carnival tradition" (ibid., 193)—darts in and out of Voigt's "Lotmanosphere."

7. From the Greek *noûs,* meaning the Aristotelian region of the highest form of rationality or mind or intellectual cosmic intuition, also approximately encompassed by Karl R. Popper's World 3 (Sebeok 1989e, 203–206).

8. This distinction between local and global has multiple and quite far-reaching implications for the doctrine of signs. Some of these are explored in more depth in chapter 1 above.

9. Vernadsky: 1863–1945; von Uexküll: 1864–1944. When I posed the question whether they knew (of) one another, Kalevi Kull, director of the Jakob von Uexküll Center at the University of Tartu, responded that "there exists a citation to Uexküll's *Theoretische Biologie* (1928 printing) in Vernadsky's manuscript on biological time, written in 1931 (but published only in 1975). From Vernadsky's sentence in this work it is also clear that he estimated Uexküll's views highly (his expression ' . . . deep considerations of v. Uexküll' seems to testify to this)" (personal communication).

10. "The Unfolding Semiosphere" is the title of Jesper Hoffmeyer's chapter in the collection by Van de Vijver et al. (1998, 281–293), with this definition: "The semiosphere is a sphere like the atmosphere, the hydrosphere or the biosphere. It penetrates these spheres and consists in signification and communication: sounds, odours, movements, colors, electric fields, waves of any kind, chemical signals, touch, etc." (ibid., 288). In the same volume, Peter Cariani writes: "The 'semiosphere', the realm of symbolically-mediated processes, envelopes [*sic*] and incorporates us at every turn" (ibid., 359).

15. The Estonian Connection

1. Five different von Uexkülls are named in this article: Jakob, his wife Gudrun, their elder son Thure, their younger son Gösta (or Gustav), and their daughter Dana. To avoid confusion, each of the foregoing is referred to mostly by his or her first name. (The Baron's grandson, Gösta's son, not mentioned below, is also named Jakob von Uexküll.)

2. In Sebeok 1988c, I argued that the concepts of "'primary' and 'secondary' modeling systems" are flawed; but, to avoid confusion, for the purposes of the present paper I retain this terminology, originally proposed in 1962 by A. A. Zaliznyak, V. V. Ivanov, and V. N. Toporov (available in English in Lucid 1977, 47–58).

3. Ariste was the president of the Finno-Ugric Congress. In my capacity as the U.S. delegate, I was member of the overall international organizing committee. Both Ariste and Lotman held the title of "Akademik," that is, were members of the Estonian Academy of Sciences (cf. Domokos ed. 1990 [after Rätsep 1990]; Voigt 1995, 199).

4. My improvised Tartu speech (in English) and the discussions in the lecture hall were routinely monitored. My wife had never been in the Soviet Union before. I, to the contrary, had traveled there quite extensively over the previous seventeen years (and in Outer Mongolia too [cf. Sebeok 1963], although not yet in the hardly accessible Baltic Republics), so I was quite inured to constant invigilation.

5. Born in 1893, Bogatyrev died a few months after I met him. Later that day in Tartu, I asked in a private conversation for his permission—which he gave at once—to translate (from the Slovak) and publish his classic 1937 monograph on the functions of folk costume. We then cornered on the spot and invited Boris L. Ogibenin (b. 1940) to write an introductory essay about the author and "Structural Ethnography" for the English edition. Bogatyrev penned and quickly sent me a gracious preface of his "heartfelt indebtedness." All these materials duly appeared the following year (Bogatyrev 1971) although, alas, too late for the author himself to see.

6. Early in June 1998 (on my second visit to Estonia), my friend Eero Tarasti and I paid joint homage to the Lotmans' grave site in the Tartu cemetery.

7. There were perhaps still another dozen men and women there whose names I didn't catch or couldn't afterwards remember; and I can't be sure whether I first met the folklorist E. M. Meletinsky there or later on in Moscow.

Several colleagues whom I met in Tartu became, as a direct result of my visit, contributors to *Semiotica*. In addition to Lotman himself, they included Egorov, Gasparov, Ivanov, Ogibenin, Piatigorsky, Revzin, Revzina, Toporov (who went on to win the Mouton d'Or Prize in 1985), and Uspensky. Rudy singled out Revzina's 1972 piece (which also contained a brief report of my long talk) as "of particular significance for the history of the Moscow-Tartu school, since it represents an effort at stock-taking at a crucial moment in the evolution of the movement" (1986, 557, n. 13).

8. It should be noted that while Lotman and his Tartu circle, with its augmentations in Moscow and, to a lesser degree, Leningrad, together constituted an extraordinary pinnacle of achievement in the domain of semiotics in the second half of our century, this group was not congruous in its extension to semiotics throughout the Soviet Union. In Moscow alone, during my stay, I was in contact with other scholars who synchronously worked in several branches of general or applied semiotics, such as the linguist R. Pazukhin, the paremiologist G. L. Permyakov, the linguist and textbook writer Y. S. Stepanov (cf. 1971) (whom I got to know better in Milano three years later), and more. In Leningrad, I especially enjoyed lively discussions with, among others, Y. V. Knorozov, a leading expert on Maya hieroglyphic writing.

9. On *semiosphere*, see also chapter 14 above and Eco's prefatory remarks to Lotman's book on pp. xii-xiii (Lotman 1990). Sturrock (1991, 10) insightfully views the semiosphere as a "semantic version of the biosphere without whose support there would be no life-forms." The international publication history of Lotman's article is detailed under Lotman 1984 in the reference list.

10. My curiosity about the work of Jakob was rekindled by a brief but suggestive passage in Klopfer and Hailman's book about the foundations of ethology (1967, 126–127).

11. For want of a ready-made term, von Uexküll dubbed his invention *Umwelt-research,* and accordingly founded the Institute for Umwelt Research at the University of Hamburg (in 1926) to carry out investigations on "the behavior of living organisms and their interaction as cells and organs in the body or as subjects within families, groups, and communities" (G. von Uexküll 1964, 145–151; Th. von Uexküll 1987, 147). The Tartu Center is the successor of the embryonic Hamburg Institute, with a program of research in biosemiotics—which merits full funding—comparable at present with that of the Biosemiotics Group at the University of Copenhagen.

In 1943, K. J. W. Craik, an Englishman, independently proposed a kindred but not empirically based and now almost forgotten "biosemiotic" theory, wherein he hypothesized that "the organism carries 'a small-scale model' of external reality and of its own possible actions within its head" (cf. Sebeok 1991e, 104–105).

12. The commonalities among C. S. Peirce, J. von Uexküll, Ernst Cassirer, Yuri Lotman, et al., can all be traced back to Kant, but to do so would require extended and meticulous monographic treatment (see also G. von Uexküll 1964, 19, 93; and for the "correspondence with Kant," 220–228). Thure has confirmed (Th. von Uexküll 1987, 150) that his father was unacquainted with the works of Peirce or Saussure, indeed, any other contributors to semiotics than Cassirer (although he must have had at least an inkling of the principal tenets of Hippocratic medical semiotics). Terminological reconciliations, often provided by Thure, were unknown to his father.

Baer sits atop a statue in a charming park by the University of Tartu. On June 2, 1998, soon after lecturing at the Jakob von Uexküll Center, I was photographed with Kull, standing in front of this famous memorial.

13. On the cognate domain of *endosemiotics,* see the fundamental article by Th. von Uexküll et al. (1993), after Sebeok 1976 (3).

14. Plenary address to the Twenty-fourth Annual Meeting of the Semiotic Society of America, Louisville, Kentucky, October 24, 1997.

References

Ackerman, D. 1991. *A Natural History of the Senses.* New York: Vintage Books.

Ader, R., D. L. Felten, and N. Cohen, eds. 1991. *Psychoneuroimmunology.* Second edition. San Diego: Academic Press.

Albone, E. S. 1984. *Mammalian Semiochemistry: The Investigation of Chemical Signals between Mammals.* Chichester: Wiley.

Anderson, M., J. Deely, M. Krampen, J. Ransdell, T. A. Sebeok, and T. von Uexküll. 1984. A semiotic perspective on the sciences: steps toward a new paradigm. *Semiotica* 52 (1/2), 7–47.

Anderson, M., and F. Merrell, eds. 1991. *On Semiotic Modeling.* Berlin: Mouton de Gruyter.

Andrews, E. 1990. A dialogue on the sign: Can Peirce and Jakobson be reconciled? *Semiotica* 82, 1–13.

Argyle, M., and M. Cook. 1976. *Gaze and Mutual Gaze.* Cambridge: Cambridge University Press.

Ariste, P. 1968. *A Grammar of the Votic Language.* Uralic and Altaic Series, vol. 68. Bloomington: Indiana University Publications.

Armstrong, E. A. 1965. *Bird Display and Behaviour.* New York: Dover.

Bacon, F. 1815. *The Works of Francis Bacon,* vols. 6–7. First edition, 1623. London: M. Jones.

Bada, J. L. 1995. Cold start. *The Sciences* 35(3), 21–25.

Baer, E. 1982. The medical symptom: philogeny and ontogeny. *American Journal of Semiotics* 1(3), 17–34.

———. 1986. Symptom and syndrome. *Encyclopedic Dictionary of Semiotics,* ed. T. A. Sebeok, 2:1033–35. Berlin: Mouton de Gruyter.

———. 1988. *Medical Semiotics.* Lanham: University Press of America.

Bailes, K. E. 1990. *Science and Russian Culture in an Age of Revolutions: V. I. Vernadsky and His Scientific School.* Bloomington: Indiana University Press.

Bakhtin, M. M. 1981. *The Dialogic Imagination,* ed. M. Holquist. Austin: University of Texas Press.

Balázs, G. 2000. Gesture jokes in Hungary. *Semiotica* 128 (3/4), 205-220.

Ballón, E. 1986. Semiotics in Peru. In *The Semiotic Sphere,* ed. T. A. Sebeok and J. Umiker-Sebeok, 387–405. New York: Plenum Press.

———. 1990. Semiotics in Peru 1980–1988. In *The Semiotic Web 1989,* T. A. Sebeok and J. Umiker-Sebeok, 195–219. Berlin: Mouton de Gruyter.

Bang, P., and P. Dahlstrom, P. 1972. *Collins Guide to Animal Tracks and Signs: A Guide to the Tracking of All British and European Mammals and Birds.* London: Collins.

Bange, P. 1979. Recherches sémiologiques dans les pays Gérmaniques. In *Le champ sémiologique. Perspectives internationales,* ed. A. Helbo, K1–22. Brussels: Editions Complexe.

Barlow, C., ed. 1992. *From Gaia to Selfish Genes Selected Writings in the Life Sciences:* Cambridge, Mass.: MIT Press.

Barnes, J. 1991. Galen on logic and therapy. In *Galen's Method of Healing: Proceedings of the 1982 Galen Symposium,* ed. F. Kudlien and R. J. Durling, 50–102. Leiden: E. J. Brill.

Barrow, J. D. 1991. *Theories of Everything: The Quest for Ultimate Explanation.* Oxford: Clarendon Press.

Barrow, J. D., and J. Silk. 1983. *The Left Hand of Creation: The Origin and Evolution of the Expanding Universe.* New York: Basic Books.

Barthes, R. 1972. Sémiologie et médicine. In *Les sciences de la folie,* ed. Roger Bastide, 37–46. Paris: Mouton.

Bateson, M. C. 1984. *With a Daughter's Eye.* New York: William Morrow.

Battisto, J. R., H. N. Claman, and D. W. Scott, eds. 1982. *Immunological Tolerance to Self and Non-Self.* Annals of The New York Academy of Sciences, vol. 392. New York: The New York Academy of Sciences.

Baum, A. F. 1981. *The Magic of Oz.* New York: Ballantine Books.

Beadle, G. W., and M. Beadle. 1966. *The Language of Life: An Introduction to the Science of Genetics.* Garden City: Doubleday.

Beadle, M. 1977. *The Cat: A Complete Authoritative Compendium of Information about Domestic Cats.* New York: Simon & Schuster.

Beckett, S. 1995. *Krapp's Last Tape, The Collected Shorter Plays of Samuel Beckett.* New York: Foxrock.

Bedani, G. 1989. *Vico Revisited: Orthodoxy, Naturalism and Science in the Scienza Nuova.* Oxford: Berg.

Behan, R. J. 1926. *Pain: Its Origin, Conduction, Perception, and Diagnostic Significance.* New York: D. Appleton.

Beniger, J. R. 1986. *The Control Revolution: Technological and Economic Origins of the Information Society.* Cambridge: Cambridge University Press.

Berkeley, G. 1732. *Alciphron, or, The Minute Philosopher.* Vol. 3 of *The Works of George Berkeley, Bishop of Cloyne,* ed. T. Jessop. London: Thomas Nelson and Sons.

Berlinski, D. 1986. The language of life. In *Complexity, Language, and Life: Mathematical Approaches,* ed. J. L. Casti and A. Karlqvist, 231–267. Berlin: Springer Verlag.

Bernard, J. 1987. Semiotics in Austria. In *The Semiotic Web 1986,* ed. T. A. Sebeok and J. Umiker-Sebeok, 143–168. Berlin: Mouton de Gruyter.

———. 1989. Semiotics in Bulgaria. *S: European Journal for Semiotic Studies* 1(2), 185–395.

Berthoff, A. E. 1999. Susanne K. Langer and the process of feeling. Chap. 10 in *The Mysterious Barricades.* Toronto: University of Toronto Press.

———. 2000. Susanne K. Langer and "The odyssey of the mind." *Semiotica* 128(1/2), 1–34.

Bettetini, G., and F. Casetti. 1986. Semiotics in Italy. In *The Semiotic Sphere,* ed. T. A. Sebeok and J. Umiker-Sebeok, 293–321. New York: Plenum Press.

Bickerton, D. 1990. *Language and Species.* Chicago: University of Chicago Press.

Bilz, R. 1940. *Pars Pro Toto.* Leipzig: Georg Thieme.

Black, I. B. 1991. *Information in the Brain: A Molecular Perspective.* Cambridge, Mass.: MIT Press.

Blacking, J. 1977. *The Anthropology of the Body.* London: Academic Press.

Bleibtreu, J. N. 1968. *The Parable of the Beast: An Exploration of the Frontiers of Biological Knowledge.* London: Gollancz.

Block de Behar, L. 1987. Semiotics in Uruguay: A very brief report for a very brief history. In *The Semiotic Web 1986*, ed. T. A. Sebeok and J. Umiker-Sebeok, 349–352. Berlin: Mouton de Gruyter.

Blumenberg, H. 1974. Ernst Cassirers gedenkend bei Entgegennahme des Kuno Fischer-Prizes der Universität Heidelberg im Juli 1974. *Revue Internationale de Philosophie* 28, 456–463.

———. 1981. *Die Lesbarkeit der Welt*. Frankfurt am Main: Suhrkamp Verlag.

Bogatyrev, P. 1971. *The Functions of Folk Costume in Moravian Slovakia*. Approaches to Semiotics, ed. Thomas A. Sebeok, vol. 5. The Hague: Mouton.

Boklund-Lagopoulou, K., and A.-Ph. Lagopoulos 1986. Semiotics in Greece. In *The Semiotic Sphere*, T. A. Sebeok and J. Umiker-Sebeok, 253–278. New York: Plenum Press.

Bonner, J. T. 1963. How slime molds communicate. *Scientific American* 209, 84–93.

Borbé, T. ed. 1978. *Semiotik III: Zeichentypologie*. München: Wilhelm Fink.

Bornet, J. 1930. *Early Greek Philosophy*. Reprint of 1892 edition. London: MacMillan.

Bouissac, P. 1973. Perspectives ethnozoologiques: Le statut symbolique de l'animal au cirque et au zoo. *Ethnologie Française* 2(2–3), 253–266.

———. 1976. *Circus and Culture: A Semiotic Approach*. Bloomington: Indiana University Press.

———. 1985. *Circus and Culture: A Semiotic Approach*. London: University Press of America.

———. 1986. Semiotics in Canada. In *The Semiotic Sphere*, T. A. Sebeok and J. Umiker-Sebeok, 59–98. New York: Plenum Press.

———. 1987. Semiotics in Canada I. In *The Semiotic Web 1986*, ed. T. A. Sebeok and J. Umiker-Sebeok, 191–251. Berlin: Mouton de Gruyter.

———. 1988. Semiotics in Canada II. In *The Semiotic Web 1987*, ed. T. A. Sebeok and J. Umiker-Sebeok, 145–203. Berlin: Mouton de Gruyter.

———. 1993. Semiotisches Wettrüsten: Zur Evolution artübergreifender Kommunikation. *Zeitschrift für Semiotik 15*, 3–22.

———, ed. 1998. *Encyclopedia of Semiotics*. New York: Oxford University Press.

Brandon, R. 1993. *The Life & Many Deaths of Harry Houdini*. London: Martin Secker & Warburg.

Brent, J. 1993. *Charles Sanders Peirce: A Life*. Bloomington: Indiana University Press.

Bridgeman, R. 1969. Horses and hounds. *The Sherlock Holmes Journal* 9(2), 59–61.

Bright, M. 1984. *Animal Language*. London: British Broadcasting Corp.

Brodeur, J.-P., and T. Pavel. 1979. Les discours sémiotiques au Canada. In *Le champ sémiologique. Perspectives internationales,* ed. A. Helbo, E1–32. Brussels: Editions Complexe.

Brooks, D. R., and E. O. Wiley. 1986. *Evolution as Entropy: Toward a Unified Theory of Biology*. Chicago: University of Chicago Press.

Buczynska-Garewicz, H. 1987. Semiotics in Poland. In *The Semiotic Web 1986*, ed. T. A. Sebeok and J. Umiker-Sebeok, 267–290. Berlin: Mouton de Gruyter.

Bühler, K. 1965. *Sprachtheorie: Die Darstellungfunktion der Sprache*. Second edition. First edition, 1934. Stuttgart: Gustav Fischer.

Burnett, J. H. 1968. *Fundamentals of Mycology*. New York: St. Martin's Press.

Busnel, R.-G., ed. 1963. *Acoustic Behaviour of Animals*. London: Elsevier.

Busnel, R.-G., and J. F. Fish. 1980. *Animal Sonar Systems*. London: Plenum.

Cairns-Smith, A. G. 1985. *Seven Clues to the Origin of Life: A Scientific Detective Story.* Cambridge: Cambridge University Press.

Carlson, M. 1990. *Theatre Semiotic: Signs of Life.* Bloomington: Indiana University Press.

Carlyle, T. 1987. *Sartor Resartus.* Second edition. First edition, 1833. Oxford: Oxford University Press.

Carrascal, A., and J. Romera. 1987. Semiotics in Spain. In *The Semiotic Web 1986,* ed. T. A. Sebeok and J. Umiker-Sebeok, 289–348. Berlin: Mouton de Gruyter.

Carreri, G. 1984. *Order and Disorder in Matter.* Menlo Park: Benjamin/Cummings.

Carrión-Wam, R. 1986. Semiotics in Venezuela. In *The Semiotic Sphere,* T. A. Sebeok and J. Umiker-Sebeok, 583–598. New York: Plenum Press.

Cartmill, M., D. Pilbeam, and G. Isaac. 1986. One hundred years of paleoanthropology. *American Scientist* 74, 410–420.

Cassirer, E. 1923. *Philosophie der Symbolischen Formen: I. Die Sprache.* Berlin: Bruno Cassirer.

———. 1944. *An Essay on Man: An Introduction to a Philosophy of Human Culture.* New Haven: Yale University Press.

———. 1946a. *Language and Myth.* New York: Harper & Brothers.

———. 1946b. Structuralism in modern linguistics. *Word* 1, 99–120.

———. 1961. *The Logic of the Humanities.* First edition, 1942. New Haven: Yale University Press.

———. 1969. *Wesen und Wirkung des Symbolbegriffs.* First edition, 1956.Darmstadt: Wissenschaftliche Buchgesellschaft.

———. 1979. *Symbol, Myth, and Culture: Essays and Lectures of Ernst Cassirer 1935–1945,* ed. D. P. Verene. New Haven: Yale University Press.

Catchpole, C. K., and P. J. B. Slater. 1995. *Bird Song: Biological Themes and Variations.* Cambridge: Cambridge University Press.

Chadwick, J., and W. N. Mann. 1950. *The Medical Works of Hippocrates.* Oxford: Blackwell.

Chamberlain, E. N. and C. Ogilvie, eds. 1974. *Symptoms and Signs in Clinical Medicine.* Bristol: Wright.

Cheraskin, E., and W. Ringsdorf. 1973. *Preventive Medicine: A Study in Strategy.* Moutainview, Cal.: Pacific Press.

Chomsky, N. 1980. *Rules and Representations.* New York: Columbia University Press.

Classen, C., D. Howes, and A. Synnott. 1994. *Aroma: The Cultural History of Smell.* London: Routledge.

Clutton-Brock, J. 1981. *Domesticated Animals from Early Time.* London: British Museum [Natural History].

Cobley, P., ed. 2001. *The Routledge Companion to Semiotics and Linguistics.* London: Routledge.

Cohen, I. B. 1994. *Interactions: Some Contacts between the Natural Sciences and the Social Sciences.* Cambridge, Mass.: MIT Press.

Cohen, M. 1988. The hounding of Baskerville: Allusion and apocalypse in Eco's *The Name of the Rose.* In *Naming the Rose: Essays on Eco's The Name of the Rose,* ed. M. T. Inge, 65–76. Jackson: University Press of Mississippi.

Cohen, T. 1999. *Jokes: Philosophical Thoughts in Joking Matters.* Chicago: University of Chicago Press.

Colapietro, V. M. 1989. *Peirce's Approach to the Self.* Albany: State University of New York Press.

Colby, K. M., and M. T. McGuire. 1981. Signs and symptoms. *The Sciences* 21(9), 21–23.

Cook, N. D. 1986. *The Brain Code: Mechanisms of Information Transfer and the Role of the Corpus Callosum*. London: Methuen.

Coquet, J.-C., and M. Arrivé. 1979. La sémiotique en France In *Le champ sémiologique. Perspectives internationales,* ed. A. Helbo, 11–26. Brussels: Editions Complexe.

Craik, K. J. W. 1943. *The Nature of Explanation*. Cambridge: Cambridge University Press.

Creasey, J. 1959. *Death of a Racehorse*. New York: Scribners.

Crews, F. 1993. The unknown Freud. *New York Review of Books,* November 18.

———. 1994. The unknown Freud: An exchange. *New York Review of Books,* February 3.

Crick, F. 1994. *The Astonishing Hypothesis*. New York: Simon and Schuster.

Croce, B. 1913. *The Philosophy of Giambattista Vico*. Translated by R. G. Collingwood. London: Howard Latimer.

Crookshank, F. G. 1938. The importance of a theory of signs and a critique of language in the study of medicine. In C. K. Ogden and I. A. Richards, *The Meaning of Meaning: A Study of the Influence of Language upon Thought and of the Science of Symbolism,* 337–355. New York: Harcourt, Brace.

Crystal, D. 1987. *The Cambridge Encyclopedia of Language*. Cambridge: Cambridge University Press.

Csikszentmihalyi, M. 1996. *Creativity: Flow and the Psychology of Discovery and Invention*. New York: HarperCollins.

Culotta, E., and D. E. Koshland, Jr. 1992. Molecule of the year: NO news is good news. *Science* 258, 1861–865.

Daddesio, T. D. 1990. William of Baskerville or the myth of the master of signs. In *Semiotics 1989,* ed. J. Deely, K. Haworth, and T. Prewitt, eds., 45–50. Lanham: University Press of America.

Damasio, A. R. 1995. *Descartes' Error: Emotion, Reason, and the Human Brain*. London: Picador.

Danesi, M. 1993. *Vico, Metaphor, and the Origin of Language*. Bloomington: Indiana University Press.

———, ed. 2000. *Encyclopedic Dictionary of Semiotics, Media, and Communications*. Toronto: University of Toronto Press.

Darwin, C. 1872. *The Expression of the Emotions in Man and Animals*. London: John Murray.

———. 1998. *The Expression of the Emotions in Man and Animals*. Introduction, afterword and commentaries by P. Ekman. New York: Oxford University Press.

Davies, P. 1995. *Are We Alone? Philosophical Implications of the Discovery of Extraterrestrial Life*. New York: Basic Books.

de Duve, C. 1995. *Vital Dust: Life as a Cosmic Imperative*. New York: Basic Books.

de Jorio, A. 1832. La mimica degli antichi investigata nel gestire napoletano. Naples: Fibreno.

———. 2000. *Gesture in Naples and Gesture in Classical Antiquity*. Translation, introduction, and notes by A. Kendon. Bloomington: Indiana University Press.

De Lacy, P. H., and E. A. De Lacy, eds. 1941. *Philodemus on Methods of Inference: A Study in Ancient Empiricism*. Philadelphia: American Philological Association.

Décsy, G. 1994. Linguistic fascination with globalism. *Eurasian Studies Yearbook* 71, 111-158.

Deely, J. 1982. *Introducing Semiotic: Its History and Doctrine*. Bloomington: Indiana University Press.

———. 1988. The semiotic of John Poinsot: Yesterday and tomorrow. *Semiotica* 69(1/2), 31–127.

———. 1994. *New Beginnings: Early Modern Philosophy and Postmodern Thought.* Toronto: University of Toronto Press.

———. 2000. *Four Ages of Understanding. The First Postmodern Survey of Philosophy from Ancient Times to the Turn of the 21st Century.* Toronto: University of Toronto Press.

Demers, R. A. 1988. Linguistics and animal communication. In *Language: Psychological and Biological Aspects.* Vol. 3 of *Linguistics: The Cambridge Survey,* ed. F. J. Newmeyer. Cambridge: Cambridge University Press.

Derrida, J. 1968. Sémiologie et grammatologie. *Social Science Information* 7(3), 135–148.

Dery, M. 1996. *Escape Velocity: Cyberculture at the End of the Century.* New York: Grove Press.

Devreotes, P. N. 1982. Chemotaxis. In *The Development of Dictyostelium Discoideum,* ed. William F. Loomis, 117–168. New York: Academic Press.

Domokos, P, ed. 1990. *Finnugor Életrajzi Lexikon.* Budapest: Tankönyvkiadó.

Dorfles, G. 1968. Mito e metafora in Cassirer e Vico. *Il Pensiero* 13, 147–158.

Doyle, A. C. 1967. *The Annotated Sherlock Holmes.* 2 vols. Edited by W. S. Baring-Gould. New York: Clarkson N. Potter.

Durling, R. D. 1991. "Endeixis" as a scientific term: (B) "Endeixis" in authors other than Galen and its Medieval Latin equivalents. In *Galen's Method of Healing: Proceedings of the 1982 Galen Symposium,* ed. F. Kudlien and R. J. Durling, 112–113. Leiden: E. J. Brill.

Dyer, F. C., and H. J. Brockman. 1996. Sensory processes, orientation, and communication: Biology of the *Umwelt.* In *Foundations of Animal Behavior,* ed. L. D. Houck and L. C. Drickamer, 529–538. Chicago: University of Chicago Press.

Eccles, J C., and K. R. Popper. 1977. *The Self and Its Brain: An Argument for Interactionism.* Berlin: Springer International.

Eco, U. 1975. *Trattato di semiotica generale.* Milano: Bompiani.

———. 1976. *A Theory of Semiotics.* Bloomington: Indiana University Press.

———. 1978. Semiotics: A discipline or an interdisciplinary method. In *Sight, Sound, and Sense,* ed. T. A. Sebeok, 73–83. Bloomington: Indiana University Press.

———. 1980a. *Il nome della rosa.* Milan: Bompiani. English translation: *The Name of the Rose.* New York: Harcourt, Brace, Jovanovich, 1983.

———. 1980b. The sign revisited. *Philosophy and Social Criticism* 7(3/4), 261–297.

———. 1983. Proposals for a history of semiotics. In *Semiotics Unfolding: Proceedings of the Second Congress of the International Association for Semiotic Studies, Vienna, July 1979,* ed. T. Borbé, 1, 75–89. Berlin: Mouton.

———. 1984. *Semiotics and the Philosophy of Language.* Bloomington: Indiana University Press.

———. 1986. Mirrors. In *Iconicity: Essays on the Nature of Culture: Festschrift for Thomas A. Sebeok on His 65th Birthday,* ed. P. Bouissac, M. Herzfeld, and R. Posner, 215–237. Tübingen: Stauffenburg.

———. 1988. Una sfida al mito delle due culture. *Saecularia nona* 2 (January-February).

Eco, U., and T. A. Sebeok, eds. 1983. *The Sign of Three: Dupin, Holmes, Peirce.* Bloomington: Indiana University Press.

Edelman, G. M. 1987. *Neural Darwinism.* New York: Basic Books.

———. 1992. *Bright Air, Brilliant Fire: On the Matter of the Mind.* New York: Basic Books.

Eder, J., and H. Rembold. 1992. Biosemiotics—A paradigm for biology: Biological signalling on the verge of deterministic chaos. *Naturwissenschaften* 79, 60-67.

Eggers, W., and S. Mayer. 1988. *Ernst Cassirer: An Annotated Bibliography.* New York: Garland Publishing.

Eibl-Eibesfeldt, I. 1989. *Human Ethology.* New York: Aldine de Gruyter.

Eisenberg, J. F., and W. S. Dillon, eds. 1971. *Man and Beast: Comparative Social Behavior:* Washington: Smithsonian Institution Press.

Ekman, P. 1985. *Telling Lies: Clues to Deceit in the Marketplace, Politics, and Marriage.* London: W. W. Norton.

Elstein, A. S., L. S. Shulman, and S. A. Sprafka. 1978. *Medical Problem Solving: An Analysis of Clinical Reasoning.* Cambridge, Mass.: Harvard University Press.

Emmeche, C. 1994a. The computational notion of life. *Teoria: Revista de teoria, historia y fundamentos de la ciencia* 9(21), 1-30.

———. 1994b. *The Garden in the Machine.* Princeton: Princeton University Press.

Ennion, E. A. R., and N. Tinbergen. 1967. *Tracks.* Oxford: Clarendon Press.

Evans, J., and J. Deely, eds. 1987. *Semiotics 1983.* Lanham: University Press of America.

Ewing, A. P., and R. R. Pattrick. 1965. A sherlockian zoo. In *West By One and By One,* 113-124. San Francisco: Privately printed.

Fabian, A. C., ed. 1988. *Origins: The Darwin College Lectures.* Cambridge: Cambridge University Press.

Fabrega, H., Jr. 1974. *Disease and Social Behavior: An Interdisciplinary Perspective.* Cambridge, Mass.: MIT Press.

Fann, K. T. 1990. Alexander Bryan Johnson: The first linguistic philosopher (1786-1867). In *The Semiotic Web 1989,* ed. T. A. Sebeok and J. Umiker-Sebeok, 31-60. Berlin: Mouton de Gruyter.

Feibleman, J. K. 1956. *An Introduction to Peirce's Philosophy Interpreted as a System.* New Orleans: The Hauser Press.

Figge, U. L. 1999. Jakob von Uexküll: "Merkmale" und "Wirkmale." Unpublished ms.

Fisch, M. 1986. *Peirce, Semeiotic, and Pragmatism.* Bloomington: Indiana University Press.

Flam, J. 1992. Passions of Matisse. *New York Review of Books,* November 5.

Fontenrose, J. 1988. *Didyma: Apollo's Oracle, Cult, and Companions.* Berkeley: University of California Press.

Foster, M. L. 1994. Symbolism: The foundation of culture. In *Companion Encyclopedia of Anthropology,* ed. Tim Ingold, 366-395. London: Routledge.

Fox, M. W. 1974. *Understanding Your Cat.* New York: Bantam Books.

———. 1982. *Love Is a Happy Cat,* with cartoons by Harry Gans. New York: Newmarket Press.

Fox, S. 1988. *The Emergence of Life: Darwinian Evolution from the Inside.* New York: Basic Books.

Francis, D. 1990. *Longshot.* New York: G. P. Putnam.

Freadman, A., and M. Morris. 1986. Semiotics in Australia. In *The Semiotic Sphere,* ed. T. A. Sebeok and J. Umiker-Sebeok, 1-17. Berlin: Mouton de Gruyter.

French, A. P., and P. J. Kennedy, eds. 1985. *Niels Bohr: A Centenary Volume.* Cambridge, Mass.: Harvard University Press.

Frutiger, A. 1989. *Signs and Symbols: Their Design and Meaning.* New York: Van Nostrand Rheinhold.

Füller, H. 1958. *Symbiose im Tierreich.* Wittenberg: A. Ziemsen.

Furnham, A. 1988. Write and wrong: The validity of graphological analysis. *Skeptical Inquirer* 13(1), 64–69.

Gadol, E. T. 1969. Der Begriff des Schöpferischen bei Vico, Kant, und Cassirer, II. *Wissenschaft und Weltbild* 2, 8–19.

Gallardo, A., and J. Sánchez. 1986. Semiotics in Chile. In *The Semiotic Sphere*, ed. T. A. Sebeok and J. Umiker-Sebeok, 99–114. Berlin: Mouton de Gruyter.

Gardiner, D. 2000. In memoriam: Herman B Wells. *REEIfication 24(2), 4.*

Gardner, M. 1957. *Fads and Fallacies in the Name of Science.* New York: Dover.

———. 1983. Margaret Mead and the paranormal. *The Skeptical Inquirer* 8(1), 13–16.

———. 1993. The Great Samoan Hoax. *The Skeptical Inquirer* 17(2), 131–135.

Garza Cuarón, B. 1988. Semiotics in Mexico. In *The Semiotic Web 1987*, ed. T. A. Sebeok and J. Umiker-Sebeok, 267–305. Berlin: Mouton de Gruyter.

Gatlin, Lila L. 1972. *Information Theory and Living Systems.* New York: Columbia University Press.

Gelb, I. J. 1952. *A Study of Writing.* Chicago: University of Chicago Press.

Geschwind, N. 1980. Some comments on the neurology of language. In *Biological Studies of Mental Processes,* ed. D. Caplan, 301–319. Cambridge, Mass: MIT Press.

Gessinger, J., and W. von Rahden, eds. 1989. *Theorien vom Ursprung der Sprache.* 2 vols. Berlin: Walter de Gruyter.

Gibson, K. R., and T. Ingold, eds. 1993. *Tools, Language and Cognition in Human Evolution.* Cambridge: Cambridge University Press.

Giles, K. 1967. *Death at the Furlong Post.* New York: Walker.

Gilot, F., and C. Lake. 1964. *Life with Picasso.* New York: McGraw-Hill.

Ginzburg, C. 1983. Clues: Morelli, Freud, and Sherlock Holmes. In *The Sign of Three,* ed. U. Eco and T. A. Sebeok, 81–118. Bloomington: Indiana University Press.

Godel, R. 1957. *Les sources manuscrites du Cours de Linguistique Générale de F. de Saussure.* Geneva: E. Droz.

Goffman, Erving. 1971. *Relations in Public: Microstudies of the Public Order.* New York: Basic Books.

Golopentia-Eretescu, S. 1986. Semiotics in Romania. In *The Semiotic Sphere*, ed. T. A. Sebeok and J. Umiker-Sebeok, 417–472. Berlin: Mouton de Gruyter.

González, C. 1986. Semiotics in Spain. In *The Semiotic Sphere*, ed. T. A. Sebeok and J. Umiker-Sebeok, 473–484. Berlin: Mouton de Gruyter.

Goodman, N. 1968. *Languages of Art: An Approach to a Theory of Symbols.* Indianapolis: Bobbs-Merrill.

———. 1978. *Ways of Worldmaking.* Indianapolis: Hackett.

Gorlée, D. 1987. Semiotics in Norway: Signs of life on the fjords. In *The Semiotic Web 1986,* ed. T. A. Sebeok and J. Umiker-Sebeok, 253–265. Berlin: Mouton de Gruyter.

Gould, S. J., and E. S. Vrba 1982. Exaptation—A missing term in the science of form. *Paleobiology B/1,* 4–15.

Gray, C. H., ed. 1995. *The Cyborg Handbook.* New York: Routledge.

Greenstein, G. 1988. *The Symbiotic Universe: Life and Mind in the Cosmos.* New York: Morrow.

Greimas, A. J. 1976. *Sémiotique et sciences sociales.* Paris: Seuil.

Greimas, A. J., and J. Courtès. 1982. *Semiotics and Language: An Analytical Dictionary.* Bloomington: Indiana University Press.

Gribbin, J. 1984. *In Search of Schrödinger's Cat: Quantum Physics and Reality.* New York: Bantam Books.

Grize, J.-B. 1979. Courants sémiologiques en Suisse. In *Le champ sémiologique. Perspectives internationales,* ed. A. Helbo, 01–14. Brussels: Editions Complexe.

Gruber, F. 1942. *The Gift Horse.* New York: Farrar and Rinehart.

Grzybek, P. 1998. Lotman, Jurij Mikhajlovic. In *Encyclopedia of Semiotics,* ed. P. Bouissac, 375–377. New York: Oxford University Press.

Guerrero, R., and L. Margulis. 1998. Stone soup. *The Sciences* 38(4), 34–38.

Guthrie, R. D. 1976. *Body Hot Spots: Anatomy of Human Social Organs and Behavior.* New York: Van Nostrand Reinhold.

Hadamard, J. 1945. *An Essay on the Psychology of Invention in the Mathematical Field.* Princeton: Princeton University Press.

Haight, M. R. 1980. *A Study of Self-Deception.* Brighton: Harvester.

Hailman, J. P. 1977. *Optical Signals: Animal Communication and Light.* Bloomington: Indiana University Press.

Hall, E. T. 1968. Proxemics. *Current Anthropology* 9, 83–108.

Halliday, M. A. K. 1978. *Language as Social Semiotic: The Social Interpretation of Language and Meaning.* London: Edward Arnold.

Handel, S. 1989. *Listening: An Introduction to the Perception of Auditory Events.* Cambridge, Mass.: MIT Press.

Hankinson, R. J. 1991. *Galen on the Therapeutic Method.* Books I and II. Oxford: Clarendon Press.

Hanna, J. L. 1979. *To Dance Is Human: A Theory of Nonverbal Communication.* Austin: University of Texas Press.

Hanson, K. 1986. *The Self Imagined: Philosophical Reflections on the Social Character of Psyche.* New York: Routledge & Kegan Paul.

Hardison, O. B., Jr., ed. 1971. *The Quest for Imagination: Essays in Twentieth-Century Aesthetic Criticism.* Cleveland: The Press of Case Western Reserve University.

Hardwick, C. S., ed. 1977. *Semiotic and Significs: The Correspondence between Charles S. Peirce and Victoria Lady Welby.* Bloomington: Indiana University Press.

Haskell, T. L. 1997. The new aristocracy. *New York Review of Books* 44(19), 47–53.

Haskins, R. 1977. Effect of kitten vocalizations on maternal behavior. *Journal of Comparative and Physiological Psychology* 91, 830–838.

———. 1979. A causal analysis of kitten vocalization: An observational and experimental study. *Animal Behaviour* 27, 726–736.

Hayles, N. K. 1984. *The Cosmic Web: Scientific Field Models and Literary Strategies in the Twentieth Century.* Ithaca: Cornell University Press.

Hediger, H. 1968. *The Psychology and Behaviour of Animals in Zoos and Circuses.* New York: Dover.

———. 1974. Communication between man and animal. *Image Roche* 62, 27–40.

———. 1980. *Tiere verstehen: Erkenntnisse eines Tierpsychologen.* München: Kindler.

———. 1985. A lifelong attempt to understand animals. In *Leaders in the Study of Animal Behavior: Autobiographical Perspectives,* ed. D. A. Dewsbury, 144–181. Lewisburg: Bucknell University Press.

———. 1990a. *Ein Leben mit Tieren im Zoo und in aller Welt.* Zürich: Werd.

———. 1990b. Vom Schmerz und seiner Ausschaltung im Naturreich der Tiere. In *Schmerz,* ed. H. J. Schulz, 156–70. Stuttgart: Kreuz.

Heidel, W. A. 1941. *Hippocratic Medicine: Its Spirit and Method.* New York: Columbia University Press.

Heims, S. J. 1991. *The Cybernetics Group.* Cambridge, Mass.: MIT Press.

Helbo, A., ed. 1979a. *Le champ sémiologique. Perspectives internationales.* Brussels: Editions Complexe.

———. 1979b. Vers des études sémiologiques: La situation en Belgique. In *Le champ sémiologique. Perspectives internationales,* ed. A. Helbo, C1–29. Brussels: Editions Complexe.

———. 1987. Semiotics in Belgium. In *The Semiotic Web 1986,* ed. T. A. Sebeok and J. Umiker-Sebeok, 169–189. Berlin: Mouton de Gruyter.

Hénault, A. 1986. Semiotics in France. In *The Semiotic Sphere,* ed. T. A. Sebeok and J. Umiker-Sebeok, 153–175. Berlin: Mouton de Gruyter.

Henle, P., ed. 1958. *Language, Thought, & Culture.* Ann Arbor: The University of Michigan Press.

Herzfeld, M. 1987. *Anthropology through the Looking Glass: Critical Ethnography in the Margins of Europe.* Cambridge: Cambridge University Press.

Hewes, G. W. 1975. *Language Origins: A Bibliography.* 2 vols. Second edition. The Hague: Mouton.

Hibbitts, B. J. 1992. Coming to our senses: Communication and legal expression in performance cultures. *Emory Law Journal* 41(4), 873–960.

Hippisley Coxe, A. 1980. *A Seat at the Circus.* Hamden: Archon Books.

Hobbes, T. 1961. *The English Works of Thomas Hobbes.* Edited by W. Molesworth. First published 1839–1845. Oxford: Oxford University Press.

Hoek, L. H. 1992. Signalizing the Netherlands. *Semiotica* 90(1/2), 1–29.

Hoffmeyer, J. 1992. Some semiotic aspects of the psycho-physical relation: The endo-exosemiotic boundary. In *Biosemiotics,* ed. T. A. Sebeok and J. Umiker-Sebeok, 101–123. Berlin: Mouton de Gruyter.

———. 1993a. *Signs of Meaning.* Bloomington: Indiana University Press.

———. 1993b. *En Snegl på Vejen: Betydningens Naturhistorie.* Copenhagen: Omverden/Rosinante.

———. 1995a. The semiotic body-mind. In *Essays in Honor of Thomas A. Sebeok,* ed. N. Tasca, 367–383. Porto: Fundaçao Eng. António de Almeida.

———. 1995b. The swarming cyberspace of the body. *Cyberspace & Human Knowing* 3(1), 16–25.

———. 1998. Biosemiotics. In *Encyclopedia of Semiotics,* ed. P. Bouissac, 82–85. New York: Oxford University Press.

Hoffmeyer, J., and C. Emmeche. 1991. Code-duality and the semiotics of nature. In *On Semiotic Modeling,* ed. M. Anderson and F. Merrell, 117–166. Berlin: Mouton de Gruyter.

Hoffmeyer, J., and C. Emmeche, eds. 1999. *Biosemiotica.* Special issue of *Semiotica* 127(1–4).

Hofstadter, D. R. 1979. *Gödel, Escher, Bach: An Eternal Golden Braid.* New York: Basic Books.

Hölderlin, F. 1959. Mnemosyne2. In *Sämtliche Werke,* vol. 1. Ed. Friedrich Beissner. Berlin: Rütten & Loening.

Holst, S. 1971. *The Language of Cats and Other Stories.* New York: McCall.

Holstein, L. S. 1970. Holmes and *Equus Caballus. The Baker Street Journal* n.s. 20(2), 112–16.

Hookway, C. 1985. *Peirce.* London: Routledge & Kegan Paul.

Howard, J. 1984. *Margaret Mead.* New York: Ballantine.

Howard, K. 1995. Guidance proteins tell nerves where to grow. *The Sciences* 35(5), 12, 47.

Humphries, W. C. 1968. *Anomalies and Scientific Theories*. San Francisco: Freeman, Cooper.

Huxley, A. 1959. Sermons in Cats. In *Collected Essays* 77–82. New York: Harper & Brothers.

Huxley, J., and L. Koch. 1964. *Animal Language: How Animals Communicate*. First edition, 1938. New York: Grosset & Dunlap.

Huxley, T. 1881. On the method of Zadig: Retrospective prophecy as a function of science. In *Science and Culture and Other Essays*, 128–48. London: MacMillan.

Immelman, K., ed. 1977. *Grzimek's Encyclopedia of Ethology*. New York: Van Nostrand Reinhold.

Immelman, K., and C. Beer, eds. 1989. *A Dictionary of Ethology*. Cambridge, Mass.: Harvard University Press.

Ingold, T., ed. 1988. *What Is an Animal?* London: Unwin Hyman.

Innis, R. E. 1985. *Semiotics: An Introductory Anthology*. Bloomington: Indiana University Press.

Ivanov, V. 1991. Self-portrait of a Russian semiotician in his younger and later years. In *Recent Developments in Theory and History: The Semiotic Web 1990*, ed. T. A. Sebeok and J. Umiker-Sebeok, 3–43. Berlin: Mouton de Gruyter.

Jackendoff, R. 1994. *Patterns in the Mind: Language and Human Nature*. New York: Basic Books.

Jacob, F. 1974. *The Logic of Living Systems: A History of Heredity*. London: Allen Lane.

———. 1982. *The Possible and the Actual*. Seattle: University of Washington Press.

———. 1987. *La statue intérieure*. Paris: Odile Jacob.

Jakobson, R. 1970. Linguistics. In *Social Sciences*. Part 1 of *Main Trends of Research in the Social and Human Sciences*. Paris: Mouton/Unesco, 419–463.

———. 1971. *Selected Writings II: Word and Language*. The Hague: Mouton.

———. 1974. *Main Trends in the Science of Language*. New York: Harper and Row.

Jakobson, R., and K. Pomorska. 1983. *Dialogues*. Cambridge, Mass.: MIT Press.

Janisse, M. P. 1977. *Pupillometry: The Psychology of the Pupillary Response*. London: John Wiley.

Jankovic, B. D., B. M. Markovic, and N. H. Spector, eds. 1987. *Neuroimmune Reactions: Proceedings of the Second International Workshop on Neuroimmunomodulation*. New York: New York Academy of Sciences.

Jerison, H. J. 1986. The perceptual world of dolphins. In *Dolphin Cognition and Behavior: A Comparative Approach,* ed. R. J. Schusterman, J. A. Thomas, and F. G. Wood, 141–166. Hillsdale, N.J.: Lawrence Erlbaum.

Jerne, N. K. 1985. The generative grammar of the immune system. *Science* 229, 1057–1059.

Jiménez-Ottalengo, R. 1986. Semiotics in Mexico. In *The Semiotic Sphere*, ed. T. A. Sebeok and J. Umiker-Sebeok, 359–367. Berlin: Mouton de Gruyter.

Johansen, J. D. 1979. Les confrontations sémiologiques au Danemark. In *Le champ sémiologique. Perspectives internationales,* ed. A. Helbo, F1–37. Brussels: Editions Complexe.

———. 1986. Semiotics in Denmark. In *The Semiotic Sphere*, ed. T. A. Sebeok and J. Umiker-Sebeok, 115–143. Berlin: Mouton de Gruyter.

Kaelin, E. F. 1970. *Art and Existence: A Phenomenological Aesthetics*. Lewisburg: Bucknell University Press.

Kanitscheider, B. 1992. Schrödinger's cat and the interpretation of quantum mechanics.

In *Erwin Schrödinger's World View: The Dynamics of Knowledge and Reality*, ed. Johann Götschl, 41–51. Dordrecht: Kluwer Academic Publishers.

Kaplan, A. 1943. Content analysis and the theory of signs. *Philosophy of Science* 10, 230–247.

Kappauf, H. W. 1991. Übersicht über derzeitige Konzepte in der Psychoneuro-immunologie. *Onkologie* 14, 10–13.

Karsh, E. B. 1983. The effects of early handling on the development of social bonds between cats and people. In *New Perspectives on Our Lives with Companion Animals*, ed. A. H. Katcher and A. M. Beck, 22–28. Philadelphia: University of Pennsylvania Press.

Kauffman, S. A. 1995. *At Home in the Universe: The Search for Laws of Self-Organization and Complexity*. Oxford: Oxford University Press.

Kawade, Y. 1992. A molecular semiotic view of biology. *Rivista di Biologia—Biology Forum* 85(1), 71–78.

Keller, E. F. 1995. *Refiguring Life: Metaphors of Twentieth-Century Biology*. New York: Columbia University Press.

Kendon, A., and S. J. Sigman. 1996. Ray L. Birdwhistell (1918–1994). *Semiotica* 112(3/4), 231–261.

Kergosien, Y. L. 1985. Sémiotique de la nature. In *Actes du IVe séminaire de l'école biologie théorique*, ed. G. Benchetrit and J. Demongeot, 11–26. Paris: Editions du C.N.R.S.

———. 1992. Nature semiotics: The icons of nature. In *Biosemiotics*, ed. T. A. Sebeok and J. Umiker-Sebeok, 145–170. Berlin: Mouton de Gruyter.

Kevelson, R. 1986. Semiotics in the United States. In *The Semiotic Sphere*, ed. T. A. Sebeok and J. Umiker-Sebeok, 519–554. Berlin: Mouton de Gruyter.

Kirk, G. S., J. E. Raven, and M. Schofield. 1983. *The Presocratic Philosophers*. Second edition. Cambridge: Cambridge University Press.

Klein, P. S. et al. 1988. A chemoattractant receptor controls development in *Dictyostelium discoideum*. *Science* 241, 1467–1472.

Kleinpaul, R. 1972. *Sprache ohne Worte*. Second edition. First edition, 1888. The Hague: Mouton.

Kling, A., J. K. Kovach, and T. J. Tucker. 1969. The behaviour of cats. In *The Behaviour of Domestic Animals*, ed. E. S. E. Hafez, 482–512. Baltimore: Williams & Wilkins.

Klopfer, P. H., and J. P. Hailman. 1967. *An Introduction to Animal Behavior: Ethology's First Century*. Englewood Cliffs: Prentice-Hall.

Kommunikation zwischen Mensch und Tier. 1993. Special issue of *Zeitschrift für Semiotik* 15(1–2).

Kraepelin, G. 1997. Mycosemiosis. In *Semiotics: A Handbook on the Sign-Theoretic Foundations of Nature and Culture*, ed. R. Posner, K. Robering, and T. A. Sebeok, 1:488–507. Berlin: Walter de Gruyter.

Krall, K. 1912. *Denkende Tiere: Beiträge zur Tierseelekunde auf Grund eigener Versuche*. Leipzig: Friedrich Engelmann.

Krampen, M. 1981. Phytosemiotics. *Semiotica* 36, 187–209.

———. 1983. Icons of the road. *Semiotica* 43, 1–204.

———. 1994a. Phytosemiotics. In *Encyclopedic Dictionary of Semiotics*, ed. T. A. Sebeok, ed., 726–730. Berlin: Walter de Gruyter.

———. 1994b. Supersign. In *Encyclopedic Dictionary of Semiotics*, ed. T. A. Sebeok, 2:1025–26. Berlin: Mouton de Gruyter.

———. 1995. Semiotics of objects. In *Advances in Visual Semiotics. The Semiotic Web 1992–93,* ed. T. A. Sebeok and J. Umiker-Sebeok, 515–535. Berlin: Mouton de Gruyter.

———. 1997. Phytosemiosis. In *Semiotics: A Handbook on the Sign-Theoretic Foundations of Nature and Culture,* ed. R. Posner, K. Robering, and T. A. Sebeok, 1:507–522. Berlin: Walter de Gruyter.

Kroeber, A. L., and C. Kluckhohn. 1963. *Culture: A Critical Review of Concepts and Definitions.* Second edition. First edition, 1952. New York: Vintage Books.

Krois, J. M. 1987. *Cassirer: Symbolic Forms and History.* New Haven: Yale University Press.

Kudlien, F. 1991. "Endeixis" as a scientific term: A. Galen's usage of the word in medicine and logic. In *Galen's Method of Healing,* ed. F. Kudlien and R. J. Durling, 103–111. Leiden: E. J. Brill.

Kudlien, F., and R. J. Durling, eds. 1991. *Galen's Method of Healing. Proceedings of the 1982 Galen Symposium.* Leiden: E. J. Brill.

Kuhn, C. G., ed. 1821–1833. *Claudii Galeni Opera omnia.* 22 vols. Leipzig: Cnobloch.

Kuhn, T. S. 1962. *The Structure of Scientific Revolutions.* Chicago: University of Chicago Press.

Kull, K. 1993. Semiotic paradigm in theoretical biology. In *Lectures in Theoretical Biology,* ed. K. Kull and T. Toomas. Tallinn: Estonian Academy of Sciences.

Labov, W., and D. Fanshel. 1977. *Therapeutic Discourse: Psychotherapy as Conversation.* New York: Academic Press.

Lacey, A. R. 1986. *A Dictionary of Philosophy.* London: Routledge & Kegan Paul.

Landau, T. 1989. *About Faces.* New York: Doubleday.

Langer, S. K. 1948. *Philosophy in a New Key.* New York: Penguin Books.

———. 1949. On Cassirer's theory of language and myth. In *The Philosophy of Ernst Cassirer,* ed. P. A. Schilpp, 381–400. Evanston: The Library of Living Philosophers.

———. 1957. *Problems of Art.* New York: Scribner.

———. 1962. *Philosophical Sketches.* Baltimore: The Johns Hopkins University Press.

———. 1982. *Mind: An Essay on Human Feeling.* 3 vols. Baltimore: The Johns Hopkins University Press.

Lange-Seidl, A. 1986. Semiotics in East and West Germany and Austria. In *The Semiotic Sphere,* ed. T. A. Sebeok and J. Umiker-Sebeok, 177–227. Berlin: Mouton de Gruyter.

Langholf, V. 1990. *Medical Theories in Hippocrates.* Berlin: Walter de Gruyter.

Langston, J. W., and J. Palferman. 1995. *The Case of the Frozen Addicts.* New York: Pantheon Books.

Latham, R. G. 1848. *The Works of Thomas Sydenham, M.D.* London: Sydenham Society.

Lauretis, T. de. 1978. Semiotics in Italy. In *The Sign: Semiotics around the World,* ed. R. W. Bailey, L. Matejka, and P. Steiner, 248–257. Ann Arbor: Michigan Slavic Publications.

Lauritzen, H. 1959. *Holmes og Heste.* Aalborg: Silkeborg Bogtrykker.

Lawrence, C. 1982. Illnesses and their meaning. *Times Literary Supplement* no. 4,148 (October 1), 1060.

Lawrence, E. A. 1985. *Hoofbeats and Society: Studies of Human-Horse Interactions.* Bloomington: Indiana University Press.

Lázár, I. 1991 *Psychoneuroimmunológia.* Budapest: Mens Sana Hungarica.

Lees, R. B. 1980. Language and the genetic code. In *The Signifying Animal: The Gram-*

mar of Language and Experience, ed. I. Rauch and G. F. Carr, 218–226. Bloomington: Indiana University Press.

Le Guérer, A. 1992. *Scent: The Mysterious and Essentials Powers of Smell.* New York: Turtle Bay Books.

Lévi-Strauss, C. 1958. The structural study of myth. In *Myth: A Symposium,* ed. T. A. Sebeok, 81–106. Bloomington: Indiana University Press.

Lewis, D. B., and D. M. Gower. 1980. *Biology of Communication.* New York: Wiley.

Leyhausen, P. 1973. The biology of expression and impression. In *Motivation of Human and Animal Behavior: An Ethological View,* ed. K. Lorenz and P. Leyhausen, 272–380. First edition, 1967. New York: Van Nostrand Reinhold.

———. 1979. *Cat Behavior: The Predatory and Social Behavior of Domestic and Wild Cats.* New York: Garland STPM Press.

Lhoest, F. 1979. Regards sur la sémiotique soviétique. In *Le champ sémiologique. Perspectives internationales,* ed. A. Helbo, R1–22. Brussels: Editions Complexe.

Li, Y.-Z. 1988. Semiotics in the People's Republic of China. In *The Semiotic Web 1987,* ed. T. A. Sebeok and J. Umiker-Sebeok, 205–216. Berlin: Mouton de Gruyter.

Lieberman, P. 1988. Voice in the wilderness: How humans acquired the power of speech. *The Sciences* 28(4), 22–29.

Liebman, R., S. Minuchin, and L. Baker. 1974a. An integrated program for *anorexia nervosa. American Journal of Psychiatry* 131, 432–435.

———. 1974b. The role of the family in the treatment of *anorexia nervosa. Journal of the American Academy of Child Psychology* 3, 264–274.

Liebowitz, M. 1984. *The Chemistry of Love.* New York: Berkeley Books.

Ljung, P. E. 1986. Semiotics in Sweden. In *The Semiotic Sphere,* ed. T. A. Sebeok and J. Umiker-Sebeok, 485–504. Berlin: Mouton de Gruyter.

Locke, J. 1975. *An Essay Concerning Human Understanding,* ed. Peter H. Nidditch. Oxford: Clarendon Press.

Loewenstein, W. R. 1999. *The Touchstone of Life: Molecular Information, Cell Communication, and the Foundations of Life.* New York: Oxford University Press.

Lorenz, K. 1954. *Man Meets Dog.* London: Methuen.

———. 1971. *Studies in Animal and Human Behaviour.* Vol. 2. Cambridge, Mass.: Harvard University Press.

———. 1973. Introduction to W. Wickler, *The Sexual Code: Social Behavior of Animals and Men,* xi-xix. Garden City: Anchor Books.

Lotman, Y. M. 1984. O semiosfere. *Sémeiótiké (Trudy po znakovym sistemam)* 17, 5–23. German versions in *Studia Russica Helsingiensia et Tartuensia* 20, 7–24 (1989), and in *Zeitschrift für Semiotik* 12, 287–305 (1990). French version: *La sémiosphère.* Limoges: PULIM (1999), from the original (1966) Russian edition.

———. 1987. On the contemporary concept of the text. *Livstegn* 3, 159–163.

———. 1990. *Universe of the Mind: A Semiotic Theory of Culture.* Bloomington: Indiana University Press.

Lotz, J. 1950. Speech and language. *The Journal of the Acoustical Society of America* 22, 712–717.

———. 1954 The structure of human speech. *Transactions of the New York Academy of Sciences,* Ser. II, 16(7), 373–384.

Lovelock, J. E. 1979. *Gaia: A New Look at Life on Earth.* Oxford: Oxford University Press.

Lucid, D. P., ed. 1977. *Soviet Semiotics: An Anthology.* Baltimore: Johns Hopkins University Press.

Lurie, A. 1981. *The Language of Clothes*. New York: Random House.

MacBryde, C. M., and R. Backlow, eds. 1970. *Signs and Symptoms: Applied Pathologic Physiology and Clinical Interpretation*. Philadelphia: J. B. Lippincott.

Magariños de Morentin, J. A. 1987. Semiotics in Argentina. In *The Semiotic Web 1986*, ed. T. A. Sebeok and J. Umiker-Sebeok, 123–142. Berlin: Mouton de Gruyter.

Mahmoudian, M. 1993. *Modern Theories of Language: The Empirical Challenge*. Durham: Duke University Press.

Majno, G. 1975. *The Healing Hand: Man and Wound in the Ancient World*. Cambridge, Mass.: Harvard University Press.

Mandelker, A. 1994. Semiotizing the sphere: Organicist theory in Lotman, Bakhtin, and Vernadsky. *Publications of the Modern Language Association* 109(3), 385–396.

Manetti, G. 1987. *Le teorie del segno nell'antichità classica*. Milano: Bompiani.

———. 1993. *Theories of the Sign in Classical Antiquity*. Bloomington: Indiana University Press.

Marantz, A. 1983. Before Babel: The misguided quest for the origins of language. *The Sciences* 23(3), 16–20.

Marcus, S. 1979. Approches sémiotiques en Roumanie. In *Le champ sémiologique. Perspectives internationales,* ed. A. Helbo, N1–10. Brussels: Editions Complexe.

Margulis, L. 1981. *Symbiosis in Cell Evolution: Life and Its Environment on the Early Earth*. San Francisco: Freeman.

———. 1993. *Symbiosis in Cell Evolution: Microbial Communities in the Archean and Proterozoic Eons*. Second edition. New York: W. H. Freeman.

———. 1998. *Symbiotic Planet: A New Look at Evolution*. New York: Basic Books.

Margulis, L., and D. Sagan. 1986. Strange fruit on the tree of life: How man-made objects may remake man. *The Sciences* 4(2), 38–45.

———. 1997a. *Microcosmos: Four Billion Years of Microbial Evolution*. Berkeley: University of California Press.

———. 1997b. *Slanted Truths: Essays on Gaia, Symbiosis, and Evolution*. New York: Springer-Verlag.

Margulis, L., and K. V. Schwartz. 1988. *Five Kingdoms: An Illustrated Guide to the Phyla of Life on Earth*. Second edition. New York: W. H. Freeman.

Markley, R., ed. 1996. *Virtual Realities and Their Discontents*. Baltimore: Johns Hopkins University Press.

Markus, R. A. 1957. St. Augustine on signs. *Phronesis* 2, 60–83.

Martin, R. 1986. Semiotics in Belgium. In *The Semiotic Sphere,* ed. T. A. Sebeok and J. Umiker-Sebeok, 19–45. Berlin: Mouton de Gruyter.

Masani, P. R. 1990. *Norbert Wiener 1894–1964*. Basel: Birkhäuser Verlag.

Maturana, H. R. 1980. Autopoiesis: Reproduction, heredity, and evolution. In *Autopoiesis, Dissipative Structures, and Spontaneous Social Orders,* ed. M. Zeleny, 45–107. Boulder, Colo.: Westview Press.

Maturana, H. R., and F. J. Varela 1992. *The Tree of Knowledge: The Biological Roots of Human Understanding*. Second edition. Boston: Shambhala.

Maynard Smith, J. 1995. Genes, memes, & minds. *New York Review of Books* 42(19), 46–48.

Maynard Smith, J., and E. Szathmáry 1995. *The Major Transitions in Evolution*. Oxford: W. H. Freeman.

Mazur, M. 1979. La sémiotique en Pologne. In *Le champ sémiologique. Perspectives internationales,* ed. A. Helbo, M1–10. Brussels: Editions Complexe.

McAlister, L. L., ed. 1996. *Hypatia's Daughters: Fifteen Hundred Years of Women Philosophers.* Bloomington: Indiana University Press.

McCormick, H. 1986. Semiotics in Venezuela. In *The Semiotic Sphere,* ed. T. A. Sebeok and J. Umiker-Sebeok, 599–611. Berlin: Mouton de Gruyter.

McFarland, D., ed. 1982. *The Oxford Companion to Animal Behavior.* Oxford and New York: Oxford University Press.

McKean, K. 1982. Diagnosis by computer. *Discover* 3(9), 60–83.

McLuhan, M. 1962. *The Gutenberg Galaxy: The Making of Typographic Man.* Toronto: University of Toronto Press.

McNeill, D. 1992. *Hand and Mind: What Gestures Reveal about Thought.* Chicago: University of Chicago Press.

McNeill, D., and P. Freiberger. 1993. *Fuzzy Logic.* New York: Simon and Schuster.

Mead, G. H. 1934. *Mind, Self, and Society: From the Standpoint of a Social Behaviorist.* Chicago: University of Chicago Press.

———. 1936. *Movements of Thought in the Nineteenth Century.* Chicago: University of Chicago Press.

Medawar, P. B., and J. S. Medawar. 1983. *Aristotle to Zoos: A Philosophical Dictionary of Biology.* Cambridge, Mass.: Harvard University Press.

Mellor, D. H., ed. 1990. *Ways of Communicating.* Cambridge: Cambridge University Press.

Merrell, F. 1991. *Signs Becoming Signs: Our Perfusive, Pervasive Universe.* Bloomington: Indiana University Press.

———. 1992. *Sign, Textuality, World.* Bloomington: Indiana University Press.

———. 1995. *Semiosis in the Postmodern Age.* West Lafayette: Purdue University Press.

———. 1996. *Signs Grow: Semiosis and Life Processes.* Toronto: University of Toronto Press.

Mertz, E., and R. J. Parmentier, eds. 1985. *Semiotic Mediation: Sociocultural and Psychological Perspectives.* Orlando: Academic Press.

Metz, C. 1974. *Language and Cinema.* The Hague: Mouton.

Milani, M. M. 1987. *The Body Language and Emotions of Cats.* New York: William Morrow.

Miller, J. 1978. *The Body in Question.* New York: Random House.

Miller, J. H. 1995. Narrative. In *Critical Terms for Literary Study,* ed. F. Letricchia and T. McLaughlin, 66–79. Chicago: University of Chicago Press.

Mivart, St. G. J. 1881. *The Cat.* New York: Scribners.

Moelk, M. 1944. Vocalizing in the house cat: A phonetic and functional study. *The American Journal of Psychology* 57, 184–205.

Monod, J. 1971. *Chance and Necessity.* New York: Alfred Knopf.

Montalverne, G. 1984. A vida secreta das plantas. *Atlantas* 4(4), 8–13.

Mooney, M. 1985. *Vico in the Tradition of Rhetoric.* Princeton: Princeton University Press.

Morris, C. 1938. Foundations of the theory of signs. *International Encyclopedia of Unified Science* 1(2), 78–137. Chicago: University of Chicago Press.

———. 1946. *Signs, Language and Behavior.* New York: Prentice-Hall.

———. 1964. *Signification and Significance: A Study of the Relations of Signs and Values.* Cambridge, Mass.: MIT Press.

———. 1971. *Writings on the General Theory of Signs,* ed. T. A. Sebeok. The Hague: Mouton.

Morris, D. 1977. *Manwatching: A Field Guide to Human Behaviour.* London: Jonathan Cape.

———. 1986. *Cat Watching.* New York: Crown.

———. 1987. *Catlore.* New York: Crown.

Morris, D., P. Collett, P. Marsh, and M. O'Shaughnessy. 1979. *Gestures: Their Origins and Distribution.* New York: Stein and Day.

Moses, P. J. 1954. *The Voice of Neurosis.* New York: Grune & Stratton.

Mounin, G. 1981. Sémiologie médicale et sémiologie linguistique. *Confrontations Psychiatriques* 19, 43–58.

Müller, H. M. 1987. *Evolution, Kognition und Sprache.* Berlin: Paul Parey.

Munro, H. H. 1982. *The Penguin Complete Saki.* London: Penguin.

Nabokov, V. 1957. *Pnin.* London: Penguin Books.

Nadin, M., and R. D. Zakia. 1994. *Creating Effective Advertising Using Semiotics.* New York: Consultant Press.

Net, M. 1990. Semiotics in Romania. In *The Semiotic Web 1989,* T. A. Sebeok and J. Umiker-Sebeok, 221–273. Berlin: Mouton de Gruyter.

Netton, I. R. 1989. *Allah Transcendent: Studies in the Structure and Semiotics of Islamic Philosophy, Theology and Cosmology.* London: Routledge.

Neuburger, M. 1906. *Geschichte der Medizin.* Vol 1. Stuttgart: Ferdinand Enke.

Nilsen, D. L. F. 2000. Body humor. In *Encyclopedia of 20th-Century American Humor,* ed. A. P. Nilsen and D. L. F. Nilsen. Phoenix: Oryx Press.

Norris, C. 1986. Semiotics in Great Britain. In *The Semiotic Sphere,* ed. T. A. Sebeok and J. Umiker-Sebeok, 229–251. Berlin: Mouton de Gruyter.

Nöth, W. 2000. *Handbuch der Semiotik.* 2nd, revised edition. Stuttgart: J. B. Metzler. English translation in preparation.

Nunberg, G. 1996. *The Future of the Book.* Berkeley: University of California Press.

Nutton, V. 1991. Style and context in the method of healing. *Galen's Method of Healing,* ed. F. Kudlien and R. J. Durling, 1–25. Leiden: E. J. Brill.

O'Flaherty, W. 1984. *Dreams, Illusion, and Other Realities.* Chicago: University of Chicago Press.

Ogden, C. K., and I. A. Richards. 1938. *The Meaning of Meaning: A Study of the Influence of Language upon Thought and of the Science of Symbolism.* Fifth edition. New York: Harcourt, Brace.

Osgood, C. E., and T. A. Sebeok, eds. 1954. *Psycholinguistics: A Survey of Theory and Research Problems.* Memoir of the *International Journal of American Linguistics.*

Osolsobé, I. 1979. Cinquante ans après . . . Ou les quatre courants de la sémiologie tchécoslovaque contemporaine. In *Le champ sémiologique. Perspectives internationales,* ed. A. Helbo, P1–5. Brussels: Editions Complexe.

O'Toole, L. M. 1975. Analytic and synthetic approaches to narrative structure: Sherlock Holmes and "The Sussex Vampire." In *Style and Structure in Literature,* ed. R. Fowler, 143–76. Oxford: Blackwell.

Otten, E. 1992. Phantom limbs. *The New York Review of Books,* January 30, 45–46.

Ousby, I., ed. 1988. *The Cambridge Guide to Literature in English.* Cambridge: Cambridge University Press.

Paci, E. 1969. Vico and Cassirer. In *Giambattista Vico: An International Symposium,* ed. G. Tagliacozzo and H. V. White, 457–473. Baltimore: The Johns Hopkins University Press.

Pagels, H. R. 1988. *The Dreams of Reason: The Computer and the Rise of the Sciences of Complexity*. New York: Simon and Schuster.

Paine, R., and W. Sherman. 1970. Arterial hypertension. In *Signs and Symptoms: Applied Pathologic Physiology and Clinical Interpretation*, ed. C. M. MacBryde and R. Backlow, eds., 272–303. Philadelphia: J. B. Lippincott.

Pais, A. 1991. *Niels Bohr's Times, in Physics, Philosophy, and Polity*. Oxford: Clarendon Press.

Palmer, S. 1937. *The Puzzle of the Red Stallion*. Garden City: Doubleday.

———. 1941. *The Puzzle of Happy Hooligan*. New York: Doubleday.

Paz, O. 1990. The power of ancient Mexican art. *New York Review of Books*, December 6.

Peirce, C. S. 1901. Implicit. In *Dictionary of Philosophy and Psychology* 1:525–526.

———. 1935–1966. *Collected Papers of Charles Sanders Peirce*, eds. C. Hartshorne, P. Weiss, and A. W. Burks. 8 vols. Cambridge, Mass.: Harvard University Press.

Pelc, J. 1974. The development of Polish semiotics in the post-war years. *Semiotica* 10(4), 369–381.

Pellegrino, P. 1992. Semiotics in Switzerland. *Semiotica* 90(1/2), 125–162.

Pentacost, H. [J. P. Philips] 1961. *Murder Clear, Track Fast*. New York: Dodd, Mead.

Petrilli, S. 1988. Victoria Lady Welby and significs: An interview with H. W. Schmitz. In *The Semiotic Web 1987*, ed. T. A. Sebeok and J. Umiker-Sebeok, 79–92. Berlin: Mouton de Gruyter.

———. 1993. Thomas A. Sebeok and semiotics in the United States in the panorama of recent developments in Italian semiotics. *Semiotica* 97(3/4), 337–372.

———. 1999. About and beyond Peirce. *Semiotica* 124, 299–376.

Petrilli, S., and A. Ponzio, eds. 2000. *Signs and Light: Illuminating Paths in the Semiotic Web*. Special issue of *Semiotica* 133.

Phillips, E. D. 1973. *Greek Medicine*. London: Thames and Hudson.

Pinker, S. 1994. *The Language Instinct: How the Mind Creates Language*. New York: William Morrow.

Platt, K. 1973. *The Princess Stakes Murder*. New York: Random House.

Pollack, R. 1994. *Signs of Life: The Language and Meanings of DNA*. Boston: Houghton Mifflin.

Polunin, I. 1977. The body as an indicator of health and disease. In *The Anthropology of the Body*, ed. J. Blacking, 85–98. London: Academic Press.

Ponzio, A. 1976. *La semiotica in Italia*. Bari: Dedalo.

———. 1993. Towards the signs of Gaia and beyond: Thomas A. Sebeok's semiotic research. *Semiotica* 97(3/4), 373–382.

Popper, K. K. 1972. *Objective Knowledge: An Evolutionary Approach*. Oxford: Clarendon Press.

Posner, R., K. Robering, and T. A. Sebeok, eds. 1997. *Semiotics: A Handbook on the Sign-Theoretic Foundations of Nature and Culture*. Vol. 1. Berlin: Walter de Gruyter.

———, eds. 1998. *Semiotics: A Handbook on the Sign-Theoretic Foundations of Nature and Culture*. Vol. 2. Berlin: Walter de Gruyter.

———, eds. 2001. *Semiotics: A Handbook on the Sign-Theoretic Foundations of Nature and Culture*. Vol. 3. Berlin: Walter de Gruyter.

Powers, R. 1991. *The Gold Bug Variations*. New York: Harper Perennial.

Prodi, G. 1977. *Le basi materiali della significazione*. Milano: Bompiani.

———. 1981. Sintomo/diagnosi. *Enciclopedia: Ricerca-Socializzazione* 12, 972–992.

———. 1988a. La biologia come semiotica naturale. In *Semiotic Theory and Practice*, ed. M. Herzfeld and L. Melazzo, 2:929–951. Berlin: Mouton de Gruyter.

———. 1988b. The material bases of signification. *Semiotica* 69(3/4), 191–241.

———. 1988c. Signs and codes in immunology. In *The Semiotics of Cellular Communication in the Immune System*, ed. E. E. Sercarz, F. Celada, N. A. Mitchison, and T. Tada, 53–64. Berlin: Springer-Verlag.

———. 1988d. *Teoria e metodo in biologia e medicina*. Bologna: CLUEB.

Propp, V. Y. 1928. *Morfologija skazki*. Leningrad: Akademia.

Proschan, F., ed. 1983. Puppets, masks, and performing objects from semiotic perspectives. *Semiotica* 47, 1–361.

Prosser, C. L. 1985. Modes of communication. In *Comparative Neurobiology: Modes of Communication in the Nervous System*, ed. M. J. Cohen and F. Strumwasser, 117–118. New York: Wiley.

Rappaport, R. A. 1999. *Ritual and Religion in the Making of Humanity*. Cambridge: Cambridge University Press.

Rauch, I. 1999. *Semiotic Insights: The Data Do the Talking*. Toronto: University of Toronto Press.

Rauch, I. and G. Carr, eds. 1980. *The Signifying Animal: The Grammar of Language and Experience*. Bloomington: Indiana University Press.

———, eds. 1989. *The Semiotic Bridge: Trends from California*. Berlin: Mouton de Gruyter.

———, eds. 1997. *Semiotics Around the World: Synthesis in Diversity. Proceedings of the Fifth Congress of the International Association for Semiotic Studies—Berkeley 1994*. Berlin: Mouton de Gruyter.

Rector, M. 1986. Semiotics in Brazil. In *The Semiotic Sphere*, ed. T. A. Sebeok and J. Umiker-Sebeok, 47–58. Berlin: Mouton de Gruyter.

Rector, M. and E. Neiva, Jr. 1979. Etudes des signes au Brésil. In *Le champ sémiologique. Perspectives internationales*, ed. A. Helbo, D1–12. Brussels: Editions Complexe.

Regan, J., S. M. Lamb, J. B. Cobb, Jr., D. R. Griffin, and A. Basu, eds. 1992. *Whitehead and Lamb: A New Network of Connection*. Claremont: College Press.

Reschke, B. 1960. *Untersuchungen zur Lautgebung der Feliden*. Unpublished doctoral dissertation, Humboldt Universität (Berlin).

Réthoré, J. 1989. Semiotic vignettes: France, 1987. In *The Semiotic Web 1988*, ed. T. A. Sebeok and J. Umiker-Sebeok, eds., 161–179. Berlin: Mouton de Gruyter.

Revzin, I. I. 1978. Notes on the semiotic analysis of detective novels: With examples from the novels of Agatha Christie. *New Literary History* 9, 385–88.

Revzina, O. G. 1972. The Fourth Summer School of Secondary Modeling Systems (Tartu, 17–24 August 1970). *Semiotica* 6(3/4), 222–243.

Rey, A. 1973. *Théories du signe et du sens*. Vol. 1. Paris: Klincksieck.

———. 1976. *Théories du signe et du sens*. Vol. 2. Paris: Klincksieck.

Ricci Bitti, P. E. 1992. Facial and manual components of Italian symbolic gestures. In *Advances in Nonverbal Communication*, ed. F. Poyatos, 187–196. Amsterdam: Benjamins.

Riffaterre, M. 1987. Hypersigns. *The American Journal of Semiotics* 5, 1–12.

Roitblat, H. L., L. M. Herman, and P. E. Nachtigall. 1993. *Language and Communication: Comparative Perspectives*. Hillsdale, N.J.: Lawrence Erlbaum.

Rosen, C. 1995. Beethoven's triumph. *The New York Review of Books* 42(14), 52–56.

———. 1999. On playing the piano. *The New York Review of Books* 46(16), 49–54.

Rosenblatt, J. S., and T. C. Schneirla. 1962. The behaviour of cats. In *The Behavior of Domestic Animals,* ed. E. S. E. Hafez, 453–488. Baltimore: Williams and Wilkins.

Rosenthal, R. 1981. Pavlov's mice, Pfungst's horse, and Pygmalion's PONS: Some models for the study of interpersonal expectancy effects. In *The Clever Hans Phenomenon: Communication with Horses, Whales, Apes, and People,* ed. T. A. Sebeok and R. Rosenthal, 182–198. New York: New York Academy of Sciences.

Ross, S. 1998. *What Gardens Mean.* London: University of Chicago Press.

Rossi-Landi, F. 1992. *Between Signs and Non-Signs,* ed. Susan Petrilli. Amsterdam: John Benjamins.

Roth, J., and D. LeRoith. 1987. Chemical cross talk: Why human cells understand the molecular messages of plants. *The Sciences* 27(3), 51–54.

Rudy, S. 1986. Semiotics in the U.S. S. R. In *The Semiotic Sphere,* ed. T. A. Sebeok and J. Umiker-Sebeok, 555–582. Berlin: Mouton de Gruyter.

Rue, L. D. 1994. *By the Grace of Guile: The Role of Deception in Natural History and Human Affairs.* New York: Oxford University Press.

Ruesch, J., and W. Kees. 1956. *Nonverbal Communication: Notes on the Visual Perception of Human Relations.* Berkeley: University of California Press.

Russell, B. 1959. *Wisdom of the West.* London: Macdonald.

Rybczynski, W. 1995. Design for living. *The New York Review of Books* 42(18), 12–15.

Sanders, C. R. 1989. *Customizing the Body: The Art and Culture of Tattooing.* Philadelphia: Temple University Press.

Santaella Braga, L. 1990. Brazil: A culture in tune with semiotics. In *The Semiotic Web 1989,* T. A. Sebeok and J. Umiker-Sebeok, 123–175. Berlin: Mouton de Gruyter.

Sapir, E. 1944. Grading: A study in semantics. *Philosophy of Science* 11, 93–116.

Sarton, G. 1954. *Galen of Pergamon.* Lawrence: University of Kansas Press.

Sartre, J. P. 1966. *Being and Nothingness.* First edition, 1943. New York: Washington Square Press.

Savage-Rumbaugh, S., and R. Lewin. 1994. *Kanzi: The Ape at the Brink of the Human Mind.* New York: John Wiley.

Sayers, D. L. 1932. *Have His Carcase.* New York: Harcourt, Brace.

Scannerini, S. 1988. The cell structures of plant, animal and microbial symbionts, their differences and similarities. In *Cell to Cell Signals in Plant, Animal and Microbial Symbiosis,* ed. S. Scannerini, D. Smith, P. Bonfante-Fasolo and V. Gianinazzi-Pearson, 143–157. Berlin: Springer Verlag.

Schandry, R. 1990. When the heart cannot be felt. *Special Science Reports* [of the German Research Service] 6(12), 4.

Scheglov, Yu. K., and A. K. Zholkovsky. 1975. Towards a "theme-(expression devices)-text": Model of literary structure. *Russian Poetics in Translation* 1, 1–77.

Schiffman, N. 1997. *Abracadabra! Secret Methods Magicians & Others Use to Deceive Their Audience.* Amherst: Prometheus Books.

Schiffrin, D. 1966. Narrative as self-portrait: Sociolinguistic constructions of identity. *Language in Society* 25, 167–203.

Schilpp, P. A., ed. 1949. *The Philosophy of Ernst Cassirer.* Evanston, Il.: The Library of Living Philosophers.

Schmitz, H. W. 1985. Victoria Lady Welby's significs: The origin of the signific movement. In *Significs and Language,* by Victoria Welby, ed. H. W. Schmitz, ix-xxxii. Amsterdam: John Benjamins.

Schneirla, T. C. 1965. Aspects of stimulation and organization in approach/withdrawal processes underlying vertebrate behavioral development. *Advances in the Study of Behavior* 1, 1–74. New York: Academic Press.

Schopf, J. W., ed. 1983. *Earth's Earliest Biosphere: Its Origin and Evolution.* Princeton: Princeton University Press.

Schroeder, R. 1996. *Possible Worlds: The Social Dynamic of Virtual Reality Technology.* Boulder: Westview Press.

Schuller, G. 1997. *The Compleat Conductor.* London: Oxford University Press.

Seabra, J. A. 1986. Semiotics in Portugal. In *The Semiotic Sphere,* ed. T. A. Sebeok and J. Umiker-Sebeok, 407–415. Berlin: Mouton de Gruyter.

Searle, J. 1992. *The Rediscovery of Mind.* Cambridge, Mass.: MIT Press.

Sebeok, T. A. 1945a. *Spoken Hungarian.* New York: Henry Holt.

———. 1945b. Linguist, informant and units. *Modern Language Journal* 29, 376–381.

———. 1946. *Finnish and Hungarian Case Systems: Their Form and Function.* Stockholm: Acta Instituti Hungarici Universitatis Holmiensis, Series B, Linguistica 3.

———. 1947a. *Spoken Finnish.* New York: Henry Holt.

———. 1947b. Two Winnebago texts. *International Journal of American Linguistics* 13, 167–170.

———. 1950. The meaning of "Ural-Altaic." *Lingua* 2, 124–139.

———. 1951. Materials for an Aymará dictionary. *Journal de la Société des Américanistes* 40, 89–151.

———. 1962. Sources for a Mari Chrestomathy. *Ural-Altaische Jahrbücher* 34, 26–40.

———. 1963. A sojourn in the Mongolian People's Republic. *The Mongolia Society Newsletter* 2, 30–31.

———. 1965. Animal communication. *Science* 147, 1006-14.

———. 1966. *Portraits of Linguists: A Biographical Source Book for the History of Western Linguistics 1746–1963.* Bloomington: Indiana University Press.

———. 1967. Discussion of communication processes. In *Social Communication among Primates,* ed. S. A. Altmann, 363–369. Chicago: University of Chicago Press.

———. 1969. The study of Finnish in the United States. In *The Finns in North America: A Social Symposium,* 170–174. East Lansing: Michigan State University Press.

———. 1972. *Perspectives in Zoosemiotics.* The Hague: Mouton.

———. 1973. Between animal and animal. *Times Literary Supplement,* No. 3,734 (October 5).

———. 1974a. Semiotics: A survey of the state of the art. In *Linguistics and Adjacent Arts and Sciences,* ed. T. A. Sebeok, 210–264. Vol. 12 of *Current Trends in Linguistics.* The Hague: Mouton.

———. 1974b. *Structure and Texture: Selected Essays in Cheremis Verbal Art.* The Hague: Mouton.

———. 1975. The semiotic web: A chronicle of prejudices. *Bulletin of Literary Semiotics* 2, 1–63.

———. 1976. *Contributions to the Doctrine of Signs.* First edition. Second edition, 1985. Lanham: University Press of America.

———. 1977a. Ecumenicalism in semiotics. In *A Perfusion of Signs,* 180–206. Bloomington: Indiana University Press.

———. 1977b. Zoosemiotic components of human communication. In *How Animals Communicate,* ed. T. A. Sebeok, 1055–1077. Bloomington: Indiana University Press.

———. 1978. *Cheremis Literary Reader with Glossary: Studies in Cheremis 10.* Louvain: Editions Peters.

———. 1979a. Prefigurements of art. *Semiotica* 27, 3–73.

———. 1979b. *The Sign & Its Masters.* Second edition, 1989. Austin: University of Texas Press.

———. 1979c. *Theorie und Geschichte der Semiotik.* Hamburg: Rowohlt Taschenbuch.

———. 1981a. Karl Bühler. In *Die Welt als Zeichen,* eds. M. Krampen, K. Oehler, R. Posner, T. A. Sebeok, and T. von Uexküll, 205–232. Berlin: Severin und Siedler.

———. 1981b. Naming in animals, with reference to playing. *Recherches Sémiotiques/ Semiotic Inquiry* 1:121–135.

———. 1981c. *The Play of Musement.* Bloomington: Indiana University Press.

———. 1983. On the history of semiotics. In *Semiotics Unfolding: Proceedings of the Second Congress of the International Association for Semiotic Studies Vienna, July 1979,* ed. T. Borbé, 1:353–354. Berlin: Mouton.

———. 1985a. *Contributions to the Doctrine of Signs.* Second edition. First edition, 1976. Lanham: University Press of America.

———. 1985b. Letter to the editor. *American Scientist* 73(1), 6.

———. 1986a. *I Think I Am a Verb: More Contributions to the Doctrine of Signs.* New York: Plenum Press.

———. 1986b. The problem of the origin of language in an evolutionary frame. *Language Sciences* 8, 169–176.

———. 1986c. Toward a natural history of language. *The World & I,* October, 462–469.

———. 1987a. Messages in the marketplace. In *Marketing and Semiotics: New Directions in the Study of Signs for Sale,* ed. J. Umiker-Sebeok, 21–30. Berlin: Mouton de Gruyter.

———. 1987b. Om teiknlæra. *Livstegn* 3, 164–180.

———. 1988a. "Animal" in biological and semiotic perspective. In *What Is an Animal?,* ed. T. Ingold, 63–76. London: Unwin Hyman.

———. 1988b. Foreword to the paperback edition of *Soviet Semiotics: An Anthology,* ed. D. P. Lucid, v-viii. Baltimore: John Hopkins University Press.

———. 1988c. In what sense is language a "primary modeling system"? In *Semiotics of Culture,* ed. H. Broms and R. Kaufmann, 67–80. Helsinki: Arator.

———. 1989a. John Lotz: A personal memoir. In *The Sign & Its Masters,* 231–247. Second edition. Lanham: University Press of America.

———. 1989b. Parasitic formations and kindred semiotic sets: Notes on the legacy of John Lotz. In *The Sign & Its Masters,* 248–252. Second edition. Lanham: University Press of America.

———. 1989c. The semiotic self. In *The Sign & Its Masters,* 263–267. Second edition. Lanham: University Press of America.

———. 1989d. The semiotic self revisited. Foreword to *Sign, Self, Society,* ed. B. Lee and G. Urban, v-xiv. Berlin: Mouton de Gruyter.

———. 1989e. *The Sign & Its Masters.* Second edition. First edition, 1979. Lanham: University Press of America.

———. 1990a. *Essays in Zoosemiotics.* Monograph Series of the Toronto Semiotic Circle 5. Toronto: Victoria College in the University of Toronto.

———. 1990b. Semiotics in the United States. In *The Semiotic Web 1989,* T. A. Sebeok and J. Umiker-Sebeok, 275–395. Berlin: Mouton de Gruyter.

———. 1991a. *American Signatures: Semiotic Inquiry and Method.* Oklahoma Project for Discourse and Theory. Norman: University of Oklahoma Press.

——. 1991b. Communication. In *A Sign Is Just A Sign*, 22–35. Bloomington: Indiana University Press.

——. 1991c. Indexicality. *American Journal of Semiotics* 7(4), 7–28.

——. 1991d. Indexicality. In *A Sign Is Just A Sign*, 128–143. Bloomington: Indiana University Press.

——. 1991e. *Semiotics in the United States*. Bloomington: Indiana University Press.

——. 1991f. *A Sign Is Just A Sign*. Bloomington: Indiana University Press.

——. 1992a. Into the rose-garden. *Ural-Altaische Jahrbücher* 64, 1–12.

——. 1992b. Tell me, where is fancy bred: The biosemiotic self. In *Biosemiotics: The Semiotic Web 1991*, ed. T. A. Sebeok and J. Umiker-Sebeok, 333–343. Berlin: Mouton de Gruyter.

——. 1992c. Uralic Studies and English for Hungarians at Indiana University: A personal view. *Hungarian Studies* 7(1/2), 149–152.

——. 1994a. *Signs: An Introduction to Semiotics*. Toronto: University of Toronto Press.

——. 1994b. What do we know about signifying behavior in the domestic cat (*Felis catus*)? *Signifying Behaviour* 1, 3–31.

——. 1995a. From Vico to Cassirer to Langer. In *Giambattista Vico and Anglo-American Science*, ed. M. Danesi, 159–170. Berlin: Mouton de Gruyter.

——. 1995b. Indexicality. In *Peirce and Contemporary Thought: Philosophical Inquiries*, ed. K. L. Ketner, 222–242. New York: Fordham University Press.

——. 1995c. Meditations on media, mediums, and mediation. Lecture delivered at a conference on "The Semiotics of the Media: State of the Art, Projects, and Perspectives," University of Kassel, March 20–23.

——. 1995d. Teaching semiotics in the United States. *Degrés* d1-d8.

——. 1996. Galen in medical semiotics. *Interdisciplinary Journal for Germanic Linguistics and Semiotic Analysis* 1, 89–111.

——. 1997a. The evolution of semiosis. In *Semiotics. A Handbook on the Sign Theoretic Foundations of Nature and Culture*, ed. R. Posner, K. Robering, and T. A. Sebeok, 436–446. Berlin: Walter de Gruyter.

——. 1997b. Global semiotics. In *Semiotics Around the World. Synthesis in Diversity. Proceedings of the Fifth Congress of the International Association for Semiotic Studies—Berkeley 1994*, ed. I. Rauch and G. F. Carr, 105–130. Berlin: Mouton de Gruyter.

——. 1998a. *Come comunicano gli animali che non parlano*. Bari: Edizioni dal Sud.

——. 1998b. The Estonian connection. *Sign Systems Studies* 26, 20–38.

——. 1999a. Foreword to I. Rauch, *Semiotic Insights: The Data Do the Talking*. Toronto: University of Toronto Press.

——. 1999b. My "short happy life" in Finno-Ugric Studies. In *Snow, Forest, Silence. The Finnish Tradition of Semiotics*, ed. E. Tarasti, 16–25. Bloomington: Indiana University Press.

——. 2000a. *Essays in Semiotics: Culture Signs*. Ottawa: Legas Press.

——. 2000b. *Essays in Semiotics: Life Signs*. Ottawa: Legas Press.

——. 2000c. The music of the spheres. *Semiotica* 128(3/4), 527–535.

——. 2000d. Semiotics and the biological sciences: Initial conditions. In *Semiotics as a Bridge Between the Humanities and the Sciences: Proceedings of the First University of Toronto Semiotics Research Unit Annual Conference*, ed. M. Danesi and P. Perron. Ottawa: Legas Press.

Sebeok, T. A., and M. Danesi. 2000. *The Forms of Meaning: Modeling Systems Theory and Semiotic Analysis*. Berlin: Mouton de Gruyter.

Sebeok, T. A., and F. J. Ingemann. 1956. *The Supernatural: Studies in Cheremis 2.* Viking Fund Publications in Anthropology No. 22. New York: Wenner-Gren Foundation for Anthropological Research.

Sebeok, T. A., and S. Petrilli. 1999. Women in semiotics. In *Interdigitations: Essays for Irmengard Rauch,* ed. G. F. Carr, W. Herbert, and L. Zhang, 469–478. New York: Peter Lang.

Sebeok, T. A., A. Ponzio, and S. Petrilli. Forthcoming. *The Semiotic Self.* English translation of *La semiotica dell'io* (Rome: Meltemi).

Sebeok, T. A., and J. Umiker-Sebeok. 1981. *Sherlock Holmes no Kigóron: C. S. Peirce to Holmes no Hikakukenkin (= Genbal-Shinsho).* Translated by Takao Tomiyama. Tokyo: Iwanami Shoten.

———. 1987–1995. Prefaces to *The Semiotic Web,* vols. 1–7. Berlin: Mouton de Gruyter.

Sebeok, T. A., and V. J. Zeps. 1961. *Concordance and Thesaurus of Cheremis Poetic Language: Studies in Cheremis 8.* 'S-Gravenhage: Mouton & Co.

Sebeok, T. A., ed. 1960. *Style in Language.* New York: John Wiley.

———, ed. 1968. *Animal Communication: Techniques of Study and Results of Research.* Bloomington: Indiana University Press.

———, ed. 1977. *How Animals Communicate.* Bloomington: Indiana University Press.

———, ed. 1994. *Encyclopedic Dictionary of Semiotics.* Second edition. First edition, 1979. Berlin: Mouton de Gruyter.

Sebeok, T. A., A. S. Hayes, and M. C. Bateson, eds. 1972. *Approaches to Semiotics.* Second edition. First edition, 1964. The Hague: Mouton.

Sebeok, T. A., and R. Rosenthal, eds. 1981. *The Clever Hans Phenomenon: Communication with Horses, Whales, Apes, and People.* Annals of the New York Academy of Sciences, vol. 364. New York: Academy of Sciences.

Sebeok, T. A., and J. Umiker-Sebeok, eds. 1976. *Speech Surrogates: Drum and Whistle Systems.* The Hague: Mouton.

———, eds. 1980. *Speaking of Apes: A Critical Anthology of Two-Way Communication with Man.* New York: Plenum Press.

———, eds. 1986. *The Semiotic Sphere.* New York: Plenum Press.

———, eds. 1987. *The Semiotic Web 1986.* Berlin: Mouton de Gruyter.

———, eds. 1988. *The Semiotic Web 1987.* Berlin: Mouton de Gruyter.

———, eds. 1989. *The Semiotic Web 1988.* Berlin: Mouton de Gruyter

———, eds. 1990. *The Semiotic Web 1989.* Berlin: Mouton de Gruyter.

———, eds. 1991. *Recent Developments in Theory and History: The Semiotic Web 1990.* Berlin: Mouton de Gruyter.

———, eds. 1992. *Biosemiotics: The Semiotic Web 1991.* Berlin: Mouton de Gruyter.

———, eds. 1995. *Advances in Visual Semiotics: The Semiotic Web 1992–93.* Berlin: Mouton de Gruyter.

Seeley, T. D., and R. A. Levien. 1987. A colony of mind. *The Sciences* 27(4), 39–42.

Segre, C. 1979. Du structuralisme à la sémiologie en Italie. In *Le champ sémiologique. Perspectives internationales,* ed. A. Helbo, L1–29. Brussels: Editions Complexe.

Seielstad, G. 1989. *At the Heart of the Web: The Inevitable Genesis of Intelligent Life.* Boston: Harcourt Brace Jovanovich.

Sekoni, R. 1989. Semiotics in Nigeria. In *The Semiotic Web 1988,* ed. T. A. Sebeok and J. Umiker-Sebeok, 187–195. Berlin: Mouton de Gruyter.

Semiotics in Switzerland. 1986. In *The Semiotic Sphere,* ed. T. A. Sebeok and J. Umiker-Sebeok, 505–517. Berlin: Mouton de Gruyter.

Sercarz, E. E., F. Celada, N. A., Mitchison, and T. Tada, eds. 1988. *The Semiotics of Cellular Communication in the Immune System*. NATO ASI Series H: Cell Biology, vol. 23. Berlin: Springer-Verlag.

Shands, H. C. 1970. *Semiotic Approaches to Psychiatry*. The Hague: Mouton.

Shannon, C. E. 1948. A mathematical theory of information. *Bell System Technical Journal* 27, 379–423, 623–656.

Sharov, A. A. 1992. Biosemiotics: A functional-evolutionary approach to the analysis of the sense of information. In *Biosemiotics. The Semiotic Web 1991*, ed. T. A. Sebeok and J. Umiker-Sebeok, 345–373. Berlin: Mouton de Gruyter.

Shklovsky, V. 1925. Novella tain. In *O teorii prozy*. Moscow: Federacija.

Short, T. L. 1992. Peirce's semiotic theory of the self. *Semiotica* 91, 109–131.

———. 1994. David Savan's defense of semiotic realism. *Semiotica* 98(3/4), 243–263.

———. 1998. What's the use? *Semiotica* 122, 1–68.

Shukman, A. 1994. Modeling system. In *Encyclopedic Dictionary of Semiotics*, ed. T. A. Sebeok, 1, 558–560. Second edition. Berlin: Mouton de Gruyter.

Siegel, R. E. 1973. *Galen on Psychology, Psychopathology, and Function and Diseases of the Nervous System: An Analysis of His Doctrines, Observations and Experiments*. Basel: S. Karger.

Sigurjónsson, Á. 1989. Semiotics in Iceland. In *The Semiotic Web 1988*, ed. T. A. Sebeok and J. Umiker-Sebeok, eds., 181–186. Berlin: Mouton de Gruyter.

Silk, J. 1980. *The Big Bang: The Creation and Evolution of the Universe*. San Francisco: W. H. Freeman.

Silva, A. 1990. Semiotics in Colombia: Within new perspectives. In *The Semiotic Web 1989*, T. A. Sebeok and J. Umiker-Sebeok, 177–193. Berlin: Mouton de Gruyter.

Singer, M. 1984. *Man's Glassy Essence: Explorations in Semiotic Anthropology*. Bloomington: Indiana University Press.

Skiljan, D., and M. Velcic 1992. Semiotic studies in Yugoslavia. *Semiotica* 90(1/2), 163–176.

Slusser, G., and T. Shippey. 1992. *Fiction 2000: Cyberpunk and the Future of Narrative*. Athens: University of Georgia Press.

Smith, W. J. 1969. Displays and messages in intraspecific communication. *Semiotica* 1, 357–369.

———. 1974. Zoosemiotics: Ethology and the theory of signs. In *Current Trends in Linguistics: Linguistics and Adjacent Arts and Sciences*, ed. T. A. Sebeok, 12(1), 561–626. The Hague: Mouton.

———. 1977. *The Behavior of Communicating: An Ethological Approach*. Cambridge, Mass.: Harvard University Press.

Snow, C. P. 1959. *The Two Cultures and the Scientific Revolution*. New York: Columbia University Press.

———. 1971. *Public Affairs*. New York: Scribners.

Sommer, R. 1969. *Personal Space: The Behavioral Basis of Design*. Englewood Cliffs, N.J.: Prentice-Hall.

Sonea, S. 1988. The global organism: A new view of bacteria. *The Sciences* 28(4), 38–45.

———. 1990. Bacterial (prokaryotic) communication. In *The Semiotic Web 1989*, T. A. Sebeok and J. Umiker-Sebeok, 639–662. Berlin: Mouton de Gruyter.

———. 1992. Half of the living world was unable to communicate for about one billion years. In *The Semiotic Web 1991*, ed. T. A. Sebeok and J. Umiker-Sebeok, eds., 375–392. Berlin: Mouton de Gruyter.

———. 1995. Oui, les bactérie communiquent! *Débats sémiotiques* l(1), 24–37.

Sonea, S., and M. Panisset. 1983. *A New Bacteriology.* Boston: Jones and Bartlett.

Sonesson, G. 1989. *Pictorial Concepts: Inquiries Into the Semiotic Heritage and its Relevance For the Analysis of the Visual World.* Lund: Lund University Press.

———. 1992. In search of the Swedish model in semiotics: Considerations on a body of literature in the process of constitution. *Semiotica* 90(1/2), 31–123.

Srivastava, R. N., and K. Kapoor. 1988. Semiotics in India. In *The Semiotic Web 1987,* ed. T. A. Sebeok and J. Umiker-Sebeok, 217–265. Berlin: Mouton de Gruyter.

Staiano, K. V. 1979. A semiotic definition of illness. *Semiotica* 28, 107–125.

———. 1982. Medical semiotics: Redefining an ancient craft. *Semiotica* 38, 319–346.

Stankiewicz, E. 1972. Problems of emotive language. In *Approaches to Semiotics,* ed. T. A. Sebeok, A. S. Hayes, and M. C. Bateson, 239–276. Second edition. The Hague: Mouton.

Steele, R., and T. Threadgold, eds. 1987. *Language Topics: Essays in Honour of Michael Halliday.* Amsterdam: John Benjamins.

Steiner, W. 1978. Modern American semiotics (1930–1978). In *The Sign: Semiotics around the World,* ed. R. W. Bailey, L. Matejka, and P. Steiner, eds., 99–118. Ann Arbor: Michigan Slavic Publications.

———. 1979. Développements de la sémiologie aux Etats-Unis. In *Le champ sémiologique. Perspectives internationales,* ed. A. Helbo, H1–27. Brussels: Editions Complexe.

Stepanov, Y. S. 1971. *Semiotika.* Moscow: Nauka.

Stephens, M. 1994. Jacques Derrida. *The New York Times Magazine,* January 23.

Stevenson, C. S. 1958. Symbolism in the nonrepresentative arts. In *Language, Thought, & Culture,* ed. P. Henle, 196–225. Ann Arbor: University of Michigan Press.

Stokoe, W. C., Jr. 1972. *Semiotics and Human Sign Languages.* The Hague: Mouton.

Stone, J. 1989. Chest pains: What do they mean? *The New York Times Magazine,* February 19, 53–54.

Storelv, S. 1986. Semiotics in Norway. In *The Semiotic Sphere,* ed. T. A. Sebeok and J. Umiker-Sebeok, 369–385. Berlin: Mouton de Gruyter.

Sturrock, J. 1991. Inside the semiosphere. *Times Literary Supplement,* May 3, 9–10.

Suess, E. 1875. *Die Entstehung der Alpen.* Vienna: Wilhelm Braunmüller.

Swenson, R., and M. T. Turvey. 1991. Thermodynamic reasons for perception-action cycles. *Ecological Psychology* 3(4), 317–348.

Swiggers, P. 1986. Semiotics in the Low Countries. In *The Semiotic Sphere,* ed. T. A. Sebeok and J. Umiker-Sebeok, 343–357. Berlin: Mouton de Gruyter.

Synott, A. 1993. *The Body Social: Symbolism, Self and Society.* London: Routledge.

Szathmáry, E., and J. Maynard Smith. 1995. The major evolutionary transitions. *Nature* 374, 227–232.

Tagliacozzo, G., ed. 1981. *Vico: Past and Present.* Atlantic Highlands, N.J.: Humanities Press.

Tagliacozzo, G., and D. P. Verene, eds. 1976. *Giambattista Vico's Science of Humanity.* Baltimore: The Johns Hopkins University Press.

Tamir-Ghez, N. 1978. Topics in Israeli poetics and semiotics. *The Sign: Semiotics around the World,* ed. R. W. Bailey, L. Matejka, and P. Steiner, 238–247. Ann Arbor: Michigan Slavic Publications.

Tarasti, E. 1986. Semiotics in Finland. In *The Semiotic Sphere,* ed. T. A. Sebeok and J. Umiker-Sebeok, 145–152. Berlin: Mouton de Gruyter.

Tarasti, E., R. Littlefield, J. Inkinen, and M. Rossi, eds. 2000. *Commentationes in Honorem Thomas A. Sebeok Octogenarii A.D. MM Editae*. Imatra: International Semiotics Institute.

Tauber, A. I. 1994. *The Immune Self: Theory or Metaphor*. Cambridge: Cambridge University Press.

Tauber, A. I., ed. 1991. *Organism and the Origin of Self*. Dordrecht: Kluwer.

Teilhard de Chardin, P. 1959. *The Phenomenon of Man*. New York: Harper & Brothers.

Tembrock, G. 1963. Acoustic behaviour of mammals. In *Acoustic Behaviour of Animals,* ed. R.-G. Busnel, 751–786. London: Elsevier.

———. 1971. *Biokommunikation: Informationsübertragung im biologischen Bereich*. Berlin: Akademie-Verlag.

Temkin, O. 1973. *Galenism: Rise and Decline of a Medical Philosophy*. Ithaca: Cornell University Press.

Thom, R. 1975. *Structural Stability and Morphogenesis*. Reading: W. A. Benjamin.

———. 1980. L'espace et les signes. *Semiotica* 29, 193–208.

———. 1983. *Mathematical Models of Morphogenesis*. Chichester: Ellis Horwood.

———. 1990. *Semio Physics: A Sketch*. Redwood City, Cal.: Addison-Wesley.

Thomas, B. 1985. *Talking with the Animals: How to Communicate with Wildlife*. New York: William Morrow.

Thomson, T. A. 1927. Review of J. von Uexküll, *Theoretical Biology*. *Journal of Philosophical Studies* 2(7), 413–419.

Threadgold, T. 1988. Semiotics in Australia. In *The Semiotic Web 1987,* ed. T. A. Sebeok and J. Umiker-Sebeok, 111–144. Berlin: Mouton de Gruyter.

Timberlake, W. 1993. Animal behavior: A continuing synthesis. *Annual Review of Psychology* 44, 675–708.

Tomkins, G. M. 1975. The metabolic code. *Science* 189, 760–763.

Topsell, E. 1607. *Historie of Four-footed Beasts*. London: W. Iaggard.

Tort, P. 1983. *La pensée hiérarchique et l'évolution*. Paris: Aubier Montaigne.

Toyama, T. 1986. Semiotics in Japan. In *The Semiotic Sphere,* ed. T. A. Sebeok and J. Umiker-Sebeok, 323–342. Berlin: Mouton de Gruyter.

Trabant, J. 1994. *Neue Wissenschaft von alten Zeichen: Vicos Sematologie*. Frankfurt: Suhrkamp.

Trabant, J., ed. 1996. *Origins of Language*. Workshop series 2. Budapest: Collegium Budapest.

Trevarthen, C. 1990. Signs before speech. In *The Semiotic Web 1989,* ed. T. A. Sebeok and J. Umiker-Sebeok, 689–755. Berlin: Mouton de Gruyter.

Trinh, H. T. 1989. Semiology in Vietnam. In *The Semiotic Web 1988,* ed. T. A. Sebeok and J. Umiker-Sebeok, 197–211. Berlin: Mouton de Gruyter.

Turnbull, D. 1989. *Maps Are Territories: Science is an Atlas*. Chicago: University of Chicago Press.

Turner, D. C., and P. Bateson. 1988. *The Domestic Cat: The Biology of Its Behavior*. New York: Cambridge University Press.

Ullmann, S. 1951. *Principles of Semantics*. Glasgow: Jackson, Son & Co.

Umiker-Sebeok, J., and T. A. Sebeok. 1981. Clever Hans and smart simians: The self-fulfilling prophecy and kindred methodological pitfalls. *Anthropos* 76, 89–165.

Umiker-Sebeok, J., and T. A. Sebeok, eds. 1978. *Aboriginal Sign Languages of the Americas and Australia*. 2 vols. New York: Plenum.

———, eds. 1987. *Monastic Sign Languages*. Berlin: Mouton de Gruyter.

Van de Vijver, G., S. N. Salthe, and M. Delpos, eds. 1998. *Evolutionary Systems: Biological and Epistemological Perspectives on Selection and Self-Organization.* Dordrecht: Kluwer Academic.

Van Dine, S. S. [W. H. Wright]. 1935. *The Garden Murder* Case. New York: Scribners.

Vardar, B. 1979. Travaux sémiologiques en Turquie. In *Le champ sémiologique. Perspectives internationales,* ed. A. Helbo, Q1–4. Brussels: Editions Complexe.

Veltrusky, J. 1940. Clovêk a predmêt v divadle [Man and object in the theatre]. *Slovo a Slovesnost* 6, 153–159.

Verene, D. P. 1976. Vico's science of imaginative universals and the philosophy of symbolic forms. In *Giambattista Vico's Science of Humanity,* ed. G. Tagliacozzo G., and D. P. Verene, 295–317. Baltimore: The Johns Hopkins University Press.

———. 1994. Ernst Cassirer (1874–1945). In *Encyclopedic Dictionary of Semiotics,* ed. T. A. Sebeok, 103–105. Berlin: Mouton de Gruyter.

Vernadsky, V. I. 1926. *Biosfera.* Leningrad: Nauka. French version, Paris, 1929.

———. 1945. The biosphere and the noösphere. *American Scientist* 33, 1–12.

Verres, R. 1986. *Krebs und Angst.* Berlin: Springer.

———. 1990. Zur Kommunizierbarkeit von Angst in der Arzt-Patient-Beziehung. In *Das Phänomen Angst,* ed. H. Lang. Berlin: Springer.

Vico, G. 1948. *The New Science of Giambattista Vico.* Translated and edited by T. G. Bergin and M. H. Fisch. Ithaca: Cornell University Press.

Vircillo, D. 1970. La fenomenologia del linguaggio nel pensiero de E. Cassirer. *Revista Rosminiana di Filosofia e di Cultura* 44, 187–202.

Voigt, V. 1983. On the history of semiotics. In *Semiotics Unfolding: Proceedings of the Second Congress of the International Association for Semiotic Studies, Vienna 1979,* ed. T. Borbé, 1:405–407. Berlin: Mouton.

———. 1986. Semiotics in Hungary. In *The Semiotic Sphere,* ed. T. A. Sebeok and J. Umiker-Sebeok, 279–292. New York: Plenum Press.

———. 1995. In memoriam of "Lotmanosphere." *Semiotica* 105(3/4), 191–206.

Voltaire. 1926. *Zadig and Other Romances.* Translated by H. I. Woolf and W. S. Jackson. New York: Dodd, Mead.

von Uexküll, G. 1964. *Jakob von Uexküll: seine Welt und seine Umwelt.* Hamburg: Christian Wegner.

von Uexküll, J. 1909. *Umwelt und Innenwelt der Tiere.* Second edition, 1920. Berlin: Springer Verlag.

———. 1973. *Theoretische Biologie.* Frankfurt: Suhrkamp. Third edition. First edition, 1920. Second edition, 1928. English version: *Theoretical Biology,* D. L. Mackinnon, trans. London: Kegan Paul, Trench, Trübner (1926).

———. 1980. *Kompositionslehre der Natur,* ed. and with an introduction by Thure von Uexküll. Berlin: Ullstein.

———. 1982. The theory of meaning. *Semiotica* 42(1), 25–82.

———. 1992. A stroll through the worlds of animals and men. *Semiotica* 89(4), 279–315.

von Uexküll, Th. 1980. Die Umweltlehre als Theorie der Zeichenprozesse. In J. von Uexküll, *Kompositionslehre der Natur,* 291–358. Berlin: Ullstein.

———. 1982a. Introduction: Meaning and science in Jakob von Uexküll's concept of biology. *Semiotica* 42(1/2), 1–24.

———. 1982b. Semiotics and medicine. *Semiotica* 38(3/4), 205–215.

———. 1986. Medicine and semiotics. *Semiotica* 61(3/4), 201–217.

————. 1987. The sign theory of Jakob von Uexküll. In *Classics of Semiotics*, ed. Martin Krampen, K. Oehler, R. Posner, T. A. Sebeok, and T. von Uexküll, 147–179. New York: Plenum Press.

————. 1990. Introduction to *Models and Methods in Biosemiotics*. Unpublished manuscript.

————. 1991. Die Bedeutung der Biosemiotik für die Medizin. *Münchener medizinische Wochenschrift* 133(41), 601–602.

————. 1992. Varieties of semiosis. In *Biosemiotics*, ed. T. A. Sebeok and J. Umiker-Sebeok, 455–470. Berlin: Mouton de Gruyter.

————. 1997. Biosemiose. In *Semiotics: A Handbook on the Sign-Theoretic Foundations of Nature and Culture*, ed. R. Posner, K. Robering, and T. A. Sebeok, 1:447–457. Berlin: Walter de Gruyter.

————. 1998. Jakob von Uexkülls Umweltlehre. In *Semiotics: A Handbook on the Sign-Theoretic Foundations of Nature and Culture*, ed. R. Posner, K. Robering, and T. A. Sebeok, 2:2183–191. Berlin: Walter de Gruyter.

von Uexküll, Th., W. Geigges, and J. Herrmann. 1993. Endosemiosis. *Semiotica* 96(1/2), 5–51.

von Uexküll, Th., and W. Wesiack. 1988. *Theorie der Humanmedizin: Grundlagen artzlichen Denkens und Handelns*. Munich: Urban & Schwarzenberg.

————, ed. 1992. *Jakob von Uexküll's A Stroll through the Worlds of Animals and Men*. *Semiotica* 89(4), 277–391.

von Uexküll, Th., R. Adler, J. M. Herrmann, K. Köhle, O. Schonecke, and W. Wesiak, eds. 1979. *Lehrbuch der psychosomatischen Medizin*. München: Urban & Schwarzenberg.

Waardenburg, J. 1994. Islamic attitudes to signs. In *Encyclopedic Dictionary of Semiotics*, ed. T. A. Sebeok, 1:392–400. Berlin: Mouton de Gruyter.

Wallace, E. 1922. *The Flying Fifty-Five*. London: Hutchinson.

————. 1930. *The Green Ribbon*. New York: Doubleday.

Wallman, J. 1992. *Aping Language*. Cambridge: Cambridge University Press.

Watson, O. M. 1974. Proxemics. In *Current Trends in Linguistics*, ed. T. A. Sebeok, 12:1, 311–344. The Hague: Mouton.

Watt, W. C. 1993. Signification and its discontents. *Semiotica* 97, 427–437.

Waugh, L. 1982. Marked and unmarked: A choice between unequals in semiotic structure. *Semiotica* 38, 299–318.

Weigel, I. 1975. Small felids and clouded leopards. In *Grzimek's Animal Life Encyclopedia*, 12:281–332. New York: Van Nostrand Reinhold.

Weinberg, S. 1977. *The First Three Minutes*. New York: Basic Books.

Welby, V. [1903] 1965. What is meaning. In *Classics in Semantics*, eds. D. E. Hayden and E. P. Alworth, 211–220. London: Vision Press.

————. 1911. *Significs and Language: An Articulate Form of Our Expressive and Interpretive Resources*. London: Macmillan.

Wemmer, C., and K. Scow. 1977. Communication in the Felidae with emphasis on scent marking and contact patterns. In *How Animals Communicate*, ed. T. A. Sebeok, 749–766. Bloomington: Indiana University Press.

Wertheimer, M. 1922. Untersuchungen zur Lehre von der Gestalt I. *Psychische Forschung* 1, 47–58.

————. 1945. *Productive Thinking*. New York: Harper & Brothers.

Wertheimer, M. 1922. Untersuchungen zur Lehre von der Gestalt I. *Psychische Forschung* 1, 47–58.

———. 1945. *Productive Thinking*. New York: Harper & Brothers.

West, M. 1991. Who said "Curiosity killed the cat"? *Semiotica* 87, 179–186.

Wheeler, J. A. 1984. Bits, quanta, meaning. In *Problems in Theoretical Physics*, ed. A. Giovanni et al., 121–141. Salerno: University of Salerno Press.

———. 1986. How come the quantum? Foreword to J. D. Barrow and F. J. Tipler, *The Anthropic Principle*, vii-ix. Oxford: Oxford University Press.

———. 1988. World as a system self-synthesized by quantum networking. *IBM Journal of Research and Development* 32(1), 4–15.

White, H. V. 1968. Giovanni Battista Vico. *International Encyclopedia of the Social Sciences*, 16:313–316. New York: The Macmillan Company & The Free Press.

White, L. A. 1940. The symbol: The origin and basis of human behavior. *Philosophy of Science* 7(4), 451–463.

Whitfield, I. C. 1984. *Neurocommunications: An Introduction*. New York: Wiley.

Whitley, R. 1984. *The Intellectual and Social Organization of the Sciences*. Oxford: Clarendon Press.

Wicken, J. S. 1987. *Evolution, Thermodynamics, and Information: Extending the Darwinian Program*. Oxford: Oxford University Press.

Wiley, N. 1994. *The Semiotic Self*. Chicago: University of Chicago Press.

Willis, R., ed. 1990. *Signifying Animals: Human Meaning in the Natural World*. London: Unwin Hyman.

Wilson, E. O. 1971. *The Insect Societies*. Cambridge, Mass.: Harvard University Press.

Wind, J., A. Jonker, R. Allott, and L. Rolfe. 1994. *Studies in Language Origins* 3. Amsterdam: John Benjamins.

Wittgenstein, L. 1953. *Philosophical Investigations*. Oxford: Oxford University Press.

Wright, C. 1996. *Listening to Music*. St. Paul/Minneapolis: West.

Wright, R. 1987. Virtual reality. *The Sciences* 67(6), 8–10.

———. 1988. *Three Scientists and Their Gods: Looking for Meaning in an Age of Information*. New York: Times Books.

Yates, F. E. 1985. Semiotics as a bridge between information (biology) and dynamics (physics). *Recherches Sémiotiques/Semiotic Inquiry* 5, 347–360.

———. 1997. Microsemiosis. In *Semiotics: A Handbook on the Sign-Theoretic Foundations of Nature and Culture*, ed. R. Posner, K. Robering, and T. A. Sebeok, 1:457–464. Berlin: Walter de Gruyter.

Yates, F. E., and P. N. Kugler. 1984. Signs, singularities and significance: a physical model for semiotics. *Semiotica* 52, 49–77.

Yllera, A. 1979. Les recherches sémiologiques en Espagne. In *Le champ sémiologique. Perspectives internationales*, ed. A. Helbo, G1–43. Brussels: Editions Complexe.

Zhinkin, N. I. 1971. Semiotic aspects of communication in animal and man. *Semiotica* 4(1/2), 75–93.

Zholkovsky, A. 1984. *Themes and Texts: Toward a Poetics of Expressiveness*. Ithaca: Cornell University Press.

Zola, E. 1963. The experimental novel. In *Documents of Modern Literary Realism*, ed. G. J. Becker, 162–196. Second edition. First edition, 1880. Princeton: Princeton University Press.

Zsirai, Miklós. 1937. *Finnugor rokonságunk*. Budapest: Magyar Tudományos Akadémia.

Index

THOMAS A. SEBEOK is Distinguished Professor Emeritus of Linguistics and Semiotics and Professor Emeritus of Anthropology, Folklore, and Uralic and Altaic Studies at Indiana University, as well as the recipient of the President's Medal of Excellence. An Honorary Member of the Hungarian Academy of Sciences, he is also Distinguished Senior Fellow Emeritus of the Institute for Advanced Study (Collegium Budapest), a recipient of the Distinguished Service Award of the American Anthropological Association, and holder of a Professional Achievement Citation from the University of Chicago. He is author or editor of hundreds of books and articles on a wide range of topics. Among his numerous semiotics publications are *The Play of Musement; A Sign Is Just a Sign; Semiotics in the United States; The Forms of Meaning: Modeling Systems Theory and Semiotic Analysis* (with Marcel Danesi); and *The Sign of Three* (with Umberto Eco).